Theology in the Present Age

Theology in the Present Age

Essays in Honor of John D. Castelein

Edited by

CHRISTOPHER BEN SIMPSON

and

STEVEN D. CONE

PICKWICK *Publications* · Eugene, Oregon

Pickwick Publications
An Imprint of Wipf and Stock Publishers
199 W. 8th Ave., Suite 3
Eugene, OR 97401

www.wipfandstock.com

ISBN 13: 978-1-62032-969-6

Cataloguing-in-Publication Data

Theology in the present age : essays in honor of John D. Castelein / edited by Christopher Ben Simpson and Steven D. Cone

xii + 310 p. ; 23 cm. Includes bibliographical references.

ISBN 13: 978-1-62032-969-6

1. Philosophical theology. 2. Theology. I. Simpson, Christopher Ben, 1973–. II. Cone, Steven D. III. Castelein, John D. IV. Title.

B1626 S567 2013

Manufactured in the U.S.A.

Did not our hearts burn within us
while he talked to us on the road,
while he opened to us the Scriptures?

Homo sum, humani nihil a me alienum puto.

Contents

THEORETICAL ESSAYS

Introduction

THESE ESSAYS ARE PRESENTED by former students and current and former colleagues of John D. Castelein in honor and celebration of his career as now Distinguished Professor of Contemporary Christian Theology at Lincoln Christian Seminary in Lincoln, Illinois. The chapters vary from the speculative to the pastoral, and so reflect the range of John's influence. (The essays included are organized into three general divisions: theoretical, practical, and personal.) They also reflect something of the man himself.

John has always dwelt on boundaries—sites of communication between one world and another where one might feel at home at times in both, at times in neither. A Belgian-American, John Castelein has been both an academic—earning his PhD at the University of Chicago Divinity School in its golden age (studying with such luminaries as Paul Ricouer, David Tracy, and Langdon Gilkey)—and a preacher—serving, at the height of his academic career, as the preaching minister at Lincoln Christian Church. He is deeply informed by both the Christian tradition (be it the Bible or the particularity of the Stone-Campbell tradition) and secular learning—be it the human sciences (with his dissertation on Peter Berger), the hard sciences (with his continued interest and teaching in "neurotheology"), the arts (with his regular and popular course on theology and film), or philosophy (from Plato to Kant to Postmodernism). All of his students have come to share something of this dual vision whether they are professors or pastors or something of both.

John has often said his *magna opera*—the great works, the marks made for which he would wish to be remembered—are his students. It is our hope that this collection of essays, a small work, might serve as a testimony to John's great and abiding work in our formation as academics and pastors, theologians and philosophers, thinkers and persons. We dedicate it to him with our gratitude.

Contributors

William Baker, Professor of New Testament, Graduate School, Hope International University

Steven D. Cone, Assistant Professor of Theology, Lincoln Christian University

Justin DeVore, Ph.D. student in Theology, University of Nottingham

Isaac Gaff, Director of Worship Arts at Calvary United Methodist Church, Normal IL; former Assistant Professor of Worship, Lincoln Christian University

Joe Gordon, Ph.D. student in Theology, Marquette University

Michael Gowin, Associate Professor of Business Administration, Lincoln Christian University

Ryan Hemmer, Ph.D. student in Theology, Marquette University

Rich Knopp, Professor of Philosophy and Christian Apologetics, Lincoln Christian University

Bob Kurka, Professor of Theology and Church and Culture, Lincoln Christian Seminary

Jarrod Longbons, Ph.D. student in Theology, University of Nottingham; Adjunct Professor, Lincoln Christian University; Associate Minister at Northside Church of Christ, Bloomington, IL

Brian Mills, Vice President of Student Development, Lincoln Christian University

David Peters, Associate Professor of Philosophy and Apologetics at Florida Christian College

Jason Rodenbeck, Senior Minister, Castle Christian Church, Cumming, GA

Justin Schwartz, Ph.D. student in Theology, University of Toronto

Christopher Ben Simpson, Associate Professor of Philosophy and Theology, Lincoln Christian University

Eric A. Teoro, Associate Professor of Business, Lincoln Christian University

Corey Tutewiler, Ph.D. student in Theology, University of Nottingham

Jeff Valodone, Campus Minister with Campus Crusade for Christ, Milwaukee, WI

THEORETICAL ESSAYS

1

Self-Transcending Life

Lonergan's Appropriation of Augustine and Aquinas on Authentic Being-in-the-World[1]

STEVEN D. CONE

IS THERE HOPE?

I will begin with a quotation from Friedrich Nietzsche, although this paper is not about him: "We don't know ourselves, we knowledgeable people—we are personally ignorant about ourselves. And there's good reason for that. We've never tried to find out who we are. How could it ever happen that one day we'd discover our own selves?"[2]

---

1. This paper forms the basis for a chapter in a book I am co-authoring with Russell Snell of Eastern University (*Authentic Cosmopolitanism: Love, Sin, and Grace in the Christian University*, forthcoming from Pickwick). The words and thoughts expressed in this paper are mine, but I wish to acknowledge his input in the proposal that forms the basis of this work.
2. Nietzsche, *The Genealogy of Morals*, 1.1.

Nietzsche testifies to an alienation all too familiar to us—are we late-born, or perhaps come too early, the children of modernity who find suspicion ensconced within our very selves.[3] But here I refer to the salutary suspicion Paul Ricoeur envisions, and I will follow his lead in examining more closely the two masters of suspicion he allies with Nietzsche—Karl Marx and Sigmund Freud.[4]

In truth this paper is not about them, either, though I will, penitential, ponder their purgative thought.[5] For what I seek is hope, a horizon for human destiny, for my own true self, that neither springs from nor ends in ideology, nor infantile desire, nor the machinations of means of production. And yet for everything to be shaken that can be shaken, I must learn the place of these many things.

The harbingers of this kingdom that will endure—the sure goal of hope—I hear in the clarion voices of Augustine of Hippo and Thomas Aquinas. This paper is about them. And yet not only about them, for to carry their insights into our time and our age, I turn also to one who walks after them, both interpreting them and speaking something new, the Canadian Jesuit Bernard Lonergan.

Lonergan argued that the masters of suspicion are in large part right with respect to the forces that they identify as constituting us. Lonergan fully acknowledged the embodiment of our being. Yet he argued that the selves that we are transcend space and time; a metaphysics of presence cannot fully define human reality. The self that constitutes itself in wonder and love forms the possibility of the self as historically constituted. The freedom of this self creatively emerges from these bounds, and it is known insofar as the self is grasped as human—a unity that both transcends and affirms any data posited about it, an identity that essentially is open to knowing and loving a world.

Being-in-love, therefore, grounds the authentic existence of the self as embodied in the world. Lonergan draws on Augustine to insist that reason finds its healing and true home in love. For reason is not an instrument that we use but rather our very conscious selves as we are struck by wonder, contemplate, and affirm the world. Lonergan also develops Aquinas' insight that the world is fully known only in charity, for charity grounds the wisdom by which the right ordering of the world can be known.

---

3. Ricoeur, *Oneself as Another*, 341ff.

4. Ricoeur, *Freud and Philosophy: An Essay on Interpretation*, 33.

5. See Merold Westphal, *Suspicion and Faith*.

SUSPICION AND THE SELF

Freud and Marx both speak of history as explaining human existence, but on quite different scales. I will begin with Freud.

Freud

In *The Interpretation of Dreams*, Sigmund Freud explains the significance of dreams according to our motivations and desires: "The dream represents a certain state of affairs, such as I might wish to exist; the content of the dream is thus the fulfillment of a wish; its motive is a wish."[6]

A wealth of meaning lies behind this simple-sounding assertion. For the desires he speaks of, in main, only masquerade as the explicit dream content, images and affects connected with the world of our waking hours.

Freud develops his case by examining a manifold of dreams, and he reveals an ingenious complexity to the human psyche. Behind the manifested level of our dreams —the "dream content"—he argues for a deep subterranean of unconscious, infantile desires, mostly though not all sexual in nature. These desires animate the true meaning of the dream—the "dream thought"—the reason why our psyche has found it worthwhile to dream.

I would like to bring out three key points with respect to Freud and the human self.

First, Freud does not consider there to be a structural difference between the sleeping and waking operation of our psyche, and this operation is a domination of what we call consciousness by the outworking of our unconscious infantile desires.[7] As he concludes his analysis: "What role is now left, in our representation of things, to the phenomenon of consciousness, once so all-powerful and overshadowing all else? None other than that of a sense-organ for the perception of psychic qualities."[8]

The main differences between sleeping and waking are that in sleep we are immobilized by a wish to sleep, due to this immobility the preconscious censor allows more of the psychic energy from our unconscious desires to come into consciousness (that is, the defense mechanisms operate in a different way), and certain logical activities are suspended. But the intellectual and artistic endeavors of our waking lives are every bit as much as the dream the outworking of our childhood history.

6. Freud, *The Interpretation of Dreams*.

7. Mitchell and Black, *Freud and Beyond: A History of Modern Psychoanalytic Thought*, 21.

8. Freud, *The Interpretation of Dreams*.

Second, this psychological outworking is absolutely deterministic. The paths of our unconscious are set in early childhood and cannot change. Freud conceived the psyche as mechanistically working out the energy states of our psychological desires. Whether we are involved in intellectual or artistic endeavor, in dreaming, in the throes of psychosis, or in any other activity or state, our psyche is working out in the most efficient way it can the energy of these desires.

Third, Freud developed this theory in the context of providing healing, and his insights were able to provide healing for many psychological and psychosomatic diseases that medical science had been ineffective in treating before him.[9] He likewise provided understandings of personality that psychology and psychiatry have used throughout their modern development.[10] We must acknowledge that the long-delayed publication of *The Interpretation of Dreams*, its development through eight editions in Freud's lifetime, and the elaboration of his psychological theories that followed it, have had a profound effect in treating mental illness.

Marx

While Freud explains human reality through the paleontology of our childhood desires, Karl Marx operates on a world-historical level. As Marx and Engels state in *The Communist Manifesto*, "the history of all hitherto existing societies is the history of class struggles."[11]

The substance of these class struggles involves quite a different type of repression than Freud envisions. "In one word, [for] exploitation, veiled by religious and political illusions, naked, shameless, direct, brutal exploitation."[12] Exploitation, that is, of those who produce by those who reap the rewards.

The world as it exists results from the historical development of economic forces.[13] The ideas one has, and one's values, are enmeshed in the economic class to which one belongs. To the bourgeois, the lower state of the workers is all too reasonable; the workers themselves have been deluded into following this myth, but the time is coming for the proletariat to awake

9. See Furst, *Before Freud: Hypnosis and Hysteria in Later Nineteenth Century Psychiatric Cases*.

10. See Millon, *Masters of the Mind: Exploring the Story of Mental Illness from Ancient Times to the New Millennium*.

11. Karl Marx and Friedrich Engels, *The Communist Manifesto*.

12. Ibid.

13. See G. A. Cohen, *Karl Marx's Theory of History*.

and arise. And this awakening will come, for it is the necessary result of the changes in the modern world of the means of production.

I will offer one more quote from Marx and then conclude, again, with three observations: "Does it require deep intuition to comprehend that man's ideas, views and conceptions, in one word, man's consciousness, changes with every change in the conditions of his material existence, in his social relations and in his social life?"[14]

So the herald of revolution proclaims.

First, Marx had no exemption from this credo for such cherished ideals as freedom and justice. Yes, the great societies of history have cherished these ideals and they are esteemed today. Yet behind these words Marx saw the specter of class conflict. *Whose* freedom and *whose* justice? That of the ruling class. That these ideals have endured means only that class conflict has endured, and their true meanings are to be found therein.

Second, Marx's economic determinism is an issue of great debate among different schools of Marxists.[15] At the least, one may say that economic determinism has been a strongly influential interpretation of Marx, and that it has had the effect, which Marx would likely have agreed with, of denying the importance and intrinsic value of the individual self.[16] For this self, instead of making its world, is the necessary consequence of a succession of social orders based on varying means of production.

Third, Marx's proclamations flow from the struggle not for equality but for survival of the poor in the modern state. Whether in the slums and villages of Central and South America, among the Czarist working class of Russia, or in areas of 75 percent unemployment in Ireland, Marx's ideas have always found a ready hearing among the downtrodden. Modern institutions such as labor unions and universal education draw much support from his works.[17] And Marx's political and social theories have shown many ways in which those who believe themselves to be living justly in a society have in fact reaped the benefits of other people's suffering. Whatever our analysis of Marx will be, we will not be able to dispense with the powerful way that our economic being conditions who we are and what we do.

14. Karl Marx and Friedrich Engels, *The Communist Manifesto*.

15. See McMurtry, *The Structure of Marx's World-View* and *contra*, Lukács, *History and Class Consciousness; Studies in Marxist Dialectics*.

16. See Breckman, *Marx, the Young Hegelians, and the Origins of Radical Social Theory: Dethroning the Self*.

17. See Lapides, *Marx and Engels on the Trade Unions*.

The Economic and Psychological Self

We may seek comfort in the face of such arguments by arguing that economics and libido have an effect on the self, but we can isolate that influence and overcome it. But here we must take care. To envision the self, sitting in its citadel, resisting the buffets of the waves of psychological and economic destiny, is quite to underestimate the power of the critique. For Marx and Freud argue that no self exists apart from these factors, that they are in fact constitutive of what we call our selves.

TRANSCENDENCE AND THE SELF

Lonergan would agree that our embodied being is constituted by the factors Freud and Marx delineate, along with many other factors, linguistic self-mediation not the least of them.[18] Yet after everything Marx and Freud have said further questions remain. In Lonergan's understanding, they totalize us according to what we are present as now. But they do not adequately take into account what makes it possible for us to be that way.

Embodied but Emergent Being

All that appears important for Freud and Marx is "us" as we are bodies, able to be completely delineated because we are fixtures in the world one can grasp and see, whether by infantile desire or economic determination. And we are arguably constituted by these realities. But there is another set of questions they do not answer. These questions ask who we are as selves who constitute ourselves in this world, providing the conditions of possibility for receiving and living as part of a world.

As I examine the analyses made by Freud and Marx, they claim that although I believe that I am asking and answering questions intelligently and reasonably, and living out these answers more or less responsibly, something else entirely is actually happening. The paths upon which my consciousness walks are set for me, either by enmeshment in socioeconomic factors or in connection with unacknowledged infantile desire. Yet the state of my wondering is in fact unrestricted. Let us envision something I would be unable (absolutely or practically) to wonder about. By even framing that hypothesis I set for myself a problem, a whole host of questions ferreting down those very paths, the product of unrestricted wonder. And no doubt

18. See Bernard Lonergan, "Prolegomena to the Study of the Emerging Religious Consciousness of Our Times."

my desire often deceives me, and the feelings that form and convey it can move me unawares. Yet can there not be a love that reorders my feelings, sets me in an authentic horizon?

There are two arguments here: first, the arguments Freud and Marx make presuppose wonder and desire, and these realities contravene the account they give of the world; and second, they themselves give witness that the account of the world known in wonder and chosen in love is right. First, neither Freud nor Marx's arguments take solipsism very seriously—they require connection to a world. Economics is a world order, and libido has to have something to desire. Yet what forms the bonds of connection in a world are arguably wonder and desire.[19] Economics presupposes motivated interest, and the substance of libido is desire. But desire and wonder do not let me lay quiet; often, no doubt, I do sleep, or act from unconscious factors, yet desire and wonder move me to arise. And do not Freud and Marx themselves presuppose this state of affairs in their writings? For within them I find clear calls to awake from my slumber, know the truth about myself and the world I had passed over before.

There is a way in which Freud and Marx are correct. For they do point out that the narcissism and hubris of human consciousness must bow before its situatedness, acknowledge it is receptive of powers in a world that go beyond it; that there is a story of this world that is greater than our conscious egos and of which we are only a part. Yet Lonergan argues that when we ask further questions—What makes this world possible and how is it possible for us to be part of it to receive from it?—we find that though we are only a tiny part of this wider world, we are an emergent, spiritual part.[20] And as emergent and spiritual, we are neither determined by what has been nor what is. We are able to be attentive, intelligent, reasonable, and responsible: free.[21]

For if we did not have this emergent, spiritual, character, how could we enact our part in the drama of forces Marx and Freud describe as shaping us? Again, do not their own works—the healing work of Freud, the prophetic destiny felt by Marx—testify that they themselves are emergent, spiritual,

19. In this respect, Lonergan draws on the work of Max Scheler to point especially to feeling to forming the intersubjective nature of human reality. See Lonergan, "What Are Judgments of Value?" 140; cf. Lonergan, "The Human Good," 336; cf. Lonergan, *Method*, 31n2.

20. Properly speaking, all of proportionate being can be described as emergent, for its immanent intelligibility is known according to what Lonergan terms "emergent probability." Human reality is both emergent and can know itself to be emergent, which Lonergan names as spiritual being. See Lonergan, *Insight*, 194–95 and 670–71.

21. See Lonergan, *Method*, 120–24.

beings, too? And can one not better understand their burdens and genius in light of a world in which there is understanding, in which the reality that is becoming can genuinely be shaped by the freedom of the real?

For just as the unity and totality of the world exceed my grasp, so I am a mystery to myself. The question that I am will not be answered by getting a better look at me, a more direct encounter with my existence. But I am a question, as is my life, and I will be known by answering that question: first with an understandable content but finally with a Yes or No.

History's Hidden Meaning

Freud and Marx both show a strong tendency to try and explain human history according to its hidden meaning. In this respect, they follow Feuerbach, who looked to show the true meaning of all human ideas on the level of immanence.[22] The full modern flower of this tendency can be seen in Hegel, who explains all of history as the history of *Geist*. (*Geist* is intended by Hegel to be transcendent, but one can wonder to what extent it is. If Desmond and others are right about tendencies in Hegel toward monism, it will be difficult for *Geist* to have an absolutely transcendent character. Note the radical difference between this conception of "*Geist* being all in all" and Christian understandings of *theosis*, in which the saved are deified but never become the divine essence.)[23]

I wonder to what extent the ancient myths and philosophies followed the same tendency, seen in these modern philosophies, and such popularizations as conspiracy theories involving the Knights Templar. Perhaps Augustine had it best when he said: "Too late have I loved you, O Beauty so ancient and so new, too late have I loved you! Behold, you were within me, while I was outside: it was there I sought you, and, a deformed creature, rushed headlong upon those things of beauty you have made."[24]

We see glimmerings of the eternal in time and try to discover, at the level of immanence, something which even natural beatitude is never intended to supply.

Aquinas, I think, would see Marx and Freud as both embracing and failing in love. They embrace love at a human level because they have genuine concern for their fellow human beings, especially the afflicted and

22. See Feuerbach, *The Essence of Christianity*.

23. On Hegel and Desmond, see Desmond, *Hegel's God: A Counterfeit Double?*; for an overview of several Christian understandings of *theosis*, see Christiansen and Wittung, eds., *Partakers of the Divine Nature*.

24. Augustine, *Confessions*, X.27.

downtrodden. However, they fail in charity because they do not see human beings as ordered to God as their final end, which is the truth of every human person, and without which there is actually a degrading of the human nature.[25] Perhaps to the extent that the causes that Marx and Freud point to are genuine, they are seeing what Aquinas would call the chain of secondary causality by which God governs the world. However, they miss the point of these causes because they deny the prime mover, who infallibly and eternally governs them.[26]

In Lonergan's terms, Freud and Marx seek explanation of human existence within space and time. But space and time are themselves in need of being explained.[27] The explanation of things is not within them, but rather they themselves—with all of history—testify to an infinite act of wisdom and love, to whose wisdom and love all ultimate explanation refers.

He would also add that who we are as a body—something present with respect to space and time—is real, but from a fully human point of view that is only data about us. To know who we are requires asking and answering questions based on that data, following the lead of wonder and love.[28]

INTELLECTUAL, MORAL, AND RELIGIOUS SELF-TRANSCENDENCE

With respect to self-transcendence, then, I am asking the question of genuine human being.

Genuine Human Being

According to Lonergan, wonder and love lead us to true self-transcendence in a two-fold way. First, led by wonder, we ask questions about our experiences and try to answer those questions. To the extent that we are genuine to the immanent norms of our questions—that is, to ourselves, as questioning beings—we will seek to know the world of being intelligently and reasonably.[29]

Yet what gives us the ability to be genuine to these questions? And what is the issue of this knowledge? Does it stay, at best, a mere intellectual

25. ST II-II Q.25.
26. ST I Q.103 (esp. a.6).
27. See Lonergan, *Insight*, 163–95.
28. Lonergan, "Mission and the Spirit," 23–33; cf. Lonergan, *Insight*, 374–98.
29. See Lonergan, "Self-Transcendence: Intellectual, Moral, Religious."

self-transcendence? Do we follow the existential and always relevant question, "How then shall we live?"

Existential questions ask about value. Truth and falsity are in the mind, but good and evil are in the world. As Terrence Malick's moving film, *The Tree of Life*, brings forth, the question of creation is not just the question of being, but of good and evil—of the arrangement of the whole.[30] But the question of value, according to Lonergan, can be asked in two ways. First, am I willing to embrace an ultimate source of value distinct from myself and my group, or do I falsely limit questions of value to my or my group's satisfactions? Second, and at a deeper level, do I embrace openness to all things—a universal antecedent willingness to know the real and commit myself to true values whatever they may be? Answering the first question establishes my moral base, but answering the second question indicates whether I have been captured by and accepted love.[31]

Wisdom and Charity

In the *Summa*, Thomas makes a fascinating pairing of wisdom and the gift of charity.[32] Wisdom is knowing first principles and thereby being able to know the right arrangement of a whole. Thomas maintains that by our natural powers we can know the world naturally, and this is significant, but only by knowing the ultimate first principle of the world—namely God—can we rightly know the arrangement of the whole. Significantly, while wisdom deals properly with knowing God, it also allows the right ordering of practical human affairs. Wisdom springs from the gift of charity, which is a special kind of friendship with God that accompanies saving grace. In this friendship we both are committed to God as our ultimate end and come to see the world, and everyone in it, as ordered to God.

Note the balance and probity with which Thomas makes his distinctions. Natural human knowledge is real, but it must deliberate its way toward the right order of things. And it does so missing the vital clue of God's ordering of the world by his wisdom and drawing all things to himself. Especially with respect to human reality, natural knowledge will fall short, because while the divinization testified to in revelation is the right ordering of every human, it is not proportionate to natural human being. Infused wisdom does not dispense with deliberation. But it gives the one animated by charity a necessary supernatural ground upon which those deliberations

30. *The Tree of Life* (Fox, 2011).
31. Lonergan, *Method*, 237–43.
32. ST II-II Q. 45.

can be made. For the gift of wisdom allows the sanctified one to know divine things and judge the affairs of this world by a kind of connaturality with divine wisdom, that is, with the Triune God who is her destiny and whose friend she has become.[33]

Lonergan refers to this infused wisdom as the knowledge that comes from the gift of love.[34] As operative, this grace prepares us to know and actively love a world by creating in us that universal antecedent willingness to bear and give ourselves to all things.[35] This gift of love becomes cooperative when we know and love. Proximately, love provides the ground for the right response to the goodness of the world. Remotely, it motivates the rectitude of our other conscious operations. How are we willing to give ourselves to the other in knowledge and responsibility? Because the gift of self is natural to one in love. Love reveals values in their true splendor.[36] Rightly valuing the world we are moved to rectitude in knowing it, to following through with the impulse of wonder in a way that brings self-transcendence because we are true to following our questions.[37]

The Order of Love

It is striking that in Thomas' Question 45 (ST II-II) on wisdom, he refers to Augustine by name nine times. In allying wisdom with charity, Thomas thereby struggles with the question of rightly ordered love. Augustine declared in his masterwork, *The City of God*,

> But if the Creator is truly loved, that is, if He Himself is loved and not another thing in His stead, He cannot be evilly loved; for love itself is to be ordinately loved, because we do well to love that which, when we love it, makes us live well and virtuously. So that it seems to me that it is a brief but true definition of virtue to say, it is the order of love; and on this account, in the

33. ST II-II Q.23, a.1 and Q.26, a.13.

34. Lonergan, *Method*, 115–18.

35. Frederick Lawrence, "The Human Good and Christian Conversation," 262; cf. Lawrence, "Expanding Challenge to Authenticity in Insight: Lonergan's Hermeneutics of Facticity (1953–1964)," 427–56.

36. Lonergan, *Method*, 243; cf. 115–19.

37. For a recent Lonerganian analysis of what it might mean for human beings to receive participation in the life of the Trinity, based on the gift of love, see the discussion between Robert Doran and Charles Hefling in the following series of articles: Doran, "The Starting Point of Systematic Theology," 750–76; Hefling, "Quaestio Disputata: On the (Economic) Trinity: An Argument in Conversation with Robert Doran," 642–60; and Doran, "Addressing the Four-Point Hypothesis," 674–82.

Canticles, the bride of Christ, the city of God, sings, "Order love within me."[38]

As Lonergan joins this conversation, he draws out the way in which the gift of love, therefore, provides human life and destiny with hope. Hope within this world is based on a mysterious destiny that goes beyond it.[39] In hope I actively say, "Yes," to the question that I am, by accepting and living out love. In hope, I can overcome the forces of determinism that would otherwise press in on me. For my debt is not to this world, but I have been set in a horizon that is ordered beyond it by the divine gift of love.

A Final Response

In this way, I think Lonergan would give his final answer to Marx and Freud (as well as to Nietzsche, although this paper is not about him). He would call them to be true to themselves and find who they truly are, and their theories' true import, in a world ordered by wisdom and love. And he would argue that the truths that they reason out would not be lessened thereby, but would rather be seen more clearly.

For reason is not some instrument that we clever animals use, but rather it is we, ourselves, as we seek to know reality based on the call of wonder. And reason is not the last word about us, nor is mere desire, for it is in rightly ordered love that we live authentically in the world. Whether we speak of the root of our personal desires, or of the social and economic forces that shape us, the self-transcendence brought by rightly ordered love reveals us to ourselves and empowers us as emergent, spiritual, beings. For authentic being-in-the-world is being-in-love.

38. Augustine, *The City of God*, XV.22.

39. Lonergan, *Method*, 117; cf. Lonergan, "Horizons," 25–26; cf. Lonergan, "Christology Today: Methodological Reflections," 94.

BIBLIOGRAPHY

Augustine. *The Confessions of Saint Augustine*. Translated by J. Ryan. New York: Image, 1960.

Breckman, Warren. *Marx, the Young Hegelians, and the Origins of Radical Social Theory: Dethroning the Self*. Cambridge: Cambridge University Press, 1999.

Christiansen, Wittung, et al. *Partakers of the Divine Nature: The History and Development of Deification in the Christian Traditions*. Grand Rapids: Baker Academic, 2007.

Cohen, G. A. *Karl Marx's Theory of History: A Defense*. Princeton, NJ: Princeton University Press, 2001.

Desmond, William. *Hegel's God: A Counterfeit Double?* Ashgate Studies in the History of Philosophical Theology. Aldershot, UK: Ashgate, 2003.

Doran, Robert. "Addressing the Four-Point Hypothesis." *Theological Studies* 68 (2007) 674–82.

———. "The Starting Point of Systematic Theology." *Theological Studies* 67 (2006) 750–76.

Farrell, Thomas J., and Paul A. Soukup. *Communication and Lonergan: Common Ground for Forging the New Age*. Kansas City, MO: Sheed & Ward, 1993.

Feuerbach, Ludwig. *The Essence of Christianity*. Translated by G. Eliot. Dover Philosophical Classics. Mineola, NY: Dover, 2008.

Freud, Sigmund. *The Interpretation of Dreams*. 3rd ed. no loc.: Pink Panda, 2007.

Furst, Lillian. *Before Freud: Hypnosis and Hysteria in Later Nineteenth Century Psychiatric Cases*. Lewisburg: Bucknell University Press, 2008.

Hefling, Charles. "Quaestio Disputata: On the (Economic) Trinity: An Argument in Conversation with Robert Doran." *Theological Studies* 68 (2007) 642–60.

Lapides, Kenneth. *Marx and Engels on the Trade Unions*. New York : Praeger, 1987.

Lawrence, Frederick. "Expanding Challenge to Authenticity in Insight: Lonergan's Hermeneutics of Facticity (1953–1964)," *Divyadaan* 15.3 (2004) 427–56. Online: http://divyadaan.in/journal/Volume%2015%20No%203%20(2004).pdf

———. "The Human Good and Christian Conversation." In *Lonergan and Communication: Common Ground for Forging the New Age*, 427–56. Kansas City, MO: Sheed & Ward, 1993.

Lonergan, Bernard. "Christology Today: Methodological Reflections." In *A Third Collection: Papers by Bernard J. F. Lonergan, S.J.,* edited by Frederick Crowe, 74–99. New York: Paulist, 1985.

———. "Horizons." In *Philosophical and Theological Papers, 1965–1980*, edited by R. Croken and R. Doran, 25–26. Collected Works of Bernard Lonergan 17. Toronto: University of Toronto Press, 2004.

———. "The Human Good." In *Philosophical and Theological Papers, 1965–1980*, edited by R. Croken and R. Doran, 336. Collected Works of Bernard Lonergan 17. Toronto: University of Toronto Press, 2004.

———. *Insight: A Study of Human Understanding*. Collected Works of Bernard Lonergan 3, edited by R. Doran and F. Crowe. Toronto: University of Toronto, 1992.

———. *Method in Theology*. Toronto: University of Toronto, 1971.

———. "Mission and the Spirit." In *A Third Collection: Papers by Bernard J. F. Lonergan, S.J.,* 374–98. New York: Paulist, 1985.

————. "Prolegomena to the Study of the Emerging Religious Consciousness of Our Times." In *A Third Collection: Papers by Bernard J. F. Lonergan, S.J.*, 55–73. New York: Paulist, 1985.

————. "Self-Transcendence: Intellectual, Moral, Religious." In *Philosophical and Theological Papers, 1965–1980*, 313–331. Collected Works of Bernard Lonergan 17. Toronto: University of Toronto Press, 2004.

————. "What Are Judgments of Value?" In *Philosophical and Theological Papers, 1965–1980*, 140. Collected Works of Bernard Lonergan 17. Toronto: University of Toronto Press, 2004.

Lukács, György. *History and Class Consciousness: Studies in Marxist Dialectics.* Translated by Rodney Livingstone. Cambridge: MIT, 1971.

Marx, Karl, and Friedrich Engels. "Works of Karl Marx and Friedrich Engel." In *The Communist Manifesto.* Mobi Collected Works. Public Domain Books, 2006. Kindle Edition.

Millon, Theodore et al. *Masters of the Mind: Exploring the Story of Mental Illness from Ancient Times to the New Millennium.* Hoboken, NJ: Wiley, 2004

Mitchell, Stephen and Margaret Black. *Freud and Beyond: A History of Modern Psychoanalytic Thought.* New York: Basic, 1995.

Nietzsche, Friedrich. *The Genealogy of Morals.* Translated by I. Johnson. Arlington, VA: Richer Resources Publications, 2009.

Philip Schaff, editor. *St. Augustine's City of God and Christian Doctrine,* In *A Select Library of the Nicene and Post-Nicene Fathers of the Christian Church. Vol. II.* Buffalo: The Christian Literature Co., 1887.

Riceour, Paul. *Freud and Philosophy: An Essay on Interpretation.* New Haven: Yale University Press, 1970.

————. *Oneself as Another.* Translated by K. Blamey. Chicago: University of Chicago, 1995.

Westphal, Merold. *Suspicion and Faith: The Religious Use of Modern Atheism.* New York: Fordham University, 1998.

2

Exceeding Immanence

An Introduction to Being in Action

JUSTIN M. DEVORE

EVERYTHING KNOWN THROUGH SELF-CONSCIOUS experience is garnered in life. Mind is predicated upon life but matter is prerequisite
for life, thus the mind itself necessitates matter. But is mind equivalent to
its prerequisite? Can the conditioned ever surpass its condition? Moreover,
is matter conditioned as well, or is it the only possible condition? If the
answer is restricted to an immanentist response, one may prefer atomiza-
tion, which reduces the phenomenon of self-conscious being into distinctly
separate non-organic material causes. Or, one might search for an *élan vital*
that, instead of dissecting the whole being into essential elements, fuses
every self-conscious being into a dynamic One. Either option results in a
vast separation between organic life and non-organic matter with a similar heterogeneity between instinctual creatures and self-conscious beings.
While living bodies are comprised of matter and minds do require bodies,
self-conscious beings, having the capacity of self-reflection and will, seem
strangely alien to the world of matter and instinctual creatures. Self-conscious life transcends the world of experience, as a merely finite world falls
short of its unlimited desires. Thus, the very phenomenon of self-conscious

being does appear to transcend its own material condition, but many restrict consciousness to the purely immanent alone.

In the present age we are faced with an awkward set of consequences resulting from immanentist incommensurabilities; and despite every attempt to overcome dualism, the Kantian dichotomy is still very much alive for the positive sciences in practical application. The knot is further tightened by the separation of theory and practice exemplified by the emancipation of scientific progress from its metaphysical grounding. As it goes, reason awards the predominant authority to formulate and answer the question of life to the positive sciences. As the study of physical reality, encompassing, but not limited to, mathematical description and cognitive analysis, the positive sciences focus on concrete knowing by methodical experimentation and theoretical extrapolation. Considering that the world is rational, the senses are reliable, and the mind is capable, modern science tends to partition (i.e., subject/object, nature/culture, mind/body) and dissect individual parts as a representation of the whole.[1] While asserting independence from metaphysics, the positive sciences still utilize the secure ontological (as well as epistemological) framework that the science of being *qua* being endows.[2]

However, the problem with conceiving such a thoroughgoing materialist immanence lies in a metaphysical notion of pure being, which is an abstraction of either primal consciousness (Hegel), or an enigmatic *a priori* existence grounded in nothingness (Heidegger), or what Alain Badiou describes as an inconsistent multiplicity. In any case, when pressed to its logical conclusions, immanentism tends to reduce all phenomena to a material cause, essentially forming a monism that reduces the many forms of being to the One of substance. And one might consider dialectical materialism as a special case of monism, for the chaotic flux (or difference) tends toward forming a singular dynamic identity. While the materialist tends to reduce form to substance, the idea of substance becomes the new synthetic form that is conditioned by an abstract notion of pure being in the most general of terms.[3]

Thus, two main options result. If self-conscious being is merely illusory, an epiphenomenon of underlying material processes, then a rigid determinism with a Freudian twist befalls us—this is the fate of scientism grounded by realism. Or, if self-consciousness itself is an outward expression of a pure spiritual unity, matter itself becomes unnecessary and banal, perhaps even an evil that captures spirit and limits its truly unlimited freedom—this is the

1. Latour, *Never Been Modern*, 10, 18, 30, 34, 43.

2. Ibid., 24. See: Spaemann, *Anthropology*, xxiii.

3. Dupré, *Passage to Modernity*, 75, 22–24, 72–75, 84.

fate of mysticism grounded in idealism. It appears that either choice erodes subjectivity and casts a hopeless future for individual self-conscious beings. The first possibility selects matter over mind and loses the self; the second choice favors mind over matter and loses the world. Either option leaves one in a hopeless state of infinite desire for something other than life itself, but the positive sciences tend toward the former.

Seeking fulfillment of such unlimited desire, the disturbing aporia of one having everything and yet desiring more is all that remains. From splitting atoms and modifying DNA to creating artificial intelligence and exploring the vast expanse of outer space, the optimistic anticipation of technological progress endeavors to fulfill our unrelenting desires by mastering the world and placing the entire universe within our grasp. But regardless of the ever-abounding practical achievements of scientific investigation, we still face the same questions as the ancients; we have not suppressed the inexhaustible perplexities that accompany the question of being.[4] And it seems that even our greatest technological advances only heighten the edge of an empty abyss because of a deeper longing for something that no particle accelerator can detect and no space telescope can find in either the vast expanse of the universe or the tiniest dissectible bit. Thus, we face a tension between faith in the promises of scientific progress and the very philosophy that makes such rational inquiry possible. For those who can see beyond simple pragmatic justifications, this disparity threatens the modern ethos and revives the most perplexing questions of life. The root of the problem is that the contemporary metaphysical ground for modern scientific *techne* falls short; it begins and ends with an illusion.[5]

Dispelling illusions and lighting the path to an alternate possibility, Maurice Blondel, most recognized for his dissertation, *Action (1893)*, examines the phenomenon of self-consciousness through human action and proposes an alternate conception of being itself. Through his philosophy of action, Blondel not only highlights the significance that living organisms exist in material reality at all, but the phenomena of specifically human life. His phenomenology of action highlights an interdependence of thought, being, and action where the self-conscious subject and material object are

4. See: Desmond, *Perplexity and Ultimacy*, xi. "Those who prefer to face forward resolutely towards the neon sun of scientific enlightenment will wonder if we are talking with nothing, or perhaps with ourselves, or our own shadow. They would have to turn from that sun to understand that the shadow cast by the question of ultimacy is thrown by an other sun. Scientific enlightenment will see only a blank emptiness in the sky, and will not see that this blank emptiness is also a shadow of the sun they do not see."

5. Desmond, *Being in the Between*, 15, 38–39.

intimately related and ordered toward a transcendent initiative. He conceives being, not as a static unity or abstract flux, but as fundamentally communal—a dialectical relation including thought, being, and action leading into the certitude of a transcendent reality that only God himself could know fully and toward which humans may only strive in their becoming.

While it is recognized that a variety of contemporary thinkers (i.e., Deleuzians) actively attempt to validate an immanentist monism, as opposed to a pantheistic monism that includes a superior transcendence, Blondel believes that any form of monism is an outright error. In *Action* *(1893)*, he argues: "Not only is every monism an error, that is, every doctrine that claims to reduce the principle of intelligibility and the principle of existence to a unity, but so too is every system, by the simple fact that it is a system, just as every action inspired by a fixed conviction is an illusion."[6] Additionally, for Blondel, "Every monism . . . is married to a dualism which it can never divorce."[7] In other words, monism is a form of reductionism that favors a static conception of ultimate reality over the dynamism of action in which self-conscious individuals must participate. But, if we remain focused on refuting either monism or dualism directly, we encounter the primary error between idealism and realism that Blondel explains in his essay *The Idealist Illusion*. The issue pertains to an attempt to seek conformity "between the idea and being," and Blondel sees a tension at work where the realist "fears taking being for the phenomenon," and the idealist "fears taking the phenomenon for being."[8] Here, the inverse reaction to our predicament is restated in different language. Blondel believes that "every dualism is a hybrid coupling of realism and idealism."[9] He argues that both realism and idealism are cut from the same *intellectualist* cloth, and he will show that one cannot "choose either one of these attitudes to the exclusion of the other."[10] The intellectualist synthesis of these seemingly opposite theories is "a generic conception of which idealism and realism in all their varied forms are only hybrid species."[11] And the monistic expression is but one example of this type of hybrid. Most importantly, the shared error occurs when "the *fact* of thinking is taken in itself separated from the very *act* of thinking."[12]

6. Blondel, *Action (1893)*, 18.

7. Blondel, *Idealist Illusion*, 80.

8. Ibid., 75, 80.

9. Ibid., 79.

10. Ibid., 75.

11. Ibid., 87.

12. Ibid.

To clarify, it is worth looking at a more lengthy section of Blondel's essay on this point:

> Whether this monster is made of the double of objects of any sort to which it relates by becoming their replica, or whether it is forbidden to brush against beings, this ideally real or really ideal monster subjects everything to its power of metaphysical construction or critical destruction: even the practical life finds itself subjected to the demonstrations it outlines. And the moral or religious prescriptions are justified or dissolved by its objective deductions alone. The abstract and the general are the rule of the concrete; the particular, the individual, the subjective are eliminated from science: nothing is taken into account except in the form of an impersonal rationalism, by means of a form of thinking that is fixed, rigid without entrails, without opening, without movement, without an inkling about the inside of things, infatuating, intolerant and despotic. And if criticism breaks this iron garrote by showing that one must give up the idea of reconciling idea with being, because it conceives of being only in the form it cannot take, then idea, not at all prepared to find the anchor it needs in the life from which it issues, loses itself in dialectical constructions and in the anarchy of intellectual individualism.[13]

This is an important point as it pertains directly to the phenomenon of self-consciousness in material reality. The tension felt between consciousness and matter can neither be resolved dualistically nor collapsed into a monism; not even dialectical materialism can reconcile the aporia without falling into the intellectualist trap. For all of these options render being into an intellectualist form that separates life from being, thought from action, and consciousness from materiality.

Continuing, Blondel argues that one has already been caught in the intellectualist trap as soon as facts are validated through appearance.[14] Such action exposes the dualism of thought and external reality.[15] He recognizes that at the same time one wishes to place trust in immediate observations, or common sense deductions, there is a desire for something more than observation or deduction can provide. Blondel believes that his philosophy of action will solve traditional problems pertaining to subject versus object (idea versus being) duality, exposing the common thread that links idealism

13. Ibid., 87–88.
14. Ibid., 75.
15. Ibid.

and realism to form the intellectualist illusion as a whole.[16] Restated simply, the illusion occurs when thought is separated from action. The resulting distortion causes a false division between subject and object that intellectualizes reality from the subjective perspective and alienates the object to its own distant and enigmatic space. "Indeed either thinking is considered the only reality, or one sees it only as a simple epiphenomenon."[17] We will see later in this essay how Blondel will approach the classification of matter; but the debate between essence and existence is the real dilemma of intellectualism, and Blondel finds fault in the formulation of the very problem itself.[18]

Demonstrating this problem, in *Action (1893)* Blondel critiques mathematics, the very foundation of the positive sciences, as a "fiction that works" by grounding itself in the One, "as if experience reached the atom or the point, and in the homogeneous and the continuum of space, size, and number, as if these were the realizable or verified limit of sensible discontinuity and heterogeneity."[19] Through this chimera, he says, "we act as if we had in hand what will always escape our grasp, unity and the homogeneous continuum."[20] Whereas the deductive sciences presuppose "at the outset the analysis to be finished," the natural sciences "always presuppose the original reality, the relative perfection, the sufficiency of each synthesis as synthesis."[21] This produces a unified totality that grounds the sciences tenuously within the experience of the object, but "we shall never deduce ... the complex nature, the discontinuity and the heterogeneity of the objects it takes as the matter of its research" through such scientific inquiry.[22] Thus, Blondel can confidently declare that: "The positive sciences are not sufficient for us, because they are not self-sufficient."[23] Affirming Oliva Blanchette's analysis of this point, Blondel shows that for science to exist at all a subjective mind must be present, and such consciousness is not accounted for by science or the immanentist philosophy that grounds it.[24]

Rejecting any mysterious notion of enigmatic being and beginning with the phenomenon of lived experience as it is, action presents itself as

16. Ibid., 76, 80.

17. Ibid., 80.

18. Ibid., 77.

19. Blondel, *Action (1893)*, 62–63

20. Ibid.

21. Ibid.

22. Ibid.

23. Ibid., 65.

24. Blanchette, *Maurice Blondel*, 66.

surely as any fact.[25] In pondering being at all we must begin to think, but such consciousness is already an enactment. Thus, action is fundamental to self-conscious being; life is being in action, but neither is fully reducible to the other. In the midst of life, self-conscious individuals must always act. We are born through action, thrust into action, and determined by our actions, hence Blondel declares: "the substance of man is action, he is what he does. *Ev τω εργω το ov* (being is in action). We are, we know, we live, *only sub specie actionis* (under the species of action)."[26]

On the first page of *Action (1893)*, Blondel observes that as a human, "I act, but without even knowing what action is, without having wished to live, without knowing exactly either who I am or even if I am."[27] And since acting is obligatory it cannot be delayed. One is forced to act; from the very moment of consciousness, choices, even those made by others, determine the path of one's life. And every action, each individual choice to act or not to act, "cuts off an infinity of possible acts."[28] But even though every act carries a universal weight, we must press forward blindly, not knowing exactly how any particular decision will shape the future.

> Practice, which tolerates no delay, never entails a perfect clarity; the complete analysis of it is not possible for a finite mind. Any rule of life that would be grounded only on a philosophical theory and abstract principles would be temerarious. I cannot put off acting until all the evidence has appeared, and all evidence that shines before the mind is partial. Pure knowledge is never enough to move us because it does not take hold of us in our entirety. In every act, there is an act of faith.[29]

Because even the purest knowledge cannot suffice for action, Blondel proposes a science of practice grounded in action itself.

Since thought itself is an action, one cannot begin with either a univocal enigma, an equivocal flux (which ultimately collapses back in on itself to form a singularity), or a dialectic that has the illusion of activity but also collapses into a form of monism, and retain any semblance of thought as living

---

25. Blondel, *Action (1893)*, 3.

26. Ibid., 191. "Not only does action manifest what we were already, but it also makes us grow and go out of ourselves, so to speak; so that after having studied the progress of action in being, and the progress of being in action, we will have to transport the center of gravity of the will consistent with the law of its progress beyond individual life."

27. Ibid., 3.

28. Ibid., 4.

29. Ibid.

thought.[30] For, thought cannot be grounded either from the side of the object as materially conditioned, nor the side of the subject as pure conscious spirit, and according to Blanchette's analysis, Blondel believes that either attempt is "a relativist point of view because it reduces thought to a theory of knowledge."[31] According to Blondel, "One must not render intelligence totally unintelligible, nor speak of an intelligible that remains intrinsically inconceivable, and this would be the case if one claims that thought proceeds from pure passivity, in the sense of inertia that one assigns to this word all too readily."[32] Likewise, if one's conception of being begins in a passive state, the possibility of self-conscious thought disappears even before it appears. As we have mentioned, for Blondel, the thought of an individual conscious subject is always already in action, and thought transcends the conscious subject insofar as the subject continuously seeks fulfillment in something beyond itself.[33] Blondel writes: "Already indispensible to the knowledge of distinct objects, rational activity underlies the subjectivity of life: yet that life, unable to isolate[34] itself, trying to justify and perfect itself, cannot raise itself to its proper level or ideal order."[35]

In its becoming, the self-conscious subject is always in the process of becoming an authentic subject. Blondel speaks of a "double efficiency" where the self-conscious individual must act, going beyond itself as it strives to "exceed its proper consciousness and its proper action."[36] This is true whether the subject actualizes its own self-motivated desires, or in accordance with the infinite nature of its willing, authenticates itself through surpassing itself in a relinquishment of those desires and embracing the transcendent order that calls it outside itself and into communal life. In either case, there is an order toward which action leads from the internal dynamism of subjective consciousness to participation in the community of being.

Ultimately, Blondel would likely agree with William Desmond that a double without dualism is possible.[37] For Desmond, "There is a difference,

30. Blanchette, *Blondel*, 421–23.

31. Ibid., 423.

32. Blondel, *La Pensée, Tome I*, 231. Special thanks to Dr. Jeffrey Courtright, who assisted with translating selections of Blondel's texts available only in the original French editions. See: Blanchette, *Blondel*, 422.

33. The theme of an infinite nature of the human will was one of Blondel's highlighted assertions in *Action (1893)*.

34. The French construction here is *s'enclore*, which translated more literally means to "fence itself off from everything else."

35. Blondel, *La Pensée, Tome I*, 174. See: Blanchette, *Blondel*, 441.

36. Ibid.

37. Desmond, *Being in the Between*, 74, 94–95, 155, 164–65, 197, 214, 216, 239–46,

a doubling, but not a dualism, between the naturing and the natured. A sense for the equivocal makes us mindful of the doubling as more than a provisional failure of univocity, but as a constitutive ambiguity in the happening of being in the between."[38] Both Desmond and Blondel critique the univocity of monism and share the idea of an in-between where ambiguity blurs the sharp contrast between the univocal reduction and equivocal abstraction of positive science on the one hand and speculative metaphysics on the other. Even in the most immanent realm of material reality, reciprocity exists between conscious subjects and material objects such that the two are irreconcilably intertwined. There is neither a univocal reduction, nor an equivocal abstraction of being. For Blondel, matter is not "an independent being from the rest and even [independent] from a creator."[39] On the contrary, matter "presents itself as in between, so to speak, of two aspects, or rather two realities, in becoming incompletely intelligible and open to various interpretations."[40] On one hand, a positive dynamism exists within thought, and specifically human thought, that cannot be reduced to mere substance or any a priori conception of thought thinking itself. On the other hand, and at the same time, there exists an intelligibility of substance that cannot be reduced to illusion any more than it can be absolutize as the only true being.

In Blondel's volume on being, he questions whether matter should be considered a being at all.[41] Importantly, Blanchette observes that Blondel does not doubt the reality of matter as Descartes did.[42] Instead, Blondel thinks that a distinction exists between the "factual idea of a substantial materiality and the necessary idea that we have of being."[43] Here, Oliva Blanchette provides an excellent summary, not only concerning Blondel's classification of matter, but also regarding the thrust of the argument for this essay as a whole:

> With this first consideration of matter as real, but not yet worthy of the name *being*, Blondel sees himself as having overcome a whole set of views that are for him inadequate in consideration of being as a whole. These include both *dualism*, which posits a second cause of being in opposition to the creator as first cause,

263.

38. Ibid., 94.
39. Blondel, *La Pensée, Tome I*, 59.
40. Ibid. See: Blanchette, *Blondel*, 425–28.
41. Blondel, *L'Être*, 63–70.
42. Blanchette, *Blondel*, 502.
43. Blondel, *L'Être, 66*. See: Blanchette, *Blondel*, 502–3, 809.

and *monism*, which fails to account for how particular finite beings can subsist in contradistinction from absolute Being in itself. At the same time he claims to overcome *idealism* as well, as a superficial form of spiritualism that only juxtaposes two kinds of substance, one material and one spiritual, each of which could be understood as subsisting in isolation from the other or as absorbing one another, whether as materialism or spiritualism, as in the opposition between Marxism and Hegelianism. For Blondel, matter cannot be understood except as it relates to spirit and finite spirit cannot be understood except as constrained by matter.[44]

Thus, Blondel grants matter an essential, yet incomplete reality of its own, but he asserts that it does not qualify to be called being. Hence, in restricting being to pure matter, and incidentally turning consciousness into an epiphenomenon, immanentism misses the larger picture and reduces the community of being to a singular part.[45]

Throughout his authorship, Blondel continues to probe for being in its truest and most absolute sense, which will move far beyond the confines of any immanent reality. He will proceed from the insufficiency of mankind's infinite willing to the fulfillment of thought in the necessary being of action within the supernatural. Through his phenomenology of action, Blondel will continue to demonstrate the essentiality of a supernatural transcendence that constitutes and surpasses the observable phenomena of material reality.[46] As cursory as it is, this brief summary has examined Blondel's theory that the true quandary for philosophy to address is not a dualistic illusion, but the reality of human life itself. His assertion is validated through a phenomenological study of the concept of action, which at the fore presents itself as a mistakenly simple concept but elucidates a reality far beyond any material immanence. Although insufficiency limits finite consciousness and shapes the mode of relation to materiality, finite consciousness is not limited to finitude *per se*. In fact, for Blondel, transcendence is implied from within the immanent realm of human action itself. He firmly situates individual

44. Blanchette, *Blondel*, 503–4.

45. Blondel, *Action (1893)*, 64 fn. 1. "But the parts are not always more simple than the whole, although they are less than the whole: the whole is resolvable, but not divisible."

46. Ibid., 40. "For all, whether they know it or not, the problem of life is a question of metaphysics, of morality and of science all at once. Action is that synthesis of willing, knowing and being, that bond of the human composite that cannot be cut without destroying what has been torn apart; it is the precise point where the world of thought, the moral world, and the world of science converge; and if these worlds do not unite in it, everything comes apart."

consciousness within a participatory community of action, and expounds upon modes of immanent action and transcendent relation. Through a painstaking undertaking, Blondel uncovers the necessity of the supernatural for human acting in the world, revealing the principle of action inherent within both human consciousness and material reality.[47] By referring to man's future fate, in order to elicit the unlimited desire of human willing, Blondel hopes that the study of action will lead toward the development of a rigorous philosophy of the supernatural. In all, we must will to act, but action always surpasses what we will to be and we must give ourselves to the eternal implication of action.[48] Such action moves from a simple act of the human will toward a transcendent reality that the immanent realm cannot contain.[49]

47. This will also involve a recovery of the term 'supernatural' that rejects its modern pejorative connotations.

48. See: Cooper, *Life in the Flesh*, 137, 148–49. "According to [Chantal] Delsol, for life to have meaning it must establish a connection with something other, something beyond itself, with 'exterior referents that go beyond it and outlive it.'"

49. Blanchette, *Blondel*, 585. "For Blondel, there is within us a power that transcends the entire universe, and that we can now characterize as 'powerful even against God,' implied in the very consciousness we have of our own initiatives."

BIBLIOGRAPHY

Blanchette, Oliva. *Maurice Blondel: A Philosophical Life*. Grand Rapids: Eerdmans, 2010.

Blondel, Maurice. *Action (1893): Essay on a Critique of Life and a Science of Practice*. Translated by Oliva Blanchette. Notre Dame: University of Notre Dame Press, 2003.

———. *La Pensée, Tome I*. Paris: Alcan, 1934.

———. *L'Être et les êtres*. Paris: Alcan, 1935.

———. *The Idealist Illusion and Other Essays*. Translated by Fiachra Long. Dordrecht: Kluwer, 2000.

Cooper, Adam G. *Life in the Flesh: An Anti-Gnostic Spiritual Philosophy*. Oxford: Oxford University Press, 2008.

Desmond, William. *Being and the Between*. Albany, NY: State University of New York Press, 1995.

———. *Perplexity and Ultimacy: Metaphysical Thoughts from the Middle*. Albany, NY: State University of New York Press, 1995.

Dupré, Louis K. *Passage to Modernity: An Essay in the Hermeneutics of Nature and Culture*. New Haven: Yale University Press, 1993.

Latour, Bruno. *We Have Never Been Modern*. Translated by Catherine Porter. Cambridge: Harvard University Press, 1993.

Spaemann, Robert. *Essays in Anthropology: Variations on a Theme*. Translated by Guido De Graaff and James Mumford. Eugene, OR: Cascade, 2010.

3

"The Incomprehensible Someone"

Hans Urs von Balthasar on the Mission of the Holy
Spirit for a Contemporary Theology of History

JOSEPH K. GORDON

INTRODUCTION

As Robert Doran contends, any contemporary[1] attempt at systematic theology must take historical consciousness seriously, and thus must present itself

---

1. It is hard for me to put into words my appreciation for John Castelein or my joy at having the opportunity to contribute to this collection of essays in his honor. This particular work, the revised fruit of one of my doctoral seminars at Marquette University, only tangentially touches on issues that have preoccupied John throughout his career as an astute interpreter and evaluator of theological texts and ideas. Nevertheless, this essay would not have been possible apart from John's teaching; I would certainly not be where I am today without his encouragement and guidance. He has encouraged me, both through his example and through his words, to always ask questions from my own horizon—after all, we always start *in via*—and to be prepared to grow and be transformed by God's truth wherever it is to be found. I am forever grateful for his sense of wonder, humble honesty, and ceaseless encouragement.

conscientiously as a theological theory of history.[2] Hans Urs von Balthasar's unique presentation of the symphonic economic work[3] of the Triune God, on Doran's recommendation, should play a significant role in the articulation of such a theology of history.[4] Doran suggests that the mission of the Holy Spirit is the "gift" around which a contemporary theology of history must revolve,[5] and Balthasar likewise affirms that "the work and position of the Holy Spirit is revealed to us as the center point of reference where all perspectives meet."[6] This is because it is the mission of the Spirit which "makes history the history of salvation" and gives history "three dimensions, a Trinitarian structure which confers upon [it] . . . a divine spaciousness and capacity for development."[7] The Holy Spirit not only reveals the Trinitarian structure of history, it also makes manifest the Triunity of God *en se*: "the Spirit who proceeds from Father and Son, since he is neither Father nor Son but their reciprocal love, introduces us to this mystery."[8]

What follows then, is an examination of the contours of Balthasar's presentation of the work/mission of the Holy Spirit in history, presented as a summary of key themes in Balthasar's pneumatology that would inform such a contemporary theology of history. In order to judiciously attend to the particularity of Balthasar's pneumatology, we must first give attention to his own unique methodological approach to theology. For Balthasar, the gift of the Holy Spirit and the concomitant indwelling of the Triune God that the Holy Spirit achieves in the believer/theologian are the necessary conditions of faithful theological reflection. "An authentic theology," Balthasar writes, "however simple or learned it professes to be, can only be developed

2. See Doran *What is Systematic Theology?* 152–53. See also Doran, "System and History: The Challenge to Catholic Systematic Theology," 652–78.

3. See Balthasar, *The Truth is Symphonic*, 15.

4 See Doran, "Lonergan and von Balthasar: Methodological Considerations," 61–84.

5 See ibid., 65–66. In his most recent monograph, Doran summarizes this pneumatological emphasis well: "A contemporary Catholic systematic theology must articulate its understanding of the mysteries of Christian faith in the context of the multi-religious and interreligious world in which we live. Concretely, this means that the central emphases in a contemporary and foreseeable Catholic systematic theology will be Trinitarian and Pneumatological, without any sacrifice of the central doctrinal thrust of the Christological dogmas . . . it is the mission of the Holy Spirit that accounts for the radical move beyond the permanent achievements of past systematic theology, a move that in no way goes back on those achievements but rather propels them forward." Doran, *The Trinity in History A Theology of the Divine Missions: I. Missions and Processions*, 10.

6. Balthasar, *A Theology of History*, 63.

7. Ibid.

8. Balthasar, *The Truth*, 12.

in the Holy Spirit."[9] Balthasar's theological method therefore emphasizes prayerful submission to this internal revelatory work of the Spirit (which is always the revelation of the Father in the form of the Son). Balthasar's pneumatology also has a broader Trinitarian context; as already noted above, the symphony which the Holy Spirit conducts in his economic mission is both grounded in and draws created history into the eternal *circumcessio* of the immanent Trinity.[10] In fact, the "Spirit is the indispensable Declarer of Trinitarian truth; in all the functions attributed to him he is the final and concluding object of *theo-logic*."[11] The following treatments of Balthasar's methodology and Trinitarian theology will thus help frame his pneumatology. We proceed with the assumption that Balthasar's thought on theological method, Trinitarian theology, and pneumatology proper remains largely consistent throughout his theological career. Even so, examining his work without giving concerted attention to its diachronic development presents risks. Balthasarian scholarship has yet to engage the development of his thought in any sustained way.[12] We will here only focus on the consistency between his earlier and later pneumatological reflections.

We will examine Balthasar's work on the mission of the Holy Spirit through four stages: 1) the immanent procession of the Holy Spirit, 2) the Spirit's work in the visible mission of the Son during the Incarnation, 3) the Spirit's sacramental universalization of the economic work of the Son in the church throughout history, and finally 4) the Spirit's work in creating the missions of the church and individual Christians as the application of Christ's universal/historical form. Finally, the essay concludes by evaluating Balthasar's work in these loci and by suggesting its value for a contemporary theology of history.

Balthasar's "Theological Style"

Balthasar is an enigmatic figure within academic theology. His oeuvre is as difficult to characterize and categorize as it is expansive.[13] Balthasar's con-

9. Balthasar, *Theo-Logic III*, 31.

10. For *"even eternal truth itself is symphonic."* Balthasar, *The Truth*, 12. Italics in original.

11. Balthasar, *Theo-Logic III*, 24.

12. For a helpful treatment of the continuity and development of Balthasar's aesthetic approach to theology from his dissertation on the apocalyptic imagination of the German people through his Trilogy, see Carpenter, "Theo-Poetics: Figure and Metaphysics in the Thought of Hans Urs von Balthasar," 7–113.

13. "So varied is [his work], so complex, usually so undidactic, so wide-ranging through different genres, that its unity is difficult to grasp, at least at first blush." De

structive theological work is littered with references to poetry, literature and contemporary and ancient philosophy. It has accordingly been compared with the work of the church fathers, a comparison Balthasar would no doubt relish. His integration of diverse theological resources—including Scripture, the Fathers and Scholastics, liturgy, philosophy, and the arts—exhibits his protest against the unchecked ascendency of an all-too-common myopia endemic to modern academic "sitting" theology. Balthasar's self-conscious intermingling of theoretical speculation and meditative/contemplative theological discourse exhibits his desire to reunite theology with prayer. Despite his prolific and erudite output, his work exhibits a prayerfulness uncommon in contemporary theological work. His own term, *kniende theologie* (praying or kneeling theology), is thus perhaps the most apt descriptor of his theological method/style.[14]

Balthasar frequently expresses his distrust of overly systematic accounts of Christian theology. While Balthasar has much praise for the rigor and creativity of Thomas Aquinas,[15] and even for scholastic theology in general,[16] he could not stomach the "sawdust Thomism" he encountered in his Jesuit education.[17] He famously described his time in the Jesuit scholasticate as a period of "languishing in the desert."[18] In Balthasar's assessment, the legitimacy and fruitfulness of truly Thomistic Scholasticism had been long lost and had been replaced with the arid pedantry of the manual

Lubac, "A Witness of Christ in the Church: Hans Urs von Balthasar," 272. For a complete bibliography of Balthasar's published works in German see Balthasar, *Bibliographie, 1925–1990* (Einsiedeln: Freiburg, 1990). For contemporary English translations see "English Translations of German Titles by Hans Urs von Balthasar," in *Hans Urs von Balthasar: His Life and Work*, 299–305.

14. See Schindler, "Preface," in *Hans Urs von Balthasar: His Life and Work*, xi. "As time went on," Balthasar explains, "theology at prayer was superseded by theology at the desk, and this brought about the cleavage now under discussion. 'Scientific' theology became more and more divorced from prayer, and so lost the accent and tone with which one should speak of what is holy, while 'affective' theology, as it became increasingly empty, often degenerated into unctuous, platitudinous piety." Hans Urs von Balthasar, *Explorations I,* 208.

15. See, for instance, *Explorations I*, 209. Also note his entirely positive assessment of Thomas's metaphysics in Balthasar, *The Glory of the Lord IV*, 393–412; and Ryan Hemmer's essay in this volume.

16. "The progress wrought by Scholasticism," Balthasar affirms, "is obvious." Balthasar, *Explorations I*, 208.

17. I have not been able to track down the source of the phrase "sawdust Thomism" in Balthasar's work, but Fergus Kerr and Edward Oakes/David Moss both attribute the quotation to Balthasar. See Kerr, *Twentieth Century Catholic Theology,* 131; and Oakes and Moss, "Introduction," in *The Cambridge Companion to Hans Urs von Balthasar*, 2.

18. Balthasar, *My Work in Retrospect*, 89. See also Henrici, "Hans Urs von Balthasar: A Sketch of His Life," 9–14.

tradition.[19] His comments on the development of dogma in *A Theology of History* capture his disdain for such theology well:

> What is entirely intolerable is the notion that the "progress of dogma" gradually narrows down the unexplored area of divine truth, continually allowing less and less space to the free play of thought within the Faith, as though "progress" consisted in first of all establishing the main outlines of the Faith, and then proceeding to the more and more detailed work required to complete the edifice until finally—shortly before the Last Judgment perhaps?—the structure would stand there complete, consisting in all its aspects of fully "used up," defined dogma.[20]

While the above explanation is undoubtedly a caricature of the kind of Neo-Scholasticism Balthasar detested—for who would be so bold as to suggest humanity could objectify and parse the content of revelation in such a way?—it does sound a clarion call against any proclivities to domesticate the mysteries of Christian faith.[21] If the Triune God has incorporated us into the fullness and fecundity of his deity in Christ through the Holy Spirit, how could we ever exhaustively analyze, compartmentalize, and categorize this fullness? Theology can never proceed with the brazen assumption that it might grasp or comprehend its "object" in its totality.

Balthasar is not wholly opposed to reasoned and philosophically sophisticated theological investigations.[22] In *Theo-Logic III*, Balthasar highlights the inescapability of the reasoned pursuit of theological truth. "Insofar as [the human person] is essentially a seeker (*fides quaerens intellectum*) and the God who finds [him or her] must continually be sought for (*ut inventus quaeratur immensus est*), this rational endeavor is never to be excluded, even from the most prayerful theology."[23] While the critical component of theology is necessary, it "can only be a constituent part of prayer's totality."[24] Critical, speculative, or systematic theology can only take place in an attitude of prayer in the counsel of the Holy Spirit.

19. "The legitimate rational method of a Thomas [had become] increasingly distorted into an unbearable rationalism by the overweening deductions of a 'theology of conclusions.'" Balthasar, *Glory of the Lord IV*, 459. The phrase "a theology of conclusions," comes from Bouyer, *Das Handwerk des Theologen*, 170–71.

20. Balthasar, *Theology of History*, 107.

21. For more on Balthasar's warnings against domesticating faith, see Hans Urs von Balthasar, *Theo-Drama IV*, 457–64.

22. "There *is* a speculative, theoretical approach in faith, in theology and in Christian life as a whole, and *it is very necessary*." Balthasar, *Prayer*, 80. Italics mine.

23. Balthasar, *Theo-Logic III*, 365.

24. Balthasar, *Prayer*, 80.

One can take "a deliberately critical view" regarding the investigation of the things of this world, provided one has the humility and openness to relevant information which critical science requires. Ultimately, though, the critical approach must not forget that the things of this world find their ultimate meaning only as they are situated within the economy of salvation.[25] Theological speculation "should take as its starting point, not man's *desiderium* as the creature's core *existeniale*, but the fire that the divine Word has fanned into flame in it."[26] The light of God's triune self-revelation must transform and transpose all critical thought and speculation. It is because of the Incarnation of the Word of God, and because of the subsequent outpouring of the Holy Spirit, that Christian theological reflection is possible at all. The manifestation and character of these truths call for a certain posture of humility.

Though Balthasar esteems the tradition of the church, he argues that "[honoring] the Tradition does not excuse one from the obligation of beginning everything from the beginning each time, not with Augustine or Thomas or Newman, *but with Christ*."[27] Though his work is saturated with approbation for traditional patristic and scholastic doctrinal *formulae*, Balthasar argues that theology must not parrot these resources; it should instead continue to unfold their inner unity in the Holy Spirit: "It is of the very essence of tradition, and so of theology, that its progress depends on a deeper, bolder exploration of the sources . . ."[28] The Triune God has given the totality of God's self in the *depositum fidei*, the inexhaustible riches of God's divine glory. Nourished and fertilized by this deposit, "the tree of tradition," Balthasar exclaims, "must put forth new branches."[29] As he frequently reminds his readers, the Holy Spirit will lead the believer "into all truth" (John 14:16).[30] When one submits to the promptings of the Spirit dwelling within, one can plumb the depths of divine being and recognize and understand, though only in a fleeting way, its form and intelligibility. Balthasar's expansive corpus, its idiosyncrasies notwithstanding, evinces the product of a powerful and synthetic mind at work. It is doubtless the kind of "new" unfolding of the tradition which the above remarks envision. It

25. Ibid.

26. Balthasar, *Theo-Logic III*, 365. "The first *desideratum* for seeing objectively is the 'letting be' of God's self-revelation. . . . This first step is not to master the materials of perception by imposing our own categories on them but an attitude of service to the object." Balthasar, *My Work*, 81.

27. Balthasar, *Razing the Bastions*, 32.

28. Balthasar, *Explorations I*, 208. See also ibid., 208–9.

29. See Balthasar, *My Work*, 15.

30. See Balthasar, *Theology of History*, 107.

has today become a fecund branch on the tree of the tradition, the fruit of which will nourish theological reflection and prayerful devotion in the church and academy for centuries. Balthasar, though, issues a caution to all who would engage the fruit of his work in the future: "Perhaps some eager soul thirsty for systematics would like to make something out of these fragments, putting the stones in order and assembling them into a mosaic. The author, however, mistrusts such undertakings. Such constructions merely try to yank the mystery from its seclusion and cast it into the glare of our light. But God dwells in inaccessible light."[31]

Balthasar is not suggesting that his work is unintelligible or incoherent, in spite of the complaints of his accusers, but is simply again reminding the reader that the subject and object of the reader's own study is not Balthasar's theology as such but instead the inexhaustible and incomprehensible mystery manifest in the revelation of the Triune God in our history. We can only approach the revelation of the Triune God with humility, ever aware of the provisionality of all of our theological reflection. For ultimately, the possibility of theology as a discipline and the ground of theological method itself is "God's love . . . poured into our hearts through the Holy Spirit who is given to us" (Rom 5:5).[32]

The Trinity: Economic and Immanent[33]

Balthasar argues that the gift of the Holy Spirit, whose very presence within us enables our theological reflection, *also* incorporates us into the Incarnate Word, returned to the Father, and thus effectuates our participation within the Triune life of God.[34] From revelation, Christian faith "knows . . . that

31. Balthasar, *Explorations IV*, 11.

32. All references to Scripture taken from the *The New Oxford Annotated Bible: New Revised Standard Version*.

33. For helpful recent summaries of von Balthasar's unique approach to Trinitarian theology, see Friesenhahn, *The Trinity and Theodicy*, 107–38; Howsare, *Hans Urs von Balthasar: A Guide for the Perplexed*, 121–44; Hunt, *The Trinity and the Paschal Mystery*; and Williams, "Balthasar and the Trinity," 37–50. For more critical perspectives see Emery, "The Immutability of the God of Love and the Problem of Language Concerning the 'Suffering of God,'" 48–52; and Kilby, "Hans Urs von Balthasar on the Trinity," 208–22.

34. With the coming of the Holy Spirit, "we are not only introduced to an 'economic' Trinity in its external relations; we are introduced to its immanent truth . . . [the Spirit] causes us to participate in the divine realm of the Father-Son relationship . . . and to participate in the Incarnation." Balthasar, *Theo-Logic III*, 74–75. "We are actually brought to participate, by grace, in the begetting of the Son from the Father." Balthasar, *Prayer*, 70.

the hypostases really exist in their relative opposition, just as it knows . . . that Father, Son, and Holy Spirit are one God."[35] "Any speculative grasp of the mystery of the identity of both aspects," he suggests, "always requires the convergence [*aufeinanderbewegung*] of two propositions—which resist every attempt to reduce them to one."[36] Such speculative approaches to Trinitarian theology, as Balthasar never tires of reminding us, are only possible because of the indwelling of the Triune God in us through the Holy Spirit. While many aspects of Balthasar's speculative Trinitarian theology are rooted in traditional patristic and scholastic expositions of the doctrine, in his own explication of the mystery of the Triune God he frequently suggests new formulations. Before examining his new controversial positions, we will first enumerate some of the "tamer" points of Balthasar's Trinitarian theology.

Balthasar affirms, with the whole of Christian tradition, that the Triune God reveals God's self in the economy; the appearance of the economic Trinity is the only *datum* from which we might proceed to some conception of the immanent Trinity.[37] "We have," he explains, "no access whatsoever to the *immanent* Trinity except as a result of the Trinity's *economic* self-manifestation."[38] Any understanding that we can have of the form of God's Triunity *en se*, therefore, can only be mediated through our creaturely language and categories.[39] As Balthasar also affirms, we must take care not to bifurcate the "economic" Trinity with the "immanent" Trinity—for there are not two Trinities but one. The "immanent" Trinity, however, cannot be univocally equated with the "economic" Trinity without remainder.[40] To equate "immanent" and "economic" absolutely would make creation necessary and would entangle God's being with God's work. As Balthasar argues, the conditions of the "immanent" Trinity allow for the very possibility of an "economic" self-manifestation of the Trinity.[41] Balthasar also upholds a traditional conceptualization of the relationship between the Trinitarian

35. Balthasar, *Theo-Logic II*, 133.

36. Ibid.

37. See Balthasar, *Mysterium Paschale*, 28; Balthasar, *Theo-Drama III*, 319–28; Balthasar, *Theo-Drama V*, 74, 258; Balthasar, *Theo-Logic II*, 138; and Balthasar, *Theo-Logic III*, 138.

38. Balthasar, *Theo-Logic III*, 210.

39. For more on this see Balthasar, *The Glory of the Lord VII*, 107.

40. Balthasar, *Theo-Drama III*, 157.

41. "The laws of the 'economic' Trinity arise from the 'immanent' Trinity." Ibid. In *Mysterium Paschale* he writes that "the exteriorisation of God (in the Incarnation) has its ontic condition of possibility in the eternal exteriorization of God—that is, in his tripersonal self-gift." Balthasar, *Mysterium Paschale*, 28.

processions and missions. For him, as for Thomas, the missions of the Son and Spirit are the "exteriorization" of their processions: each mission is a procession plus a created external term.[42] The missions are the economic "modalities" of the Son and Spirit.[43] Balthasar also stresses that the missions are identical to the processions, though again, not without remainder.[44] Additionally, he affirms the unity of the work of the Triune God *ad extra*.[45] In each of these areas, Balthasar's work clearly exhibits his commitment to traditional articulations of Trinitarian faith.

Beyond this "common ground," however, Balthasar suggests a number of unique and controversial contributions to Trinitarian theology. Balthasar posits the existence of "infinite distance" between the persons of the Trinity,[46] describes a type of "surprise" experienced by the persons within the immanent Trinity,[47] and offers a unique treatment of the *triduum mortis*—focused primarily on Christ's passivity in death—in its relationship to Trinitarian theology.[48] He is also openly critical of traditional

42. See Balthasar, *Theo-Drama I*, 646; Balthasar, *Theo-Drama V*, 63–65; and Balthasar, *Theo-Logic III*, 201.

43. Balthasar, *Theo-Drama III*, 226.

44. "Once we presuppose the creation, *processio* within the Godhead and *missio* outside it are one and the same as far as the Divine Persons are concerned, even at the point where the Son and Spirit enter the visible realm of creation." Balthasar, *Theo-Drama V*, 63; See also ibid., 80; and Balthasar, *Theo-Drama IV*, 55.

45. "The one Triune God effects the work that is, and remains, the central thing in the whole of human history: Those who are by nature finite, and have fallen captive to decay because of having turned away from God, are presented, through the calling back of the One into eternal life, with the hope, indeed, the certainty, of following after him." Balthasar, *Credo*, 59. See also Balthasar, *Explorations III*, 108; Balthasar, *Theo-Logic II*, 11; and Balthasar, *Theo-Drama IV*, 327. Balthasar's formulation of appropriation is complex and fragmentary, and would require more attention than can be given at this juncture.

46. See Balthasar, *Glory VII*, 322. See also Balthasar, *Theo-Drama III*, 228ff; and Balthasar, *Theo-Drama IV*, 323.

47. "In his trinitarian life he is continually being surprised by the 'ever-greater' that he is." *Theo-Logic III*, 30. See also O'Hanlon, *The Immutability of God in the Theology of Hans Urs von Balthasar*, 76, 79, 120–21, 168.

48. See Balthasar, *Mysterium Paschale*, passim; and Balthasar, *Theo-Drama IV*, 317–61. Balthasar's treatment of Christ's passive descent into hell has received a great deal of attention already, and discussion of the descent would take us too far afield of our present concern. For summary and defense of Balthasar's position see Hunt, *Trinity*, 68–76; and Friesenhahn, *Trinity and Theodicy*, 126–31. For an argument asserting the heretical nature of Balthasar's position see Pitstick, *Light in Darkness*. Pitstick and Edward Oakes also had a lively print exchange over this topic in *First Things*. For bibliographic information on this exchange see Friesenhahn, *Trinity and Theodicy*, 185.

"psychological" approaches to Trinitarian theology.[49] Balthasar suggests that analogies based on the *imago trinitatis* within the individual human subject are incomplete because they cannot convey the dynamism of love intrinsic to God's triune being. For Balthasar, "Love alone is credible."[50] Balthasar argues that an interpersonal analogy is needed to complement the psychological approaches to understanding the immanent Trinity.[51] In Balthasar's estimation, an interpersonal analogy of lover, beloved, and fruit of love is needed to do justice to the love that the Triune God is as it is manifested in God's self-revelation in the economy.[52] The themes of dynamism and love hold pride of place in his reflections on the Trinity.

Each of Balthasar's "new" Trinitarian convictions, then, can be traced to his desire to conscientiously relate every aspect of his Trinitarian theology to the fact of the Triune God's self-revelation as love—the revelation of the love of the Father in the Incarnate Word through the Holy Spirit. "God is not," he suggests, "in the first place, 'absolute power,' but 'absolute love,' and his sovereignty manifests itself not in holding on to what is its own but in its abandonment."[53] Balthasar's Trinitarian theology is thus a presentation of the divine mystery of love,

> which relates the event of the kenosis of the Son of God to what one can, by analogy, designate as the eternal "event" of the divine processions. It is from this supra-temporal yet ever actual event that, as Christians, we must approach the mystery of the divine "essence." That essence is forever "given" in the self-gift of the Father, "rendered" in the thanksgiving of the Son, and "represented" in its character as absolute love by the Holy Spirit.[54]

In Balthasar's understanding of the mystery of Christian faith, divine life itself must contain the possibility of kenosis for the Son to experience the kenosis into and within the economy. The Son's economic kenosis, as the fitting outworking of his procession, reveals that love is at the heart of the immanent Trinity. As Balthasar clarifies elsewhere, however, "this does not mean . . . that God's essence becomes itself (univocally) 'kenotic,' such

49. On this, see Hunt, *Trinity*, 57.

50. Balthasar, *Love Alone Is Credible*. See also Balthasar, *Credo*, 29.

51. In a particularly candid passage he exclaims, "Augustine's triadic logic calls for a complementary counter *image*, which bursts open the narrow confines of the self-enclosed subject, *even as it fails to maintain the unity of the divine substance* because of its emphasis on interpersonal love." Balthasar, *Theo-Logic II*, 40.

52. See ibid., 59, 62.

53. Balthasar, *Mysterium Paschale*, 28.

54. Ibid., viii.

that a single concept could include both the divine foundation of the possibility of kenosis, and the kenosis itself. . . . What it does mean . . . is that the divine 'power' is so ordered that it can make room for a possible self-exteriorization even to the utmost point."[55]

Balthasar's supposition of a sort of *analogia vacuandi* ("analogy of emptying") allows him to argue that every legitimate dynamism intrinsic to creation finds its ground in the supratemporal kenotic dynamism intrinsic to the immanent Trinity.[56] The "ever-greater" of God's Triune life contains within it the possibility of the "other" which is the created order.[57] Though Balthasar's rather novel contributions to trinitarian theology have given and will continue to give many traditional theologians pause, he nevertheless achieves a rather stunning portrayal of the Triune God which communicates the axiomatic Christian conviction that "God is love" (1 John 4:16). Hence Balthasar's trinitarian theology is dually radical: it is so in his fixation upon the *radix* of God's love—its foundation and guiding principle—and in the profligate liberality of Balthasar's idiom in his expression of this love. Though his trinitarian exposition is bold, and though he exhibits a great deal of confidence in his formulations, Balthasar consistently draws attention to the insufficiency of his Trinitarian reflections. His theology consequently possesses a pronounced apophatic element: "The Trinity is and remains an absolute mystery," he avers, and "any approach to the mystery must proceed by statements running in opposite directions."[58] Balthasar's expressiveness bespeaks his embrace of the paradox that the unknowable Triune God has clearly communicated God's self to us. While the Triunity of God remains a mystery, it is nevertheless an economically revealed mystery which attests to the fact that God is—in God's immanence—love. The "form" in which this mystery appears in our economy is the kenotic form of Christ. As the Apostle John writes, "God's love was revealed among us in this way: God sent his only Son into the world so that we might live through him" (1 John 4:9). As we will now see, it is only through the work of the Holy Spirit that the mystery of this love is accessible. The Holy Spirit enfolds us into the infinite mystery of the Triune God, drawing us into God's self to participate in his masterful direction of his interminable self-giving love in our own history.

55. Ibid., 29.

56. "We endeavored to locate all the genuine dynamisms of creation, but also the positive impulses of faith and hope, in the infinite life of God." Balthasar, *Theo-Drama V*, 181.

57. See Balthasar, *Credo*, 32.

58. Balthasar, *Theo-Logic III*, 157.

THE PROCESSION AND MISSION OF THE SPIRIT[59]

With our outlines of Balthasar's methodology and Trinitarian theology delineated, we now proceed to attempt to integrate the pneumatological insights scattered throughout his broad work into a coherent whole. This is no easy task for multiple reasons. The sheer quantity of Balthasar's work demands that we not approach it superficially. The subject matter of pneumatology also complicates things. As Balthasar admits in *Explorations III*, "one of the most difficult and rare things of all is a theology that permits the Holy Spirit himself [sic] to become the very theme of theology."[60] The difficulty of producing a cogent pneumatology, Balthasar suggests, is due to the Spirit's reluctance to cooperate with our plans: "The Spirit is breath, not a full outline, and therefore he wishes only to breathe through us, not to present himself to us as an object; he does not wish to be seen but to be the seeing eye of grace in us, and he is little concerned about whether we pray to him, provided that we pray with him, 'Abba, Father,' provided that we consent to his unutterable groaning in the depths of our soul."[61]

The Spirit is "the most mysterious aspect of God."[62] We affirm the existence and divinity of the Spirit because we discover these truths in revelation, but it seems impossible to pin down or circumscribe the Holy Spirit for closer examination. The Spirit was, is, and remains, the "incomprehensible someone" in the Godhead who is closer to us than we are to ourselves, yet still remains utterly indefinable.[63] As Balthasar rightly discerns, the only way we can come to a remotely satisfactory understanding of the Holy Spirit is through surrendering ourselves completely to his internal work in the depths of our souls: "To him, the most delicate, vulnerable, and precious one in God, we must open ourselves up, without defensiveness, without thinking that we know better, without hardening ourselves, so that we may undergo initiation by him into the mystery that God is love."[64] Initiation into the mystery of God's love by the Spirit conforms one to the likeness of divine love and infuses that person's speech and action with the economic

59. For lengthier treatments of Balthasar's pneumatology, see Sachs, "*Deus semper major—Ad majorem Dei gloriam*," 631–57; Balthasar, "Spirit and Life: The Pneumatology and Spirituality of Hans Urs von Balthasar"; Tossou, *Sreben nach Vollendung*; and Vogel, "The Unselfing Activity of the Holy Spirit in the Theology of Hans Urs von Balthasar," 16–34.

60. Balthasar, *Explorations III*, 11.

61. Ibid., 111.

62. Balthasar, *Credo*, 75.

63. Ibid.

64. Ibid., 76.

"form" of the divine love manifest in the Son. The Spirit does not execute his tasks within us in a coercive way, and so we always run the risk of resisting or ignoring his promptings. If we are able to defer to the Spirit's work in our being, he will shine the divine light of Triune love through us as if through a prism.

The Objective and Subjective Procession of the Holy Spirit

As noted above, for Balthasar, the immanent Trinity grounds the economic Trinity. Before we proceed to examine Balthasar's expositions of the missional work of the Holy Spirit, we must offer a brief overview of his beautiful yet paradoxical understanding of the procession of the Holy Spirit. Within the immanent Trinity, Balthasar describes the Holy Spirit as both the "Person-al" unity of the immanent love of Father and Son, and the fruit of their loving reciprocal exchange. The Spirit is both simultaneously, and has been so from eternity: "If the Father generates the Son in love, there is no moment at which the Son would not already also, in the same love, both be allowing himself to be generated and returning this love in the Holy Spirit; so that the Spirit would already, from the first, be flaring up as the flame of love between the two of them, thus being simultaneously both origin and result of that love."[65]

Elsewhere he describes the Spirit as "both the innermost crucible of movement of love between Father and Son and its product and fruit—the objective testimony to that fire and love."[66] These two aspects of the Spirit—as the subjective experience and objective product of the reciprocal love of the Father and Son—allow Balthasar to hold in tension the distinct shape of the love of the Triune God and its irreducible profundity; in doing so he is able to draw attention to both the intelligibility and boundlessness of the divine mystery made visible through the invisible work of the Spirit. In expressing the subjective love between Father and Son, the Spirit manifests the form of God's love as it is revealed in the economic mission of the Son. As the objective fruit of this unending love, the Spirit explodes every metaphorical and analogical container. As such, the Spirit attests to the fathomless mystery of the Triune God. We are drawn into this mystery in the Holy

---

65. Ibid., 78. Balthasar takes care to note that "the *taxis* must not be understood in any temporal sense whatsoever, because the processions of the Son and the Spirit are just as eternal as their existence." Balthasar, *Theo-Logic III*, 58. See also Balthasar, *Theo-Logic II*, 136.

66. Balthasar, *Theo-Logic III*, 307.

Spirit's economic work; through the Spirit we are incorporated into Christ and thus become the vessels of his presence through subsequent history.

From the Incarnation to Resurrection

Balthasar argues that the truth of God's triunity is economically manifested for the first time in the conception of the Incarnate Son, sent by the Father, through the Holy Spirit.[67] Within the immanent Trinity, Balthasar argues that the Holy Spirit proceeds from both the Father and the Son.[68] However, Balthasar writes, "when the Son becomes human, he, the indivisible Spirit of both, becomes, in the Father, the Spirit who issues directives and, in the Son, the Spirit who receives directives."[69] Balthasar draws attention to this submission of the Son to the Holy Spirit as an economic "inversion" of the Trinity.[70] The Incarnate Son submits himself fully to the guidance of the Holy Spirit during his earthly, visible mission.[71] For Balthsar, Christ's visible mission is a mission of obedient love and passivity. From the beginning, it is a mission ordered to the cross.[72] From before his birth through his crucifixion and death, the Son expresses resolute commitment to this mission.

The Outpouring of the Spirit

For Balthasar, the Son's historical/economic mission, culminating in his crucifixion, resurrection, and ascension, reveals the intelligibility of history. "By recapitulating history," he writes, "[Christ] becomes its norm."[73] The singular historical existence of the Incarnate Word, however, must still be universally extended to "every individual existence."[74] The Son's departure from the stage enables the entrance of the Spirit, who takes up the work of the universal mediation of the Son: "It is [the Holy Spirit] who sets his

---

67. See Balthasar, *Explorations III*, 118–19.

68. For his discussion of the *filioque*, see Balthasar, *Theo-Logic III*, 207–18.

69. Balthasar, *Credo*, 46. See also Balthasar, *Mysterium Paschale*, 30.

70. See Balthasar, *Theo-Drama III*, 191; see also ibid., 183–220. For an early articulation of "inversion" see Balthasar *Explorations IV*, 230–31.

71. "When the Son becomes human, he, the indivisible Spirit of both [Father and Son], becomes, in the Father, the Spirit who issues directives and, in the Son, the Spirit who receives directives." Balthasar, *Credo*, 46.

72. "The world was created with a view to the Son, who was to be born as a man and to die as the Lamb of God." Balthasar, *Theo-Logic III*, 415.

73. Balthasar, *Theology of History*, 81.

74. Ibid., 82.

stamp upon the church and on the individual believer, and on the history of both, by interpreting the life of Jesus (which is itself an interpretation of the Father), giving it the form and force of an unfailing valid norm."[75] In sovereign freedom, the Spirit reiterates the form through "endless variations."[76] The Son's return to the Father is the necessary condition of the fullness of the Son's own manifestation through the work of the Holy Spirit. For Balthasar there is no question of a supercession of missions; the Son and the Spirit together effect the Triune God's offer of participation in divine life to humanity.[77] In complete cooperation and equality, the Father's two hands accomplish the economic tasks entrusted to them by the Father. The Spirit's outpouring allows the Son's "bestowal of the Father [to] become effective[,] . . . [abolishing] the kenotic 'inhibition' and [letting] the eternal mutuality of the breathing of the Spirit be actual and real in the world. . . ."[78] The end of the visible activity of the Son leads into this invisible activity of the Holy Spirit,[79] and the economic "inversion" which began at the Incarnation comes to an end.[80]

As we have noted above, Balthasar argues compellingly that the Incarnation of the Word is the first historical event in which God's triunity is fully manifest. The outpouring of the Spirit after Christ's death—first on the disciples by the risen Christ, and second on "all flesh" at Pentecost—provides the theologian with a further insight into the mysterious nature of the Holy Spirit within the immanent Trinity. In these two events, Balthasar suggests: "The mystery of the economic Trinity . . . unites in an incomprehensible manner [the objective and subjective aspects of the Spirit] thereby permitting us to see into the depths of the mystery within the Godhead, where the Spirit comes into being in divine-sovereign freedom as the personal 'We' beyond the 'I'-'Thou' of Father and Son, as the product of the union and as its fruit and attestation."[81]

75. Ibid.

76. Balthasar, *Explorations III*, 10.

77. "The sending of the Word of God (the Son) and the lending of the divine Spirit are only two phases of a single process in which divine truth and life are offered to man." Balthasar, *Prayer*, 68. See also Balthasar, *Credo*, 33; 64.

78. Balthasar, *Explorations IV*, 235.

79. Balthasar, *Theology of History*, 90.

80. "The 'economic' inversion changes nothing with regard to the *taxis* of the Divine Persons. What it does do . . . is to point to the simultaneity of the missions of the Son and Spirit, whose mutual relations change according to the needs of the *oikonomia*: first, the Spirit is sent to incarnate the Son and to accompany the man Jesus to his death; then, the Risen One can resume charge of the Spirit and, together with the Father, send him upon the Church." Balthasar, *Theo-Logic III*, 182.

81. Balthasar, *Explorations III*, 127.

It is only in the Spirit's outpouring that we can come to see the Spirit as the simultaneous subjective and objective love of the Father and Son. For Balthasar, this duality of the Holy Spirit is manifest in the economy through the Spirit's work in the church. The Spirit instantiates the "objective" norms and structures of the visible church and makes possible and nurtures the subjective holiness of the church in her sacrificial witness of God's love to the world. The Spirit creates and sustains the offices of the church.[82] In his perpetual unity with the risen Christ, the Spirit reigns sovereign over both tradition and Scripture.[83] The Spirit also accomplishes the "liquefaction" of the earthly substance of Jesus into the Eucharist.[84] Just as the Spirit quickens the flesh of the dead in resurrection, he also quickens the elements of the sacraments, infusing them with the living Word. In the sacraments of the church, "as everywhere,"

> [the Spirit] is subsistent event: the *liberator who charges the waiting form with infinite content.* He is the Lord of the sacraments, because he is the Spirit who is both hierarchical and personal. As the Spirit of the Church, the hierarchical Spirit, he prepares the vessels, sets up the universal, valid framework, forming out of the life of Christ these seemingly lifeless rigid images. As the personal Spirit of Love he breathes the life of Christ into them, and fills them with all the uniqueness and historical reality of the divine encounter.[85]

The Holy Spirit orders and quickens the physical elements of water, stone, bread, wine, and bodies to continue and universalize Christ's presence in the world. The Spirit "breathes through the finite structures of human life as that which is incomprehensibly open."[86] In his sacramental actions, the Spirit shatters of the boundaries of temporality.[87] Through utilizing these finite structures to convey the infinity of the Triune God, Balthasar argues that the Spirit confirms the conjunction of obedience and love evidenced in Christ's own mission as normative for Christians. Just as Christ consented to a life of humble submission to the promptings of the Spirit in creation,

82. The Spirit is "most definitely Lord of ecclesial office . . . a prominent form of charism." Balthasar, *Theo-Logic III*, 319. See also Balthasar, *Theology of History*, 111.

83. Balthasar, *Theo-Logic III*, 319.

84. See Balthasar, *Explorations IV*, 227–43.

85. Balthasar, *Theology of History*, 100. Italics mine. See also Balthasar, *Theo-Logic III*, 335–52.

86. Balthasar, *Explorations III*, 10.

87. "[The Spirit] cannot be tied down definitely to any duration of the past and the present." Balthasar, *Explorations III*, 151.

so too must his followers submit to the Spirit in the Spirit's use of the materials of creation.[88] For Balthasar then, the objective organs of the Roman Catholic Church represent the necessary material scaffolding of the Spirit's unfolding work.[89] The ecclesial objects and offices which the Spirit maintains and advances, however, are incomplete without the Spirit's work of inculcating subjective holiness in the church.

The Mission of the Holy Spirit and Subjective Holiness of the Church and Saints

The Spirit creatively weds the normative revelation of the Son and the variegated data of historical processes to accomplish the mission of spreading the message of the gospel to the ends of the earth. In this act of "supreme, divine freedom, . . . it rests with him . . . to dispose of the infinite wealth in the life of Christ that it can blossom out of the variousness of history, and that at the same time history, thus made subject to this norm, shall be able to discover the fullness within itself."[90] The Spirit works from inside the creaturely finite freedom of the human subjects whom he indwells to conform the adopted sons and daughters of God to the likeness of the perfect obedience of the true Son of the Father. Having composed the Body of Christ in the church, the Spirit "goes forth from the unity of Christ and the Church" carrying the Triune love of God to a waiting world.[91] As the Spirit drove Christ into the wilderness, so the Spirit impels the church out into a resistant world: "The Spirit . . . is ready, out of the intimacy of love, for every confrontation with the world, for every collision, every provocation, every risk and adventure of the mission. He directs and takes responsibility for the continuation of the transcendence of God into the world . . . and lets the 'little flock,' 'the sheep among the wolves,' give its testimony where they can encounter only opposition."[92]

Given Balthasar's stress on the importance of the missions of the Son and Spirit, it should come as no surprise that he devotes significant attention to the Spirit's creation of the special missions of individual Christians. "The Spirit who breathes where he will," Balthasar declares, "is not the mild, diffused, timeless beacon of the Enlightenment always present in the same fashion. Rather he is the Spirit of missions and special functions

88. See Balthasar, *Credo*, 47.
89. Balthasar, *Theology of History*, 105.
90. Ibid., 103.
91. Balthasar, *Explorations III*, 9.
92. Ibid., 384.

within the mystical body."[93] The individual Christian's "existence is to be an ever-creative translation in the Holy Spirit, an ever-new future of God."[94] Balthasar's *Theology of History* concludes with a beautiful homage to the subjective holiness of the Spirit manifest in the saints:

> The Spirit meets the burning question of the age with an utterance that is the key word, the answer to a riddle. Never in the form of an abstract statement . . . almost always in the form of a new concrete supernatural mission: the creation of a new saint whose life is a presentation of his own age of the message that heaven is sending to it, a man [or woman] who is, here and now, the right and relevant interpretation of the Gospel, who is given to this particular age as its way of approach to the perennial truth of Christ. How else can life be expounded except for living?[95]

Through the objective structures and subjective holiness of the Body of Christ, the Spirit works to effect the reconciliation of the world with its Creator. Even with his thoroughly positive depiction of the Spirit's work in the church, however, Balthasar clearly indicates that the Spirit can and does encounter resistance in his mission from within the Ecclesia.[96] Balthasar also affirms that the Spirit's mission can and does take place outside of the boundaries of the Roman Catholic Church.[97] Though Balthasar's notion of the universal mission of the Holy Spirit is underdeveloped, he offers a number of insights which suggest his openness towards more development in this area. Just as the Son's work cannot be confined to the church, the Spirit too operates in the broader world.[98] The Spirit blows wherever he will, impelling creation onward to its eschatological transformation in the bosom of the Trinity.

93. Balthasar, *Explorations I*, 158.

94. Balthasar, *Explorations III*, 385.

95. Balthasar, *Theology of History*, 109–10.

96. "All these concrete norms in which the Holy Spirit expounds the Word of God to the Church are subject to many kinds of perils and contingencies: resistances in those who are thus chosen: resistances in their environments which hinder their work; resistances, finally, in the Church, who may not listen to their message or only listen skeptically." Ibid., 110–11.

97. On the "world-wide operation" of the Spirit, see Balthasar, *Theo-Logic III*, 415ff.

98. "[J]ust as there is a *logos spermatikos* among the latter, we must assume that there is something like a *pneuma spermatikon* that corresponds to it. Finally, over and above the perspective of world history, there opens up the panorama of the Spirit's activity in the whole of creation." Balthasar, *Theo-Logic III*, 20.

A Brief Summary

The Christian does not gaze into the mystery of Triune Love at a distance; God's being cannot be disinterestedly discerned.[99] One can only *grasp* this mystery in contemplative or speculative thought if one has first been *grasped into* it by the Holy Spirit. The Spirit, as the gift of the Father and Son, takes up residence in the deepest recesses of the human person, incorporating her into the inexhaustible and ineffable mystery of Triune Being. From the perspective of the divine economy, this revelation has unfolded in stages. As Balthasar summarizes: "The Spirit appears (first) essentially as the common fruit of the Father and the Son, which (secondly) can become autonomous in relation to them (the result is 'sent'), and, further (thirdly), as the gift of God to the world, once again permits the whole sovereign freedom of God to be known in the manner in which it holds sway in creation, in the covenant, and in the Church."[100]

The Spirit of mission, the subjective and objective love of the Triune God, takes us up into this mystery, allowing us to penetrate to the depths of divine truth. The indwelling of the Spirit makes possible the apperception of theological truth and a fruitful knowledge of the Divine Trinity: "Through the Son's glory we glimpse the abyss of the invisible Father's love-glory in the Holy Spirit's twofold love. Born of the Spirit as we are, we exist in the fire of love in which Father and Son encounter each other; thus, together with the Spirit, we simultaneously bear witness and give glory to this love."[101]

CONCLUSION: TOWARDS AN INTEGRATED THEOLOGICAL ACCOUNT OF HISTORY

In the preface to the second edition of his short work *A Theology of History*, Balthasar indicates that his work should have instead "been called the *nucleus* of a theology of history," because it "took for granted created things as the content which is given its form by the christological categories." Balthasar highlights the "from above" character of this work, which "was only intended to be about the relation of Christ, as belonging christologically within time, to time in general, the time of human history." Because of this "from above" character, Balthasar admits that could not adequately treat the ordered

---

99. "Intimacy with the Holy Spirit of truth thus cancels out the spectator's uninvolved objectivity, with its external, critical attitude to the truth, and replaces it with an attitude which one can only describe as prayer." Balthasar, *Prayer,* 79.

100. Balthasar, *Explorations III*, 125.

101. Balthasar, *Theo-Logic III*, 448.

history of creation from below in the same work.[102] Balthasar's expansion of his theology of history in the last three volumes of the *Theo-Drama* carries forward and deepens his "from above" christological account, but he again gives scant attention to the horizontal "meanings" of history which can be discerned apart from the vertical dimension of history revealed in Christ.[103] This represents—on his own admission—a lacuna in his massive work.[104] For Bernard Lonergan and for Robert Doran, as for Balthasar, the meaning of history is unveiled in the economic revelation of the Triune God in the work of Christ universalized through the Holy Spirit. History requires this revelation of the Triune God of love for its intelligibility. Lonergan and Doran, however, offer the resources for a "from below" account of history which are lacking in von Balthasar's work.[105]

In addition, Protestants will likely balk at Balthasar's high estimate of the importance of the perpetuity of ecclesial offices. For Balthasar, the Holy Spirit *both* conforms individual Christians and the church as a whole to the holiness manifest in Christ, *and* sustains the church through apostolic succession. These two dimensions of the Holy Spirit's economic work are inseparable for him. One wonders if either of these dimensions of the Spirit's work has priority. Does the Spirit work outside the boundaries of the Roman Catholic Church, in Protestant communities or even in the broader world, to bring about the fruit of love, joy, peace, patience, kindness, goodness, gentleness, faithfulness, and self-control? If Balthasar would answer in the affirmative—and this seems likely given his comments in some places—then why are ecclesial offices necessary? Also, one wonders how Balthasar would reconcile what appears to be, at least on the surface, the incongruity of duly ordained bishops and priests not only failing to manifest Christ's holiness out of ignorance but even in willful ways.

In spite of the seemingly disjointed nature of his work, Balthasar provides a powerful synthetic exposition of Christian truth which is grounded in the revelation of the Triune God in history and combines methodological rigor with contemplative prayerfulness. His exposition of trinitarian theology, while idiosyncratic, remains within the boundaries of orthodoxy. The dynamistic, interpersonal and love-centered account of Triune life *en se*

102. Balthasar, *Theology of History*, 7.

103. Balthasar's *Theo-Logic Theological Logical Theory: I. Truth of the World* does contain helpful resources for the "from below" dimensions of a theological understanding of history, yet the work lacks the clarity and thoroughness of the works of Bernard Lonergan and Robert Doran mentioned below.

104. See Balthasar, *Theology of History*, 7.

105. See Lonergan, *Insight*, 287–88; Lonergan, "Mission and the Spirit," 23–34; and Doran, *Theology and the Dialectics of History*.

which he accomplishes offers a counterbalancing—albeit analogously limited—perspective to traditional "psychological" analogies of the Trinity. Finally, his scripturally and traditionally grounded account of the procession and mission of the Holy Spirit provides the resources for a comprehensive foundational account of the Holy Spirit's work in the economy of the created order. Though Balthasar's theology is impressionistic and often seems disorderly, his account of the mission of the Holy Spirit—from the Spirit's immanent procession, into the Incarnation, through the Spirit's objective and subjective sacramentalization of Christ's presence through time and concluding in the Spirit's creation of the missions of the church and the saints—offers a helpful framework for organizing the necessary components of a foundational account of the revealed meaning of created history.

BIBLIOGRAPHY

Balthasar, Hans Urs Von. *Credo: Meditations on the Apostle's Creed*. Translated by David Kipp. San Francisco: Ignatius, 2005.

————. *Explorations in Theology: I. The Word Made Flesh*. Translated by A. V. Littledale and Alexander Dru. San Francisco: Ignatius, 1989.

————. *Explorations in Theology III: Creator Spirit*. Translated by Brian McNeil. San Francisco: Ignatius, 1993.

————. *Explorations in Theology IV: Spirit and Institution*. Translated Edward Oakes. San Francisco: Ignatius, 1995.

————. *The Glory of the Lord A Theological Aesthetics: IV. The Realm of Metaphysics in Antiquity*. Translated by Brian McNeil et al. Edinburgh: T. & T. Clark, 1989.

————. *The Glory of the Lord A Theological Aesthetics: VII. Theology: The New Covenant*. Translated by Brian McNeil. San Francisco: Ignatius, 1989.

————. *Love Alone Is Credible*. Translated by David C. Schindler. San Francisco: Ignatius, 2004.

————. *Mysterium Paschale: The Mystery of Easter*. Translated by Aidan Nichols. San Francisco: Ignatius, 2005.

————. *My Work in Retrospect*. Translated by Brian McNeil and Kenneth Batinovich. San Francisco: Ignatius, 1990.

————. *Prayer*. Translated by Graham Harrison. San Francisco: Ignatius, 1986.

————. *Razing the Bastions*. Translated by Brian McNeil. San Francisco: Ignatius, 1993.

————. *Theo-Drama Theological Dramatic Theory: I. Prolegoumena*. Translated by Graham Harrison. San Francisco: Ignatius, 1988.

————. *Theo-Dramatics Theological Dramatic Theory: III. Dramatis Personae: Persons in Christ*. Translated by Graham Harrison. San Francisco: Ignatius, 1992.

————. *Theo-Drama Theological Dramatic Theory: IV. The Action*. Translated by Graham Harrison. San Francisco: Ignatius, 1994.

————. *Theo-Dramatics Theological Dramatic Theory: V. The Last Act*. Translated by Graham Harrison. San Francisco: Ignatius, 1998.

————. *Theo-Logic Theological Logical Theory: I. Truth of the World*. Translated by Arian J. Walker. San Francisco: Ignatius, 2000.

————. *Theo-Logic Theological Logical Theory: II. The Truth of God*. Translated by Adrian J. Walker. San Francisco: Ignatius, 2004.

————. *Theo-Logic Theological Logical Theory: III. The Spirit of Truth*. Translated by Graham Harrison. San Francisco: Ignatius, 2005.

————. *A Theology of History*. San Francisco: Ignatius, 1994.

————. *The Truth is Symphonic: Aspects of Christian Pluralism*. Translated by Graham Harrison. San Francisco: Ignatius, 1987.

Bouyer, Louis. *Das Handwerk des Theologen*. Einsiedeln: Johannes Verlag, 1980.

De Lubac, Henri. "A Witness of Christ in the Church: Hans Urs von Balthasar." In *Hans Urs von Balthasar: His Life and Work*, 271–88. San Francisco: Ignatius, 1991.

Doran, Robert. "Lonergan and von Balthasar: Methodological Considerations." *Theological Studies* 58.1 (1997) 61–84.

————. "System and History: The Challenge to Catholic Systematic Theology." *Theological Studies* 60.4 (1999) 652–78.

————. *Theology and the Dialectics of History*. Toronto: University of Toronto Press, 1990.

———. *The Trinity in History A Theology of the Divine Missions: I. Missions and Processions.* Toronto: University of Toronto Press, 2012.

———. *What is Systematic Theology?* Toronto: University of Toronto Press, 2005.

Emery, Gilles. "The Immutability of the God of Love and the Problem of Language Concerning the 'Suffering of God.'" In *Divine Impassibility and the Mystery of Human Suffering*, 48–52. Grand Rapids: Eerdmans, 2009.

Friesenhahn, Jacob. *The Trinity and Theodicy: The Trinitarian Theology of Hans Urs von Balthasar and the Problem of Evil.* Burlington, VT: Ashgate, 2011.

Henrici, Peter. "Hans Urs von Balthasar: A Sketch of His Life." In *Hans Urs von Balthasar: His Life and Work*, 9–14. San Francisco: Ignatius, 1991.

Howsare, Rodney. *Hans Urs von Balthasar: A Guide for the Perplexed.* London: T. & T. Clark, 2009.

Hunt, Anne. *The Trinity and the Paschal Mystery: A Development in Recent Catholic Theology.* Collegeville, MN: Liturgical, 1997.

Kerr, Fergus. *Twentieth Century Catholic Theology: From Neoscholasticism to Nuptial Mysticism.* Malden, MA: Blackwell, 2007.

Karen Kilby, "Hans Urs von Balthasar on the Trinity." In *The Cambridge Companion to the Trinity*, 208–22. Cambridge University Press, 2011.

Lonergan, Bernard. *Insight: A Study of Human Understanding,* The Collected Works of Bernard Lonergan, vol. 3. Toronto: University of Toronto Press, 1992.

———. *Method in Theology.* New York: Herder & Herder, 1972.

———. "Mission and the Spirit." In *A Third Collection*, 24–34. Mahwah, NJ: Paulist, 1985.

Oakes, Edward and David Moss. *The Cambridge Companion to Hans Urs von Balthasar.* Cambridge: Cambridge University Press, 2004.

O'Hanlon, Gerald. *The Immutability of God in the Theology of Hans Urs von Balthasar.* Cambridge: Cambridge University Press, 1990.

Pitstick, Alyssa. *Light in Darkness: Hans Urs von Balthasar and the Catholic Doctrine of Christ's Descent into Hell.* Grand Rapids: Eerdmans, 2007.

Sachs, John R., S.J. "Deus semper major—Ad majorem Dei gloriam." In *Gregorianum* 74.4 *The Pneumatology and Spirituality of Hans Urs von Balthasar* (1993) 631–57.

———. Spirit and Life: The Pneumatology and Spirituality of Hans Urs von Balthasar. Ph.D. diss., Tübingen, 1984.

Tossou, Kossi K. Joseph. *Sreben nach Vollendung: Zur Pneumatologie im Werk Hans Urs von Balthasar.* Freiburg: Herder, 1983.

Vogel, Jeffery A. "The Unselfing Activity of the Holy Spirit in the Theology of Hans Urs von Balthasar." *Logos* 10.4 (2007) 16–34.

4

Breaking Forth from Form's Interior

Hans Urs Von Balthasar
on the Aesthetics of St. Thomas Aquinas

RYAN T. HEMMER

INTRODUCTION

In the two decades since his death, the vast theological corpus of the Swiss Catholic theologian, Hans Urs von Balthasar, has arguably received more attention than it did during the five decades of his theological career. There are, as one might expect, a manifold number of reasons and conditions that have contributed both to Balthasar's former neglect, and to his more recent lionization. In spite of the emerging rapprochement between his thought and the theological mainstream, however, his work remains enigmatic and—as a result—prone to misunderstanding and misappropriation. This is perhaps especially true with respect to the way that Balthasar reads and interacts with the Western literary, philosophical, and theological canons, which he employs so prodigiously. One of the distinctive aspects of Balthasar's theological method is his abiding belief in the dialogical nature of the theological task. Theology, for Balthasar, is conversation, and the gratuity of God's goodness means that the theologian can find conversation partners within every diverse interval of the human experience: the literary, poetic, and philosophical; the scientific, musical, and dramatic.

While scholars have spent not a little ink exploring the sets of relations between Balthasar and these multifarious avenues of thought, there are several lacunae in the existing body of scholarly work concerning the major sources of Balthasar's theology. His interpreters, for instance, have long recognized that Balthasar's medieval theological inheritance focuses principally on the thought of Maximus, Dionysius, and especially Bonaventure, yet there is a basic tendency not to ignore the dependence upon Thomas Aquinas that so suffuses Balthasar's work.[1] This neglect is—to say the least—odd, given the claims of some scholars that, "The influence of Thomas Aquinas on the formulation of Balthasar's theology and philosophy is clear and shows that Balthasar regarded him with perhaps more esteem than any other theologian in history."[2] While such claims are at least potentially hyperbolic, the truth of the matter is that, for Balthasar, Thomas Aquinas is at the very center of *sapientia christiana*; he is the pivotal figure situated between the ages, and the embodiment of intellectual sophistication and spiritual maturity. Of his encounter with Thomas, Balthasar proclaims, "What a wealth of material is to be found in Thomas, what a variety of approaches and aspects he suggests, how numerous the hints and promptings scattered at random through his works, compared with the dry bones of a modern textbook!"[3]

Throughout Balthasar's massive authorship, the influence of Thomas is evident both explicitly—through the hundreds of references that Balthasar makes to him—and implicitly to all those with the Thomistic ears to hear. Yet unlike individuals such as Irenaeus, Origen, Dionysius, or Maximus the Confessor who are all given singular focus both in the *Trilogy* and in monographs, Thomas rarely is the subject of such attention. At least one time, however, in Balthasar's magisterial *Trilogy*, he turns his erudite gaze upon

1. Fr. Robert Doran has tried to show, through a provisional set of complimentary analyses of the work of Balthasar and his Jesuit contemporary, Bernard Lonergan, that the Bonaventurian and Thomistic theological frameworks truly require one another in order to achieve a synthesis capable of establishing what Lonergan calls the general (applicable to broader human knowing) and special (specific to theology) categories of theology. See Doran, "Lonergan and Balthasar: Methodological Considerations," 569–607.

2. Campodonico, "Il pensiero filosofico di Tommaso d'Aquino nell'interpretazione di H. U.Von Balthasar," 187. [Eng. Trans.: "Hans Urs von Balthasar's Interpretation of the Philosophy of Thomas Aquinas," 33.]

3. Balthasar, *Explorations I*, 208.

Thomas' doctrine with a sharp focus and with a view toward sustained exposition.[4] The surprise is that the doctrine in question is neither the Trinity, nor Christology, nor ethics, but is rather—to borrow a phrase from Étienne Gilson—the doctrine of the "forgotten transcendental," that is, of the doctrine of *pulchrum*, beauty.[5]

This essay seeks to clarify the manner in which Balthasar reads and appropriates the aesthetics of Thomas Aquinas. While never developing an original aesthetic theory, St. Thomas Aquinas inherited and appropriated an aesthetic tradition in order to answer the relevant questions of theology. In expositing this appropriation, Hans Urs von Balthasar shows that Thomas' aesthetic synthesis elucidates the sets of relations that comprise the beautiful object and mediate its meaning; it identifies the faculty of apprehension whereby the beautiful is meaningfully understood, and gets to the heart of Thomas' understanding that the beautiful is the metaphysical, an insight in which created and uncreated being are skillfully demarcated, related, and revealed.

THE MOST RELUCTANT AESTHETE: ST. THOMAS' AESTHETIC APPROPRIATION

It is a well-established trope of Thomistic scholarship that Thomas Aquinas simply does not articulate a fully formed theory of theological aesthetics.[6] While his *opera omnia* is replete with discussions of aesthetics in relation to a myriad of other doctrines, the discussions in themselves do not constitute a theory. This fact is not lost on Balthasar; in fact, he is acutely aware of

4. While the best known exposition of Aquinas occurs in *Glory of the Lord IV*, this is not the only time Balthasar undertook a serious study of Aquinas. In 1954, he wrote a commentary on Aquinas' exposition of Christian charism entitled *Thomas von Aquin, Besondere Gnadengaben und die zwei Wege menschlichen Lebens: Kommentar zu Summa Theologica II-II, 171–82.*

5. Gilson, *The Elements of Christian Philosophy,* 174.

6. See, for example, Copleston, *A History of Philosophy II,* 422: "One cannot say that there is a formal discussion of aesthetic theory in the philosophy of St. Thomas, and what he does have to say on the matter is mostly borrowed from other writers, so that through his remarks may be taken as the starting-point of an aesthetic theory, it would be a mistake to develop an aesthetic theory on the basis of his remarks and then attribute that theory to him, as if he had himself developed it." While not in any way contradicting this statement, Beardsley helpfully observes, "Considering the vast number of difficult and fundamental problems that are dealt with so extensively in the greatest system of scholastic philosophy, that of Thomas Aquinas (1225–74), it is perhaps surprising that he is so short with aesthetics. But what he says is penetrating, and its significance is out of ordinary proportion to its length," in *Aesthetics from Classical Greece to the Present,*100.

the manner in which Thomas' use of aesthetics functions in relation to his larger arguments, as well as the sources from which Thomas draws in order to make judgments about aesthetic dimensions. In *The Glory of the Lord IV*, Balthasar attempts a sustained exposition of Thomas' aesthetics, and makes it clear from the very beginning of the analysis that Thomas is not an aesthetician by trade: "Beauty is seldom a central concern for St. Thomas Aquinas, and for the most part his discussion is dependent on material presented to him by tradition. He calmly reviews this inherited material and tries to harmonise the elements that pour in upon him from Augustine, Denys, Aristotle, Boethius, and his master, Albert, without, so it would seem, making an original contribution of his own to aesthetics in the strict sense."[7]

While not developing an original theory, Thomas is the heir of at least three major streams of aesthetic convention, all of which have a discernable and significant impact on the way he reasons through the transcendental structure of *pulchrum* in relation both to human consciousness and to the being of things. These sources—unsurprisingly for anyone familiar with Thomas' standard *magisterium*—are Aristotle, Augustine (Albert inhabits this tradition), and Dionysius. In Balthasar's view, these aesthetic traditions are essentially three ways of understanding, developing, and relating the terms that constitute *pulchrum*: integrity, consonance or proportion, and clarity.[8]

This three-fold structure, however, is conditioned by discrete developments in the theological and philosophical traditions of Thomas' own formation. The final two terms—consonance (*proportio sive consonatia*) and clarity (*claritas*)—derive especially from Dionysius' *Divine Names*, a text from which Thomas never strays very far. As Balthasar observes, "Denys says (in *Div. nom.* iv, 7) that God, as the cause of all that is beautiful, gives to everything *consonatia et claritas*: *consonatia* is the concord among parts, which therefore essentially the same as harmony, proportion, order, fairness of aspect; *claritas* is the brilliant light that descends vertically upon this horizontally ordered structure."[9] Of these two Dionysian terms (consonance

---

7. Balthasar, *The Glory of the Lord IV*, 393.

8. For Aquinas, integrity, proportion, and clarity are three constituting elements of aesthetic constitution. The ability of an object to be beautiful (a separate issue from being perceived by a subject as beautiful) depends upon its integrity, proportion, and clarity. For Thomas, this three-fold relation functions as a Trinitarian analogy. See Thomas Aquinas, *The Summa Theologica*, translated by Fathers of the English Dominican Province, second, revised edition, 22 vols. (London: Burns, Oates & Washbourne, 1912–36; reprinted in 5 vols., Westminster, MD: Christian Classics, 1981) I.39.8. Unless otherwise noted, all quotations of the *Summa* (hereafter *ST*) are from this translation.

9. Balthasar, *Glory of the Lord IV*, 397. Pseudo-Dionysius states, "But the Super-Essential Beautiful is called 'Beauty' because of that quality which It imparts to all

and clarity), *claritas* is the most illusive.[10] In Balthasar's reading, Thomas' understanding and use of *claritas* bridges the gaps between the different traditional sources of his aesthetics, and exemplifies Thomas' ability and tendency to synthesis disparate aesthetic traditions. In at least one sense, as Balthasar shows, Thomas tries to utilize Augustine's description of beauty—which Balthasar sees as flowing from the Stoic tradition—and synthesizes it with the Plotinian qualities of Dionysius (*pulchritude corporis est partim convenientia cum quasam coloris suavitate*).[11] Additionally, the metaphysics of Albert the Great, Thomas' teacher, also informs the way that Thomas understands *claritas* in terms of light and form.[12] Thomas' understanding of *claritas* serves as an example of how different philosophical and theological traditions with respect to beauty intersect in a Thomistic synthesis. The indebtedness to these traditions, and the creative manner of synthesis and interpretation is characteristic of Thomas' aesthetic appropriation.

Beyond this very specific example, Balthasar explores a number of different emphases in Thomas' aesthetics and shows how they transpose, augment, or develop particular theological and philosophical traditions. He argues, for instance, that Thomas' insistence on the objectivity of beauty (that a thing is not beautiful because it is loved, but rather is loved because it is beautiful) is adopted from Augustine, as well as the idea (found in Augustine, Hilary, and Peter Lombard) that beauty corresponds to the second person of the Trinity.[13] In his commentary on Dionysius, Thomas expands upon the consonance-clarity structure of the Areopagite's aesthetics with Aristotle's concept of beauty in terms of appropriate size.[14] As Balthasar

things severally according to their nature, and because It is the Cause of the *harmony* and *splendour* in all things, flashing forth upon them all, like light, the beautifying communications of Its originating ray; and because It summons all things to fare unto Itself (from whence It hath the name of 'Fairness'), and because It draws all things together in a state of mutual inter penetration" (emphasis mine). See Pseudo-Dionysius, *Dionysius, the Areopagite, On the Divine Names, and, Mystical Theology.*

10. James F. Anderson, for example, argues, "*Claritas*, a word which seems to be untranslatable literally, includes the notion of intelligibility, since it means the cognitive—and not only intellectual—manifestness of the thing's form." See, Thomas Aquinas, *An Introduction to the Metaphysics of Thomas Aquinas*, 89n.4.

11. Balthasar, *Glory of the Lord IV*, 397–98.

12. Ibid., 398. "Thomas's predecessors had already amplified this definition (limited initially to the corporeal plane) in a transcendental manner by understanding *coloris suavitas* as the material mode of appearance of *claritas* in general. This can be seen quite clearly in, for example, Albert's metaphysics of form and light. Thomas does the same. He extends the concept of beauty transcendentally to the point where he can even apply it to truth itself."

13. Ibid., 398–99.

14. *In Div. Nom.* 4, lect. 10. "The Philosopher adds a third aspect to these

comments on this text, "it gives [Thomas] an opportunity of quoting and inserting the Aristotelian definition alongside the Dionysian and Augustinian. For in addition to *symmetria* Aristotle laid down a further criterion for beauty: appropriate size, without which something can at best be 'pretty' but not beautiful."[15] Balthasar argues that Thomas understands this notion of appropriate size in terms of perfection or integrity.[16] Thus, in question 39 of the *Prima Pars*, Thomas combines the Dionysian components of beauty (consonance and clarity) with Aristotelian perfection (integrity) in order to relate beauty to the different aspects of hypostatic differentiation in intra-Trinitarian operations. He argues not simply that beauty relates to the person of the Son, but that the truth of this association can be seen in the sets of relations between the three-fold nature of beauty and the characteristics of the Son.[17]

From Dionysius, Augustine, Albert, and Aristotle, Thomas is able to appropriate, synthesize, develop, and formalize his three-fold structure of understanding beauty. This structure, however, is not the only important inheritance that was bequeathed to Thomas from his ancient forebears. Of particular importance is the transcendentality of beauty, that is, its inability to be situated within Aristotle's categories, and thus its convertibility with the good, the true, the one, and even with being itself. Yet, the transcendental quality of beauty is a difficult concept to fully understand in Thomistic terms, because beauty itself is a synthesis of the good and the true. For Balthasar, this places Thomas again within the tradition of Dionysius and many other theologians. He asserts that "Thomas adopts the idea of placing the *pulchrum* within and yet beyond the transcendentals, the *verum* and the *bonum*, in that, like Denys, he presupposes the fundamental unity of the good and the beautiful and, with Alexander, William of Auvergne and

---

[*consonantia* and *claritas*] (*Ethics* IV, 6) when he says that beauty is only present in a large body—hence small men may be called well-proportioned and pretty [*formosi*] but not beautiful." Quoted from Bourke, *The Pocket Aquinas*, 267.

15. Balthasar, *Glory of the Lord IV*, 399.

16. Ibid. "Thomas generally interprets this aspect of beauty (again in the spirit of Aristotle) in terms of *perfectio*, which is an anticipation of his later, central concept of ordered being. This in the principle passage dealing with aesthetics in the Commentary on the Sentences Thomas lets all the diverse streams of thought converge: the divine person of the Son is 'beautiful' as species (Hilary), as perfect image (=*aequalitas and consonantia cum Patre*: Augustine), as possessor of the *perfecta nature Dei* (Aristotle); but as 'perfect Word of the Father' he has *claritas* (Denys), which shines upon all things and which all things reflect back (Albert)."

17. *ST* 1.39.8.

Albert, makes a conceptual distinction between the two, a distinction which brings the beautiful closer to the true."[18]

In all of this, what Balthasar helps us to see is that Thomas is consciously, intentionally, and carefully synthesizing different tributaries of aesthetic tradition into a confluence that is original. Balthasar, however, is not simply trying to map out the genealogy of Thomas' aesthetic appropriation, but rather, having explored the inheritance of Thomas, is seeking to show how this inheritance and synthesis relate to the larger intentions of Thomas' philosophy; namely, how beauty helps to explicate his philosophy of being.

THE BEAUTIFUL FORM: CAUSALITY, APPREHENSION, AND INTELLIGIBLE RELATIONS

The affective aesthete may well decide to cease the exploration at this point. "How," he might ask, "can such an existential and tacit thing as beauty be reduced to mere definitions of various terms?" In this objection, of course, he is correct. The aesthetic experience is not one of terminological clarification, but rather one of wonder. It is precisely at those intervals at which one falls silent before glory that beauty is objectively grasped. Balthasar is far from insensitive to these concerns. In fact, he makes many of the very same points himself. Yet, as he consistently argues, to the degree that beauty is transcendentally convertible with the true, the good, and even being itself, it is not simply that which provokes sets of affective moods within individuals, but is itself a locus of concrete intelligibility, of form, of meaning.

Describing the genius of Josef Pieper, Balthasar exuberantly recalls the words of Goethe, who insists, "'A word from the treasury of home-grown human language contains more reality than a technical term.' And then follows this astounding but accurate statement: 'Improbable as this may sound, we can say that not only Lao Tzu, Plato and Augustine but even Aristotle and Thomas Aquinas used no technical terminology.'"[19] Despite the element of poetic hyperbole in this statement, it nevertheless contains a fundamental insight into the way that Balthasar reads Thomas on the issue of aesthetics; namely, that Thomas keeps always before him the *wonder* of the mystery of being, whereas subsequent theology and philosophy flattens out being to such a degree that wonder is no longer the appropriate response.[20]

18. Balthasar, *Glory of the Lord IV*, 400.

19. Balthasar, "Forward" to Pieper, *The Josef Pieper Anthology*, ix.

20. See ibid., xii: "Perhaps because Christian theology has likewise set up shop as the (equally specialized) 'science' that deals with the manner in which the divine *Urgrund* has revealed itself in Christ. But this turn of events can be dated back only to a

Despite the general scholarly consensus that Thomas has no theory of the beautiful, scholars nevertheless tend to converge on the same points of emphasis when attempting to exegete the various texts in which Thomas performs certain kinds of aesthetic analyses. In general terms, the standard structure of the beautiful, for Thomas, concerns a specific set of relations within form in and through which the beautiful is meaningfully established and understood. These relations have been mentioned previously: *integritas* (integrity and perfection), *proportionalitis* (proportion, harmony), and *claritas* (a term without a precise translation, but variously translated as splendor or clarity). While in the previous section, we set out to show how Balthasar traces the genealogical history, reception, and synthesis of these terms, we now must turn to the terms themselves, and to the way in which Balthasar exposits their meaning within Thomas' philosophical and theological reflection.

There is a whole network of interrelations that one must consider with respect to Thomas' philosophy of beauty. The first question one must answer in this investigation is the question of causality. Within the causal structure of Aristotelian doctrine, it is not immediately clear to which cause beauty most meaningfully relates. Thomas himself takes great care to show how one can reasonably assert the divine causality of the human person, and yet cannot make God the complete causal explanation for actually existing human being. In response to the objection that God enters into composition with all contingent being, Thomas replies, "The Godhead is called the being of all things, as their efficient and exemplar cause, but not as being their essence."[21] From this Balthasar rightly asserts that "Thomas sees *esse* as the non-subsistent fullness and perfection of all reality and as the supreme 'likeness of divine goodness,' and so God can no longer in any way be re-

---

rationalist Late Scholasticism and to the influence of Descartes, whereas for the Fathers and High Scholasticism the 'awe' of the philosopher before the 'holy and manifest mystery' had always been the basis and presupposition for the Christian's love for the God who gives himself wholly in the Old and New Covenants." This theme is a recurring one in Balthasar's work. In his analysis of Thomas' notion of being he remarks, "The period following Thomas was not able to sustain this state of tension and either reduced *esse* to a supreme and completely vacuous concept, which—as pure being 'there'—can be derived, abstracted, effortlessly from essences: this is rationalism. The other response was so to consolidate *esse* in itself that it coincides with God and now generates essences from itself in the divine cosmic process: this is pantheistic idealism" (Balthasar, *Glory of the Lord IV*, 405). In *Glory of the Lord V*, Balthasar offers an extended meditation on the wonder the being elicits in the contexts of his discussion of "the miracle of being and its fourfold distinction." He argues—with Heidegger—that wonder before being is the beginning of thought, but he also insists—contra Heidegger—that such wonder is response to something wondrous. See Balthasar, *The Glory of the Lord V*, 613ff.

21. *ST* Ia.3.8c, rep. 1.

garded as the being of things, except in the sense that he is their efficient, exemplary and final cause."[22] One rightly notices that, for Thomas, God is not the formal or material cause of humanity. When we move to the question of causality with respect to the beautiful, however, Thomas indicates that the beautiful can be understood as having the aspect of formal cause.

In a question concerning the status of the good in terms of formal cause, Thomas' interlocutor argues that goodness must be understood to have an aspect of formal causality because of its convertibility with the beautiful, which even the interlocutor understands to be related to formal cause. By reasoning from the major premise of the convertibility of the good and the beautiful (in which anything predicated of the one can be predicated of the other) and the minor premise that the beautiful has an aspect of formal cause, the interlocutor concludes that the good has an aspect of formal cause.[23] The *responsio* reveals the key to understanding the way in which Thomas differentiates between the transcendental notions. He appeals to Aristotle to show that, properly speaking, the good is that toward which all things tend, meaning that it must be understood in terms of final rather than formal cause.[24] The reply to the first objection shows the way in which Thomas makes this differentiation. He argues that indeed while the good and the beautiful are the same in terms of metaphysical form, they differ in terms of logical priority. The logical differentiation has to do with the

22. Balthasar, *Glory of the Lord IV*, 393.

23. *ST* 1.5.4, ob. 1. "It seems that goodness has not the aspect of a final cause, but rather of the other causes. For, as Dionysius says (Div. Nom. iv), 'Goodness is praised as beauty.' But beauty has the aspect of a formal cause. Therefore goodness has the aspect of a formal cause." On this point Étienne Gilson rightly argues, "if in our estimation goodness is goodness because it is to be beautiful, we should consider it a formal rather than a final cause, and, of course, what it true of goodness itself is also true of God. The answer to this objection [that beauty has an aspect of *final* cause] establishes both that beauty truly is a convertible property with being and also that it is distinct from the point of view of reason" (Gilson, *Elements of Christian Philosophy*, 174).

24. *ST* 1.5.4. rep. 1, "I answer that, Since goodness is that which all things desire, and since this has the aspect of an end, it is clear that goodness implies the aspect of an end. Nevertheless, the idea of goodness presupposes the idea of an efficient cause, and also of a formal cause. For we see that what is first in causing, is last in the thing caused. Fire, e.g., heats first of all before it reproduces the form of fire; though the heat in the fire follows from its substantial form. Now in causing, goodness and the end come first, both of which move the agent to act; secondly, the action of the agent moving to the form; thirdly, comes the form. Hence in that which is caused the converse ought to take place, so that there should be first, the form whereby it is a being; secondly, we consider in it its effective power, whereby it is perfect in being, for a thing is perfect when it can reproduce its like, as the Philosopher says (Meteor. iv); thirdly, there follows the formality of goodness which is the basic principle of its perfection."

faculties of apprehension:[25] the good, as that toward which all things tend, is the intentional object of the appetite (appetite being the faculty of movement toward), whereas the beautiful is the intentional object of intelligence of the cognitive faculty.[26]

Balthasar intricately extrapolates the philosophical and cognitive significance of this indirect analysis of beauty as he focuses in both upon beauty in terms of form, and beauty in terms of intelligible relations. That beauty is understood to have an aspect of formal cause allows Thomas to focus on the appearance of form within the world of created being as a participation in the transcendental fullness of divine goodness (goodness is praised as beauty). Indeed, as Balthasar shows, the earthly locations of beauty must be understood through this doctrine of participation, in which divine freedom and intellect changes indeterminate potential being into actual existence through the application of divine knowledge to potency. As Balthasar states, "Confronted with the infinite range of the possible that can participate in the act of being, only the divine intellect is able to 'discover' and posit the circumscribed forms, even if they are not joined to the act of being as an external addition, but are so to speak, stamped out from its constantly infinite fulness. In an image reminiscent of Grosseteste, Thomas says that the forms are 'nothing other than a kind of seal of the divine knowledge in things.'"[27]

Such an affirmation allows the formal aspect being to be experienced as the splendor of being. For though *species* and *lumen* are discrete aspects of the beautiful, Balthasar argues that they necessarily relate to each other as a unity. He asserts early on in the first volume of *The Glory of the Lord*, that, "The beautiful is above all a *form*, and the light does not fall on this form from above or from outside, rather it breaks forth from the form's interior. *Species* and *lumen* in beauty are one, if the *species* truly merits that name."[28] One senses a certain plasticity in the way in which the term "form"

25. For Balthasar's discussion of apprehension and its relation to transcendental notions, see Balthasar, *Glory of the Lord I*.

26. *ST* 1.5.4, ad. 1. "Beauty and goodness in a thing are identical fundamentally; for they are based upon the same thing, namely, the form; and consequently goodness is praised as beauty. But they differ logically, for goodness properly relates to the appetite (goodness being what all things desire); and therefore it has the aspect of an end (the appetite being a kind of movement towards a thing). On the other hand, beauty relates to the cognitive faculty; for beautiful things are those which please when seen. Hence beauty consists in due proportion; for the senses delight in things duly proportioned, as in what is after their own kind—because even sense is a sort of reason, just as is every cognitive faculty. Now since knowledge is by assimilation, and similarity relates to form, beauty properly belongs to the nature of a formal cause."

27. Balthasar, *Glory of the Lord IV*, 403. See also, *De veritate* 2.1, ad. 9.

28. Balthasar, *Glory of the Lord I*, 146. Earlier in this volume, Balthasar argues that,

is used both in Balthasar and in Thomas: sometimes it refers to causality; sometimes it refers to intelligibility; sometimes it refers to that which allows truth to be understood in dynamic and even ecstatic terms. Form, in the sense of splendor, gives truth depth, dimension, shape; it allows for truth to be expressed in fully personal terms. As Balthasar asserts, "If the *verum* lacks that *spendor* which for Thomas is the distinctive mark of the beautiful, then the knowledge of truth remains both pragmatic and formalistic. The only concern of such knowledge will then merely be the verification of correct facts and laws, whether the later latter are laws of being or laws of thought, categories and ideas."[29]

The sensorial dimension of form is, for Balthasar and for Thomas, the key insight through which human subjectivity is able to discern between what is given in truth and in beauty, and the good toward which all being tends. Commenting on one of the most alluded to aesthetic passages of the Thomistic corpus, Balthasar insists,

> We strive after the good as a goal to be attained, while the beautiful is admired and loved for the sake of its form; it is that which is pleasing not for me but in itself as it is seen; *pulchra dicuntur quae visa placent, id cuius ipsa apprehensio placet*. It is its "relation to the cognitive faculty" that distinguishes it from goodness and causes it to shine forth from the true as *pulchritudo veritatis*. This last point is in line with Aquinas's inspired insight: *maxima pulchritudo humanae naturae consistit in splendore scientiae* ["The supreme beauty of human nature consists in the splendour of knowledge"]. For Wisdom plays before the face of God, but "this playful action is not performed for the sake of extrinsic goals, but happens for its own sake. This is also true of the delights of Wisdom."[30]

"We may, however, without prejudice distinguish and relate to each other, albeit in a very preliminary way, two elements in the beautiful which have traditionally controlled every aesthetic and which, with Thomas Aquinas, we could term *species* (or *forma*) and *lumen* (or *spendor*)—form (*Gestalt*) and splendour (*Glanz*)." (*Glory of the Lord I*, 115)

29. Ibid., 406.

30. Balthasar, *Glory of the Lord IV*, 400. The standard phrase that Thomas expresses is *"pulchra dicuntur quae visa placent,"* see *ST* I.5.4, ad 1. Commenting on these Thomistic understandings, Copleston helpfully shows that "Nevertheless, it may well be as well to point out that when he remarks that *pulchra dicuntur quae visa placent*, he does not mean to deny the objectivity of beauty. The beautiful consists, he says, in proper proportion and belongs to the formal cause: it is the object of the cognitive power, whereas the good is the object of desire. For beauty three elements are required, integrity or perfection, proper proportion and clarity: the form shines out, as it were, through colour, etc., and is the object of disinterested (non-appetitive) apprehension (Copleston, *A History of Philosophy*. Vol. 2, 422). Balthasar concludes, "The essentialist

The movement of desire toward the good is not, in itself, a movement of intelligence. The manner of apprehension is not sensorial in the idiom of sight, but rather is an internal movement of appetite toward the final cause of being. Beauty, on the other hand, though convertible with the good in transcendental terms, differs in terms of the faculty of apprehension. As that which *seems* pleasing, beauty is apprehended intelligently and understood in terms of relations and sets of meanings.

For Thomas, the form of the beautiful is communicated to human intelligence through the dynamic relations of integrity, proportion, and clarity, meanings which avail themselves to the light of agent intellect, and thus to understanding.[31] As Balthasar notes: "It should be clear why, for Thomas, the definitive aesthetic concepts do not centre around 'form' (with its essential parts and its interior light) but have to be concepts implying comparative relation: *ordo, ordinatio, dispositio, proportio, proportionalitas.* Reality realizes only in a proportionality which, while incomprehensible in itself, is the foundation of all order and thus of all form."[32]

The sets of relations that these terms denote are relations not merely between the parts and the whole of a particular form of beauty, but are sets of relations that allow for the meaningful apprehension of being in both human and divine terms. What emerges, however, is that the human subject perceiving the intelligible relations of integrity, proportion, and clarity within the world of experience is himself a relation, both in himself and in relation to God. He is thus a relation to a relation, a suspension of a suspension. This suspended suspension called man, and the world of being that is mediated to him through the meaningful relations of created existence, are rightfully understood in terms of being, but this being is itself always already a relation to the absolute as a likeness to God. For Balthasar, the true achievement of Thomas' aesthetics is the insight that finite human being is situated in the tension between *esse* and *essentia*, that the concrete experience of intelligible relations as formally beautiful reveals the truth that the being of human subjectivity exists only in a "non-reciprocal relation of

---

aesthetics of 'size, number and weight,' of *covenientia* and *claritas*, is completely justified by the fact that reality realizes itself only in essences. Moreover, since human knowing in every case starts off from concrete sense-experience, the starting point of aesthetics will necessarily be (more than ever) corporeal beauty, experienced on the sensory, empirical plane: *pulchra sunt quae visa placent*" (*Glory of the Lord IV*, 407).

31. For instance, Thomas argues, "Hence beauty consists in due proportion; for the senses delight in things duly proportioned, as in what is after their own kind—because even sense is a sort of reason, just as is every cognitive faculty. Now since knowledge is by assimilation, and similarity relates to form, beauty properly belongs to the nature of a formal cause" (*ST* I.5.4, ad 1).

32. Balthasar, *Glory of the Lord IV*, 408.

dependence" to the divine.[33] This relation is the transcendental condition for both the objects of aesthetic sense, and the proverbial beholder in whose eye the relations are grasped.

GOD AND CREATION: *ESSE, ESSENTIA*, AND "THE DISTINCTION"

To understand the function of beauty within the constructive theological universe of Thomas Aquinas requires an analysis of Thomas' greatest philosophical achievement: his masterful delineation of *esse* from *essentia*.[34] Beauty, to the degree that Thomas maintains its transcendentality and convertibility with the good, the true, and thereby with being, occasions insights into the intelligible relations between God and creation, revealing the uncreated glory that appears in the world of finite being as the radiated love of the good beyond being. For Balthasar, the genius of Thomas' aesthetics is only realized when understood within the context of this radiating glory flowing outward from within being. Balthasar argues, in essence, that Thomas' aesthetics is his metaphysics, that his aesthetics must be understood as metaphysical aesthetics.

In light of the nature of the inheritance and appropriation of the different streams of aesthetic tradition that inform Thomas' mature speculation, Balthasar shows how the world of aesthetic concerns informing Thomas' horizon is not a discrete meditation on the transcendental quality of beauty as a *quaestio* of theological pedagogy, but rather is an explication of being itself, its uncreated origin, its created appearance, and the relations and distinctions between the two.

For Thomas, the term "God" can be defined in at least two nominal senses: *ipsum esse* and *ipsum intellegere*, being itself and understanding itself, meaning that God can in some sense be understood as the unrestricted

---

33. This phrase is used in the sense given by David Burrell. See "Analogy, Creation, and Theological Language," 77–98. Burrell nuances the phrase from its original form in Grant, *Towards an Alternative Theology*. It is an insight from the concept of non-duality in the thought of Sankara. See also Burrell, "Distinguishing God from the World," 20–33.

34. As David Burrell has shown, the first instance of the philosophical demarcation of essence from existence occurs with the Muslim philosopher Avicenna's distinction between the nature proper to a thing, i.e., its truth, and its existence or the affirmation that it is the case. Burrell states, "This is the first clear formulation of a distinction between essence and existence, and it is the text of Avicenna's to which Aquinas has recourse in his early essay which has provided the framework for subsequent discussion in the West: *De ente et essentia.*" See Burrell, *Knowing the Unknowable God*, 19.

act of existing and the unrestricted act of understanding.[35] With respect to existing, the heart of Thomas' metaphysics is to state in emphatic fashion that whatever it means "to be" in the world of finite being, it is simply not an infinite act, but rather is a kind of suspension, a set of relations. The intelligibility of finite being, however, cannot be grasped simply in terms of the meaningful relations in themselves, but must be related to the infinite act of existing beyond all finitude.

In this way, as Balthasar shows, being must be understood as a likeness to God, proceeding from the infinite act of existing not as a blind Plotinian emanation, but the intelligent and dynamic emanation or act of love. Balthasar thus argues, "Consequently, Thomas expresses here not a specifically Platonic point of view but his own constant and fundamental position. The procession of being—Thomas also speaks repeatedly of its emanation from God—is the procession of act-uality (it is not, as it were, just a naked being 'there')."[36] This procession of actuality does not imply that being is self-subsisting, but rather that it is only intelligible as it adheres in and with actually existing subjects. Of *esse*, Balthasar insists, "In itself it has no subsistence but inheres in natures: *esse non est subsistens sed inharens*. Thomas is adamant that this self-realisation of the real must not be understood as the actualisation of a potency. 'On the contrary,' natures are potential *vis a vis* the realising act of being."[37] That being is a non-subsistent act that cannot be understood in the terms of potencies means that actually existing natures are not simply a necessary result of the act of existing, but rather, "it is only in them that [*esse*] comes to 'standing' and subsistence."[38] For Thomas, as Balthasar argues: "Confronted with the infinite range of the possible that can participate in the act of being, only the divine intellect is able to 'discover' and posit the circumscribed forms, even if they are not joined to the act of being as an external addition, but are so to speak, stamped out from its constantly infinite fulness. In an image reminiscent of Grosseteste, Thomas says that the forms are 'nothing other than a kind of seal of the divine knowledge in things.'"[39]

---

35. For an analysis of Thomas' understanding of *Ipsum Intellegere*, see Lonergan, *Verbum: Word and Idea in Aquinas*, 192–97.

36. Balthasar, *Glory of the Lord IV*, 401.

37. Ibid., 403.

38. Ibid.

39. Ibid. See Thomas Aquinas, *De veritate* 2.1, ad 9: "Whenever there is anything which corresponds to the concept we have of the word knowledge, of it we know not only that it is but also what it is, for knowledge is a distinct reality. But, as Damascene says, 'we cannot know what God is, but only that He is.' Therefore, in God there is nothing corresponding to our concept expressed by knowledge. Knowledge, therefore,

The divine seal on the infinite range of being that constitutes substantial forms within the world of finite being indicates a doctrine of participation. Where at first, the absolute transcendence and difference of the infinite act of existing seems remote from the existing forms of this world, when these forms are rightly understood, the absolute is present at hand. Balthasar insists,

> It is precisely here that a new kind of intimacy of God in the creature becomes clear, an intimacy which is only made possible by the distinction between God and *esse*. Allowing natures to participate in reality—God's most proper prerogative—is not to be understood as the disintegration or diminution (on the part of the creature) of God's being and unicity (which is how it is invariably seen outside the Christian tradition) and the essences of things must not appear as simply the fragmentation of reality, in a negative sense, but must be seen positively as posited and determined by God's omnipotent freedom and therefore are grounded in the unique love of God.[40]

This play of participation in which being is given as a gift of intentional donation through the outpouring of the love of the infinitely free absolute is a revelation in two senses. It shows that creation is only intelligible in relation to that which is beyond it, and it makes plain the truth that there is what Robert Sokolowski calls "the distinction" between God and creation.[41] Drawing attention to this, Balthasar observes, "In what we might call the 'real distinction' (circumspectly, because here we are dealing with an inexplicable mystery) God contemplated his Creation with free, so to speak, stereoscopic sight, which means at the same time that God preserves for the creature this wholly new plasticity. . . ."[42] For Thomas, Balthasar argues, being is thus fully affirmed as complete fullness (it is the proper effect of God) and total nothingness (it is non-subsistent), and through this

---

does not exist in God." Aquinas' responds, "The intellect is said to know what a thing is when it defines that thing, that is, when it conceives some form of the thing which corresponds to it in all respects. From our previous discussion, it is clear that whatever our intellect conceives of God falls short of being a representation of Him. Consequently, the quiddity of God Himself remains forever hidden from us. The most we can know of God during our present life is that He transcends everything that we can conceive of Him—as is clear from Dionysius."

40. Ibid., 404

41. See Sokolowski, *The God of Faith and Reason*.

42. Balthasar, *Glory of the Lord IV*, 405.

understanding of fullness and nothingness, we receive sets of insights into the good beyond being.[43]

Human subjectivity, perception and understanding into that which is beyond the self, is not simply placed on one side of the divide or the other. The intellectual spirit is situated in the midst of the tension between existence and essence, seeking that which all things desire not simply as object of the will but as an object of understanding; the human subject seeks in intelligence and being the one who is called *ipsum esse* and *ipsum intellegere*. A grasp of the real distinction—between God and the world, and between essence and existence—occasions the insight that God is not simply another being, but is something simultaneously wholly other and wholly familiar. We are at home in this distinction between fullness and nothingness because the light of understanding itself is the fruit of the tension in human subjectivity as the nothingness of possible intellect gives way to the light of agent intellect. This play, both cosmic and intimate, is revealed in Thomas' aesthetics as the heart of his metaphysics. For Balthasar, distinction, participation, and understanding are all interrelated in this insight. He states,

> The real distinction between existence and essence necessarily opens our eyes to the truth that God is self-subsistent being but it also closes our eyes and forbids us to cling on to what we have seen. For quite obviously the created intellectual spirit (if it is going to be able in any sense to know reality) is situated precisely within this distinction, in that active, illuminate fulness (*lumen intellectus agentis*) which at the same time remains nothingness (*intellectus possiblis*). In this distinction created spirit encounters the real whenever the real attains subsistence, i.e. In the subsistence of finite, material essences (*omnis cognitio incipit a sensu*). But these in their turn can only be the object of thought if they exist, if they participate in *the* reality which contains in itself all that is real, which compenetrates and dominates it and, as it were, indifferently transcends it.[44]

43. Ibid., 404. "Thus *esse*, as Thomas understands it, is at once both total fulness and total nothingness: fulness, because it is the most noble, the first and most proper effect of God, because 'through being God causes all things' and 'being is prior to and more interior than all other effects.' But being is also nothingness since it does not exist as such, 'for just as one cannot say that running runs,' but rather that 'the runner runs,' so 'one cannot say that existence exists.'" See *In. Div. Nom.* 5.1; *De Pot.* 3.7; *In Boeth. De. Hebd.* 2.

44. Balthasar, *Glory of the Lord IV*, 405. The nothingness of the possible intellect must be understood in the Aristotelian sense of potency. Thomas argues, for instance, that, "As potentiality to sensible being belongs to corporeal matter, so potentiality to intellectual being belongs to the 'possible' intellect. Wherefore nothing forbids habit to be in the 'possible' intellect, for it is midway between pure potentiality and perfect act"

Balthasar sees Thomas' achievement as a permanent one. He goes as far as to argue that late medieval and early modern metaphysics suffer from an inability to be attentive to the tension of the distinction, resulting in the tendencies to either flatten out being into merely that which can be reasonably abstracted from essence, or to conflate being with God. These twin tendencies, for Balthasar, are the philosophical postures of rationalism and idealism respectively.[45] The God of Aquinas, the one who reveals himself in through the intelligible and mysterious relations of understanding and wonder cannot be collapsed into the being of the world. To do so—to close the distinction, to resolve the tension—is to lose God, the world, and the self in the univocity of being, which is merely a crude euphemism for non-being. For Thomas and for Balthasar, being, in its fullest and most coherent sense, is likeness to God. Balthasar insists, "When God, in his knowing and omnipotent love, is seen freely choosing to create, there can be no question of a restrictive fragmentation of being into finite essences. *Esse*, can be suspended without confusion or limitation, in creaturely, free infinity and perfection, before the free God and only thus become the allusive likeness of divine goodness: *ipsum esse similitudo divinae bonitatis*."[46] These metaphysical terms such as suspension and harmony of relations are themselves already aesthetic ways of apprehension, and as such disclose the truthfulness of the beautiful as convertible with being; the metaphysical *is* the beautiful.

Being as the likeness of God takes metaphysical intuition and speculation out of merely intuitive and merely speculative modes of reason; it directs thought beyond merely thinking in itself and directs it toward that which is beyond being. God's revelation of God's self is also the revelation of creation, which, though being wholly contingent upon the freedom and love of God, is meaningfully related to the absolute in a way that bestows upon it not simply dignity, but also meaning. Being as likeness to God

---

(*ST* I-II.50.4, rep 2.).

45. Ibid., 405. "The period following Thomas was not able to sustain this state of tension and either reduced *esse* to a supreme and completely vacuous concept, which—as pure being 'there'—can be derived, abstracted, effortlessly from essences: this is rationalism. The other response was so to consolidate *esse* in itself that it coincides with God and now generates essences from itself in the divine cosmic process: this is pantheistic idealism."

46. Ibid., 406. See Aquinas, *De Ver.* 22.2, ad 2: "The good which is desired by all things is, in the opinion of the Philosopher, existence, as the Commentator maintains. But God is not the existence of all. Then God is not the good which is desired by all." To this objection, Aquinas responds, "Created existence is itself a likeness to the divine goodness. So in desiring to be, things implicitly desire a likeness to God and God Himself." In this one can see how the distinction between existence and essence, God and creation is intelligible according to a likeness that mediates between the divine and the human.

means that the finite notes of the harmony of created being participates in the mysterious and uncreated symphony of divine life. Balthasar concludes,

> The metaphysics of Thomas is thus the philosophical reflection of the free glory of the living God of the Bible and in this way the interior completion of ancient (and thus human) philosophy. It is a celebration of the reality of the real, of that all-embracing mystery of being which surpasses the powers of human thought, a mystery pregnant with the very mystery of God, a mystery in which creatures have access to participation in the reality of God, a mystery which in its nothingness and non-substance is shot through with the light of the freedom of the creative principle, of unfathomable love.[47]

To reflect on the metaphysical aesthetics of St. Thomas is to be concerned with the really real, with the sets of meaningful, glorious, and mysterious relations that show simultaneously that the being of the world is not the absolute, and that the absolute is present in every intelligible sense. The relations of size, color, order, perfection, harmony, and structure reveal to the world of created being the truth of itself and the truth of that which is beyond it. These relations are not subject to the mastery of created cognition; they both reveal the truth of the interrelatedness between the creation and God, and yet couch the same meaning in always-greater mystery. In reflection on the way in which the transcendental notions of being are meaningfully understood, both meaning and mystery begin with authentic human subjectivity, that is, with authentic acts of self-transcendent understanding, which moves from the data of experience toward insight into phantasm, and to the wonder of being.[48]

CONCLUSION

Subsequent generations of the faithful have universally recognized the life, thought, and achievements of St. Thomas Aquinas as a prodigious and fecund source of understanding with respect to the whole catalogue of the

47. Ibid., 406–7.

48. Ibid., 411–12 "The circumscription of the beautiful, through such allusive concepts as *integritas* (*perfectio*), *proportio* (*harmonia, convenientia*), *claritas, ordo*, is a circle that does not permit any running off in one direction or univocal construction. The circle can be entered through the sensory experience of beauty, which has an irreducible primacy. However, it is clear that, like the other transcendentals, beauty too, even sensory beauty, can only be recognised by a free and rational mind: *solus homo* (as opposed to the animals) *delectatur in ipsa pulchritudine ensibilium secundum se ipsam*." See *ST* Ia.93.3, ad 3.

mysteries of faith. When it seems that no more accolades may be directed his way, the incisive and brilliant mind of Hans Urs von Balthasar illuminates the aesthetic aspect of Thomas' theology in way that others have not. For Balthasar, Thomas' explorations in aesthetics are not discrete questions through which the theological student must pass on the way to understanding, but rather are extensions of his philosophy of being. Balthasar traces the different traditions of aesthetic insight that Thomas synthesizes and appropriates in order to advance his arguments about the structure of creation and the difference between God and the world. This appropriation discerns the intelligible relations between objects of aesthetic value and the perception of that beauty through acts of intelligence. Aesthetic experience is communion in which the finitude of created being finds itself enraptured in the warmth, glow, and mystery of the unrestricted act of being and understanding, the God of love who orders all things to himself, in whose presence we discern the paradox that he is unknowable and yet makes himself known.

BIBLIOGRAPHY

Aquinas, Thomas. *An Exposition of the On the Hebdomads of Boethius*. Translated by Janice L. et al. 1992. Reprint. Leonine 50. Washington, DC: Catholic University Press of America, 2001.

———. *An Introduction to the Metaphysics of Thomas Aquinas*. Edited and translated by James F. Anderson. 1953. Reprint. Washington, DC: Regnery, 1997.

———. *On the Power of God*. Translated by the English Dominicans. 1949. Reprint. Westminster: Christian Classics, 1952.

———. *The Summa Theologica*. Translated by Fathers of the English Dominican Province. 2nd rev. ed. 22 vols. 1912–36. Reprint. Westminster, MD: Christian Classics, 1981.

———. *Truth*. Translated by Robert W. Mulligan (Vol. 1: qq. 1–9); James V. McGlynn (vol. 2: qq. 10–20), Robert W. Schmidt (vol. 3: 21–29). 1952–54. Reprint. Indianapolis: Hackett, 1994.

Balthasar, Hans Urs von. *Explorations in Theology*, Vol. 1: *The Word Made Flesh*. Translated by A. V. Littledale and Alexander Dru. San Francisco: Ignatius, 1989.

———. *The Glory of the Lord: A Theological Aesthetics*, Vol. 1: *Seeing the Form*, 2nd ed. Translated by Erasmo Leiva-Merikakis. New York: Crossroad, 2009.

———. *The Glory of the Lord: A Theological Aesthetics*, Vol. 4: *The Realm of Metaphysics in Antiquity*. Translated by Brian McNeil C.R.V. et al. San Francisco: Ignatius, 1989.

———. *The Glory of the Lord A Theological Aesthetics*, Vol. 5: *The Realm of Metaphysics in the Modern Age*. Translated by Oliver Davies, et al. San Francisco: Ignatius, 1991.

———. *Thomas von Aquin, Besondere Gnadengaben und die zwei Wege menschlichen Lebens: Kommentar zu Summa Theologica II-II, 171–182*. Gemeinschaftsverlag F. H. Kerle/A. Pustet Heidelberg und Granz-Wein-Salzburg, 1954

Beardsley, Monroe C. *Aesthetics From Classical Greece to the Present: A Short History*. Tuscaloosa, AL: University of Alabama Press, 1966.

Bourke, Vernon J., editor. *The Pocket Aquinas*. New York: Washington Square, 1960.

Burrell, David, C.S.C. "Analogy, Creation, and Theological Language," In *The Theology of Thomas Aquinas*, 77–98. Notre Dame, IN: University of Notre Dame Press, 2005.

———. *Faith and Freedom: An Interfaith Perspective*. Challenges in Contemporary Theology. Malden, MA and Oxford: Blackwell, 2004.

———. *Knowing the Unknowable God: Ibn-Sina, Maimonides, Aquinas*. Notre Dame, IN: Notre Dame University Press, 1986.

Campodonico, Angelo. "Hans Urs von Balthasar's Interpretation of the Philosophy of Thomas Aquinas." Translated by Joseph G. Trabbic. *Nova et Vetera* 8.1 (2010) 33–53.

Copleston, Frederick, S.J., *A History of Philosophy*. Vol. 2: *Medieval Philosophy: From Augustine to Duns Scotus*. New York: Doubleday Image, 1993.

De Bruyne, Edgar. *The Esthetics of the Middle Ages*. Translated by Eileen B. Hennessy. New York: Frederick Ungar, 1969.

Doran, Robert M., S.J. "Lonergan and Balthasar: Methodological Considerations." *Theological Studies* 58.1 (1997) 569–607.

Eco, Umberto. *The Aesthetics of Thomas Aquinas*. Translated by Hugh Bredlin. Cambridge: Harvard University Press, 1988.

Gilson, Etienne. *The Elements of Christian Philosophy*. New York: Doubleday, 1960.

Grant, Sara, R.S.C.J. *Towards an Alternative Theology: Confessions of a Nondualist Christianity*. Bangalore: Asian Trading Corp., 1991.

Lonergan Bernard, S.J. *Verbum: Word and Idea in Aquinas*. Collected Works 2. Toronto: University of Toronto Press, 1997.

Pieper, Josef. *The Josef Pieper Anthology*. San Francisco: Ignatius, 1989.

Pseudo-Dionysius. *Dionysius, the Areopagite, On the Divine Names and Mystical Theology*. Translated by C. E. Rolt. London: New York: Macmillan, 1951.

Sokolowski, Robert. *The God of Faith and Reason*. Washington, DC: Catholic University of America Press, 1995.

5

On the Conceptual Relationship between Religion and Science

Considerations from a Christian Perspective

RICHARD A. KNOPP

U NLIKE MOST AUTHORS IN this volume, I never had Dr. Castelein as a professor. But that does not mean that he was never my teacher. We have been close friends and colleagues for over thirty years. His educational impact on me stemmed from team-taught college classes; faculty presentations and retreats; numerous sermons that he preached in chapel and at my local church; conference travels together; and personal conversations about life, the universe, and everything. He presided or prayed at the weddings of my three children; and years before then, he even instructed us all on how to get past those tough spots in the Atari version of Mario Brothers. About twenty years ago, we collaborated on a *festschrift* in honor of our seminary major professor, Dr. James Strauss.[1] Now it is Dr. Castelein's turn to be deservingly honored, and my privilege to contribute.

While Christian theology is Dr. Castelein's area of expertise, he's always had a keen interest in science, and he incorporates scientific issues

1. Knopp and Castelein, *Taking Every Thought Captive.*

and developments in his lectures. He properly understands that doing contemporary theology without interacting with science is not doing theology adequately. With that in mind, I want to discuss the conceptual relationship between science and religion. I believe that this material will be beneficial for those who profess little, if any, religious faith, but I also hope that it will be profitable for religious believers, especially those who align themselves with the core tenets of Christian theology.

One of the central issues is whether science and religion should be seen as *overlapping* or as *non-overlapping*. These two perspectives correlate with two prominent alternatives that are advocated by both religious believers and non-believers: science and religion do overlap and necessarily *conflict*; or science and religion *cannot conflict*, because their methods, their respective languages, and their subject matter are entirely different. If they do not overlap, then two corollaries follow: nothing from science could ever count *against* religious faith, and nothing within the scope of science could ever count *for* a religious belief. For some, this would be tremendously consoling; for others, it would be terribly disturbing. On the other hand, if science and religion *do* overlap, then the prerequisite is in place for unavoidable conflict, and the relationship between science and religion easily becomes extremely *negative* in nature—a sentiment that is widely held in our culture today.

So how can there be such disparity in how science and religion are viewed? One main reason is that many discussions of their relationship give woefully inadequate attention to the nature of religion and to the nature of science. Both religion and science are often treated far too monolithically, as though we can somehow simply discuss the relationship between "religion" and "science" *per se*. But such attempts make two false assumptions: that different religions and religious traditions are essentially the same in their nature and in the kinds of claims they make; and that science itself is a uniformly perceived and practiced enterprise. Elsewhere, I have argued that science is not so monolithic in its methods or its mindsets; and it is not as purely objective, empirical, and rational as it is prominently portrayed.[2] Here, I want to emphasize the diversity of *religion* and the distinctiveness of biblical Christianity in terms of how this should affect our view of the conceptual relationship between science and religion. If we want to understand how science and religion relate, we must recognize that religions significantly differ in their nature. If this is the case, then how science relates to religion will greatly depend on what religion, and even what religious tradition, we are referencing.

2. I pursued this consideration in the Strauss *festschrift*, "On the Value of the Philosophy of Science," in *Taking Every Thought Captive*, 239–70. A more recent presentation is my "Lessons from the Philosophy of Science."

My primary contention is that *biblical Christianity is distinctive among religions and religious traditions, and it uniquely offers a strong basis for recognizing a very "positive" relationship between science and religion.* While historical[3] and philosophical[4] considerations are also important to demonstrate this point, this chapter will concern itself with the *conceptual* relationship between science and religion. It will survey and evaluate four basic models for relating science and religion (the Conflict Model, the Compartmentalized Model, the Complementarian Model, and the Coordination Model), arguing that *a Christian worldview,[5] when consistently applied, offers its strongest endorsement to the Coordination Model, which best fosters a positive and potentially productive relationship between science and religion.*

3. Historically speaking, in spite of the widely held notion that science and religion (especially Christianity) are intrinsically hostile, most pioneering scientists in the early modern period were Christians (or Creationists) who operated with a very positive understanding of the relationship between their science and their faith. Fred Heeren lists and discusses fifty such scientists (*Show Me God*, 268–97). Geisler and Anderson list fifteen individuals who are "most of the founders of the various disciplines of modern science" (*Origin Science*, 39–40). And Henry Schaefer discusses five scientists of the seventeenth century, six who were born before 1900, and nine contemporary scientists who are distinctively Christian (*Science and* Christianity, 7–35). Examples include Francis Bacon, Kepler, Robert Boyle, Isaac Newton, Michael Faraday, James Maxwell, J. J. Thompson, Charles Coulson (not to be confused with the late Charles Colson), John Suppe, John Polkinghorne, Allan Sandage, and Francis Collins. Even the notable case of Galileo and the Roman church was a clash over how to *interpret* Scripture (as well as a "complex interplay of untoward political circumstances, personal ambitions, and wounded prides"). Galileo himself still had great respect for Scripture and its role in sanctioning his science. See Shea, "Galileo and the Church," 118–21, 124–32.

4. Philosophically speaking, some kind of a creationist perspective provides the theoretical foundation for the necessary and basic presuppositions that make science possible—assumptions that science itself cannot justify. Moreland and Craig list ten such assumptions, including the existence, orderliness, and knowability of a theory-independent, external world; the laws of logic; the basic reliability of sense perception; and the uniformity of nature (*Philosophical Foundations*, 348–49).

5. Unfortunately, whatever terminology is adopted to identify this viewpoint is unavoidably problematic. Words like "Christian," "worldview," and even "biblical" carry considerable and confusing baggage. By "Christian worldview," I intend to highlight the theological core of the Christian faith as it is communicated in the Bible and as it is expressed in the classic Christian creeds. Minimally, a Christian worldview holds that God exists; that He created the universe and life; that He created humans in His image; that He has acted providentially and miraculously in history and ultimately in and through Jesus Christ; that He has revealed truths in a variety of ways to various people; and that He has uniquely guided the authors of the Bible books to communicate what He intended.

ON THE NATURE OF RELIGION AND THE UNIQUENESS OF A CHRISTIAN WORLDVIEW

Those who do not know much about religion have every right to think that it is a confusing mess. Those who do know a lot about religion, *know* it's a mess! The number of religions in our world is mind boggling. David Barrett's two-volume, 1700 page *World Christian Encyclopedia* identifies 10,000 distinct religions and 33,830 denominations within Christianity![6] The spectrum of beliefs represented here is enormous. Are we to lump them all together in trying to understand the relationship between science and *religion per se*? That would only make sense if they all say pretty much the same thing. Yet even if we consider only six of the world religions (i.e., Hinduism, Buddhism, Taoism, Judaism, Christianity, Islam), we encounter fundamental differences. And if we focus exclusively on Christianity, we discover a complex array of perspectives. There are different "branches" (e.g., Roman Catholic, Eastern Orthodox, Protestant, Anglican), different "denominations" (e.g., Baptist, Lutheran, Presbyterian, Church of Christ), and different theological "wings" (e.g., liberal, neo-orthodox, existential, fundamentalist, evangelical).

While it may be important for some purposes to analyze and evaluate the various Christian branches and denominations, my focus here is on the extent to which a religion or religious branch, denomination, or theological wing makes specific truth-claims about *nature and history*. It's what I call the "*empirical content*" of religious belief. Why is this important in understanding the conceptual relationship between science and religion? Because science is primarily seen as an activity concerned with the empirical world—the world we can access with our physical senses and with various instruments that extend our senses, like telescopes and subatomic colliders. If religion is understood as making no claims about the empirical world, then there can be no overlap between it and science. On the other hand, if religion is viewed as making empirical claims about history and nature, then the stage is set for possible, if not inevitable, conflict with science. When we consider the issue of empirical content, we can detect significant differences among religions and among Christian denominations and theological wings. Basically, the point is this: when compared to other religions and various theological perspectives within Christendom, a Christian worldview offers a unique perspective on the nature of religion due to its distinctive claims about nature and history. Here are several claims to consider:

6. Barrett, *World Christian Encyclopedia*, 1:3, 2:3.

1. *When compared to other religions, the worldview expressed in biblical Judaism and Christianity is unique when it comes to the issue of empirical content.*

Of course, Hinduism, Buddhism, Taoism, and Islam have a "history"; they can point to some historical origin and to various historical documents regarded as sacred. But their belief system—their worldview—is not based *on* history and *in* history the way Judaism and Christianity are. Biblical Judaism and Christianity have historically founded their beliefs and practices on fundamental claims that are directly connected to history and nature. The biblical worldview not only makes truth-claims about what *is* the case in nature and history, it asserts by implication that some states of affairs *cannot* be the case if the biblical worldview is true. For example, if God created the universe, it cannot be eternal, self-originating, or self-explanatory. If God created humanity in His image, humans have some distinctive qualities that are not fully explainable in purely materialistic terms. God acted in history and on nature (e.g., by producing a great flood as a judgment on human sin; by bringing a series of plagues on the Egyptians to effect Israel's release from captivity; by parting the Red Sea; by miraculously helping the Israelites conquer their promised land against incredible odds; by taking the form of human flesh and doing signs and wonders through Jesus of Nazareth; by providing miraculous powers to the early leaders of the Christian faith). God also communicated prophecies about future events and revealed specific information *within* time and space and *about* time and space (e.g., by speaking to Abraham, to Moses, to the Old Testament prophets, to John the baptizer, to Jesus, to the New Testament preachers). In sum, the propositional truth-claims of biblical Judaism and Christianity entail substantive empirical content about nature and history.[7]

Other religions have no comparable touchstone in history or nature. The diverse philosophical beliefs of Hinduism do not depend on any particular history, people, or person. And while Buddhism, Taoism, and Islam can point to a founding historical figure,[8] their respective beliefs do not *require* any specific claims about events in space and time.[9] Even if one

7. This does not mean, however, that biblical theism includes *nothing but* propositions or that it can be reduced to propositions. The biblical literature consists of *much more* than propositions (e.g., praise passages, lamentations, parables). But, the Bible cannot rightly be characterized *without* these propositional truth-claims about nature and history.

8. Buddhism points to Siddartha Gautama (c. 560–480 B.C.); Taoism was founded by Lao-Tzu (604–517 B.C.); and Islam was initiated by Muhammad (570–632 A.D.).

9. David Clark rightly adds that religions like Buddhism, Taoism, and Confucianism do not even have a logical place for supernatural miracles, because their belief system rejects the existence of a God/god who could perform them. Also, while later traditions attributed miracles to the founders of these religions, the founders themselves

accepts the reports that some founders performed miracles, their miracles were never regarded as necessary for the truth of the religion itself.[10]

With Christianity, however, the contrast could not be clearer. The apostle Paul says, "If Christ has not been raised, then our preaching is vain, your faith also is vain" (1 Cor 15:14), and "if Christ has not been raised, your faith is worthless; you are still in your sins" (1 Cor 15:17). Biblical Christianity stands or falls on the occurrence of the miracles performed by Jesus and the great "sign of Jonah"—as Jonah was in the belly of the earth for three days, so the Son of Man (Jesus) will be in the belly of the sea monster for three days and nights (Matt 12:38–41). And it is not just the miracles of Jesus that are essential to the truth of Christianity. The truth of Christianity would never have been boldly preached or accepted had it not been for the miraculous events associated with the lives of its apostles and prophets. Christianity as it is known from the New Testament would not exist without the miracle of Pentecost (Acts 2) or the miraculous blinding and healing of Saul (Acts 9) or the miraculous visible sign given to Gentiles (non-Jews) of speaking in different languages (Acts 10). The Bible in general and Christian theology in particular profess an amazing level of "empirical content" that intersects with history and the natural world.

2. When compared to the sacred writings of other religions, the Bible is unique in its historical character.

The sacred literature of Hinduism, Buddhism, Taoism, and Islam is categorically different from that of the Bible. The Bible presents God's miraculous interaction with nature and humanity in a historical narrative, with a discernible chronology of real people, places, and events. Yet one would look in vain to find all of these qualities in the sacred writings of Hinduism, Buddhism, or Taoism (not to mention other religions like Jainism, Sikhism, Confucianism, Shinto, and Zoroastrianism).

---

discouraged the practice of such marvels. See "Miracles in the World Religions," 202–5.

10. The production of the Qur'an, the holy book of Islam, is regarded by Muslims as a great miracle. And Muslims believe that Muhammad performed some miracles. Yet most of the information about Muhammad comes not from the Qur'an but from the *haddith* (tradition), which presumably contains Muhammad's spoken judgments, and the *sunna*, which describe Muhammad's behavior or practice (see Noss, *Man's Religions*, 5th ed., 529–32). Even so, the miracles later attributed to Muhammad are not considered critical to the truth of Islam. Clark makes the point that "virtually all ancient miracle stories outside the Bible are described in texts written long after the events they report." But the documents describing Jesus' miraculous works were composed "within a generation of his life" ("Miracles in the World's Religions," 211).

Hinduism has a large body of sacred texts, the most important ones being the four *Vedas* and the *Upanishads*.[11] In neither the *Vedas* nor the *Upanishads* do we find a detectable historical narrative that makes persistent claims about specific divine action in history as we do in the Old Testament with Abraham, Moses, the prophets, etc.

Buddhism has a large and wide array of writings that are valued differently by diverse sects. But the basic Buddhist canon is the *Tripitaka* (or *Tipitaka*), which contains three groups of writings that were first written down in the mid-third century B.C. and collected in three "baskets" (*pitaka*). The writings present rules for the monks, discourses on doctrine and ethics by the Buddha, as well as additional teachings about ethics and refutations of other teachings in other schools. In general, the writings are arranged by type and, in some cases, by length. But it presents no integrated historical narrative, much less one that covers decades or centuries as does the Bible. And it offers no divine action that could be construed as a miracle. In fact, Buddhism categorically rejects the concept of a transcendent God who could perform such acts.[12]

Taoism professes the *Tao Te Ching* ("The Way and Its Power") as its initial sacred text. Information about its date and its author is uncertain, although it was probably written between the sixth and fourth centuries B.C. Tradition holds that it presents the sayings of Lao Tzu. It discusses the *Tao* (the "Way"), which is some eternal, impersonal, mystical but supreme principle of the universe. The *Tao* is extremely nebulous. The book even says that "the Tao that can be conceived is not the real Tao." The *Tao Te Ching* provides instructions on how to tap in to The Way through creative quietude, humility, a life of simplicity without ceremony, and working with and not against nature. But Taoism includes no historical narrative; nor does it make any claims about a God who acts in space and time.[13]

Islam differs significantly from these religions, because it professes a transcendent God (Allah) who reveals his message to prophets and

---

11. The *Vedas* were composed from 1500–1000 B.C. and primarily consisted of hymns to the gods and mythology about the gods and rulers. They especially emphasized priestly ritual and sacrifice and were composed in complicated poetic form. They "show no systematic development, ordering, or single mythological framework." The earliest extant manuscripts we have of the Vedas date back to the eleventh century A.D. The *Upanishads* were appended to the *Vedas* after 1000 B.C. They gave less emphasis to ritual and incantation and more to meditation and ascetic practices. They present significant concepts for Hinduism, including the idea that the world is *maya* (illusion) and that the true underlying reality behind this illusion is *Brahman*. See Esposito, *World Religions Today*, 280.

12. See Bush, et al., *The Religious World*, 117–19.

13. See ibid., 181–82.

messengers. Muhammad claimed that Allah recited the contents of the book to him in Arabic through the angel Gabriel from A.D. 610 to the year of his death in 632. The Qur'an seems more "historical," because it mentions Old and New Testament characters like Noah, Abraham, Moses, Jonah, and Jesus (see 4:163–64), and it presents Muhammad as "the last" of these prophets (33:40). But aside from a shorter opening chapter, the 114 *surahs* (chapters) are arranged by length, from longest to shortest. The Qur'an offers no coherent historical narrative or context like the Bible, although the *surahs* do identify whether their respective recitations were received by Muhammad in Mecca (which was earlier) or in Medina (which was later).[14]

Paul Maier, a long-time professor of Ancient History at Western Michigan University, captures this point well about the unique historical nature of the Bible when he says,

> Because Judeo-Christianity has so thoroughly influenced Western culture, we are prone to imagine that all other world religions have a similarly solid historical base. This is by no means the case. It can, in fact, be argued that *every* religious system before or since Judaism and Christianity has avoided any significant interaction with history, and instead has asked its followers to believe, by sheer faith alone, the claimed revelations of its founder(s). . . . The founder may well have been historical, of course, but one looks in vain for true correlations with secular history in the founder's holy book.[15]

3. When compared to unbiblical "Christian" theologies, a truly biblical worldview presents specific claims about nature and history that are empirically "checkable."

Not only does the biblical worldview contrast with other religions on the matter of empirical content, those who profess some form of Christian theology substantively differ among themselves on its fundamental nature. I contend that any "Christian" theology that reduces Christianity to mere subjective states of mind or inner feelings (like that of Schliermacher or Tillich) has abandoned *biblical* Christianity that possesses significant empirical content. Any "Christian" theology that preaches a divine revelation with no propositional content that can be empirically checked or rationally criticized (like that of Karl Barth's neo-orthodoxy) has abandoned the biblical worldview that makes specific truth-claims about nature and history. Such theologies construct a Christianity that is necessarily *separate from* the

14. See Bush, et al., *The Religious World*, 318.
15. Maier, *In the Fullness of Time*, xv.

realm of empirical science. As a result, they are rightly subject to the charge of resorting to an *absolute commitment* that is *irrational*. W. W. Bartley, a philosopher of science offered this insightful and devastating criticism of much of modern theology in his book, *The Retreat to Commitment*.[16] In essence, Bartley argued that theologies like those of Tillich and Barth are "irrational" because they have totally removed themselves from the plane of any possible rational or empirical criticism. *No* rational arguments or empirical considerations, even in principle, can count *for* or *against* their theologies. Of course, this is a "safe" position, since nothing can prove such theologies to be false, but it has also helped foster the widespread intellectual sentiment that religion is *irrelevant* to the "real world" of time and space—that religion is totally different from science.

The question about the empirical content of religious belief was classically raised in the 1940s by the philosopher John Wisdom and prominently flaunted in the 1950s by Antony Flew who described an intriguing parable about an "invisible gardener." When two explorers came to a clearing that had flowers and weeds, one—the "believer"—thought that there must be a gardener. The other explorer—a skeptic—denied it. The two tried various ways to check for the existence of this gardener (e.g., an electrified fence, bloodhounds). But nothing worked. Yet the believer was not dissuaded. He asserted that there *is* a gardener, but he is "invisible, intangible, insensible to electric shocks, a gardener who has no scent and makes no sound, a gardener who comes secretly to look after the garden which he loves." Then the skeptic thrusts his fatal blow in the form of a question: "Just how does what you call an invisible, intangible, eternally elusive gardener differ from an imaginary gardener or even from no gardener at all?"[17]

This short and simple parable cuts like a surgical instrument through the body of religion. But it is important to see that not all religious perspectives are equally "hurt" by this. To be sure, *most* religions and *many* "Christian" theologies leave us with no empirically discernible difference between *believing in* a God who has no contact with history and nature and *not believing in* a God at all. On the other hand, this is *not* true for the *biblical* worldview. Specifically, the Christian worldview affirms that God is not purely invisible, intangible, and speechless. God has truly entered the garden of nature and history, and He was specifically revealed in the person of Jesus Christ. In responding to Phillip's request to "show us the Father," Jesus said, "Anyone who has seen me has seen the Father" (John 14:9). And then Jesus says, "Believe me when I say that I am in the Father and the Father is

16. See Bartley, *The Retreat to Commitment*.
17. See Flew, "The Falsification Challenge," 356 (originally published in 1955).

in me; or at least believe on the evidence of the miracles themselves" (John 14:11). God has become flesh in the form of Jesus Christ, God's Son (John 1:1–3, 14; 3:16–18; Phil 2:5–11; 1 John 4:1–3). And this Son of God was accessible to the physical senses of men and women. They saw him with their eyes and touched him with their hands (1 John 1:1–3). Even some skeptical followers of Jesus (like Thomas) who demanded empirical evidence of his resurrection were satisfied with what they were allowed to see and touch (John 20:24–30).[18] The God of biblical Christianity is not a mere transcendent spirit, or nebulous idea of the "Absolute," or a subjective projection of our minds or inner wishes. The Jesus of history gives us the "exact representation" of God's nature (Heb 1:1–3). He is described as the "image" of God (Col 1:15), a translation of a Greek word that spells "icon" in English. As a result, we might coin an instruction using a modern computer analogy: click on the icon of Jesus and the application will open to God.

Now what does this discussion have to do with the conceptual relationship between science and religion? First, it helps us understand why *some* religions and "Christian" theological perspectives *must* take a *non-overlapping* approach. Religion according to them is purely about subjective feelings and values. It is merely about meaning and purpose. It gives ethical direction on individual behavior and social action. But it has nothing to do with the empirically-accessible world of "facts" in history or nature. Second, it helps us understand why *biblical Christianity* must adopt some kind of *overlapping* approach to science and faith. Like science, the biblical worldview makes specific truth-claims about the physical world and historical events.[19]

DIFFERENT MODELS FOR RELATING SCIENCE AND RELIGION

While numerous texts survey various ways to relate science and religion, Ian Barbour's four-fold way of classifying their possible relationship has been very influential and widely utilized. He speaks of conflict, independence,

---

18. The closest followers of Jesus were *all* skeptical of his resurrection from the dead. Yet each one became convinced of it because they were allowed to see him, touch him, fish with him, and eat with him over a period of forty days prior to his ascension to heaven (see John 20:10–18; 20:19–22; 21:1–13; Matt 28:1–10; Mark 16:1–14; Luke 24:1–12, 13–35, 36–48).

19. Of course, biblical Christianity also addresses matters like ethics, meaning, and purpose. But what it claims about ethics, meaning, and purpose is *based* on its truth-claims about God's historical action in *this* world.

dialogue, and integration.[20] I want to revise the terminology and specifically discuss and evaluate four different models for relating science and religion *from the standpoint of a professing biblical Christian.* Science and religion (a) inevitably and necessarily *conflict*; (b) they are *compartmentalized* by being totally separate from one another; (c) they *complement* one another by addressing different "levels" of reality; or (d) they are *coordinated* in the sense that each can legitimately critique the other and productively contribute information to the other.

A. The Conflict Model

The "conflict model" undoubtedly receives the most notoriety. Viewing science and religion at "war" has a long history, and it is deeply etched in our culture.[21] Two opposing mentalities dominate when Christianity and science are seen in unavoidable and irresolvable conflict: some are confident that *science trumps religion*—science wins and Christianity is wrong; and some are convinced that *religion trumps science*—Christianity wins and science is wrong.

Many people see science as the Cinderella of the modern world. It's been repressed in times past, primarily from religious zealots, but now the legitimate king of truth rules. And this kingdom of science shows little respect for religious believers. This view is reflected by a prominent group of "new atheists" like Richard Dawkins, Sam Harris, Christopher Hitchens, and Victor Stenger who wield science as their primary weapon against religious fundamentalism.[22] For example, Richard Dawkins, perhaps the current self-proclaimed prince of science, says, "I think a case can be made that faith is one of the world's great evils, comparable to the smallpox virus but harder to eradicate."[23] Science trumps religion.

Many Christians implicitly convey their own fairy tale imagery. They see themselves as Little Red Riding Hood with nothing but goodies to share

20. See Barbour, *Religion in an Age of Science*, 3–30. McGrath refers to it as "the most widely used typology" (McGrath, *Science and Religion*, 45). Carlson (*Science and Christianity: Four Views*) highlights creationism, independence, qualified agreement, and partnership.

21. Andrew White, the first president of Cornell University, wrote *A History of the Warfare of Science and Theology* (1896) and John Draper stressed *The History of the Conflict between Religion and Science* (1874). Both White and Draper were highly critical of religion and of dogmatic theology.

22. See Dawkins, *The God Delusion*; Harris, *The End of Faith*; Hitchens, *God is Not Great*; and Stenger, *God: The Failed Hypothesis*.

23. Richard Dawkins, "Is Science a Religion?" 26.

with grandma (and the rest of the world!). But science is the Big Bad Wolf that is out to get them. As a result, many Christians are afraid or highly suspicious of science, and they don't want to be affected by it. After all, the wolf in Darwin's clothing has ravaged their culture and devoured untold numbers of Christians. This view seems especially exemplified by those whose decisive authority begins and ends with the Bible. For example, Ken Ham not only attests to this singularly important biblical authority, he claims that it requires a youth-earth understanding of creation: "The authority of Scripture is a central point of faith. If you don't get the first two chapters of the sacred text right, you cannot get the rest right either. . . . A young earth is a corollary for trusting the Bible as the authority . . ."[24] Religion (i.e., the Bible) trumps science.

This conflict model is not just a *position* that acknowledges conflict; it is a *disposition* that incites it. And from practical experience we know that when we are in "conflict mode," we don't make many friends or much headway. Even if genuine conflict does exist, it would undoubtedly be more pleasant and potentially more productive if we would at least adopt an attitude of mutual respect. Unfortunately, both religious believers and skeptics often decline genuine dialogue for a diatribe. But Christians should reject name calling and disparaging adjectives as simply "un-Christian"; and skeptics, especially those who pride themselves on the use of logic, should recognize that such a practice commits a variety of logical fallacies.[25]

If science and biblical Christianity overlap, then it is possible, perhaps even likely, that there will be inevitable conflict—either apparent or genuine. Here are some observations on why this is the case and how we might best respond to it.

(a) As successful as science has been, anyone with a basic awareness of the history of science realizes that the scientific consensus has changed through time.[26] If this is taken to mean that science is "getting it more right" as it

24. Ham and Hall, *Already Compromised*, 33, 35.

25. For example, the *ad hominem* fallacy is the illegitimate move of dismissing the position by attacking the person (e.g., "You shouldn't believe him; he's a Christian"). The "fallacy of association" rejects a position on the basis of its association with something or someone else that is regarded as inferior or unacceptable (e.g., "She's just one of those skeptics"). The "genetic fallacy" dismisses a position based on its unacceptable origin (e.g., "That absurd idea comes from the Bible"). For a comprehensive discussion of such fallacies, see Kreeft, *Socratic Logic*, 68–122.

26. For example, astronomy and physics have moved from (a) Ptolemy's geocentric (earth-centered) model to (b) Copernicus's heliocentric (sun-centered) model with circular orbits, to (c) Newton's model of elliptical planetary orbits around the sun based on a property of mass that produces gravitational attraction, to (d) Einstein's view that the so-called "attraction" is a property of curved space rather than mass. Physics has

goes along, it also implies that it *did not* have it quite right before. While those who hold that *science trumps religion* may say that science *does* have it right *now*, it is certainly appropriate, based on historical precedent, not to be dogmatic about it.

Those who think that *religion trumps science* often highlight the changes in science. It's not so much that they are *against* science per se, but they do oppose a view coming from science that, *at the present*, seems incompatible with their understanding of the world as it is informed by their religion. Yet they should be careful not to summarily dismiss widespread scientific consensus because it opposes *what they take to be* the Bible's position.

(b) Christianity also appears to conflict with science because scientists do not always speak *as scientists* but *as philosophers*. If this is true, then one important objective is to detect when this occurs. Atheist Carl Sagan wrote a chapter on "the fine art of baloney detection," and Phillip Johnson, thought of as the father of the Intelligent Design movement, emphasized the need to use a "baloney detector."[27] What I'm recommending is that we manufacture and utilize "hat detectors."

For example, when molecular biologist Francis Crick, one of the co-discoverers of the structure of the DNA molecule, says, "The ultimate aim of the modern movement in biology is in fact to explain *all* biology in terms of physics and chemistry,"[28] he is not speaking as someone who is making *empirical* descriptions or generalizations; he is making a *philosophical* claim that necessarily goes beyond what he can know *empirically*. He is claiming that biology is fully reducible to physics and chemistry; it is reducible to *pure matter*. This is a *philosophical* position of *materialism*. As a result, Crick is no longer wearing his "*science* hat"; he has now donned a "*philosophy* hat."

When Oxford chemist Peter Atkins asserts that "there is no reason to suppose that science cannot deal with every aspect of existence," he is not wearing a "*science* hat"; he is making a claim that goes far beyond the empirical confirmation capability of science. When biologist Jacque Monod says, "Man knows at last that he is alone in the universe's unfeeling immensity,

---

moved from a view of indivisible atoms, to atoms that can be "split"; from a view of the atom that has nicely orbiting electrons (like the sun has nicely ordered planets) to the idea that electrons are like waves *and* particles whose position and momentum cannot be simultaneously determined. Geology has moved back and forth between "uniformitarianism" (where changes occur at a uniform rate over time) and "catastrophism" (where changes periodically occur rapidly, for example, through the effects of meteors).

27. See Sagan, *The Demon Haunted World*, 201–218; and Johnson, "Tuning Up Your Baloney Detector," 37–52.

28. Crick, *Of Molecules and Men*, 10.

out of which he emerged only by chance,"[29] he is not wearing a "*science* hat." He is expressing a *philosophical* viewpoint on human origins that cannot be known on empirical grounds.

In reference to the biologist Richard Dawkins and his book, *The God Delusion*, one's "hat detector" has to work overtime! He exclaims that "any creative intelligence, of sufficient complexity to design anything, comes into existence only as the end product of an extended process of gradual evolution. Creative intelligences, being evolved, necessarily arrive late in the universe, and therefore cannot be responsible for designing it. God . . . is a delusion . . ."[30] Because Dawkins is such a world-famous evolutionary biologist, many will assume that he is expressing ideas that are based solidly, if not exclusively, on "scientific" grounds. But empirical science alone cannot know that all creative intelligences evolve or that God is a delusion. In saying such things, Dawkins is wearing a "philosophy hat"—and a big one at that.

Christians should not be opposed to "science," but it should be obvious that they can be rightly expected to protest an incompatible *philosophy* that attempts to wear scientific clothes. Such a view has been referred to as "scientism"—a view that fuses scientific methodology with a philosophical worldview of naturalism or materialism. The Christian worldview certainly opposes *scientism*, but not science. And it is critical to expose scientism when its advocates are presumably speaking for science. As John Lennox puts it, "Statements by scientists are not necessarily statements of science."[31]

(c) Christianity can also appear to conflict with science because religious believers mis-interpret or inappropriately apply Scripture. Of course, it's relatively easy for some Christians to dismiss or devalue science because of its changing nature or to reject ideas expressed by scientists because they are really incompatible philosophical views. It's harder to face the possibility that their biblical interpretations could actually be mistaken. But here, historical precedent should create a considerable sense of humility for Bible believers.

At one time, some contended that the Bible taught that the world was flat and did not move. For example, in the sixteenth century some used the Bible to contend (against Copernicus) that the earth cannot move as a planet and orbit the sun.[32] Yet these views have now almost universally been

29. Monod, *Chance and Necessity*, 180. (At least Monod acknowledges this in the subtitle of this book: *An Essay on the Natural Philosophy of Modern Biology*.)

30. Dawkins, *The God Delusion*, 31.

31. Lennox, *God's Undertaker*, 19.

32. This view seemed justifiable based on a literal interpretation of various biblical

repudiated, even by those who take a very literal interpretation of Scripture. So the growing consensus of science *has*, in fact, prompted changes in our understanding of the Bible. The big questions, of course, are these: Are there any *other* interpretations of Scripture, particularly about history, life, or the universe, that might be incorrect or over-extended? If so, which ones? Such questions can only be answered on a case-by-case basis. And they may not be easy to determine. For now, however, we should at least acknowledge the *possibility* that some conflicts between science and Christianity exist because of mistaken biblical interpretations.

B. The Compartmentalized Model

The Compartmentalized model proposes a *non-overlapping* view of science and religion. Stephen Gould (1941–2002), a Harvard paleontologist, called this view NOMA for "non-overlapping magisteria."[33] This means that science and religion do not share any territory in common and that each rules its own domain with its unique purposes and methods. Religion concerns values, meaning, and morality; while science is concerned with empirical facts. Earlier in this chapter, I discussed why this view is to be expected, if not required, by *some* approaches to religion—because many skeptics and religious believers maintain that religion makes no empirical claims like science does. Religion and science are entirely different. Their subject matter is different; their methods are different; their languages are different; and so on.

This view is widely held. Although I am not aware of any surveys on this, my sense is that, among scientists who are atheistic or agnostic and among religious believers who are academically or professionally involved in science, this is the *dominant* view. This view may be espoused by those who think that science is *better* than religion because it deals with the "real" world, but it may also be championed by those who see religion and science as *equally important* because they respectively address unrelated spheres of equal significance.

---

passages. The earth is "firmly established, and cannot be moved" (1 Chr 16:30); and the "sun rises" and goes "down" (e.g., Josh 12:1; Pss 50:1; 104:19; Isa 45:6; Mal 1:11; Rev 7:2). Some interpreters would even have had biblical grounds for claiming that the earth is flat because it has "four corners" (Isa 11:12; Rev 7:1; 20:7). See Westman, "The Copernicans and the Churches," 90–93.

33. Gould says that "the net, or magisterium, of science covers the empirical realm" but "the magisterium of religion extends over questions of ultimate meaning and moral value." See his *Rocks of Ages*, 5–6.

One way this view is often expressed is through the adoption of "methodological naturalism" in science. Methodological naturalism sees science, *by definition*, as concerned *exclusively* with empirical observations and explanations.[34] That is, science in its *method* is restricted to describing only "natural" or physical phenomena, and it can appeal only to "naturalistic" or physical causes in its explanations. One consequence of this is that science, by definition, can say nothing about the existence or non-existence of God or the soul, since neither of them is considered empirical. This approach is attractive to atheists and skeptics because it can conveniently help them keep creationism out of the science classroom.[35] But methodological naturalism is also adopted by many scientists who are Christians, in part because it "keeps science in its place" and lets religion "do its thing" by talking about God, meaning, and morality.

Methodological naturalism is an important concept that is the focus of much current debate. Intelligent Design supporters like Phillip Johnson, Bill Dembski, and Stephen Meyer argue that methodological naturalism should *not* be a fundamental principle of science, because it necessarily excludes potentially legitimate explanations from science (like an act or a process of intelligence). Furthermore, they contend that some sciences like archaeology, cryptology (deciphering codes), and forensics *do* consider "intelligence" as a legitimate explanation for what they study. In fact, in many cases, their primary objective is to determine whether an object or a series of sounds or a death is the result of some cause that possessed intelligence or the mere by-product of combined chance and natural law.

While methodological naturalism deserves a more comprehensive treatment, I want to focus some comments toward those who accept both methodological naturalism in science *and* the basic principles of a Christian worldview.[36] On the one hand, methodological naturalism does appear

---

34. *Methodological* naturalism should not be confused with "*metaphysical* naturalism," which is a philosophical view that the physical world (i.e., nature) is all that is real—that nothing supernatural exists.

35. In the landmark Pennsylvania court decision against Intelligent Design, Judge Jones particularly appealed to methodological naturalism: "Science has been limited to the search for natural causes to explain natural phenomena. . . . While supernatural explanations may be important and have merit, they are not part of science. . . . This self-imposed convention of science, which limits inquiry to testable, natural explanations about the natural world, is referred to by philosophers as 'methodological naturalism' and is sometimes known as the scientific method. . . . Methodological naturalism is a 'ground rule' of science today which requires scientists to seek explanations in the world around us based upon what we can observe, test, replicate, and verify" (Jones, "Memorandum Opinion," 65).

36. For a clarification on what is meant by a "Christian worldview," see footnote 5.

capable of keeping "science in its place." Because science, by definition, is restricted to what is *empirical*, science cannot make the move into the distinctive territory of religious or philosophical concerns like God, meaning, or morality. On the other hand, the principle of methodological naturalism seems to ignore the question of whether the truth-claims of the Christian faith cross over into the realm of science. If they do, then science is arguably forced to deal with them; yet according to the definition of science given by methodological naturalism, science *cannot* (and *should not*) deal with them.

For example, a Christian worldview assuredly entails that the universe is not eternal and that it did not begin through any set of mere natural properties or principles; that life is not explicable solely in terms of natural processes; that the capacities of the human mind cannot be accounted for by purely materialistic evolution; that Jesus had powers that transcended natural explanation and that he was raised from the dead. But if methodological naturalism is adopted by a believing Christian, then such considerations are, by definition, excluded from any kind of scientific relevance. Yet that consequence seems to result in the inference that such Christian worldview entailments make no claims about what has occurred, or is occurring, in the realm of nature and history—a view that can only problematically be reconciled, if at all, with Scripture or the historic Christian tradition.

The NOMA view is partially true because science and religion *do* have distinctive areas of concern. And it correctly describes the relationship between science and many forms of religion. But a biblical worldview cannot rightly be characterized by NOMA. As Stephen Meyer puts it, "The writers of the Bible did not see fit to limit their claims about God to the nonfactual domain that NOMA has allocated to religion. Now, there might be some religions that can fit comfortably with NOMA. But biblical Christianity—because it's built not just on faith, but on facts—simply cannot."[37]

A problem with methodological naturalism is manifested more specifically for evangelical Christians who opt for a full-blown form of theistic evolution.[38] When methodological naturalism is comprehensively applied to biology (with a presumed acceptance of Darwinism) and combined with a Christian worldview, it seems to produce a situation where there is no substantive difference between the *empirical* expectations of theistic evolutionism and the *empirical* expectations of non-theistic Darwinism. And

---

37. Cited in Strobel, "Where Science Meets Faith," 76.

38. I think people like Francis Collins and Karl Giberson (*The Language of God*), Denis Lamoureux (*I Love Jesus and I Accept Evolution*), and Ted Peters (*Can You Believe in God and Evolution?*) would fit this description.

this appears to render God's activity in the origin and development of life as "superfluous," "undetectable," and "scientifically irrelevant."[39]

As a result, Christian evangelical theistic evolutionists [ETE] who accept the mechanism of Darwinism (i.e., mutation and natural selection), face a challenging dilemma: (1) If the biological evolutionary directives were "*built in*" at God's initial creation, it seems difficult for the ETE to reconcile their view of chemical and biological *continuity* required by Darwinism with the entailed sense of *discontinuity* that seems demanded by their theology (e.g., the incarnation, biblical miracles, the resurrection of Jesus, and the relevance of intercessory prayer). (2) On the other hand, if the biological evolutionary directives were "*not* built in"—if God somehow *continued* (and *continues*) to act in ways that transcend "natural" evolutionary capacity—then the ETE seems forced to admit that a naturalistic (Darwinian) mechanism is *not sufficient* to account for the origin and diversity of life. According to the dilemma's first horn, the ETE's position emerges as significantly *inconsistent*. According to the second horn, the ETE's position is not distinct, in principle, from the Intelligent Design advocates whose views the ETE typically reject. In other words, the position of the ETE either appears to be inevitably indistinguishable from the Darwinist or inevitably indistinguishable from the Intelligent Design theorist. Perhaps a better move would be to reevaluate the application of an all-encompassing Methodological Naturalism to the area of biology and to acknowledge that adopting Methodological Naturalism or accepting Darwinism may not be the best options for someone who professes a Christian worldview.

C. The Complementary Model

A confusion of words might lead some to think that the "complementary" model motivates scientists and religious believers to persistently tell one another how good they look. While these "compliments" might be good for their egos, this picture misunderstands the point. The "complementary" model views science and religion, at least at times, as referring to the same subject matter, but *at different levels*.[40]

A good illustration of this comes from thinking about a large electronic sign that consists of thousands of small colored lights. If we describe the sign *as a physicist*, we would talk about its atoms, electrons, and elements.

39. See Meyer, "Teleological Evolution," 102.

40. This approach was prominently espoused by Donald MacKay, a neuroscientist and professing Christian. See his *Brains, Machines, and Persons*, 15–24; *Human Science and Human Dignity*, 26–34; and *The Clockwork Image*, 36–39, 90–92.

If we describe the sign *as an electrician*, we would refer to ohms, amps, and volts. If we describe the sign *as an artist*, we would comment on its colors and hues. But even after all of these descriptions, we would not know *what it says!* Understanding the *meaning* of the sign requires yet another level of consideration. To understand its meaning, one needs the following: (1) a broader perspective to "see it all"; (2) the existence of a message by some intelligent agent that is expressed in a symbolic system or language that can carry information and (3) the presence of some intelligence who can interpret those symbols as intended.

If one were to ask, "What is the 'truth' about this [sign]?" would the truth be described in terms of electrons and atoms; or ohms and amps and volts, or different colors; or a message of some sort? Well, the "truth" is, it is *all* of these things. Each description is offering truth about this object, but none of them provides the *whole* truth. Their respective approaches are "complementing" each other by describing different "levels" of this reality.[41] No single description is complete, but each one is nonetheless "true."

The complementarity approach has considerable insight and value. Christians as well as skeptics should have little difficulty accepting much truth in this view. We *do* describe the world at different "levels"; and as a result we have different "truths" at these respective levels. However, it is important that we *not* infer from this that truth, *per se*, is "relative." Some Postmodernists may affirm something like this. But not all truth *within* a level is determined by one's personal or cultural perspective. If I describe the electronic sign *as an electrician*, the "truth" is not something I *project* or *impose* from my personal or cultural or linguistic context; it is something that I had better *discover* and *recognize*. (I have yet to hear of an electrician who is a Postmodernist at work! If I do, I will feel philosophically obliged to recommend that he keep his life insurance premiums current.)

Recognizing different "levels of truths" can have genuine benefit when applied to science and religion. A scientist can express many truth-claims *within* the level of empirical description without implying anything about God, human value, or meaning. A religious believer can express many truth-claims about God and meaning without implying anything about the way electrons should behave. In other words, there are *distinct* areas of subject matter for science and religion, and sometimes these distinct areas can be seen as operating at different levels of reality.

---

41. The "complementarity principle" of Niels Bohr offers an analogy. Two explanations of light (as particles or as waves) offer distinctive and complete descriptions; yet neither description adequately accounts for the reality in question. See Polkinghorne, *Science and Theology*, 31.

But a primary problem with the Complementarity approach is that it can easily collapse into a Compartmentalized model that, I have suggested, should not be acceptable to a Christian theist. To the extent that we make these different levels sharply *distinct*, we separate them to the point where there is no overlap whatsoever between them. And this results in a Compartmentalized (NOMA) view of science and religion with non-overlapping areas of concern. As such, while this NOMA approach may be appropriate, if not necessary, for some religions and some views of Christianity, it does not accurately capture the comprehensive nature of a biblically-grounded worldview. Biblical Christianity does not merely offer truth-claims about meaning and morality; it presents truth-claims about "facts" in history and about the nature of the universe and humanity.

D. The Coordination Model

The *Conflict* model sees overlap, and therefore potential conflict, between science and religion. It emphasizes that when conflict exists, one side has to be wrong—the *other* one. Atheistic scientists think religion is wrong; and conflict-oriented religious believers think the scientists are wrong. Neither side is open to modifying its views in light of what the other has to say. The Conflict model, therefore, involves a "spirit" of opposition and hostility. The "other side" is "the enemy" that must be defeated.

The *Compartmentalized* model has the scientific lions and the religious lambs getting along just fine—because they are not in the same field! Because the subject matter of science is entirely different from the subject matter of religion, science cannot learn anything from religion, and religion cannot learn anything from science.

The *Complementarity* model initially seems to provide hope for how science and religion can address the same subject matter without becoming enmeshed in hostility. Like the Compartmentalized model, science and religion have distinct "levels" of concern. Science, for instance, addresses the "what"; and religion answers the "why." While this may be mutually enlightening for individual scientists and religious believers, and it may desirably tone down the rhetoric of those with a Conflict view, it's not clear why it should prompt anyone to modify their positions on science or on religion, based on what either might say to the other.

The *Coordination* model proposes a spirit of cooperation between science and religion. It holds that sufficient overlap exists between the legitimate perspectives of science and religion such that religion can sometimes instruct science and that science can sometimes instruct religion. By consequence, this means that, at times, our views of science and religion may need to be modified, based upon what each might learn from the other. Of course, accepting what the "other side" has to say may not be easy, but it could be productive.

Before I develop this idea further, I want to offer a reminder about what *kind* of religion I am talking about. Earlier in this chapter, I stressed that religions are not equal when it comes to their claims about empirical matters and that a biblical worldview uniquely exceeds other religions and alternative Christian theologies in terms of its empirical content. With that in mind, I will focus on the *Christian* worldview rather than speaking of "religion" in general.

(1) *The Christian worldview can inform science and facilitate scientific progress.* My guess is that this point will generate more cheers from Christians than from skeptics. This is both expected and understandable. Some Christians would relish the opportunity to "set science straight." But I'm not interested in pontificating truths for science from a theological chair. Instead, I want to offer some proposals.

On the assumption that the Christian worldview is true, what would it entail that could be informative for science? First, it would have something substantive and specific to say about the events of *history*. This follows from the point emphasized earlier about the unique "empirical content" of the biblical worldview. The biblical worldview offers countless claims about the existence of particular nations, individual people, cultural practices, specific places, linguistic terminology, and past events. By consequence, it provides a variety of direct and indirect *predictions* about what to expect and what not to expect within the sciences of *history* and *archaeology*. For example, when the Gospel of John says (John 9:1–11) that Jesus healed a blind man at the *Pool of Siloam* in Jerusalem, it makes a specific claim about a definite place. As a result, it makes a set of predictions that can potentially be confirmed or falsified. It does not predict that the pool will be found at some future time, but it does implicitly predict that (a) it is quite possible that archaeologists will eventually discover the pool and that (b) no definitive archaeological or historical information will ever be uncovered to prove that this pool did not exist. As it turns out, a significant discovery was made in 2004 in the oldest part of Jerusalem that decisively reveals the existence of the Pool of Siloam in the first century.[42] This is just one notable example to indicate that, and how, a biblically-guided worldview can inform the historical sciences.

42. See "Archaeologists Identify Traces of 'Miracle' Pool" and Shanks, "The Siloam Pool." For an online summary of the Shanks' article, see http://www. biblicalarchaeology.org/daily/biblical-sites-places/biblical-archaeology-sites/

What about other sciences? Can the Christian worldview inform sciences like cosmology? In principle, it's not that difficult to see that it can. Cosmology attempts to analyze the nature and origin of the universe. Since the biblical worldview holds that the universe was created by God and is not eternal, it makes some predictions about what cosmologists should and should not expect to discover. For example, they should expect to discover that the universe is *not infinitely old*, because it had a *beginning*. And they should not expect to discover any principles or equations that would *completely* account for the existence of universe *within* the universe itself. Cosmologists certainly have the prerogative to pursue whatever research direction they choose, but they could benefit by the available guidance from the biblical worldview. Had they done so in the past, they would not have resisted the idea of a "Big Bang" as many of them did when the idea was mathematically and scientifically launched back as the 1920s. Einstein might not have committed his "biggest blunder"[43] by injecting an arbitrary constant into his equations to avoid a "big bang" implication. And cosmologists might not have had to wait for the *accidental* discovery of cosmic background radiation by Pensias and Wilson in 1965 before the general consensus about a "beginning" of the universe began to change.[44] Without question, scientific discoveries have sometimes occurred by accident. But in principle, scientific advancement would be accelerated by having reliable direction on "what to expect" and "what not to expect." And in the area of cosmology, a biblical worldview could provide such direction.[45]

The same point can be made for *biology*. As with cosmologists, biologists certainly have the right to pursue whatever research direction they choose, but they could benefit from the available guidance given in the biblical worldview.[46] The biblical worldview proposes that God was *necessarily*

---

the-siloam-pool-where-jesus-healed-the-blind-man/.

43. See Gamow, *My World Line*, 44.

44. For introductory discussions, see McGrath, *Science and Religion*, 151–56; Ross, "Astronomical Evidences," 141–72; and Gonzalez and Richards, *The Privileged Planet*, 169–81.

45. Even if a religious believer rejects the notion of a "big bang" because it requires an unacceptable old age for the universe, such a "young-earth creationist" would still agree with "old-earth creationists" that a purely "naturalistic" explanation of the universe's origin will never be demonstrated.

46. I am not suggesting that biologists should frame their hypotheses based on the mere *authority* of the Bible. Such a reliance on *authority* in scientific matters has been strongly and specifically repudiated since the time of Galileo. Yet even though such biblical guidance might not be theoretically preferred, I am suggesting that it could be *pragmatically profitable*. That is, *if* scientists acknowledged the best theologically attested principles pertaining to nature and biology, they could become more efficient in

involved with the generation of life and that God was *necessarily* involved in the formation of the "basic kinds" of life (Gen 1:11–12, 21, 24–25). These *theological* ideas have *scientific* implications. In a sense, they predict that a completely naturalistic explanation of the origin and diversity of life will never be definitively demonstrated. They predict that purely unguided, unintelligent processes cannot produce life from non-life, and they cannot construct kinds of life from fundamentally different kinds of life.[47] If this is true, then scientists will inevitably have more success at determining the *limits* of purely naturalistic changes than in the futile attempt to establish a comprehensive evolutionary thesis that maintains that life evolved from non-life and that *all* current forms of life can be completely explained by some purely naturalistic, unguided mechanism.[48]

Given these considerations, I suggest that the Christian worldview *can* legitimately and productively inform science. The question now is: can science legitimately inform and even modify our theological understanding?

(2) *Science can sometimes inform our understanding of Christian theology.* Galileo once claimed that "the holy Bible can never speak an untruth—whenever its true meaning is understood."[49] Clearly, if the Bible is true in its affirmation about a particular subject, then it cannot be false. That seems logically certain. The problem is: the Bible must always be *interpreted*. It says that God "created," but what does that mean? It says that God created the heavens and the earth in "six days," but what does that mean? It says that "all of the trees of the field will clap their hands" (Isa 55:12), but what does that mean? It says that Jesus healed a blind man at the Pool of Siloam (John 9:1–11), but what does that mean? It says that Jesus was raised from the dead, but what does that mean? How can we be certain that our *interpretations* are in line with the truth that God intended in Scripture?

My emphasis on the necessity of *interpretation* is not intended to imply that our interpretations cannot be correct or that we cannot have very good

---

their work by pursuing more promising lines of research rather than pursuing eventual "dead ends." On the other hand, if scientists want to invest their energies (and monies!) to *verify* "dead ends," that would still contribute to scientific "progress."

47. What constitutes a "kind" of life is subject to considerable debate, both theologically and scientifically. While it may be theologically tempting to hold that a "kind" should be equated with a "specie"—which has often been defined by the capacity to reproduce fertile offspring—my suggestion is that we restrict our claims to the most fundamentally different "kinds" of life. I would rather *understate* what a biblical worldview of creation entails than *overstate* it.

48. See Meyer's extensive discussion in his *Signature in the Cell.*

49. The statement appears in Galileo's 1615 *Letter to the Grand Duchess Christina*, cited in Hummel, *The* Galileo Connection, 105.

grounds for the ones we have. But to say that our interpretations *on some things* are well established and true is not to say that *all* of them are well established and true.

As a personal confession, I believe that, without God, the universe would not exist. I believe that a real person named Jesus actually brought sight to someone who could not previously see. I believe that Jesus was physically dead and in a tomb and was subsequently brought to life, repeatedly seen, talked to, and even touched by others. And I believe that my basic *interpretation* of these events is what the writers of Scripture intended to communicate.

However, I concede that some biblical passages and concepts are not so decisively understood, and plausible linguistic and historical arguments can be offered for *more than one* interpretation. Now I may still believe that there is but one *correct* interpretation of such passages, but I should not be dogmatic about which one it is, based on the evidence of Scripture alone. For example, what is Paul talking about when he refers to those who are "baptized for the dead" (1 Cor 15:29)? Who or what was Paul's "thorn in the flesh" (2 Cor 12:7)? Who were the "sons of God" who married the "daughters of men" (Gen 6:2)? These are tough questions. Even the apostle Peter admitted that the apostle Paul's letters "contain some things that are hard to understand" (2 Pet 3:15–16).

One big question here is this: does the Bible leave some things ambiguous in what it says about history and nature on which science could help us achieve a more definitive *biblical* interpretation? The general answer to this must be "yes." For example, based *solely* on what the Bible says about the nature of the earth and the objects of the heavens, one common sense biblical interpretation is that the earth is flat and stationary, and the sun moves around the earth. The earth has "four corners" (Isa 11:12; Rev 7:1; 20:8 NASV); it "cannot be moved" (Ps 93:1; 96:10; 104:5); and the sun "rises" (Ps 104:22; Eccl 1:5; Matt 5:45; Jas 1:11). Now I am convinced that these are examples of "phenomenological" language. That is, the descriptions are expressed from the perspective of how these "phenomena" *appear to a human observer*; they are not intended as literal, physical descriptions of the way things really are. However, why am I so willing to accept a *phenomenological* interpretation in these passages and not a *literal* one? If *all* I had to go on is what the Bible says, and if I were living in, say, the seventh century A.D., would I not be completely rational in interpreting these passages literally? What's the difference now? The difference is that the science of astronomy has decisively informed and influenced my view of the natural world—so much so that I am fully convinced that the earth is neither flat nor stationary and that it orbits the sun while rotating on its own axis. This information *from science* has decisively and properly affected my *biblical interpretation* and theological understanding.

If we acknowledge the principle of this example, then the next big question is this: in what *other* ways can science constructively inform theology? Can it—should it—be used to inform our biblical understanding, for example, of whether God used 144 hours or billions of years to create the heavens and earth? whether God employed evolution (at least partially) to "create" various species? whether Noah's flood was global or regional? Raising these questions quickly propels us into hotly contested waters! So what's the answer? My first response is that these issues need to be evaluated on a case-by-case basis. It may well be that Scripture speaks definitively about each of these questions and that *my* interpretation of the Bible is correct in each case. On the other hand, if the Bible is not so definitive in what God intends to reveal on these matters, then I should, in principle, be open to allowing God's revelation *in nature* to help inform, enhance, and even correct my biblical interpretation.

Of course, I am fully aware that many Christians are dogmatically confident that the Bible *does* speak definitively about these issues and that, where science disagrees, then science is wrong. And I am fully aware that many non-Christian scientists are dogmatically sure that *science* speaks definitively about these issues and that, where the Bible disagrees, then the Bible is wrong. But the Coordination Model of relating science and Christianity should prompt us all to *re*-examine the issues and be open to the real possibility that our views might need to be modified in light of what the "other side" has to say. It directs us to guard against extending our dogmatic contentions beyond what is truly warranted, whether those contentions are constructed from science or from Scripture.

Trying to come to grips with science, especially for a Christian believer, is a theological and cultural imperative. In spite of much clamor about postmodernism these days, we still live in a world that is dominated by the power and perspectives of science. Only to their detriment will Christians ignore it, relegate it to irrelevance, or simply oppose it. And only to their detriment will those who are scientifically minded dismiss the basic principles and revelatory information from the Lord of creation. May science and Christian theology be stimulated and blessed by each other. I think Dr. Castelein would appreciate this important and potentially productive pursuit.

BIBLIOGRAPHY

"Archaeologists Identify Traces of 'Miracle' Pool." No pages. Online: http://www.msnbc. msn.com/id/6750670/#.UNt4-rYmS7O. Author

Barbour, Ian. *Religion in an Age of Science*. New York: HarperCollins, 1990.

Barrett, David. *World Christian Encyclopedia: A Comparative Survey of Churches and Religions in the Modern World*. 2 Vols. New York: Oxford University Press, 2001.

Bartley, W. W. *The Retreat to Commitment*. 2nd ed. LaSalle, IL: Open Court, 1984.

Bush, Richard A., et al. *The Religious World*. 2nd ed. New York: Macmillan, 1988.

Clark, David. "Miracles in the World Religions." In *In Defense of Miracles*, edited by R. Douglas Geivett and Gary Habermas, 199–213. Downers Grove, IL: InterVarsity, 1997.

Crick, Francis. *Of Molecules and Men*. Washington: University of Washington Press, 1966.

Dawkins, Richard. *The God Delusion*. Boston, MA: Houghton Mifflin, 2006.

———. "Is Science a Religion?" *The Humanist* 57 (1997) 26–29.

Esposito, John, et al. *World Religions Today*. New York: Oxford University Press, 2006.

Flew, Anthony. "The Falsification Challenge." In *Philosophy of Religion: Selected Readings*, edited by Michael Peterson, et al., 354–56. New York: Oxford University Press, 1996.

Gamow, George. *My World Line*. New York: Viking, 1970.

Geisler, Norman, and Kerby Anderson. *Origin Science*. Grand Rapids: Baker, 1987.

Gould, Stephen. *Rocks of Ages: Science and Religion in the Fullness of Life*. New York: Ballantine, 1999.

Ham, Ken, and Greg Hall. *Already Compromised: Christian Colleges Took a Test on the State of Their Faith and the Final Exam is In*. Green Forest, AR: Master, 2011.

Harris, Sam. *The End of Faith: Religion, Terror, and the Future of Reason*. New York: Norton, 2004.

Heeren, Fred. *Show Me God*. Wheeling, IL: Searchlight, 1995.

Hitchens, Christopher. *God is Not Great: How Religion Spoils Everything*. New York: Grand Central, 2007.

Hummel, Charles. *The Galileo Connection*. Downers Grove, IL: InterVarsity, 1986.

Johnson, Phillip. "Tuning Up Your Baloney Detector." In *Defeating Darwinism by Opening Minds*, 37–52. Downers Grove, IL: InterVarsity, 1997.

Jones, John. "Memorandum Opinion." Kitzmiller vs. Dover Area School District, 2005. Online: http://ncse.com/files/pub/legal/kitzmiller/highlights/2005-12-20_ Kitzmiller_decision.pdf

Knopp, Richard A. "Lessons from the Philosophy of Science on the Perceptions and Practice of Science." (November 2011). No pages. Online: https://itunes.apple. com/itunes-u/center-for-research-in-science/id421902830#ls=1.

Knopp, Richard A., and John Castelein, editors. "On the Value of the Philosophy of Science for Christian Faith and Ministry." In *Taking Every Thought Captive: Essays in Honor of James D. Strauss*, 239–70. Joplin, MO: College, 1994.

Kreeft, Peter. *Socratic Logic*. 3rd ed. South Bend, IN: St. Augustine's Press, 2010.

Lennox, John. *God's Undertaker: Has Science Buried God?* 2nd ed. Oxford: Lion, 2009.

MacKay, Donald. *Brains, Machines, and Persons*. Grand Rapids: Eerdmans, 1980.

———. *The Clockwork Image: A Christian Perspective on Science*. Downers Grove, IL: InterVarsity, 1974.

————. *Human Science and Human Dignity*. Downers Grove, IL: InterVarsity, 1979.

Maier, Paul. *In the Fullness of Time: A Historian Looks at Christmas, Easter, and the Early Church*. Grand Rapids: Kregel, 1997.

McGrath, Alister. *Science and Religion: A New Introduction*. 2nd ed. Malden, MA: Wiley-Blackwell, 2010.

Meyer, Stephen. *Signature in the Cell: DNA and the Evidence for Intelligent Design*. New York: HarperCollins, 2009.

————. "Teleological Evolution: The Difference It Doesn't Make." In *Darwinism Defeated? The Johnson-Lamoureux Debate on Biological Origins*, 91–102. Vancouver: Regent College, 1999.

Monod, Jacques. *Chance and Necessity*. New York: Knopf, 1971.

Morris, Henry. *The Long War Against God*. Grand Rapids: Baker, 1986.

Noss, John. *Man's Religions*. 5th ed. New York: Macmillan, 1974.

Polkinghorne, John. *Science and Theology: An Introduction*. Minneapolis, MN: Fortress, 1998.

Ross, Hugh. "Astronomical Evidences for a Personal Transcendent God." In *The Creation Hypothesis*, 141–72. Downers Grove, IL: InterVarsity, 1994.

Sagan, Carl. *The Demon Haunted World: Science as a Candle in the Dark*. New York: Ballentine, 1996.

Schaefer, Henry. *Science and Christianity: Conflict or Coherence?* Watkinsville, GA: The Apollos Trust, 2003.

Shanks, Hershel. "The Siloam Pool: Where Jesus Healed the Blind Man." *Biblical Archaeology Review* 31 (2005) 16–23.

Shea, William R. "Galileo and the Church." In *God and Nature: Historical Essays on the Encounter between Christianity and Science*, 114–35. Berkeley, CA: University of California Press, 1986.

Stenger, Victor. *God: The Failed Hypothesis. How Science Shows That God Does Not Exist*. Amherst, NY: Prometheus, 2007.

Strobel, Lee. "Where Science Meets Faith: An Interview with Stephen C. Meyer." In *The Case for a Creator*, 69–92. Grand Rapids: Zondervan, 2004.

Westman, Robert. "The Copernicans and the Churches." In *God and Nature: Historical Essays on the Encounter between Christianity and Science*, edited by David C. Lindberg and Ronald Numbers, 76–113. Berkeley, CA: University of California Press, 1986

6

The Stone-Campbell Understanding of Conversion

A Misunderstood Sola Fide

ROBERT C. KURKA

AUTHOR'S PREFACE

In the circles of Lincoln Christian Seminary, John Castelein has developed a well-earned reputation in the area of contemporary theology but among evangelical scholars, his most recognized contribution may be in the area of systematics. This notoriety is due in no small part to his essay and corresponding rejoinders in a 2007 Zondervan publication, entitled *Understanding Four Views on Baptism*.[1] In this John Armstrong-edited volume that appeared in Zondervan's "Counterpoints" series, Castelein articulated the theological distinctives that are held by Restorationists in a careful and sensitive manner, arguing that baptism is an inseparable element in the "conversion process," not a symbolic additive to faith or a form of water re-

1. Castelein, "Christian Churches/Churches of Christ View: Believer's Baptism as the Biblical Occasion of Salvation," 129–48.

generationism.[2] The subsequent responses from his Baptist, Reformed, and Lutheran counterparts sufficiently demonstrate that while not necessarily convinced by all of Castelein's arguments, they, nonetheless, did consider his (Stone-Campbell) understanding to be a legitimate evangelical viewpoint.[3] Suffice to say, this positive assessment had not been so commonplace in many conservative Protestant evaluations of Restorationist baptismal theology, and most certainly an essay presenting such as an identifiable option would have been nearly unthinkable in earlier times. Indeed, the inclusion of a Church of Christ/Christian Church position statement was itself, a "paradigm shift" in the perception of this tradition by fellow evangelicals. Not too many years before, Stone-Campbell adherents were seen at best, at the outer fringes of evangelicalism, and at worst, simply ignored.[4] The recognition of a distinctive, Restorationist understanding of baptism in the Zondervan volume was a definitive statement that this often-"marginalized" group was truly in the conservative Protestant orb, and the selection of Professor Castelein to write the representative essay was a recognition that properly degreed and competent theologians were to be found in the Campbellite tradition.

In a modest way, I would like to believe that my own scholarly work in the circles of the Evangelical Theological Society helped pave the way for the Castelein article. Several years before the Zondervan book was published, I had delivered a paper at a national ETS meeting in which I attempted to correct common evangelical misconceptions about the Stone-Campbell view of baptism. This paper, in turn, contributed to later academic responses by Baptist theologians, notably Canadian theologian, Stanley K. Fowler.[5] The 2002 publication of the William Baker-edited, *Evangelicalism*

2. Ibid., 134.

3. As evidence of Castelein's careful and theologically comprehensible (to evangelical ears) essay, note the words of Reformed scholar, Richard Pratt, in his response to the essay: ". . . Castelein is to be commended for presenting a positive portrait of his tradition's doctrine of baptism. He has clarified the intent of the doctrine and how it fits within a view of salvation by grace" (153).

4. Restorationists have no doubt, contributed to this alienation. Baptist scholar, Ardel Caneday has noted that the acerbic Alexander Campbell, "alienated opponents and set a pattern for subsequent generations, both for followers and for opponents. Some of his followers took Campbell's beliefs on baptism to extremes, inciting sustained alienation from without and prolonged strain within that resulted in schisms. American Evangelicalism's exclusion of Christians and of churches within the Stone-Campbell tradition has injured both traditions." (Caneday, "Baptism in the Stone-Campbell Restoration Movement," 288.)

5. Stanley K. Fowler, "Baptists and Restorationists in Search of a Common Theology of Baptism." In this paper, Fowler cites my 2001 ETS paper (upon which this essay is based) as a "significant contribution" towards providing "some of the clearest

and the Stone Campbell Movement, further promoted a fresh understanding of Restorationist baptismal theology and its general agreement with the English Baptist tradition, in general, and specifically, a new endeavor to read the primary works of Alexander Campbell on the part of Southern Baptist theologians.[6] The most positive fruits of this rapprochement would be seen in another 2007 publication, *Believer's Baptism: Sign of the New Covenant in Christ*, which featured a most irenic chapter on "Baptism in the Stone-Campbell Restoration Movement."[7] In this essay, author Ardel Caneday, encouraged by his dialogue with several of us Stone-Campbell adherents in the ETS, engages the writings of Alexander Campbell and firmly exonerates him from any charge of baptismal regeneration.[8] The waters have clearly begun to part.

In tribute to Dr. Castelein's essay, I have revised this earlier ETS paper, which hopefully both provides further historical context for the occasion of John's fine articulation of Restorationist belief, and further complements his argument that baptism is inseparable to any New Testament discussion of saving *faith*.[9]

---

evidence of the refinements in Restorationist thinking that signify a convergence with Baptist thought" (13).

6 See Baker, *Evangelicalism and the Stone-Campbell Movement*. Both Caneday and Fowler credit the essays in this volume as representing "the theological formulations of the clearest, most careful, and most articulate representatives of the Stone-Campbell tradition" (Candeay, "Baptism in the Stone-Campbell Restoration Movement," 327).

7. Caneday, "Baptism in the Stone-Campbell Restoration Movement," 285–328. In this chapter, Caneday gives a charitable and historically-sensitive reading to Campbell's own words, recognizing that the tenor of the Restorationist's writings were heavily flavored by his indebtedness to a post-Enlightenment hermeneutic as well as the polemics of early-nineteenth century theological discourse. Prof. Caneday credits the chapters by John Mark Hicks and myself in the *Evangelicalism and the Stone-Campbell Movement* volume for helping him "contextualize" Campbell.

8. Caneday writes: "From the beginning of the Restoration movement, Alexander Campbell was careful to articulate his beliefs concerning baptism, making it clear that he did not hold that baptism itself regenerates" (Ibid., 327).

9. Castelein observes: ". . . Christian churches and churches of Christ see no tension between faith and baptism. Tensions and confusion result only when baptism is divorced from faith and then set over against it. Some Restorationist leaders view baptism as actualized faith and, therefore, see no conflict between baptism for the remission of sins and justification by faith" (Castelein, "Christian Churches/Churches of Christ View," 133).

INTRODUCTION

I have been lecturing recently in colleges of the Church of Christ and the Disciples of Christ those followers of Alexander Campbell, the Scottish Presbyterian preacher who was active in West Virginia and southwestern Pennsylvania during the early part of the nineteenth century. He founded a community known simply as the Disciples of Christ because he so opposed the divisive nature of denominational Christianity. Of course, the outcome of his efforts to try to persuade all Christians to join one community was that he created three new groups: The Disciples of Christ, the Christian Church and the Church of Christ. These are wonderful Christians—*and also part of the evangelical fold.* They form an immense community of perhaps five million members in the United States. According to George Gallup, they also profess to being *born-again Christians*. Yet, most historians continue to overlook the Disciples of Christ when they come to a study of American evangelicalism, despite the fact that their churches dot the landscape of America from Pittsburgh to Abilene . . . I am using the term (evangelical) to denote those historic American religious communities that are united by a commitment to Biblical authority, a belief in the necessity of conversion or new birth, and an emphasis upon worldwide evangelism.[10]

Timothy Smith's words have a particular relevance to evangelical scholars who seemingly have spent the past decade determining the parameters of evangelicalism's boundaries.[11] Recent ETS meetings have engaged new construals on the doctrines of God, justification, creation, and even the defining article of inerrancy. During this period of time, evangelical scholarship has been challenged to reconsider who or what is the meaning of the term "evangelical," given that not a few of our conservative "heroes" do not fit comfortably into the historic (at least in North America) conclaves of conservative theology due to more catholic understandings of revelation, tradition, and the sacraments.[12] This new openness to revisiting old themes has also contributed to a fresh attitude towards the legitimacy of conservative traditions who, too often, because of theological *misunderstanding*— a fault of both parties—have been kept at the margins of evangelicalism.

10. Smith, "The Evangelical Contribution," 68–69.

11. Expressed in these conference themes for ETS national meetings: "Defining Evangelicalism's Boundaries" (2001); "What is Truth?" (2004); "Text and Canon" (2008); "Justification by Faith" (2010); "Caring for Creation" (2012); and perhaps, the most telling indicator of evangelical re-definition, "Evangelicalism, Inerrancy, and the Evangelical Theological Society: Retrospect and Prospect" (2013). The winds—as well as the *waves*—of conservative Protestantism are clearly shifting.

12. Anglican New Testament scholar and theologian, N. T. Wright, immediately comes to mind.

As a member of such a *"marginalized fellowship"*—the Stone-Campbell Movement—this new environment in the ETS has presented a welcome opportunity for me to address the kind of theological concern that has continually created suspicion about this tradition; namely the issue of conversion, and more specifically, the place of baptism in this process. Regrettably, the general absence of constructive dialogue on this already controversial topic (i.e., baptism) has produced some unfortunate caricatures among both Stone-Campbellites and the larger evangelical community, thereby restricting what could be a potentially beneficial theological *construal*, not to mention the cause of Christian Unity.

The modest purpose of this essay, then, is to attempt to present what I believe, is a theologically-responsible understanding of the Stone-Campbell Movement's doctrine of conversion, which, despite claims to the contrary, stands within, if not actually *exegetes* evangelicalism's historic (and biblical) commitment to *sola fide*.[13] This contention will be argued using the following perspectives:

1. *Historical Perspective*: A brief analysis of evangelical conversion doctrine will be undertaken, noting the general tendency to separate baptism from any direct relation to "saving faith." In "contrast," we will describe the Stone-Campbell insertion of baptism within the scheme of belief—too often in a theological awkward fashion—which is then interpreted to be a form of a "sacramental" model instead of a distinct (and thoroughly *evangelical*), baptismal paradigm, itself;

2. *Exegetical Perspective*: A proposal will be made that the Stone-Campbell perspective actually presents a natural if not better reading of the New Testament text, if one allows didactic and narrative passages to inform each other;

3. *Systematic Perspective*: In reference to the above, I will suggest that an adequate definition of "New Testament faith" should include the element of baptism; and

4. *Practical Perspective*: The practical results that a Stone-Campbell conversion understanding brings are numerous, including a healthier ecclesiology (a great evangelical *need!*), greater connection with

---

13 I am not questioning the biblical legitimacy of "faith alone," only the biblically and historically unwarranted associations that have come to define this *locus classicus* of the Reformation.

mainline Christianity (notably the "non-born-again" varieties), and a viable, test-driven model for participating in the "dramatic action" of God.[14]

THE HISTORICAL PERSPECTIVE

The Stone-Campbell doctrine of conversion may not be all that new to orthodoxy. In actuality it may be "restoring" the faith/baptism integration that was largely held until the *sixteenth century*.[15] In fact, it can be reasonably argued that what might be called the contemporary *"evangelical consensus"* on the nature of conversion is in large part due to the theology of Ulrich Zwingli.[16] This faith model in turn, generally excludes baptism from having any real value in the appropriation of God's saving grace. In dramatic verbiage that would have (did?) made Martin Luther wince, much less than the Catholic Church, the Swiss Reformer declared: "In this matter of baptism all the doctors have been in error from the time of the apostles. . . . For all the doctors have ascribed to the water a power which it does not have and the holy apostles did not teach."[17]

While these words certainly resonated with a Reformation spirit intent on breaking with the Roman Catholic sacramental system, they hardly did

14. This term is appropriated from the essay of Vanhoozer, "The Voice and the Actor," 94.

15. See the magisterial study of Ferguson, *Baptism in the Early Church: History, Theology, and Liturgy in the First Five Centuries*. Ferguson notes in his conclusion: "The New Testament and early Christian literature are virtually unanimous in ascribing a saving significance to baptism. If anything, the early church exaggerated this aspect of baptism's significance. . . . The main variation among mainstream Christian authors was in how strongly different individuals affirmed the necessity of baptism for salvation" (854).

16. Cincinnati Christian Seminary's Jack Cottrell has forcefully argued that Zwingli's doctrine of baptism was a "radical reversion" in Christian thinking in an excellent (and generally ignored) chapter "Baptism According to the Reformed Tradition," in *Baptism and the Remission of Sins*, 39–81.

This article is based upon Cottrell's 1971 doctoral dissertation (Princeton) entitled "Covenant and Baptism in the Theology of Huldrich Zwingli." Leading Zwingli scholars (e.g., Peter Stephens) are aware of Cottrell's work and interact with it respectfully, but unfortunately evangelical systematicians have failed to give it much of a hearing. In his somewhat controversial 2001 work, *Most Moved Mover*, Clark Pinnock makes reference to Cottrell's "ignored thesis" as he chastises evangelicalism's reticence (in fact the Fletcher chapter) to revisit hallowed traditions: "Are we not aware (for example) that Zwingli overturned a virtual consensus in tradition with regard to baptism as a means of grace in his own views about it? He turned a sacrament into a mere ordinance and major novelty" (109).

17. Zwingli, "Of Baptism," 130.

justice to the *previous fifteen hundred years of ecclesiastical history.* While it can be certainly demonstrated that the church fathers did see a linkage between baptism and the power of God (a connection that Zwingli denounced as unbiblical), it can also be readily seen that for the most part, these patristics were not "water regenerationists," but squarely placed the salvific work in the blood of Christ.[18]

In actuality, it was not the "doctors" who performed the doctrinal adjustment but rather Zwingli, himself, relegating baptism to a position of relative insignificance in the "faith principle." In words quite unlike any uttered by Augustine, Aquinas, and even Luther, the Zurich sage bifurcated belief and baptism in a manner which not only remains, but in fact has come to define the "orthodox" notion of receiving Christ. Consider these declarations: "Christ himself did not connect salvation with baptism; it is

---

18. Ibid., 134. The witness of baptism's integral connection with faith (and hence, appropriating the work of Christ) is multitudinous—until the sixteenth-century Reformers. A representative reading includes these statements:

(commenting on John 3:5)

- Justin Martyr: "We have learned from the apostles this reason in order that we . . . may obtain in the water the remission of sins" (*The First Apology*)
- Irenaeus: "The faith above all teaches us that we have received baptism for the remission of sins." (*Dem.* 3)
- Tertullian: "Happy is our sacrament of water, in that, by washing away the sins of our early blindness, we are set free and admitted into eternal life" ("Of Baptism")
- "When we have entered the water, we make profession of the Christian faith in the words of the rule."
- Cyril of Jerusalem: "Great is the Baptism that lies before you. A ransom to captives; a remission of offences; a death of sin; a new-birth of the soul; a garment of light; . . . a welcome into the kingdom; the gift of adoration . . ." (*Catechetical Lectures*, 111:4)
- Augustine: "(It is the) apostolic tradition, by which the Churches of Christ maintain it to be an inherent principle, that without baptism . . . it is impossible for any man to attain to salvation and everlasting life." ("A Treatise on the Merits and Forgiveness of Sins," 1:34)
- Thomas Aquinas: "Men are bound to that without which they cannot obtain salvation. Now it is manifest that none can obtain salvation but through Christ. . . . But for this end is baptism conferred on a man, that being regenerated thereby, he may be incorporated in Christ . . ." (*Summa Theologica*, 68:1, 2398)
- Martin Luther: "Sins are drowned in baptism, and in place of sin, righteousness comes forth." (LW 35, pars. 4–5)
- "In it (baptism) God allies himself with you and becomes one with you in a gracious covenant of comfort" (LW 35, par. 9)

The above citations are adapted from the following surveys: Cottrell, "Historical Backgrounds to Reformed Theology" 28–35; Finney, *Studies in Early Christianity*, Vol. XI, 352–66; and Bromiley, *Historical Theology: An Introduction*, 268–72.

by *faith alone*. Faith is the only thing through which we are blessed. We are saved by faith only."[19]

Although contemporary evangelicals would generally see very little dispute with these Zwinglian statements, his *contemporaries* (Protestant as well as Catholic) would have certainly detected an *unfamiliar* note to his concept of belief; i.e., the idea that faith was merely an "inward enlightenment" (Zwingli's terminology) wholly unrelated to the baptismal experience.

Consequently baptism, for Zwingli, is given and received for the sake of fellow-believers, not for a supposed effect in those who receive it.[20] Jack Cottrell has perceptively commented on the effect of Zwingli's presentation:

> Zwingli's doctrine of baptism was a radical revision of fifteen hundred years of Christian thinking. It was practically a complete substitution of one view for another. The biblical consensus had described baptism as a work of God, the time at which God applies the benefits of Christ's work to the believing, submitting sinner. Zwingli, however, abandoned this view for the idea that God's saving work as applied to the individual occurs as a rule prior to baptism. The result was that baptism itself came to be regarded not as the work of God but as almost exclusively the work of man.[21]

There appears to be a number of reasons—*both theological and political*—for Zwingli's "great reversal" towards baptism's role in conversion. Let me suggest several: (1) It seems that his distancing of baptism from faith is a logical accompaniment to Zwingli's well-known understanding of the Lord's Supper, in which Christ's "presence" is not beheld in any special way—it is a *memorial*; a remembrance of what He has done for His people. One does not have to rehearse how dramatically different this was from the Eucharistic theology of Luther not to mention the transubstantiationalism of the Roman Catholic Church. In his zealous efforts to *"de-sacramentalize"* the sacraments, Zwingli moved in a direction that virtually denied any spiritual

19. Zwingli, "Of Baptism," 134. Zwingli notes the cases of Nicodemus, Joseph of Ramoth, Gamaliel, and the thief on the cross, as examples of persons "saved" without baptism. While this, a somewhat common evangelical argument against the rite today, it is difficult to find this line of reasoning prior to Zwingli.

20. Zwingli writes: "As used in this context the word sacrament means a covenant sign or pledge. If a man sews on a white cross, he proclaims that he is a confederate. . . . Similarly the man who receives the mark of baptism is the one who is resolved to hear what God says to him, to learn the divine precepts and to live Life in accordance with them" ("Of Baptism," 131).

21. Cottrell, "Baptism according to the Reformed Tradition," 62.

benefits to the participant, either in communion or in baptism.[22] In perhaps a more politically-motivated situation—the dispute with the Anabaptists over infant baptism—the Swiss Reformer constructed a paedo-baptist apologetic that *necessarily* removed the rite from any supposed efficacy. In short, his opposition to Hubmaier, et al.'s insistence on believer's baptism could no longer be done upon traditional terms; i.e., that infant baptism (the preferred mode) was performed to remit sin. Obviously, this understanding would have to be jettisoned in order to fit Zwingli's anti-sacramentalism. In its place, the Reformer proposed a unified *covenant of grace* in which Christians stand essentially in the same covenant to God as did Abraham and Old Testament Israel.[23] This covenant is Christological in focus and recognizes a continuity between the People of God, Old Testament and the People of God, New Testament. While there are many today, within the Stone-Campbell Movement (myself, included) who would not object to Zwingli's unified approach to redemptive history, virtually all would raise a "red flag" at the extension of this "oneness" to include a *common sign*. We *would* reject the notion that God had instituted covenant infant circumcision with Abraham as a sign of divine ownership, that would *continue* to mark the New Israel (church) of the present time, albeit in the form of *infant baptism*. Zwingli's development of this concept is certainly theologically coherent, if not a bit creative. Whereas circumcision had been a "bloody mark" of the covenant in its pre-Christian form, the once-for-all shedding of *Christ's blood* had brought about a "bloodless transformation" to this rite in baptism. While the details of the sign were now modified by the cross, its essential meaning and recipients (infants) remained unchanged.[24]

22. Zwingli's "de-sacramental" theology of baptism and the Lord's Supper is receiving a needed challenge today, thanks in no small part to our postmodern culture's "recovery of symbolic communication." Helpful contributions to restoring *God's action* in the sacraments include Robert Webber's *Ancient-Future Faith*; see especially 107–15; 141–45.

23. This is seen in Zwingli's "A Reply to Hubmaier." Cottrell, "Reformed Tradition," 50–52. Cf. the discussion on baptism and the covenant in W. P. Stephens, *The Theology of Huldrych Zwingli*, 206–17.

24. Stephens, *The Theology of Huldrych Zwingli*, 206–7. A theological point to ponder: While it has often been posited that there is a parallel between infant circumcision and infant baptism, it is difficult to find this in Scripture, itself. Perhaps, a better theological connection is seen between the sacrificial system of the Old Testament and believer's baptism in the New. What I mean by this is while "faith" is the appointed means of appropriating God's salvation (Christ) in both testaments, that belief is "pictured" in the Old Testament as ones "heartfelt" bringing of sacrifices to the promising God (a daily occurrence). While the prophets denounce the offering of sacrifices without genuine repentant hearts (cf. Isa 1:11–17), one can hardly conclude that Yahweh would have been pleased with an "inward trust" *without* the "blood of bulls and lambs

Certainly one can understand if not even appreciate Zwingli's desire to disentangle the sacraments from the almost "magical" properties that had come to be associated with them in the Catholic Church of his day. Salvation had been given over to the grace-bestowing acts of the church instead of centering upon the finished work of Christ on the cross. In his letter to Fridolin Lindauer, Zwingli boldly asserted the removal of sin "is the function of the blood of Christ alone,"[25] a contention that correctly answers the question, "What must I do to be saved?" ("Nothing, salvation is accomplished solely in Christ's death.") This is a critical observation, for too often evangelicals, especially Stone-Campbell adherents fall prey to a blurring of the distinction between the *completed work of salvation* (Christ) and the *personal appropriation* of that work (faith). In fact, Zwingli himself, appears to have confused this line of demarcation when he argued that "absolutely no sin is taken away by the *washing of baptism*,"[26] which while true, creates the impression that baptism effects the salvific process rather than is a *response to* the *hapax* work of Jesus. I will return to this issue shortly.

Zwingli's desire to excuse baptism from conversion brought about some rather "creative" exegetical expressions. Obviously, "baptism" passages

---

and goats" (Isa 1:11). Rather, sacrifices performed by a sincere, humble believer were efficacious in procuring God's forgiveness in anticipation of the final full work of Christ (Heb 9:23–28). In essence, this is "putting on Christ" in the Old Testament. On the other hand, with the completion of Jesus' atoning work, one no longer has to express this outward trust repeatedly, but only once in the waters of baptism. There seems to be a cogency between Paul's appeal to Abraham's faith (Gen 15:6; Rom 4) and the believer's "baptism into Christ" (6) that is tighter than simply some internal element; i.e., a "justified faith" has always been seen, Cf. W. Kaiser's chapter on "The Old Testament as the Plan of Salvation" in his *Toward Rediscovering the Old Testament*, 121–35. "Paradoxically" the New Testament Second sacrament, the Lord's Supper which corresponds to/fulfills the Passover meal, is celebrated *often* in contrast to the feast's *annual* occurrence. The final sacrifice of the Lamb ushers in frequent eating and drinking (cf. Acts 2:42,46; 20:7; 1 Cor 11:17–34). On the "visible" character of saving faith, see the article on "*Aman*," by R. W. L. Moberly (esp. 431–32). In commenting on Gen 15:6 (cited of course, three times in the New Testament) the author notes "that the verb here is a perfect with a *waw consecutive*, which most naturally implies 'constant continuance in a past state' (GKCS 112ss). The point appears to be therefore, that Abraham's trusting response to God's promise in 15:4–5 is one notable example of the response to God that characterized his life, already in Gen 12:1–4; 13:14–17. . ." (432). Abraham's "faith" is enacted in his journey to Haran, and in 13:14–17 (18) in accepting ("walking through") the Lord's gift of land. Note in each case how belief in God's promise was expressed in an altar sacrifice (12:7; 13:18; 15:9ff). In this last instance, the sacrifice is specifically *God's guarantee* of His promised blessing to Abraham (not unlike God's "*Pledge*" in Christian baptism?).

25. *Zwingli's Works VIII* 2363–13; cited in Stephens, *The Theology of Huldrych Zwingli*, 182.

26. Zwingli, "On Original Sin," 27.

which had been traditionally understood in connection with faith in Christ had to be read in a different light. In a 1523 letter to Thomas Wyttenbach, The Swiss Reformer describes baptism as a figure of speech (*katachresis*), which much like the bread and wine in the Lord's Supper *symbolizes* something outside of itself (in the latter case, the body and blood of Jesus, in the former, [inward] faith).[27] (It is also worth noting that in this same correspondence, Zwingli actually suggests that baptism is more necessary for those "*weak in faith*"—as a confirmation of the inward reality—whereas, for those who are "strong," the sacrament is really not needed.) Zwingli's October 1524 letter to Lindauer reveals a similar way in which he justified his faith/baptism bifurcation citing 1 Peter 3:20–21, as he argues that the "baptism that now saves you" is not in actuality a reference to water baptism at all but a *metonymy* for faith.[28] Consequently, this and other major baptismal passages (e.g., Rom 6:3–4; Gal 3:27; Eph 5:26; Tit 3:5) are to be understood *figuratively*, for any notion that water has any connection to the cleansing of our sin, has been ruled out of place.[29] As Cottrell has pointed out, Zwingli's "penchant for appealing to figures of speech" made it possible, then for him to occasionally make strong (seemingly paradoxical) statements about baptism; e.g. "We are baptized in order to be new creatures."[30] This bold declaration then, could be made without fear of contradiction if it was understood that the "water" was being used symbolically to represent faith.

Zwingli even carried this baptism hermeneutic a step further, when he distinguished three meanings to the New Testament's use of *baptizo*. First, as mentioned earlier, he assigned a metaphorical meaning to the term—it was a reference to *inward faith*.[31] Second, he posited a baptism definition that again, avoided a clear association to water but rather was indicative of *ex-*

27. *Zwingli's Works VIII* 194:14–15; cited in Stephens, *The Theology of Huldrych Zwingli*, 195.

28. Stephens, *The Theology*, 195. In "On Original Sin," Zwingli writes: "baptism is sometimes used for the blood and passion of Christ. This again, by metonymy, the name of the sign being transferred to the things signified, for metonymy is a transposition of names. For instance, when I Peter 3:20 and 21 teaches that we are saved through baptism in the same way that men were saved of old in the ark, we are not to understand . . . the washing of baptism, but Christ Himself. . . . We see here again incidentally the sign used for that of which it is the sign." (28).

29. Zwingli, "On Original Sin," 28.

30. Cottrell, "Baptism according to the Reformed Tradition," 47.

31. Zwingli, "Of Baptism," 132. Actually, Zwingli, himself, refers to "four different senses" as he delineates "an immersion in water whereby we are pledged individually to the Christian Life" ("Of Baptism," 132). In our estimation this is not really distinct from the "metaphorical meaning." Cf. also Cottrell's discussion, in "Baptism According to the Reformed Tradition," 47–48.

ternal teaching, especially the teaching of John the Baptist. No doubt, John's prophetic activity did include the literal water baptism of repentant persons, yet his "baptism" was much larger that the agency of water. John could/did "baptize" individuals without the physical element, and furthermore, this same kind of waterless baptism (teaching) occurred in Acts 19:1–7 (5) with the Ephesian disciples. In essence, this nuance sees baptism functioning as a substitute term for preaching/teaching the gospel.[32] Finally, and perhaps most importantly, Zwingli asserted that baptism was often to be read in terms of a *Holy Spirit baptism* which of course is what Jesus brought in difference to the lesser, water version of John (Luke 3:16).[33] This definition, of course, was related to Zwingli's Augustinian view of the gift of faith to the elect, a *spiritually regenerative baptism* that enables one to personally appropriate the saving work of Christ. This Spirit baptism can come after water baptism or before, can precede teaching baptism or follow it; it really does not matter. There is no fixed sequence to the baptisms, but one thing is very clear: only "this (i.e., Spirit) baptism none can give save God."[34]

Geoffrey Bromiley comments that Zwingli's treatment of baptism contained two surprising omissions:

> (a) He makes no clear provision of external baptism, whether of water or even teaching, as a means of inner grace. The sign seems to be disjointed from the thing signified even if it is rightly perceived that baptism in the full sense embraces both. (b) More particularly, Zwingli does not seem to do justice here to the work of the Word, which one would have expected him to relate to external teaching. The Word inwardly understood and believed (p. 154) plays an important role, but again in disjunction from the outer form. The underlying problem seems to be the *extreme spiritualizing* in which the external and the internal

---

32. Zwingli, "Of Baptism." 132–34; 161–75.

33. Ibid., 132–33; 146–50. Zwingli comments: "Now we see here that the baptism of John and of all those who have even baptized or taught can only baptize outwardly. St. John (47) himself refers to this fact when he says in Luke 3: 'He shall baptize you with the holy Ghost and with fire.' Hence, it follows that baptism is an initiatory sign which we administer even to those who do not employ the inward baptism of the Spirit and without knowing whether they have that Spirit and without knowing whether they have that inward baptism or not" (149).

34. Ibid., 137. This statement reveals that any distinction between *the gift* (salvation) and an individual's response to that grace has now been eliminated. As in Augustine, Faith (inward) is now itself the gift, although unlike the great Bishop of Hippo, baptism is relegated to merely a human (non-salvific) act. Obviously, Zwingli is articulating a form of what later Calvinists will refer to as "Irresistible Grace."

are almost fully separated, even though both are integral to baptism in its full New Testament sense.[35]

It is my hope that the reader of this essay will not miss the significance of this rather lengthy, historical survey of Ulrich Zwingli's conversion theology. This Swiss Reformer is in many ways, the creator of the Protestant context in which the Stones, Campbells, and their adherents found themselves in the nineteenth century. It was *Zwingli's bifurcation of faith and baptism*, not to mention his *Augustinian assimilation of faith and salvation* that set the agenda for the subsequent centuries of theological thought, including our own time.[36] It is not a "stretch" to see contemporary evangelicalism's program of conversion—an unexplained move of the Holy Spirit, praying a sinners prayer of faith, and *perhaps* a later public demonstration of that belief in baptism—as at least an indirect descendent of Zwingli's teaching. Furthermore present-day evangelicalism's difficulty in constructing a well-defined *ecclesiology*, is also understandable when faith is so divorced from its symbolic expressions. Thus, it should not be entirely surprising when new converts are less-than-enthusiastic in embracing the commitments of church membership since baptism—and the Lord's Supper—appear to be so optional to following Jesus. Such an *individualized* concept of faith is hard to find in the first fifteen hundred years of Christianity, much less the literature of the New Testament. Yet, we evangelicals who claim to rest our teaching upon the authority of Scripture, alone, continue to uncritically follow the Zwinglian model as we define "trust in Christ" as fundamentally an *internal*

35. Bromiley, *Historical Theology*, 278–79.

36. Bromiley also notes that "in baptismal doctrine Calvin makes no very distinctive Reformation statement" on this subject, as he does so many others. Cottrell also comments that, "John Calvin . . . owes much more to Zwingli than is usually recognized. This is especially true with regard to his understanding of the sacraments, including baptism. Calvin followed Zwingli's lead in rejecting the Biblical consensus regarding the meaning of baptism, and he accepted the Zwinglian idea of covenant unity as the basic framework for his own explanation of the purpose and result of baptism" ("Reformed Theology" 68–69). This is also the conclusion of John T. McNeill in his classic, *The History and Characteristics of Calvinism*. McNeill writes that while the "sacramental doctrine was developed by Bullinger," it was from the "groundwork laid by Zwingli" (89). This is also witnessed in numerous evangelical writings on "faith" including J. I. Packer's recent article in *The Dictionary of Biblical Theology*. Packer denotes three elements "circumscribing" the biblical idea of faith: (1) Right belief about God; (2) resting upon divine testimony; and (3) supernatural divine gift (432–53). Both Zwinglian themes—inwardness and divine gifting—are present in this competent but "exclusively" reformed treatment. Indeed, the author cannot help but depict Arminianism's view of faith (human response) as a "person's contribution to his or her own salvation. This would be in effect a Protestant revival of the doctrine of human merit" (433).

moment—"something done with my heart."[37] This failure to be constantly critical of our own doctrinal construals has led us to marginalize further reform movements (let me add Pentecostalism, as well as the Stone-Campbell tradition) that might push us in better biblical *application* of the core beliefs which are held in agreement.

It was thus, in this Protestant environment, articulated by Zwingli, that Alexander Campbell's "new version" of conversion was presented, and often misunderstood. As a result of a theological pilgrimage that took him through both Presbyterian and Baptist associations, this Irish immigrant called into question the Reformed notion of saving faith (and its "popular" frontier expression) and in turn offered a *process* in which one "put on" the work of Christ. In a work reflecting his more "mature" views on the subject Campbell wrote:

> Faith and truth, repentance and death unto sin, baptism or a burial and resurrection with Christ, are as much antecedents and consequences respecting one another as are oxygen, calories, and light to animal life and comfort. But we do not separate these, in nature nor in operation, from one another: no more can we separate faith, repentance, and baptism, in regeneration or conversion, according to the spiritual agencies concurrent in forming a new man out of an old man. We are, indeed, enlightened, quickened, regenerated, justified, adopted, sanctified, and saved by the truth believed and obeyed. Faith and obedience are in embryo, twin sisters in the heart of a convert; and are developed, manifested, and perfected by the overt acts of confession and profession, or by faith and baptism.[38]

Using the logic of "Scottish Common Sense Realism," (and its fondness for Baconian science) Campbell challenged what had become an unassailable "staple" of Protestant theology, i.e., the relative insignificance of baptism in one's response to Christ. But this was not all. Instead of viewing baptism as simply a *human* pledge of allegiance, Campbell revived a pre-Reformation (and he would contend, biblical) emphasis upon *God's activity* in the rite. However, this divine work was not simply a non-catholic version

37. In a very helpful chapter on conversion (in which he tightly holds together faith and repentance), Wayne Grudem nonetheless, defines "true saving faith" as "something done with my heart, the central faculty of my entire being that makes commitments for me as a whole person (*Systematic Theology*, 712). As is the case with most evangelical (Calvinistic) theologians, baptism is relegated to a section in the "Doctrine of the Church" (966ff), which inadvertently contributes to a popular notion that church membership is somewhat "optional" to conversion.

38. Alexander Campbell, *Christian Baptism*, 275.

of baptismal regeneration as is so often charged, but rather an *objectification of God's promises* to the penitent believer. For Campbell, baptism replaced the subjectivity of the "mourner's bench" with a more "*sensible*" expression of God's forgiveness: "Therefore, as was said of old, 'according to this faith, so be it unto thee,' so we say of immersion. He that goeth down into the water to put on Christ, in the faith that the blood of Jesus cleanses from all sin, and that He has appointed immersion as the medium, and the act of ours, through and in which he actually and formally remits our sins, has when immersed, the actual remission of his sins."[39]

Two things must be noted about the above statement. One, Campbell puts full stress upon the *blood of Christ* as that which effects the forgiveness of sins. This is not the contention of a water regenerationist. Second, baptism is not seen as magical cleansing that miraculously transforms the recipient but rather *God's pledge*, "the witness of the Spirit which resides not only in the individual's heart who believes in God's promises in the gospel, but also in the communal and objective character of the action itself."[40] Hicks' description suggests a third important element in Campbell's baptismal theology; its connection with entrance into the *community of God's people*.[41] In a *Millennial Harbinger* (a Campbell periodical) article published in 1833, this nineteenth-century "reformer" connected the individual and corporate dimensions of faith: "First century believers brought together personal faith and baptism as its public declaration into one undifferentiated reality both in practice and in their understanding of conversion. This composite view of conversion explains the otherwise difficult statements that seem to make baptism essential for salvation (Mark 16:16; 1 Pet 3:21).[42]

Obviously, in the context of a Protestant environment used to a conversion model of "*interiority*" and *individuality*, these were strange words. Not surprisingly, Campbell found himself constantly under the charge of promoting a Catholic-like sacramentalism. Because the "inward faith

39. Alexander Campbell, "Ancient Gospel—No. IV," *Christian Baptist* 5 (April 1828) 222, cited in John Mark Hicks, "God's Sensible Pledge," 22.

40. Hicks, "God's Sensible Pledge," 24. In this emphasis on God's pledge, Campbell is "reversing" three centuries of Zwinglian influence, especially concerning the meaning of the word *eperotéma* and the Reformed Tradition has largely viewed this term in terms of a human "pledge of allegiance" to God, Campbell preferred to see *eperotéma* as signifying God's confirmation of an enacted covenant (Campbell, *Christian Baptism*, 255–56). See also Cottrell, "Historical Backgrounds to Reformed Theology," 25–27.

41. Hicks, "God's Sensible Pledge." Hicks cites theologian Stanley Grenz as well as pastor-teacher, John MacArthur, as contemporary evangelicals who recognize baptism's "communitarian" significance.

42. Campbell, *Millenial Harbinger* 4 (November 1833) 560; cited in Hicks, "God's Sensible Pledge," 25.

experience" of Zwingli had become so ingrained in evangelical dogma, Campbell's opponents also included many Arminians. A Methodist writer, T. Mck. Stuart called the "Campbellite" doctrine of baptism *"papistic,"* allegedly supporting his contention with references from the Council of Trent.[43] He furthermore declared that Campbell's conversion theology was in actuality a "justification by works" and a more subtle version of water regenerationism. In fact, for Stuart, *Campbellism* represented a "repudiation of the Reformation idea of justification by faith alone, indeed of Protestantism itself."[44] No less vehement, were Campbell's detractors in more conventional Reformed circles, both Presbyterian and Baptist.[45] Unfortunately, this less-than-accurate, somewhat polemical reading of Campbell's "composite conversion" model is still seen in comments of evangelicals today.[46]

Although in my own experience there have been some Stone-Campbell adherents that have recklessly bordered upon a baptismal regenerationism (not a few through simple theological ignorance), evangelical critics would be hard pressed to ground that sentiment in Campbell himself. Baptism does not save, only Jesus' atoning work can do that. Again, note the "Restorationists" *own words*: "He that is immersed does nothing, any more than he who is buried. In immersion as in being born, and in being buried, the subject is always *passive*. . . . When we talk of the act of immersion we

43. T. Mck. Stuart, *Errors of Campbellism* (Cincinnati: Cranston and Stone, 1890) 25; cited in Tristano, *The Origins of the Restoration Movement*, 92.

44. Tristano, *The Origins of the Restoration Movement*, 92.

45. Bill J. Humble has documented numerous examples of Reformed (Presbyterian and Baptist denominations of Alexander in his classic 1952 study, *Campbell and Controversy*. Also Baptist historian, Robert Torbet chronicles less-than-charitable characterizations of Campbell from the late 1820s as he "was attacked by charges as varied as being a Unitarian, a Diest, and even an immoral man" (*A History of the Baptists*, 274). "Campbellism" became a popular (and non-flattering) handle for this new, non-denominational movement.

46. In a recent review of Cottrell's Romans commentary, a noted evangelical New Testament scholar could not resist making the following remark; "The strand of Arminian tradition to which Cottrell belongs is more comfortable with the concept of 'original grace' than 'original sin.' In the Campbellite tradition, water baptism is necessary for salvation" (Carson, *New Testament Commentary Survey*, 74). While it is true that Cottrell has stated that "baptism is for salvation" (*Baptism: A Biblical Study*, 166), his words must be understood in the context of appropriating the finished work of Christ, much in the sense of Millard Erickson's well-known definition: "Salvation is the application of the work of Christ to the lives of humans" (*Christian Theology*, 902). If we accept Erickson's definition (i.e., "application") then it is true that Cottrell and Stone-Campbell adherents believe that baptism is salvifically necessary for conversion—"necessary element in receiving Jesus as Lord" (faith)

have the agent, not the subject in our eye. He, however, who is acceptably immersed, has been immersed as one that is dead—not as one that is alive."[47]

It is difficult for me to see a much stronger emphasis upon the regenerative work of *God* even in Calvin; clearly the act of being baptized is not in itself, salvific, but rather part of the faith appropriation of what has been done in Christ. While it is true that Campbell did insist upon the immersion of penitent believers as a requirement for membership in his "nondenominational" churches, he nonetheless disavowed the notion that the unbaptized were lost in their sin. In an 1837 article in the *Millennial Harbinger*, he wrote: "But he that thence infers that none are Christians but the immersed, as greatly errs as he who affirms that none are alive but those of clear and full vision."[48]

To sum up this historical perspective, it is my contention that the historic (and sometimes contemporary) evangelical suspicion about the Stone-Campbell understanding of conversion is actuality rooted in Ulrich Zwingli's questionable separation of baptism from the response of faith. This *"paradigm shift"* in conversion theology, subsequently affected the following centuries of Protestant thinking and practice (a clear departure from that of earlier Christianity) and by the time of the nineteenth century had attained virtually dogmatic status. Alexander Campbell's call to "restore" baptism into a more biblically based *composite model*, was then seen by many to be a water regenerationism—*due to this Zwinglian context*. While Campbell's thinking in the matter may not always be expressed in the best systematic sense, it is clear that he is not a baptismal regenerationalist. Indeed, he is not adding a new work to faith but actually clarifying what New Testament "trust in Jesus" genuinely looks like. Campbell's twentieth-century heir, Jack Cottrell has well summarized what conversion means in the Stone-Campbell tradition: "Baptism . . . (is) the concrete embodiment of all this new *faith-content* (i.e., the Triune Godhead, the birth, ministry and redemptive work of Christ, the gift of the Holy Spirit) . . . a humble confession that one indeed believes these things; thus in a real sense baptism is a kind of extension of faith itself."[49]

47. Campbell, *Christian Baptism*, 256. See also Hicks, "Alexander Campbell on New Testament Christians Among the Sects," 183. Campbell also vigorously argued for restoring the mode of baptism ("immersion") and against the practice of infant baptism (cf. ibid., 116–246; 313–438). While immersion of repentant believers is a "core value" for Restorationists, this essay is only concerned with the theological significance of *baptizo*—as part of saving faith.

48. Campbell, *Millennial Harbinger* 8 (1837), 414; cited in Hicks, "Alexander Campbell Among the Sects," 189.

49. Cottrell, "Baptism," 139.

THE EXEGETICAL PERSPECTIVE: THE NARRATIVES OF CONVERSION

In G. R. Beasley-Murray's classic and still unparalleled study, *Baptism in the New Testament*, the author identifies six key "conversion elements" that are associated with baptism by the New Testament writers. These are: grace, faith, the Holy Spirit, the church, ethics, and hope. Summarizing Scripture's witness on the subject, Beasley-Murray concludes that "the idea that baptism is purely symbolic rite must be pronounced not alone unsatisfactory but out of harmony with the New Testament itself."[50]

The above statements represent this English Baptist scholar's honest attempt to evaluate the data of the text without an *a priori* system to either spiritualize or even dispose of the exegetical evidence. In this venture he was essentially retracing the earlier steps of Alexander Campbell as the latter attempted to reconcile his findings from the New Testament with "inward faith" model that he had inherited in his Reformed upbringing. As we have previously noted, this "reconciliation" was largely unachievable. This lack of resolution was due in significant part to an examination of the conversion accounts in the book of Acts, a work which for Campbell (and many other "Restorationists" regardless of denominational stripe) portrayed a "*divine*" *design* for what the church of all ages should emulate.[51] While many contemporary Stone-Campbell scholars would eschew this rigid pattern, we would affirm that the Lukan narrative is at least a helpful insight in how the first generation(s) of Christians actually understood conversion theology.

Even a cursory reading of the Acts of the Apostles reveals that baptism was tightly integrated into the notion of receiving Christ. From the direct commands to "repent and be baptized" (2:38; cf. 22:16) to the narrative accounts describing the conversion of both Jewish and Gentile hearers (2:41; 8:12, 13, 16, 36–38; 9:18; 10:47–48; 16:15, 33; 18:8; 19:5). Luke's story of the church's explosive growth includes a rite which can hardly be deemed peripheral. Interestingly also, is the placement of these "composite" conversions within appropriate "church progress panels" that provide the seam

50. Beasley-Murray, *Baptism in the New Testament*, 263–96. While the author's assessment of the New Testament's presentation of baptism is well-known, his call to make baptism integral to the gospel conversion and church membership (393–95) has not been a major preoccupation of evangelicalism. In a later work, *Baptism Today and Tomorrow*, Beasley-Murray "connects" God's gifts (i.e., forgiveness of sins, union with Christ, possession of the Spirit, church membership, inheriting the kingdom, justification/supplication, sonship, holy living) with faith and baptism (cf. for example, "forgiveness of sins" is promised to faith [1 John 1:9; Acts 15:9] and "put on" in baptism [Acts 2:38; 22:16]).

51. Beaslet-Murray, *Baptism in the New Testament*, 263.

of this book (i.e., 6:7; 9:31; 12:24; 16:5; 19:20; 28:31), thus, making Acts a *chronicle of baptism* (rather than merely recitations of a "sinner's prayer").[52] While it has long been noted that the *sequence* of these conversion records is hardly uniform (cf. 2:38–41 and 8:4–17 in which the Holy Spirit's indwelling is promised upon baptism in the first instance, whereas, in the second, there is a time gap between baptism and the reception of Spirit; also in the conversion of Cornelius and his household [10:44–48; 11:15–17] the Holy Spirit proceeds [their baptism] it is still nevertheless impressive that baptism is mentioned in virtually every instance).[53] For Luke, water baptism is not merely a symbol of an inward reality nor something inconsequential to belief in Christ, but rather an integral, and *transcultural element* in trusting Jesus; in fact a "summary expression" for that which we call "faith." Instead of resorting to the Zwingli-like tendency to minimize baptism's role by "spiritualizing" it, the Acts reader should *appreciate* the author's simple and straight forward connection between baptism in the water and that of the Holy Spirit. Beasley-Murray comments:

> we may cite Edward Schweitzer, who draws attention to the twice repeated utterance of the Lord, that John baptized with water but the disciples will be baptized with the Holy Spirit (1:5; 11:16); this shows that the surprisingly important matter was the outpouring of the Spirit and that baptism in water was the "accident" of the greater gift. "In which case," writes Schweitzer, "2:38 teaches no other than that for Luke baptism belongs to the much more important fact of conversion." This judgment is surely true to theology of Acts. It will counsel offence to none who refuse to make conversion small . . . to such conversion baptism "belongs" as its embodiment, its completion and its seal.[54]

All too often Acts has been subordinated to the supposed "richer" theological propositions of the epistles, especially those of Paul.[55] Con-

52. Campbell writes of a "law of baptism" which he sees in the New Testament. This law is given by Christ in the Great Commission (Matt 28:18–20) and carried out in "the divinely-recorded practice of the Apostles. . . . There is one historical book in the sacred writings of the Christian Institution that records the Acts and deeds of the Apostles under this commission . . . the Acts of the Apostles. . . . The Apostles did accordingly first preach the gospel to every individual. . . .Then they immersed just so many as said they believed the gospel. . . . This is the uniform and immutable practice during the apostolic age" (*Christian Baptism* 244, 230–31)

53. See Beasley-Murray, *Baptism in the New Testament*, 93–125. Cf. also Longebecker, "Acts" for an excellent introduction into Luke's "Missionary panels."

54. Ibid., 121–22.

55. A long-cherished principle of biblical hermeneutics has been to give precedence

sequently, the *drama* of conversion is often "hushed" by the intimidating thunder of the Romans letter. On the other hand, "Restorationists" such as Pentecostals and Stone-Campbell adherents have *"retaliated"* by giving a place of prominence to the Lukan narratives that seem to best justify their particular theological emphases. Recent evangelical calls for a *"canonical-linguistic"* approach for doing theology offer some promise of breaking down these "adversarial relationships" within the biblical text by allowing Paul and Luke a much-needed conversation with each other.[56]

Paul's grand presentation of "justifying faith" (Romans) should not be read in isolation from the Acts' conversion narratives but rather as the *very theological convictions* that ground the latter. When the apostle argues "that a man is justified by faith apart from observing the law," he is not asserting anything different from Peter's call to repent and be baptized in the name of Jesus Christ for the forgiveness of your sins" (Acts 2:28). This Petrine call in effect, *exegetes* what this justifying faith looks like. In fact, Paul's discussion of justification and its character-building consequences (5:3–5) is tightly woven to the eloquent baptismal imagery of chapter 6, that much like the accounts in Acts, gives the *visual depiction of conversion*—a "burial in Christ" (note the aorist tense verbs). This in turn, "unites" us with the One who gives us our standing in grace, hope of glory and the perspective of a renewed life. Furthermore, as we continue to read Romans and Acts in tandem, we come across another strong belief/baptism connection in the tenth chapter of the epistle—the "confession of the believing heart" (10:9). When these two documents are allowed to inform each other, this heartfelt confession must be seen as that which accompanied baptism (cf. Acts 2:38, 39; 8:36, etc.).

It is beyond the scope of this essay to explore in detail the wealth of New Testament material that describes baptism in *"faith-type"* terms (e.g., 1 Cor 6:11, 12:13; Gal 3:26, 27; Eph 1:13; 2:8; 3:17; 4:30; Col 2:11ff; 3:1ff; Tit 3:5; 1 Pet 3:20, 21; 1 John 1:9). The point should be clear, though, that these

---

to the "didactic" over the "narrative" passages in Scripture. While this practice is unquestionably true, it has too often minimized the story-line. Recent developments in speech-acts theory as well as new theological constructs (e.g., "Openness of God") have renewed a concern to give the narratives a better hearing.

56. Perhaps, there is a type of "intertextual" dialogue going on between Luke and Paul—in a number of places. Since the composition of Acts postdates Romans, could it be that Luke is "intentionally" narrating Paul's eloquent "justification by faith" discussion in the letter? Might we not also see the Third Gospel's well-known emphasis upon female disciples as an intertextual clarification of some misappropriations of Paul's severe words to women in 1 Tim 2:11–15? We have already discussed another way of "silencing narrative" reading didactic passages through well-defined theological paradigms (e.g., Zwingli on "faith").

texts do not have a great difficulty to present to the evangelical theologian if he/she is open to having one's definition of "faith" exegetically expanded. Even First Peter's seemingly troublesome statement, "baptism that now saves you" (*nun sozei baptisma*; 3:21) does not need to be played down if baptism is not divorced from its rightful place in conversion. Beasley-Murray, however, cautions us to not miss the real significance of this passage:

> Observe carefully; it is not said that the giving to God of an answer saves; the Risen Lord does that, "baptism saves . . . through the resurrection of Jesus Christ." But the response is at the heart of the baptism wherein the Lord makes the resurrection effective. Surely we are not interpreting amiss in believing that once more we have the representation of baptism as the supreme occasion when God, through the Mediator Christ, deals with a man who comes to Him through Christ on the basis of his redemptive acts. It is a meeting of God and man in the Christ of the cross and resurrection; it is faith assenting to God's grace and receiving that grace embodied in Christ.[57]

The above observation brings a needed point of clarification to an argument that is often set in terms of baptism's salvific role. Beasley-Murray has reminded us that this ("baptism saves") in fact, is an inappropriate connection if we fail to note that baptism's efficacy is solely dependent upon the "redemptive acts" of Christ. The *cross* and the *empty tomb* are the true means of salvation; and where as we say *"amen"* to this gift in this composite form of conversion (summed up in baptism) the *power of the resurrection* becomes our own.

Therefore, while we can give ready assent to the question, "Is baptism necessary for saving *faith*?" (at least as the New Testament discusses the subject), we must be careful not to confuse this means of salvific appropriation with the redemptive, divine act itself.

THE SYSTEMATIC PERSPECTIVE

Systematic theologians may still be unconvinced that the Stone-Campbell conversion theology is actually *amending* a biblical and orthodox standard— "justification by faith"—as it insists upon baptisms role in acknowledging

---

57. Beasley-Murray, *Baptism in the New Testament*, 262. Robert Stein notes that this verse (1 Pet 3:21) is "notoriously difficult for non-sacramentalists," but is "quite understandable if baptism is understood as part of a "repentance-faith-confession-regeneration-baptism conversion" (Stein, "Baptism and Becoming a Christian in the New Testament," 2:1:11).

the saving work of Christ. Many evangelicals contend that they detect a bit of a "faith-plus" in this "unusual" (*at least in the last five hundred years*) emphasis upon a "sacrament's" role in *sola fide*. Regrettably, Stone-Campbell proponents have not always been clear on this matter. Popular polemic against "faith only" (i.e., baptism is not essential for conversion) teaching is not only theologically irresponsible but only fuels the larger evangelical suspicion that we are water regenerationists in Protestant clothing—and not even sophisticated enough to recognize their own heterodoxy. Even Campbell, himself, could be somewhat confusing, as when he referred to baptism as "faith perfected."[58] Surely such a definition would have been as foreign to the Apostle Paul as John Wesley. Yet, in spite of these rather awkward theological construals, it is disengenuous to simply dismiss the Stone-Campbell view of conversion as a *redividus* sacramentalism. The astute *Roman Catholic* critic of Restorationism's intellectual roots, Richard Tristano has perceptively noted the true "uniqueness," to this position.

> It could be said that Alexander Campbell's opinions on baptism was a *via media* between the evangelical and Roman Catholic views on the subject. Regarding both form and subject, Campbell was entirely in agreement with the Baptists, since he advocated immersion of penitent believers only, his whole reasoning up to a point was representative of Protestant orthodoxy . . . but onto this orthodoxy Campbell grafted an opinion, namely the remission of sins through baptism. In other words, he advocated that a real change of state is effected by the sacrament and ordinance *which at first glance seems very Catholic*.[59]

Tristano's words, thus, accurately describe a conversion model (especially, baptism) which is thoroughly evangelical at its "boundaries" but generally more "sacramental" than its Protestant family's usual articulation of that faith. It clearly is *not* Roman Catholic. On the other hand, this "unusual" faith configuration is hard for evangelicals to *plot* in their traditional models of orthodoxy. For one thing, it often does not appear

---

58. Campbell, *Christian Baptism*, 284. Much better is the approach of New Testament Scholar Robert Stein who sees baptism in a "constellation" (my term) of conversion. He writes: "In the New Testament conversion involves five integrally related components or aspects, all of which took place at the same time, usually on the same day. These five components are repentance, faith, and confession by the individual, regeneration, or the giving of the Holy Spirit by God, and baptism by representatives of the Christian Community. ("Baptism and Becoming a Christian in the New Testament," 2:1:6). Stein's understanding of "composite conversion" strongly resembles Restorationist Walter Scott's "Five Finger Exercise." Also see the revised and edited version of this article in Stein, "Baptism in Luke-Acts," 35–66.

59. Tristano, *The Origins of the Restoration Movement*, 91.

as a separately—identified paradigm but is either ignored or written off as a "sect" that has tacked on baptism to some *ad hoc* manner.[60] Baptist theologian Millard Erickson is fairly typical of evangelical systematicians as he delineates *three* basic views of baptism among Christian tradition: (1) "Sacramental;" in both its Roman Catholic and Lutheran expressions; (2) "Sign and Seal of the Covenant," the traditions Reformed and Presbyterian understanding; and (3) "Token of Salvation," the model adopted by Baptist and Mennonite groups.[61] In this otherwise competent dismission of "the initiatory rite of the church" (Erickson's chapter title), the author omits any discussion of the Stone-Campbell tradition's baptismal theology (even negatively!), which as the Catholic Tristano notes, needs to be recognized for the peculiar *genus* that it really is. In my own teaching of undergraduates on this subject, I have taken the liberty to describe yet a *fourth* baptismal model—"the Stone-Campbell model" for lack of a better label—which identifies baptism as an integral element of *saving faith*, thereby distinguishing it from both sacramental and Baptist versions, although it bears some general resemblance to each.[62] Church of Christ missiologist and former Lincoln professor, Rees Bryant, has fundamentally expressed the same concept (i.e., "element of saving faith") as he terms baptism "*the sacrament of conversion*."[63] He further notes that: "Baptism should be seen as *faith expressed* or faith embodied . . . we should regard baptism as an *act of faith* by which sinners accept what God has done for them through Christ, and we should also regard it as a sacrament of conversion through which God gives the benefits symbolized by the rite."[64]

Bryant's statements reflect Beasley-Murray's earlier admonishment to "make baptism integral to *conversion*," as this English Baptist despaired of the inadequacy of his contemporary evangelical baptism models.[65] Indeed, if Erickson's aforementioned three versions are the *only paradigms* available, there appears to be much in New Testament material on baptism that needs to be read in seemingly unnatural ways. On the other hand, if we sus-

---

60. In a footnote, Wayne Grudem acknowledges "Churches of Christ" (along with many Episcopalians and many Lutherans) as among those denominations that stress the necessity of Baptism for salvation (*Systematic Theology*, 981). It is not an independently identifiable baptismal perspective but merely a Protestantized version of Roman Catholic water regenerationism.

61. Erickson, *Christian Theology*, 1098–1106.

62. This "fourth way" has now been recognized and given public expression in John Castelein's essay in the Zondervan volume.

63. Rees Bryant, *Baptism, Why Wait?* 191–93.

64. Ibid., 192.

65. Beasley-Murray, *Baptism in the New Testament*, 393–95.

pend judgments on what *saving faith* must look like (i.e., "inward spiritual quickening") and allow the text to form our faith-impression, we can read the New Testament's eloquent baptismal theology within the "boundary" of *faith*. Therefore, "justification by faith" is a biblical non-negotionable which can never be compromised in ecumenical dialogue. Yet, we must be careful about carrying pre-conceived notions about *pistis* to the discussion, that tend to suppress "uncomfortable" elements which Scripture through its "minority voices" would call us to face. In its best articulation, then, the Stone-Campbell view of conversion—*baptism as part of saving faith*—is not a repudiation of *sola fide*, but its *exegete*.

THE PRACTICAL PERSPECTIVE

The Stone-Campbell understanding of conversion offers *practical promise* to the church of Jesus Christ on several levels:

(1) It presents a *normal* model of conversion in a generally *natural* reading of the New Testament text. I choose the term, "*normal*" purposely, as we attempt to define biblical faith. On the issue of what is needed for human redemption, Scripture is most decidedly clear: once-for-all death and resurrection of Jesus Christ (cf. Rom 3:23–24; 5:6–8; 6:23, et al.). On the other hand, when the issue of how one individually appropriates this saving action, faith is the fairly obvious answer. Yet as we have seen in two millennia of Christian history, the exact nature of this faith is not so certain. I hope that I have perhaps contributed in some way to moving beyond the sense of ambiguity in voicing a Stone-Campbell critique of an "inward belief" portrayal. While my colleagues in the Restoration movement have very few questions about the *Christ-centeredness* of common evangelical conversion practices (i.e., "Sinner's Prayer"), we do have some serious reservations that this is what Scripture describes. As we read the New Testament narratives of conversion (Acts), we cannot help but note the tight relationship between belief, repentance, confession and baptism as persons respond to the invitation of the gospel. Consequently, we observe in these texts (and more didactic ones, as well) a *normal model* of what saving faith looks like, or at least how the initial generations of Christians understood a life-changing trust in Jesus. We have no desire to question the veracity of other (more prominent) conversion schemes; such is audacious and unprofitable. Rather, we would call upon our brothers and sisters to engage us in dialogue around the New Testament allowing Word and Spirit to modify our present paradigms to more faithful

readings. Hence, I used the more guarded term, (a modifiable one to be sure) "normal" to describe our understanding of the text. If we are in any way accurate in seeing a New Testament connection of baptism with conversion, then we invite others to follow the apostolic practice; i.e., if the first century "put on Christ" in this manner. *Why not* continue this model?

(2) There is another advantage to the Stone-Campbell view. There is no shortage of critics from the *mainline churches* when it comes to assessing our typical evangelical conversion theology.[66] These "not-so-friendly-to-biblical authority voices" are nonetheless, hard to dismiss when they challenge evangelicalism's "sacramentless" practice when we so adamantly defend the Bible's inerrancy and absolute rule over the Christian life. The "preferred" (Zwingli) model cannot really answer this stinging charge. "*Sola fide baptism*," on the other hand, meets and potentially silences this criticism.

(3) This raises yet another practical issue, an *ecclesiological* one. It has long been noted that while evangelicals have a strong and vibrant doctrine of salvation, they also have a *notoriously weak doctrine of the church*— if they have one at all. This is due, at least in part, to a conversion theology that distinguishes between a *visible* and *invisible* church. Since baptism has been in large part relegated to the role of inconsequential symbol, it cannot play the role of identifying the regenerate believer who has crucified the old person in Christ (cf. Rom. 6:3ff) who in turn contributes to the well-being of the Christian community. When this natural, biblical "link" between the individual Christian and his/her community is severed from a discussion of (applied) *soteriology* and simply assigned to a subcategory of the church's rites, *ecclesiology* inevitably suffers. Consequently, many contemporary evangelical "laypersons" consider church membership fairly peripheral to their

---

66. Non-evangelicals such as James Barr have painfully (and often rightly!) rebuked "Bible believers" for our own lack of biblical fidelity. Not only do we mute the spiritual witness of baptism to our pre-set "conversion models," but strong prophetic issues such as poverty and social justice, rarely make in into our discussions or sermons. Barr has rightly (if not over zealously) criticized evangelicals ("fundamentalists") for celebrating the "centrality and infallibility of the Bible" but refusing to "make careful exegetical examination of the meaning of the passages" (*Fundamentalism*, 38). This has led in Barr's assessment that evangelicals adopted a "fossilized theology" that was constructed after the evangelical revivals, coupled with nineteenth-century Calvinism, and is critically "conserved" (16). More recently, evangelical scholars like Peter Enns have echoed this criticism. (See his *Inspiration and Incarnation*.) In short, evangelicals may not be as *biblical-oriented* as we would like to suppose.

"relationship with Jesus."[67] If they are in fact baptized (and many no doubt are) this baptism does not generally "*tie*" them into a Christian community as an accountable kingdom citizen but rather merely "*symbolizes*" the inward, born again experience they have undergone that is wholly unrelated to the *ecclesia*. Unfortunately, as the Reformers rightly confronted the "*faithless ecclesiology*" of Roman Catholicism, they substituted a "*church-less faith*" in its place. A Stone-Campbell conversion model has better prospects of bringing together these biblically inseparable doctrines.[68]

(4) Finally, let me suggest that there is a *missiological* practicality in a conversion understanding that regards baptism in its *sola fide*. Too often, in the saga of missions, baptism has been withheld from new believers in favor of some length of catechetical instruction. Not only is there scant biblical warrant for this practice, but there are also scores of sincere seekers who have been *excluded* from the Community of Christ because they lacked sufficient knowledge. While baptism should not be given to persons who are unwilling to surrender to the lordship of Christ and the cost of discipleship, it should not be the exclusive domain of some "spiritually elite" who demonstrate their worthiness by a mastery of the missionary's manual. The New Testament knows of no significant "time delay" between initial belief and baptism—even when the candidates were heretofore unbiblically-schooled pagans (e.g., the Philippian jailer in Acts 16:27–34). Fuller Seminary's Dean Gilliland recalls a sorrowful example from his own missionary experience when baptism was placed into the category of "*reward*" instead of conversion:

> I shall never forget my disappointment as a first-term missionary when . . . I took a day's journey by foot to a small village church. The purpose of the trip was to examine and to baptize supposedly new Christians. One who was brought in for her baptismal examination was an old woman. She had been coming for three consecutive years and asking for baptism, but had been refused each time because she could not read the Bible or recite the catechism. On this trip, her fourth attempt, she

---

67. It is not surprising that Stone-Campbellites generally have a more well-formed ecclesiology than most other evangelical groups, although this can sometimes degenerate into a rigid patternism, In Everett Ferguson's work, *The Church of Christ*, the subject of church membership is discussed in relation to the doctrine of salvation (135–205)—a Stone-Campbell distinctive. Hopefully, this may suggest a "better way" to do our systematics.

68. Bryant, *Baptism, Why Wait?* 183–99.

was refused again. As a recent arrival, I had little to say. Sadly "knowledge" was given a higher value than faith.[69]

Rees Bryant notes that Gilliland's silence that day has been controverted by a *teaching career* that has regularly denounced this practice and called for "the importance of baptism to our understanding of conversion."[70] The Stone-Campbell Movement's insistence on a "composite conversion" (i.e., belief-baptism) helps meet this serious missiological concern.

CONCLUSION

In Kevin Vanhoozer's aforementioned essay, "*The Voice and The Actor*," this perceptive Reformed theologian reminds us of becoming paralyzed in "that kind of systematic mind whose thoughts are restless until they find their rest in a *totalizing* conceptual framework." With kudos towards Emanuel Lévinas, Vanhoozer cautions that "A totalizing system acknowledges only what conforms to its conceptual scheme, it therefore absorbs the 'others' into the 'same' (i.e., into my categories). . . . Indeed, the cynic might say that Lévinas has written the perfect job description for the systematic theologian."[71]

It has been the intent of this essay to propose that due to such a "*totalizing scheme*" (Zwingli's "inner faith" model), evangelical scholars (as well as pastors and laity) have reacted with suspicion when a fellow legitimate, orthodox body has questioned the adequacy of "received truth." Certainly there are elements of Christian Faith that defy negotiation (e.g., Creation, Trinity, substitutionary and satisfactory work of Christ, salvation appropriated by faith, etc.), but this is not to say that our *prior formulations* of these beliefs are beyond modification. As evangelicals committed to the authority of Scripture, we should be more than willing to give a hearing to "*minority voices*" who ask us to question whether our traditional exegesis has been less that objective on a particular topic. We should be the first to admit that specific theological emphases are born out of specific historical contexts, in which the theologians task has often been *corrective* rather than *comprehensive*. Vanhoozer rightly warns us against "locating interpretive authority in community consensus, for even believing communities, as we know the Old Testament narratives, often get it badly wrong, and to locate authority

---

69. Dean Gilliland, *Pauline Theology and Mission Practice*, 15; cited in Bryant, *Baptism*, 198.

70. Ibid., 199.

71. Vanhoozer, "The Voice and The Actor," 78.

in the community itself is to forgo the possibility of prophetic critique."[72] It is unfortunate that the proponents of "*sola scriptura*" have so often (contradictorily) elevated the "*community voice*" (be it Reformed, Lutheran, or even Stone-Campbell) to an equivocal status with Scripture, thus spending more time in "intra-faith" polemic rather than in the biblical "policing" of cherished positions. As such, we have created both an evangelical "*center*" and a "*periphery*," which often denies that these other perspectives might help us move towards a much deeper and richer center. The theme, "defining evangelicalism's boundaries" will hopefully begin a new chapter in evangelical dialogue rather than be a continuation of several centuries of marginalizing somewhat different presentations of the "one faith" from our usual understandings, but construals, nonetheless, that force us to listen to the "whole canonical dialogue" (Vanhoozer). Are we ready to reconsider what a *whole canon-driven "sola fide"* might really look like? (This also includes Stone-Campbell adherents who have become too confident in our own patterns).

One of the key themes of Alexander Campbell's "Restoration Movement" was its vision for Christian unity; a cessation of denominational strife and a return to the "plain teaching" of the Scriptures. In retrospect, it is easy to accuse the leader of this heritage as a naïve utopian, for his own movement has itself, fractured three times and the supposed perspicuity of Scripture is much less difficult to espouse in theory than perform in practice. However, the issue of denominational rancor should not be so readily dismissed. While *denominationalism* is fundamentally a sinful attitude, a *hostility towards denominations* does not have to necessarily accompany this. The existence of a plethora of evangelical traditions does not require that there be discord and lack of fellowship among these bodies, but rather, in the true spirit of Christ, a willingness to revisit Christian doctrine through some different, perhaps, even refreshing eyes.

In fact, the Christian world may be better off in the end for its seemingly diverse, yet potentially *complementary* readings of the biblical message. In a plea that Campbell would resonate with *in spirit* (although perhaps not in exact verbiage, and one that one could well imagine Castelein penning) Vanhoozer casts the tone for defining *sola fide* specifically and our "evangelical boundaries," generally:

> I for one would be sorry if everyone thought just like me. I would deeply regret if there were no Mennonite, Lutheran or Greek Orthodox voices in the world. Why? Because I think that truth would be better served by their continuing presence. To

72. Ibid., 80.

some, this may be a shocking way of thinking about truth. Is not truth one? Must not our confessions of faith contain not only affirmations but denials? Yes. Yes! But my question concerns whether a systematics that employs only a single conceptual system can fully articulate the truth.[73]

May Luke's words then, serve to accurately describe today's evangelical doctrinal journey: "Now the Berean Jews were of more noble character than those in Thessalonica, for they received the message with great eagerness and examined the Scriptures every day to see if what Paul [or *Zwingli, Luther, Calvin, Campbell, etc.*] said was true."[74]

---

73. Ibid., 81. If the "catholic elements" of the Christian Faith (e.g., Trinity, birth, death, resurrection, ascension of Christ, salvation by grace, etc.—the Apostles' Creed, for instance) are acknowledged, can we, as evangelicals, permit a certain degree of tolerance for new construals of these core beliefs? Recent disputes in Restorationist schools over new and potentially constructive models of how biblical history was recorded, the historicity of Adam and Eve, and the apparent discord in Paul's writings seems to suggest that a tradition that has been shown a fair amount of theological intolerance in spite of its orthodoxy is itself, guilty of marginalizing voices that affirm historic Christian beliefs in unfamiliar terms. Well-respected evangelical historian, Mark Noll (who wrote the forward to *Evangelicalism and the Stone-Campbell Movement*) has recently offered a measured defense for the much-maligned work of Peter Enns, who despite Noll's disagreements with him on a few specific issues, reminds conservatives that "Enns's proposals do not contradict traditional affirmations about the inspiration, reliability, and authority of Scripture." He then adds, "To be sure, he (Enns) does challenge many of the exegetical conclusions that believers in a high view of Scripture often take for granted, but not trust in Scripture itself" (Noll, *Jesus Christ and the Life of the Mind,* 145. Evangelicals and particularly Restorationists, would do well to heed these sage words.

74. Acts 17:11[TNIV], emendation, mine.

BIBLIOGRAPHY

Baker, William R., editor. *Evangelicalism and the Stone-Campbell Movement*. Downers Grove, IL: Inter Varsity, 2002.

Barr, James. *Fundamentalism*. Philadelphia: Westminster, 1978.

————. *Inspiration and Incarnation: Evangelicals and the Problem of the Old Testament*. Grand Rapids: Baker, 2005.

Beasley-Murray, G.R. *Baptism in the New Testament*. Exeter: Paternoster, 1962.

————. *Baptism Today and Tomorrow*. London: St. Martin's, 1966.

Bromley, G. W. *Historical Theology: An Introduction*. Grand Rapids: Eerdmans, 1978.

Bryant, Rees. *Baptism, Why Wait?: Faith's Response in Conversion*. Joplin, MO: College, 1999.

Campbell, Alexander. *Christian Baptism with its Antecedents and Consequents*. 1852. Reprint. Nashville: Gospel Advocate, 1951.

Caneday, A.B. "Baptism in the Stone-Campbell Restoration Movement." In *Believer's Baptism: Sign of the New Covenant in Christ*. NAC Studies in Bible and Theology Series, 285–328. Nashville, TN: B&H Academic, 2006.

Carson, D. A. *New Testament Commentary Survey*. 5th ed. Grand Rapids: Baker, 2001.

Castelein, John D. "Christian Churches/Churches of Christ View: Believers Baptism as the Biblical Occasion of Salvation." In *Understanding Four Views on Baptism*, 129–60. Grand Rapids: Zondervan, 2007.

Cottrell, Jack. "Baptism according to the Reformed Tradition." In *Baptism and the Remission of Sins: An Historical Perspective*, 39–81. Joplin, MO: College, 1990.

————. "Baptism." In *Essentials of Christian Faith*, 129–50. Joplin, MO: College, 1992.

————. *Baptism: A Biblical Study*. Joplin, MO: College, 1989.

————. "Historical Backgrounds to Reformed Theology." In *Baptism and the Remission of Sins: An Historical Perspective*, 28–35. Joplin, MO: College, 1990.

Erickson, Millard. *Christian Theology*. Grand Rapids: Baker, 1998.

Ferguson, Everett. *Baptism in the Early Church: History, Theology, and Liturgy in the First Five Centuries*. Grand Rapids: Eerdmans, 2009.

————. *The Church of Christ: A Biblical Ecclesiology For Today*. Grand Rapids: Eerdmans, 1997.

Finney, Paul Corby, et al., editor. *Studies in Early Christianity*, Vol. XI: *Conversion, Catechumenate, and Baptism in the Early Church*. Garland, 1993.

Fowler, Stanley K. "Baptists and Restorationists in Search of a Common Theology of Baptism." Paper given at the ETS National Meeting, Atlanta, 2003.

Gilliland, Dean. *Pauline Theology and Mission Practice*. Grand Rapids: Baker, 1983.

Grudem, Wayne. *Systematic Theology*. Grand Rapids: Zondervan, 1974.

Hicks, John Mark. "Alexander Campbell on Christians Among the Sects." In *Baptism and the Remission of Sin: An Historical Perspective*, 171–201. Joplin, MO: College, 1992.

————. "'God's Sensible Pledge': The Witness of the Spirit in Early Baptismal Theology." *Stone-Campbell Journal* 1.1 (1998) 5–26.

Humble, Bill J. *Campbell and Controversy*. 1952. Joplin, MO: College, 1986.

Longenecker, Richard N. "Acts." In *The Expositor's Bible Commentary 9*, edited by Frank E. Gaebelein, 207–573. Grand Rapids: Zondervan, 1981.

McNeill, John T. *The History and Characteristics of Calvinism*. Oxford: Oxford University Press, 1954.

Moberly, R. W. L. "Aman." In the *New International Dictionary of Old Testament Ttheology and Exegesis*, edited by Willem VanGemeren, 1:427–33. Grand Rapids: Zondervan, 1997.

Noll, Mark A. *Jesus Christ and the Life of the Mind*. Grand Rapids: Eerdmans, 2011.

Packer, J. I. "Faith." In *The New Dictionary of Theology*, edited by Sinclair B. Ferguson, J. I. Packer, and David F. Wright, 246–47. Downers Grove, IL: Inter Varsity, 1997.

Pinnock, Charles. *Most Moved Mover*. Grand Rapids: Baker, 2001.

Robert Webber. *Ancient-Future Faith*. Grand Rapids: Baker, 1999.

Smith, Timothy. "The Evangelical Contribution." In *The Evangelical Landscape: Essays on American Evangelical Tradition*, 61–75. Grand Rapids: Zondervan, 1996.

Stein, Robert "Baptism and Becoming a Christian in the New Testament." *The Southern Baptist Journal of Theology* 2.1 (1998) 6–17.

———. "Baptism in Luke-Acts." In *Believer's Baptism: Sign of the New Covenant in Christ*, 35–66. Nashville, TN: B & H Academic, 2006.

Stephens, W. P. *Theology of Huldrych Zwingli*. Oxford: Clarendon, 1986.

Torebt, Robert. *A History of the Baptists*. Valley Forge, PA: Judson, 1963.

Tristano, R. M. *The Origins of the Restoration Movement: An Intellectual History*. Atlanta: Glenmary Research Center, 1988.

Vanhoozer, Kevin. "The Voice and the Actor." In *Evangelical Futures: A Conversation on Theological Method*, edited by John G. Stackhouse, 61–106. Grand Rapids: Baker, 2000.

Zwingli, Huldrich. "Of Baptism." In *Zwingli and Bullinger*, edited by Samuel Macauley Jackson and William John Hinke, 129–75. Durham, NC: Labryinth, 1983.

———. "On Original Sin." In *On Providence and Other Essays*, 1–32. NC: Labyrinth, 1983.

7

Post-Protestantism

A Postmodern Ecclesiastical Approach[1]

JARROD LONGBONS

IT WAS A WARM, summer evening in Krakow, Poland.[2] I joined a group of approximately thirty philosophers, theologians, and publishers in the heart of a thriving Jewish district,[3] enjoying a delectable meal of fish soup and grass-fed steak. During the feast, I discussed all things faith and culture with theologian John Milbank, political scholar Marcia Palley,[4] and editor

1. This essay is dedicated to two men, both important to my theological develop-ment. First, my father, Jeff Longbons, baptized Catholic, worshipped with the rest of his family in a non-Catholic setting. He always taught me the beauty of the Catholic tradition but never denied the sincerity of my non-Catholic, Christian faith. His greater emphasis was always for me to just be a Christian. The other is Prof. John Castelein. He was the first learned theological figure working in a particular tradition that took the time to teach me the beauty and strength of other traditions. To the both of you: I am in your debt.

2. This meal took place during the Krakow conference of the "Centre of the The-ology and Philosophy" in 2011. http://theologyphilosophycentre.co.uk

3. I took great delight in the Jewish setting, which flourishes in spite of Auschwitz looming just outside of the city.

4. Of note for this essay, Marcia Pally has recently published a very important book called *The New Evangelicals: Expanding the Vision of the Common Good*. In this

Robin Parry.[5] The conversation was lively and the soup transcendent. After discussing the films of Terrence Malick, Marcia Palley looked to me and asked, "In which religious tradition do you pastor?"

I hate being asked that question at such conferences. For one thing, such gatherings are highly international, while my tradition is confined mainly to the US. Moreover, even amongst theologians, I am an odd ecclesiological specimen. Often, even the informed do not know how to categorize me. But it is not their fault. How can I blame them, when I struggle to categorize myself?

I responded the usual way: "It is called the Restoration Movement, or the Stone-Campbell Movement. It started during the revival days on the American frontier, and claims neither to be Protestant nor Catholic. Instead, each church is autonomous, thus non-denominational, and rather than asking members to adhere to creedal statements, the aim, however naively, is to go back to the primitive church found in the 'Acts of the Apostles.' We are weird. We are sacramental about Baptism, and non-sacramental about the Lord's Supper, but you better do it every week!"

Professor Milbank interrupted, "Oh, you are Post-Protestant, then."

"Excuse me, what is that?" I replied.

He explained, "Post-Protestants are non-Catholic Christians who no longer protest Catholicism, but also, at times, are open to its practices and doctrine." It is deeper than interdenominationalism, because it crosses the widest frontier within Western Christianity—the Protestant/Catholic lacuna. "Post-Protestant sensibilities," Milbank informed me, "are increasing all over the world."

Is it true? Am I Post-Protestant? And is my tradition? I surveyed the current state of affairs in my own congregation. I discovered that some communion presiders colored their meditations with sacramental language, while book clubs discuss Schmemann's *For the Life of the World*, and Cavanaugh's *Being Consumed: Economics and Christian Desire*. These books,

---

work, Pally introduces the "New Evangelicals" by showing their historic break from the "religious right" and reconnection to historic evangelicalism, which was often radical and quite progressive. For an introduction to Pally's work see my interview with her on my theological blog, "The Art of the Good Life," at: http://theartofthegoodlife.blogspot.com/2011/11/interview-marcia-pally-on-new.html. Her work, though not cited, has shaped some of my ideas for this essay; I am immensely indebted to her research.

5. I remain indebted to Regius Prof. of Theology, Graham Ward (Oxford) for noticing that I was sitting at the end of the table by myself. He was so gracious as to trade places with me, so that I could sit in the middle of the table and near my own professor, John Milbank. His charity has been doubled in my own work and ministry just by that invitation. I owe him many thanks, for I was able to sit and talk with people far more cultured than I am. For this, I will be forever grateful.

Eastern Orthodox and Roman Catholic, respectively, shape the theological imagination of my own people.

How could I have overlooked this? I do live in a Post-Protestant world and always have; after all, I was born in 1981 at the tail end of Generation X and on the horizon of the Millennial generation—a time when boundary lines are blurred for sport. Thus, I wish to introduce this Post-Protestant phenomenon in this essay and, in due course, argue that it represents something of a postmodern ecclesiology. And in the end, I will claim that it offers many ecumenical cues for the contemporary ecclesiological situation, though not without some disadvantageous aspects to avoid.

FROM PROTESTANTISM TO POST-PROTESTANTISM

Understanding a word with the prefix "post-" (i.e., postmodern or Post-Protestant) first requires knowledge of the root word, if only to bring aware-ness of the idea that preceded it. Moreover, understanding postmodernity and understanding Post-Protestantism go together, since modernity, and Protestantism coexisted for some time. Some even go so far as to say "mo-dernity is . . . the consequence of the Reformation and the development of human inwardness."[6] Whatever modernity's cause and origin, there is a clear enough relation to conclude that these two bedfellows—modernity and Protestantism—can only be understood together and so it is consequently with postmodernity and Post-Protestantism.

Protestantism began in 1517 when Luther posted his Ninety-Five The-ses on a church door in Wittenberg.[7] As stated in the name, Protestants are protesters, and generally of the Catholic Church. But at its beginning, at least with Luther, the protest was over specific church abuses surround-ing soteriology. As part of a financing effort, certain clerics were selling indulgences as acts of penance.[8] Luther questioned this as a form of grace through merit. Corruption was the catalyst for Luther's elucidation of the so-called "Protestant Principle"—the need for the church to undergo con-stant critique and reform.[9] This principle is based on a theory of revelation called *sola scriptura*, and following it was Luther's emphasis on *sola gratia*

---

6. Gillespie *The Theological Origins of Modernity*, 189.

7. There are, of course, antecedents to the Protestant Reformation existing for about two centuries, but Luther's action serves, as Martin Marty suggests, as a "sym-bolic date for the genesis of Protestantism" (*Protestantism*, 21).

8. Indeed, the question for the Reformers was over: penance or true repentance?

9. See Schlabach *Unlearning Protestantism*, 24.

through *sola fidei*.[10] Luther's reading of the Psalms, Galatians, and Romans caused him to claim that the Bible taught salvation by grace through faith alone. Simply, righteousness is not attainable through human merit; grace only comes by one's faith in Christ. It is attained through God's righteousness, not the believer's. In short, Luther rejected merit-based grace, and thus he rejected all grace-imbuing artifacts such as indulgences and sacraments.[11] Interestingly, many heirs of the Reformation minimized grace to faith alone,[12] thus separating grace from nature; something Luther would have no doubt rejected.

Originally, Luther worked for church reform and had no interest in starting a new ecclesiastical communion.[13] But this is exactly what happened, as his movement played the first note in a chorus of schisms to follow. Soon after, Protestants would be called Lutherans, Calvinists, Presbyterians,

10. Jaroslav Pelikan argues, "For the Reformation had as its central Protestant principle the doctrine of justification by faith alone, the uselessness of human or ecclesiastical merit in the process of salvation, the free forgiveness of sins for the sake of Jesus Christ" (*Obedient Rebels*, 17). To add to this, the Protestant principle is a co-mingling of *sola gratia* and *sola fidei* based on Scripture alone.

11. Now Luther did not explicitly reject the sacraments; he altered their meaning. Rather than transubstantiation—elements imbued with the real presence of Christ— Luther promoted consubstation, wherein the presence of Christ is simply "with" the elements. The main point, real presence or no, is that Luther said that grace comes to the fallen only through faith and not by a sacramental system.

12. There is another argument that could be introduced here, but I lack the space to develop it. Perhaps it will serve as a follow up project in the future. The argument I am referring to hails from Historical Jesus studies and Christian origins concerning the seeming inconsistency between Jesus and Paul. Jesus' notion of the gospel surrounds his identity as the royal Davidic Messiah whose purpose is to bring in the kingdom of God. Jesus' message is communal and about a new order or a new people living by God's ways and means. On the other hand, Paul preaches a message of justification by grace through faith. This message seems to be more central to the individual's salvation. Indeed, Paul rarely wrote concerning the kingdom and Jesus rarely spoke of justification. For our purposes, Christians in the Reformation tradition seemed to have focused on justification while Roman Catholics seemed to focus on kingdom theology. That is to say, salvation is centered more on the individual for Protestantism and is more communal, even political for Catholicism. One possible answer to clarify this perceived dichotomy is that Paul carried Jesus' message that was originally for the Jews out into a Gentile world; Paul does not deny the kingdom, rather for Gentiles to enter into it as such, there is need for their personal justification.

13. Another important thing to note as one attempts to interpret the Reformation is that Luther was not working as a Lutheran or a Protestant, but a Catholic when he first began his protest. So to understand Luther one must understand the wider Catholic world in which he was engaged.

Methodists, etc. Now, the number of denominations that followed exceeds 30,000 world-over.[14]

Through time and a Counter-Reformation, Protestants held to Luther's *sola fidei* but penned new creeds for each individual denomination. Some creeds were robust, others were minimized to *sola scriptura*—no extra biblical content standing as a rule of faith—while in other cases it meant the denial of tradition for theological knowledge. Indeed, tradition and hierarchy came to be seen as a way of diminishing the role of the Holy Spirit in the life of such communions; each communion sought to make disciples within its particular context through the Spirit's unique leading. This pneumatic denial of tradition, too, became part of the "Protestant Principle."[15] Later, the Reformation was blended with the politics of Western Liberalism, rendering it possible for contemporary Christians to emphasize individualism and choice over authority and tradition.

How did Protestantism rise up during modernity? First, we date its origins back to the early modern period—the sixteenth century.[16] Culturally, this was a time of enlightenment, rationality, and science. Religiously, nominalism was on the rise, thus people began to envision God as an abstract principle. This differed greatly from the earlier analogical/participational models of God.[17] While a complex history of ideas is at play here, one basic result was that nominalism distanced God from the world and thus shifted sites for religious mediation. For the analogical imagination, God was mediated to people through creation, the church, tradition, Scripture, and even art.[18] For late medieval, modern, and eventually the Protestant imagination (all shaped by nominalism) God was only mediated through the inner self and Scripture: "the Reformation took its altars out of the churches and placed them in the human heart."[19] This move, along with biblical translation and an increasingly literate population, would eventually, though un-intentionally, lead to individualist interpretations of Scripture.

---

14. http://www.religioustolerance.org/christ7.htmn.

15. An important criticism of such thought involves the following: if you deny the work of the Holy Spirit by denying tradition, do you not actually diminish the Holy Spirit's role by implying that the Holy Spirit could not have worked or spoken in the past? One who only looks to fresh interventions of the Holy Spirit in the life of a contemporary ecclesial setting actually deprives the Holy Spirit of His power through time and space.

16. Gillespie, *Theological Origins of Modernity*, 4–5.

17. For a helpful summary of Luther's relationship with Nominalist philosophy see Michael Allen Gillespie *The Theological Origins of Modernity*, 101–28.

18. Szerszynski, *Nature, Technology, and the Sacred*, 16–23.

19. Lilla *The Stillborn God*, 197.

Lilla concludes that the Reformation, "taught men that they will be justified (or not) according to their interior faith, and that the Scriptures are open to them without the authoritative interpretation of the church."[20] Luther's attempt at reform spawned an entire "Reformation," which in turn provided the foundation for more schisms to follow.[21]

Catholic responses like the Council of Trent helped solidify division between Catholic and Protestant. And reactively, Protestantism took on various new flavors. Generally, Protestants rejected Catholic sacramentality and sometimes replaced it with ordinances.[22] In other cases, sacramentality was neutered, because "grace through faith" remained the main mantra of the Reformation and the sacraments of Rome imbued grace, *ex opere opera-to*.[23] Additionally, Scripture was prioritized over the liturgy and priesthood,[24] a change which arose with the advent of the printing press and Protestant accusations that Catholics add to Biblical revelation with their tradition and the papacy. Paramount for the Protestant was to only read the Bible to discern God's will for humanity.

The building of modern statecraft drove the wedge even further. This is most clearly the case with the first real national experiment—The

20. Ibid., 198. Gillespie says something similar: "Luther was able to transform the abstract and distant God of nominalism into an inward power that suffused individual human being" (*Theological Origins*, 107).

21. This is the reason why many consider the Reformation to be the ideological bedrock for capitalism; it highlighted individual will, interpretation, and eventually, choice.

22. Noll, *Is the Reformation Over*, 91. Sacraments are church practices that impart grace, while ordinances are church practices that merely memorialize moments of grace.

23. It is interesting to note that the Catholic theologian Herbert McCabe describes a sacrament, such as baptism, as needing faith in Christ from the participant in order for the act to mean anything at all. He argues that without this faith as a primal element, baptism is nothing more than magic. He writes, "Such a baptism would be play-acting, a pretence, and not a sacrament at all. It is important to see that it is a denial of Faith, and not just wickedness, that invalidates baptism" (*New Creation*, 44). This insight is not only interesting in that it seems to go against Protestant caricaturing of the sacramental system, but also because McCabe also argues that Catholics, historically, used language other than the language of Protestantism because they feared falling into the heresy of Protestantism. Today, he notes, certain language and focus on the Bible is making a comeback within the Catholic Church away from the manualist, anti-Protestant style of theology.

24. Simply, the ministry of the word became primary over the ministry of the table, holy orders, and systems of prayer, confession and song.

United States of America.[25] America is largely a Protestant nation,[26] and so it consequently feared the Catholic Church as a rival political ideology. Protestantism, like the American ideology, is fundamentally modern in the sense that it prizes individual liberty over tradition, ecclesial authority (i.e., the magisterium), and all other forms of non-representational hierarchical authority. These supposed conflicting ideologies spurred Protestant civil mistrust in the United States for many years.[27] Consider the fact that it took around 185 years for America to elect its first Catholic president.[28] With much suspicion, an overwhelmingly Protestant nation thought that a Catholic president would take all of his governing cues from the Vatican.

Ultimately, the varying flavors of Protestantism surged and overflowed in the late twentieth century with ever-increasing new ecclesial brands, including the so-called non-denominational church. These "free churches" reject bishops and other forms of hierarchy while still accepting the fundamentals of the "Protestant Principle." With ever-increasing new liturgical expressions, approaches to evangelism and the like, most of these non-denominational churches still fit within only a few particular Protestant theological traditions.[29]

But this is where our story makes a dramatic shift. Today, many Protestants no longer protest the Catholic Church. In some cases they work alongside Catholics in mutual ministry. Some go further to actually utilize Catholic teaching in congregational life. Not to say that complete acceptance of Catholic teaching abounds in Protestant life today, but more and more non-Catholic churches exhibit openness toward Catholic teaching.

25. On how the modern nation state, not least of all America, has impacted Christian faith see William Cavanaugh's two works *Theopolitical Imagination* and *Migrations of the Holy*.

26. Although, it seems now that this is more of a historical argument since a recent study has shown that Protestantism is no longer a majority group in America. See http://articles.latimes.com/2012/oct/09/local/la-me-protestants-20121010. Of note is the rise of people describing their religious background as "no religion," which might follow from Protestantism's loose connection between faith and commitment to church.

27. Noll, *Is the Reformation Over?* 45.

28. Of note, Joe Biden, Vice President since 2008, is the first Roman Catholic V.P. in American History.

29. Marty, *Protestantism*, 26–27. Recently, I spoke to a student about his ecclesiological background. He informed me that he was from a non-denominational church and his church thus did not suffer the sectarian problems that other churches do. I asked him more about the teaching of the church or at least the "statements of belief" found in its weekly bulletin or website. In only a matter of moments, I was able to show my student that his theological heritage was still very indebted to the works of John Calvin and other Calvinistic or "Reformed" churches.

Instead of starting with protest, there is a growing trend toward unity and mutual respect.

POST-PROTESTANTS

Though it took time for Post-Protestantism to reach its current maturity, its starting point goes back a few centuries. Gestating during American revivalism, it emerged first from churches with names like "Church of . . ." such as the Church of Christ, Church of God, and Church of the Bible.[30] So the foundation of the Post-Protestant phenomena dates back as far as the second great awakening. For example the Church of God calls itself "The Church of God reformation Movement (Anderson)." Notice the small "r" in reformation. It does not claim to be the historic Reformation of Luther, Calvin or Zwingli, but it does seek reform by unifying Christian groups on the basis of Scripture and holiness. Though often rejecting Catholic piety, and rooted in the Wesleyan Arminian Holiness tradition, unity is the C.O.G's stated goal. More potent in this respect, however, is the "Stone-Campbell Movement," often called, "The Restoration Movement."[31] This movement claims neither Catholicism nor Protestantism as its starting point. Like the "Church of God," it aims to get behind the schism of creedal separation by restoring the primitive church found in the book of Acts.[32] These two traditions, and others like them, have had varying success levels, but their aim has always been for unity over division.

Skipping forward past the early and middle twentieth century to the late twentieth and early twenty-first centuries—ecclesial life, both for Protestants and Catholics, has changed dramatically. Catholics live in the aftermath of Vatican II, a council that innovated its liturgy and even mandated more openness to Protestantism. In short, after Vatican II, the Catholic stance toward Protestantism was more open and communicative.[33] This move engendered an openness to dialogue from the Protestant side as well.[34]

30. http://en.wikipedia.org/wiki/Post-Protestant

31. It is comprised of the Churches of Christ, Christian Churches and Churches of Christ, and the Disciples of Christ communions.

32. While this has been heralded as a good and noble task, others like Gerald Schlabach argue that there is a danger in the desire to go back to the beginning and bypassing all inherited traditions. "Where does it end?" he asks. Does reforming or restoring cause "the unstable prospect of perpetually starting over . . . ?" (Schlabach, *Unlearning Protestantism*, 35).

33. One bit of evidence for this was the Vatican's invitation of Protestant observers to the Council; perhaps, most notably, was Lutheran theologian, George Lindbeck.

34. For a list of ecumenical dialogues between Rome and Protestant churches see

Indeed, late twentieth century theologians from both sides began engaging more with one another's thought.[35] From a theological school and movement perspective, the late twentieth century witnessed Post-Liberalism, Radical Orthodoxy, Ecumenical meetings, etc., that have all—in their own distinctive ways—tried to look to the "great tradition" of Christianity as a whole, as opposed to remaining firm within particular theological ghettoes.

Also, and more than ever, Protestants have broken ties with traditional denominations, forming community churches, non-denominations, house churches, and new spin-offs (such as the emergent church[36]) which promise an orthodox Christianity free of the trappings of denominationalism.[37] This further splintering is still a result of the Reformation's schism. But what is truly interesting is the emergence of a Protestantism that seeks unity, ceases protest, and even, at times, utilizes Catholic teachings.

Groups like "Catholics and Evangelicals Together"[38] and the "Ekklesia Project"[39] are now commonplace. Still, more interesting than ecumenical talks, is that many non-Catholics actually read Catholic writers. Low-level examples are the fantasy of J. R. R. Tolkien, the spirituality of Henri Nouwen and Thomas Merton, and the politics of Mother Theresa and Dorothy Day. On a more formative level, however, we can note the inspiration gained by Protestants from the Catholic Church calendar,[40] sacramental theology, and Catholic social teaching.

If you'll permit another anecdote, I'd like to share a story from my book club. Every winter I lead an intergenerational group through three or four theological books. We've read Bonheoffer, Chesterton, Augustine, William Cavanaugh, Norman Wirzba, Hauerwas, and others. At the close of one of our meetings, an eavesdropper and fellow patron of the restaurant called me over and asked, "What kind of group are you?"

Noll, 75–114.

35. For example, the conversation between Karl Barth and Hans Urs von Balthasar concerning the notion of *analogia entis.*

36. For a source that attempts to foster dialogue within the so-called "emergent" style of churches see the emergent village: http://emergentvillage.org

37. Take for example Brian McLaren's *A Generous Orthodoxy*. Famously, he wrote this book to describe his piety and other like-minded emergent types with a smattering of adjectives such as: missional, evangelical, post/protestant, liberal/conservative, mystical/poetic, biblical, charismatic/contemplative, fundamentalist/Calvinist, Anabaptist/Anglican, Methodist, catholic, green, incarnational, depressed-yet-hopeful, emergent, unfinished *Christian.*

38. http://www.leaderu.com/ftissues/ft9405/articles/mission.html

39. http://www.ekklesiaproject.org

40. An example of this can be seen in the "Ancient Future" work of evangelical liturgist Robert Webber, http://www.ancientfutureworship.com

I replied, "What do you mean?"

"Are you Catholic?" I said, "No."

"Are you Eastern Orthodox?" "No," I said again.

"OK," he replied, "Well you must be Anglican, then."

"Nope."

Before I could end the questioning myself, he gave up and asked, "What are you?"

When I told him "We worship at a Church of Christ," I mused with a sense of pride that we may have been the first "Restoration Movement" church confused as Eastern Orthodox. But in truth, this story is not unique. Today, it is common for Protestant/non-Catholic Christians to draw inspiration from the Catholics and Orthodox, although they rarely fully convert to these other, ancient communions. The Post-Protestant world smacks of postmodernity. It seems possible to hold various viewpoints together without endangering the sanctity of any of them, or without the need of full conversion; one can be Catholic or Orthodox without entering into either particular church. "What some call the 'postmodern' situation," Schlabach explains, "encourages a crossing of boundaries in hopes of mutual enrichment among communities and traditions."[41]

Let's summarize some things one might find within Post-Protestantism. Individual Bible reading remains important, yet it need not be read exclusively: community necessarily helps with interpretation.[42] To this, we can add that art and tradition have been revalued. First, consider art. For much of the Protestant imagination art was a pragmatic tool for preaching the gospel; rarely was art an end unto itself.[43] But many Post-Protestants have rediscovered an aesthetic imagination indebted to Catholicism, where art is its own end and at times functions as a bit of heavenly revelation.[44] Sec-

41. Schlabach, *Unlearning Protestantism*, 22.

42. Take for example, N. T. Wright's assertion on how the Bible is authoritative. He says much is gained from both the Catholic and Protestant perspectives. See: http://ntwrightpage.com/Wright_Bible_Authoritative.htm

43. See http://firstthings.com/blogs/evangel/2010/02/the-beauty-of-god/. Anecdotally: whenever I enter into a Protestant Christian bookstore and look at the art, what I find is usually some picture of Christ carrying a lamb, or a wounded boy who is carrying a hammer and nail. It seems that each painting or portrait is meant to give a sense of comfort by conveying a straightforward interpretation of the gospel. Must art have an explicit message in order to function as revelation?

44. Film maker, Scott Derrickson, a one time evangelical, is now promoting the aesthetic imagination of Catholics such as Flannery O'Connor and Ingmar Bergman, most recently at the "Glen West" workshop: http://imagejournal.org/page/events/the-glen-workshop/, where he offered a class on filmmaking and Christianity. Other presenters at the workshop cited the Orthodox and Catholic thought as primary inspirations for their artistic imaginations. It is important to note that the "Glen workshops" are

ondly, traditional worship, theology, and even "tradition as revelation" are given a higher footing than once imagined by the Reformation's heirs. Some are reviving use of sacred calendars[45] while others wish to get behind modernism by having the church fathers speak to our current concerns, as is the case with those in the Radical Orthodoxy sensibility. It is not uncommon to see a broadened sacramental imagination applied to church practice within Protestantism that tastes of Catholicism or Eastern Orthodox tendencies.

RESOURCES FOR POST-PROTESTANTISM

There are many reasons for this Post-Protestant situation. Post-Vatican II Catholicism heralded in a time of openness within the Catholic Church. One outcome was its re-evaluation of Protestantism. Protestants are no longer deemed heretical according to the Vatican; now, it is willing "to address non-Catholic Christians as 'brothers' . . ."[46] Or as McCabe argues, "we should, to my mind look upon the vast majority of non-Catholic Christians . . . simply as fellow Catholics who have the misfortune to be deprived of the full sacramental life of the Church."[47]

But other Catholic developments were equally important, namely John Paul II's pontificate. As stated, America's base ideology is liberty, leading it to deny communism's atheistic force throughout the twentieth century. Concurrently, JPII, the most popular modern pontiff, was a driving force for subverting European communism. This no doubt made him popular even amongst Protestant Americans. And to this we should note that he penned a best seller that endeared the Protestant world to the Church of Rome.[48] In other terms, he became a veritable "rock star" for religious and cultural liberty, and thus positive ecumenical feelings.[49]

inundated with "recovering" evangelicals working within the arts. For this information, I am indebted to Ryan Stewart, a student in the Seminary of Lincoln Christian University, who attended the workshops in honor of his M.A. thesis in Theology—under the direction of Prof. John D. Castelein—called "Toward a Theological Appropriation of Cinematic Horror."

45. For example, the "Salt of the Earth: A Christian Seasons Calendar" http://www.thechristiancalendar.com. It is a calendar based on the Christian year with art and meditations on the different seasons. Some leaders who promote it include Brian McLaren, Stanley Hauerwas, Walter Brueggemann, Phyllis Tickle, and Marva Dawn.

46. Noll, *Is The Reformation Over?* 60.

47. McCabe *The New Creation*, 49.

48. Noll, *Is The Reformation Over?* 28.

49. John Paul II wrote a best seller called *Crossing the Threshold of Hope*. In addition to JPII's work, we can cite the work of Mother Theresa of Calcutta; Christians of all stripes too praised her for her work with the poor.

Another catalyst for change was the ecumenical dialogue convening after Vatican II. Presciently, The Vatican invited non-Catholic observers to the council.[50] This openness was a good foundation for future dialogue; the years that followed got even better. Beginning in the 1960s, until recently, there have been various invitations from the Vatican to a broad range of Protestant denominations for the purposes of ecumenical dialogue.[51]

But perhaps the sharpest catalyst came from the fruits of modernity itself: secularity. In the West, modernity took shape most fully as a secular worldview.[52] This is evidenced within Protestantism by the appearance of the "Death of God," secular, and even the atheist theologies.[53] If it is true that there are no atheists in foxholes, then it is even truer that there are no denominations there. If you doubt this, then ask graduate students in modern, liberal theology programs, or at least ask those who speak politically about issues of faith, such as the pro-life movement. Increasing secularity has brought Catholics and Protestants together in various ways to protect religious freedoms and shared commitments concerning faith in Christ.

But most intensely—and with the most ingenuity—the major factor underpinning Post-Protestantism is the base of theologians and church leaders who relied on and introduced Catholic teaching to a Protestant world in which secularity held much sway. In other words, there were those who introduced and put into practice Catholic thought for the service of the church as a whole, beyond sectarian dispute.

THEOLOGICAL DEVELOPMENTS AND POST-PROTESTANTISM

Surveying theological development is arduous and always incomplete. Thankfully, our goal is not a full-fledged genealogy. I wish to highlight just

50. For an interview with one ecumenical observer of the Vatican II on his experiences see http://www.firstthings.com/article/2007/01/re-viewing-vatican-iian-interview-with-george-a-lindbeck-2

51. Noll, list the dates for ecumenical dialogue between 1966 through 1988 in *Is the Reformation Over?* 77–83. As for the non-denominational, free church, and Post-Protestant veins, this has been a little more challenging since they often lack a hierarchy for such representation.

52. See Stanley Hauerwas' and William Willimon's personal experience with this phenomenon in *Resident Aliens*, 15–19.

53. Consider this list of thinkers: Thomas J. J. Altizer, John A. T. Robinson, John Shelby Spong, Don Cupitt and the theo-blog: An Und Für Sich: http://itself.wordpress.com, spearheaded by Adam Kotsko, Anthony Paul Smith, and Brad Johnson; this blog represents the work of a new wave of "radical theologians" in the style of Altizer et al.

a few shifts in the theological development of Western Christianity that catalyzed Post-Protestantism. First, it is important to note that much modern theology, especially in America, has been dominated by the German, Protestant theological tradition.[54] On one level, this brings the hegemony of Systematics, whereby theology typically imposed systems of thought onto divine revelation in order to categorize doctrines and practices. Only recently in America have alternative theological methods such as the essay and occasional treatise reached prominence.

How does Systematic Theology work? Beginning with a cultural question generated from philosophy or the social sciences, this approach applies certain constraints upon revelation in order to show how Christianity fits within a cultural framework, or how it answers questions prevalent to a given era. This is evidenced by Schleiermacher's attempt to make the Christian faith compatible with Kantian dualism,[55] or with Tillich's method of correlation.[56] As a result, Protestant theology adopted an air of modern liberalism mounting into radical forms of thought, becoming downright atheistic at times. By the 1960s some theologians went so far as to ask, "is God dead?"[57]

What were the faithful to do? For Protestants, options were scant. One approach was to deny cultural criticisms in favor of a *fideistic* faith. This attempt can be seen in the premodern faith of many fundamentalist churches. Premoderns insist on the complete inerrancy of Scripture, adopting statements like "If something is not in the Bible, it cannot be true" and its converse "If it is in the Bible, it must be true." The Premodern's creed: "The Bible says it, I believe it, that settles it." Another adverse approach to theological modernizing is antimodernism. This is the approach of many contemporary apologists. Ironically, they use modern tools such as enlightenment epistemology and science to dispute modernism and to prove Christian claims. Simply put, they accept the modern field of engagement, and try to prove Christianity with it.[58] Others go further. They follow the modern

54. See John Milbank's "The Eastward Movement of Western Theology," http://youtu.be/-TO_McoDehA

55. Schleiermacher's two-volume systematic theology *The Christian Faith* focused the ground of faith on the feeling of "absolute dependence." Doctrinal elements that defy that category, such as the Holy Trinity, only receive treatment within the appendix.

56. Tillich famously attempted to bring theology into correlation with existentialist philosophy.

57. This cover was highlighted in the Roman Polanski's film, *Rosemary's Baby,* which depicted the birth of the antichrist and which also highlighted the anxious spirit of the time in wonderful, horror-cinematic fashion. It seems that the American theological landscape of the 1960s caught up with Nietzsche's nineteenth century proclamations.

58. They would do well to read Bruno Latour *We Have Never Been Modern.* Latour argues that we have never been modern, so how can we follow it and be

path into postmodern criticism, thereby reducing their commitments to one story to be lived alongside other stories. Their faith reduces dogmatic statements down to existential life cues.[59] But where is one able to find a faith that is neither neglectful of modernity's questions nor fully accepting of them, while still holding on to foundational doctrinal commitments? In the Protestant milieu some found assistance in the neo-orthodoxy of Karl Barth.[60] But while this was a powerful force in rejecting modern liberalism, it unsatisfactorily reduced the gospel to its *kerygma* leaving some dissatisfied with how much of modernity could be addressed.

However, in the modern, liberal (thus, diminutive) theological world, other voices sprang up. During the height of the 1960s radical theology there were a few Anglophone theologians impacting top tier universities such as Cambridge. It was there, under the tutelage of Donald McKinnon, that Rowan Williams would face modern theology and ask, "but I believe, is there more?"[61] Other current theological leaders just as disenchanted as Williams would follow and they, too, were forced to ask similar questions. Among these thinkers were Janet Martin Soskice and Sarah Coakley, not to mention a powerful theological pupil of Williams, John Milbank.[62] Milbank would later start a movement (Radical Orthodoxy) that not only rejected modernity, but also introduced a "catholic" style of doing theology to people who were steadfastly Protestant. And perhaps by virtue of being English, these emerging theological leaders wrote in a more essayistic manner than a systematic one, thus they were not forced to impose narrow paradigms on revealed knowledge.

The American scene was different, but not unrelated. During the height of modernistic theology, the diamond in the rough was the Yale school. Barthians such as Hans Frei and George Lindbeck dominated Yale at the time. Their work was more narrative than systematic, and like their British counterparts they were not afraid to engage culture. Their movement is known

---

"postmodern" or precede it as "premoderns?" Or how can we oppose it as is the case with the "antimoderns?"

59. My system of categorization—premodern, modern, anti-modern, postmodern, and postmodernism—is indebted to Prof. John D. Castelein. He developed this scheme for his class "Insights for Ministering to Contemporary Minds," a class he regularly taught at The Seminary of Lincoln Christian University.

60. Barthian theology is still prominent within American, British and Australian theological circles.

61. On Rowan Williams and his rejection of Radical Theology, Anglophone Protestantism, and a brief assessment about Donald MacKinnon, see Short *God's Advocates,* 17–18. Nota Bene: the question in quotes is not attributed to Rowan Williams, it is simply the author's method of describing Williams' biography.

62. Short, *God's Advocates,* 18.

as Post-Liberalism.[63] Post-Liberalism took seriously the idea that cultural situations shaped theology, yet it did not deny the importance of tradition. It also combined cultural and biblical narratives in dialogue, resulting in a higher valuation of Scripture. But more importantly for our query, however, is a student at Yale during this time (though it would be a mistake to say that he fits into the Post-Liberal school, solely) by the name of Stanley Hauerwas.

On September 10, 2001 Hauerwas was named America's best theologian.[64] Mennonite pacifism, Barthianism, Catholic social thought, and the importance of storytelling communities distinctively shape Hauerwas' uniquely, ecumenical theological approach. The reason for highlighting Hauerwas in particular is that his work may have done more to introduce Protestants to Catholic ideas than any other American thinker. One way this was achieved was through the co-writing of a popular-level book called *Resident Aliens: Life in the Christian Colony.*[65] It has provided help to Protestant's of all stripes, beyond the influence of the ivory tower. Since largely read in local churches by clergy and lay leaders, its impact was quicker than the trickle-down effect of the academy. Indeed, *Resident Aliens* was a gateway drug for Hauerwas' more academic and ecumenical writings.

One teaching post—lasting for more than a decade—which may have been quite providential for Hauerwas was at Notre Dame. And though there is much made of his influence by the Mennonite John Howard Yoder, it was there that he grew interested in Catholic Social teaching and the Catholic philosophy of Alasdair McIntyre and developed a deeply formative friendship with Catholic theologian and priest David Burrell. A provocateur *par excellence*, Hauerwas employed Catholic moral thought even though at

63. Post-Liberal theology was developed by George Lindbeck, Hans Frei, and to a lesser extent, David Kelsey. It drew inspiration from Thomas Aquinas, Karl Barth, and the *Nouvelle Theologie* movement, so its inspiration is manifestly ecumenical. But it also drew from the philosophies and sociologies of Wittgensten, MacIntyre, Geertz, and Berger. Some who followed the Post-Liberal theological school of thought or who are at least heavily influenced by it include R. R. Reno, Ephraim Radner, George Sumner, Christopher Sietz, Garrett Green, William Placher, Bruce Marshall, Kathryn Tanner, Fr. Robert Barron, and Stanley Hauerwas.

64. This appraisal was done by *Time* magazine: http://www.time.com/time/magazine/article/0,9171,1000859,00.html. In sad irony, this issue printed one day before 9/11/01 attacks, and Hauerwas is a promoter of Christian pacifism. This feature, along with the events of 9/11, catapulted Hauerwas to the heights of "public intellectual" status (one of the first theologians to be consider a public intellectual, in America, since Tillich and the Niebuhr's). One can appreciate his reported response to receiving the title of America's Best Theologian: "'Best' is not a theological category," http://en.wikipedia.org/wiki/Stanley_Hauerwas

65. Hauerwas and Willimon, *Resident Aliens*.

the time he was a self-identified Methodist ethicist.[66] His work introduced American Protestants to a wider theological world, and in the end it proved useful for developing a fresh faith, once confounded by Protestant Modern Liberalism, not to mention its result—postmodernist relativism.

Hauerwas also played a part in introducing Americans to the work of John Milbank and his championed sensibility called "Radical Orthodoxy."[67] Milbank's work (and Radical Orthodoxy's), as hinted to above, is driven first by "out-narrating" the modern story. Second, its roots are British and are thus non-systematic. Third, Milbank's influences are wide. They are not limited to German Protestant thought or any one particular tradition. Milbank regularly draws from French sources such as the Catholic movement *nouvelle theologie*.[68] Radical Orthodoxy is refreshing because it considers all academic subjects as theological and worthy of engagement. There is no separation between academic fields or between culture and theology; indeed, everything is theological. Milbank et al. work toward a particular end, one of "catholic" theology, that is to say a more orthodox, historical, and ecumenical expression. And because secularity is the enemy, schismatic thought is not valued. Therefore, Christians who read Radical Orthodox works are asked to reconsider modernity, look to church history, and utilize broad orthodox claims in order to deal with modern/postmodern ones. Though there is not enough room to analyze all of this sensibility here, we can say that many Protestants, evangelical[69] and mainline,[70] have been drawn to this movement and

66. For a fascinating account of Hauerwas' life, work, and theology see his memoir *Hannah's Child: A Theologians Memoir*.

67. For an interesting exposé on the theological relationship between Hauerwas and Milbank, see their discussion mediated by Luke Bretherton on the occasion of Hauerwas' recent memoir: http://podcast.ulcc.ac.uk/accounts/kings/Social_Science/ Milbank_Hauerwas_Bretherton.mp3

68. Proponents of this school of thought include Yves Congar, Hans Urs von Balthasar, Henri de Lubac, Jean Daniélou, and Josef Ratzinger, etc.

69. A list of evangelical thinkers who fit within the Radical Orthodox sensibility includes but is not limited to: Anthony D. Baker, Eric Austin Lee, Christopher Ben Simpson, James K. A. Smith, and D. Stephen Long. Now it is true that many of these thinkers have adopted other ecclesiological stances later in their development, and maybe they would not like the pigeonhole title "evangelical," but they all discovered R.O. as Nazarenes, Stone-Campbellites, conservative Methodists, and Reformed thinkers.

70. A list of mainline Protestants or non-Catholics includes, but is not limited to Graham Ward, Brent Driggers, and John Hughes. To be sure, there are many Catholics and Eastern Orthodox thinkers who are attracted to Radical Orthodoxy, and are thus put into conversation with non-Catholic thinkers on a regular basis. A short list of such thinkers in this realm: William Desmond, Jeffery Bishop, David Bentley Hart, Fr. John Behr, David L. Schindler, D. C. Schindler, Conor Cunningham, and Fergus Kerr, etc.

others like it, because they can continue to profess faith while questioning the hegemony of modern/postmodern thought.

In part because of the work of people such as Hauerwas, Williams, Milbank, etc. (all non-Catholics) the Protestant world—within the waste land of modernity—has been given tools, both Catholic and Protestant, for using Christian grammar to negotiate an increasingly secular world. And there are others, to be sure, from the fields of biblical studies, philosophy, and sociology that have contributed to a similar kind of work.[71] But for our purposes, the thinkers mentioned above serve as first-level signposts in rejecting modernity, surpassing the sectarian theological world of Protestant vs. Catholic.

In summary, Post-Protestantism arrived on the scene most fully within postmodernity, because it is in such a world that theological party lines may be questioned and blurred. One could argue that Protestantism has followed its cultural milieu throughout all the epochs of modernity right down to the current milieu that doubts exclusive narratives, absolute truth claims, political hegemony, etc. If these items necessarily accompany postmodernity, then they apply to Post-Protestantism as well. For it too rejects boundary lines, denominational truth claims, objective knowledge, single power structures, and like other postmodern expressions of belief, they blend the contemporary with the ancient.[72] This last point is evidenced in Post-Protestantism with the following examples: Radical Orthodoxy,[73]

71. Indeed there are many religious thinkers from various fields who represent Catholic and Protestant views, but whose work has been formative for Protestant use of Catholic teaching. In the case of biblical studies some examples include the work of N. T. Wright, Margaret Barker, Marcus Bauckham, Ellen F. Davis, and Scot McKnight, etc. As for philosophers, Alasdair MacIntyre, Charles Taylor, Albert Borgmann, William Desmond, and Bernard Lonergan represent such blending. In the case of sociology some examples are Jacques Ellul, Robert Bellah, Peter Berger, and Bruno Latour.

72. This particular insight I gleaned from Prof. John D. Castelein. It is evidenced in television shows such as *Lost*, *Buffy the Vampire Slayer* and *Supernatural*; films such as *Exorcism of Emily Rose*, *Avatar*, and the *Indiana Jones* series; and in religious and philosophical systems such as *neo-paganism*, *Wicca*, and *eco-philosophy*. The point is that postmodernism blends the contemporary and the ancient into one-textured narrative or belief system.

73. Radical Orthodoxy wishes to answer modern/postmodern questions with ancient sources such as Augustine, Aquinas, the Cappadocian fathers, Maximus the Confessor, etc.

Paleo-Orthodoxy,[74] the Ancient-Future worship movement,[75] and even the Ancient Christian Commentary series.[76]

THE PROS OF POST-PROTESTANTISM

There is much to praise of such a movement. For one thing, the Post-Protestant appeal to unity is a Christian idea faithful to Christ's "High-Priestly" prayer in John 17, in keeping with biblical orthodoxy. But unity is good on a pragmatic level as well. As Christians negotiate interaction with a secular society, it is certainly helps present a unified, Christian front regarding issues that impact Christianity's basic teachings. Clearest are issues like how Christians value life and procreation. Since most Christians place a high value on life, overcoming divisions concerning the importance of Scripture and tradition with unified voice is, no doubt, a good thing.

Another praise is for theological enrichment. The days of reading only your tradition's teachers are gone; Christians of all stripes are now learning from other traditions. In some cases this learning deepens one's prior commitments, while in others it has caused some new commitments. An example of the former involves the renewed interest in daily Bible reading now practiced by Catholics. Mark Noll suggests that growing Protestant-Catholic dialogue pushed some Catholics to reinvigorate individual Bible study.[77] Catholics have always valued the Bible, but that value was deepened on an individual level as a result of ecumenical dialogues. On the other hand, sometimes entire church communities convert to an entirely different tradition.[78] In these cases, wider reading and ecumenical thinking has caused some to say that if they are to be consistent in their thinking then

74. Thomas Oden wrote a work that is central to the movement called "Paleo-Orthodoxy" in his *Classic Christianity: A Systematic Theology*. This work seeks to explain Christian doctrine by quoting the comments of a wide variety of historical Christian figures on topics in a systematic fashion. Its main aim is to show that there is something unified within "Classic Christianity" much like the fundamental notion of C. S. Lewis' *Mere Christianity* (vii–xvi). The "mere" in the title seeks to explain Christian faith outside of denominational/traditional parochialism, that is, simply the main essence underlying all Christian traditions.

75. Spear-headed by Robert Webber, this movement aims to bring ancient liturgical thought into the contemporary, evangelical liturgical expression.

76. This commentary series examines biblical texts by compiling ancient interpretations and quotes on each given text. IVP, an evangelical publisher, produces this series of commentaries. http://www.ivpress.com/accs/

77. Noll, *Is the Resformation Over?* 60–63.

78. For example, see http://www.stlukeorthodox.com/html/innews/congregation-follows.htm

they could no longer hold the same commitments, they must rejoin more ancient forms of Christian expression. On the whole, these phenomena are undoubtedly beneficial to the wider Christian faith, because they represent a united front to another wise suspicious world. Additionally, wider and deeper understandings of Christianity have helped to communicate deeper responses to all the questions that surround us.

THE CONS OF POST-PROTESTANTISM

Conversely, several things cause alarm relating to this new development. One is the dubious nature of unity. Even if we create unity-seeking communities, who is to say that these new communities do not cause more division? There is little evidence to suggest that unity movements such as the Church of God or the Restoration Movement have resulted in more unity over mounting diversity; indeed, both have matured into "line-drawing" communities and have even produced internal schisms of their own.[79] Additionally, unity based on a common enemy is dangerous. St. Basil the Great says, "we have in common with each other that we hate our common opponents, but whenever the enemies leave, we then harm each other as enemies."[80] If Christendom were ever realized again, Post-Protestant unity will not be enough. We run the risk of continuing older, deeper divisions. Restoration, over unity, ought to be the *telos*.

Also, an oft manifested truth states that if you are everything, you cannot be anything. In other words, one who accepts all views actually possesses none of them. To be fair, most Post-Protestants do not accept every other view. It is hard to imagine, for instance, that they'd accept both Christ and another deity in the same manner. But they do often accept a multitude of aspects of differing theological traditions, as in the case with the emergent church. In the end, many of these positions cannot actually be held together unless violence is done to other parts.[81] Some theological ideas

79. One example, with the Restoration Movement, is the case of the International Church of Christ. This group represents a sub-group that has disconnected from the mainstream forms of the Church of Christ.

80. St. Basil, *On the Holy Spirit,* 119.

81. One example of this is found in a local church within my own community. It blends Calvinistic pre-destination with Charismatic "health and wealth." On one Sunday a member noted that they it heard said, "if you are having difficulty now, God has willed that into your life." On the following Sunday, the preacher said, "if you are struggling, then perhaps your faith is weak; strengthen your faith and God will bless you in all ways. You need to pray more, and harder." These two views seem to be at odds with one another.

are incompatible; holding them together results in internal inconsistency. Real unity does not mean that all groups throw away everything that defines them or accepts in full everything of another group. Real dialogue, and at times disagreement, is necessary, if the Christian church is going to find non-schismatic unity.

Ultimately, Post-Protestants must think about ecumenical thought beyond what will serve the life of one congregation or communion. The sole motivator cannot be self-service. Unity has to be in the service of the whole as much as the parts, otherwise Christianity will be further divided, albeit adorned with stranger and more interesting divisions. What I wish to say is that if the theological diversity of Post-Protestantism remains solely for the individual congregation, then the wider Christian world will look more schizophrenic than it already does.

CONCLUSION

As modernity's chicks come home to roost with the emergence of postmodernity,[82] so it is with Protestantism. We live in the Post-Protestant milieu, for good and for ill. It seems that there is little for non-Catholics to protest over, and new boundary lines are being drawn away from denominational differences and around the frontlines between secularity and faith in the risen Christ. But how far will this go? Protestants must ask themselves if they are no longer protesting the Church of Rome, should they consider entering into either it or the Eastern Orthodox communion? Likewise, Catholic and Orthodox churches must ask if they ought to extend fellowship and brotherhood to Protestants in a more robust and inclusive manner. These are big ideas, however, and ones that are not addressed in this essay. They include issues about authority, and hierarchy, two things I am confident will not be settled anytime soon. That said, however, the current state of openness is a breath of fresh air in the direction of reconciliation that we should note and strive to build.

82. I owe this line to the teaching and thought of Christopher Ben Simpson.

BIBLIOGRAPHY

Ancient Future Worship. No pages. Online: http://www.ancientfutureworship.com.

Benson, Christopher. Review of *The Beauty of God: Theology and the Arts*, by Daniel J. Treier, Mark Husbands, and Roger Lundon. *First Things* blog *Evangel* (Monday, February 15, 2010) http://firstthings.com/blogs/evangel/2010/02/the-beauty-of-god/.

Bretherton, Luke. "Stanley Hauerwas, John Milbank & Luke Bretherton in Conversation." King's College, London, October 18, 2010. Audio recording. Online: http://podcast.ulcc.ac.uk/accounts/kings/Social_Science/Milbank_Hauerwas_Bretherton.mp3.

Cassidy, Edward Idris Cardinal. "The Christian Mission in the Third Millennium." *First Things* 79 (January, 1998). No pages. Online: http://www.leaderu.com/ftissues/ft9801/articles/cassidy.html.

Cavanaugh, William. *Being Consumed: Economics and Christian Desire*. Grand Rapids: Eerdmans, 2008.

———. *Migrations of the Holy: God, State and the Political Meaning of the Church*. London: T. & T. Clark, 2003.

———. *Theopolitical Imagination: Christian Practices of Space and Time*. London: T. & T. Clark, 2003.

"Denominations." No Pages. Online: http://www.religioustolerance.org/christ7.

Ekklesia Project. No Pages. Online: http://www.ekklesiaproject.org.

Elshtain, Jean Bethke. "Theologian: Christian Contrarian." No pages. http://www.time.com/time/magazine/article/0,9171,1000859,00.html.

Gillespie, Michael Allen. *The Theological Origins of Modernity*. Chicago: University of Chicago Press, 2009.

Hauerwas, Stanley. *Hannah's Child: A Theologians Memoir*. Grand Rapids: Eerdmans, 2010.

———."Memoir Hannah's Child." Podcast. http://podcast.ulcc.ac.uk/accounts/kings/Social_Science/Milbank_Hauerwas_Bretherton.mp3

Hauerwas, Stanley, and William Willimon. *Resident Aliens: Life in the Christian Colony*. Nashville: Abingdon, 1989.

Latour, Bruno. *We Have Never Been Modern*. Cambridge: Harvard University Press, 1993.

Lewis, Brian. "Congregation will follow pastor's lead in converting." No pages. http://www.stlukeorthodox.com/html/innews/congregationfollows

Lewis, C. S. *Mere Christianity*. San Francisco: Harper Collins, 2001.

Lilla, Mark. *The Stillborn God: Religion, Politics and the Modern West*. New York: Vintage, 2007.

Marty, Martin. *Protestantism: Its Churches and Cultures, Rituals, and Doctrines, Yesterday and Today*. Chicago: Holt, Rinehart, and Winston, 1972.

McCabe, Herbert. *New Creation*. London: Continuum, 2010.

McClaren, Brian. *A Generous Orthodoxy*. Grand Rapids: Zondervan, 2004.

Milbank, John. "The Eastward Movement of Western Theology" http://youtu.be/-TO_McoDehA.

Noll, Mark. *Is the Reformation Over: An Evangelical Assessment of Contemporary Roman Catholicism*. Grand Rapids: Baker Academic, 2005.

Oden, Thomas. *Classic Christianity: A Systematic Theology*. New York: HarperOne, 2009.

Palley, Marcia. *The New Evangelicals: Expanding the Vision of the Common Good*. Grand Rapids: Eerdmans, 2011.

Paul, John II. *Crossing the Threshold of Hope*. New York: Knopf, 1995.

Pelikan, Jaroslav. *Obedient Rebels*. New York: Harper Row, 1964.

Polanski, Roman. *Rosemary's Baby*. Film. Produced by William Castle. Paramount Pictures, 1968.

"Post-Protestantism." No Pages. Online: http://en.wikipedia.org/wiki/Post-Protestant.

"Salt of the Earth: A Christian Seasons Calendar." No Pages. Online: http://www.thechristiancalendar.com.

Schlabach, Gerald. *Unlearning Protestantism: Sustaining Christian Community in an Unstable Age*. Brazos: Grand Rapids, 2010.

Schleiermacher, Friedrich. *The Christian Faith*. London: T. & T. Clark, 1999.

Schmemann, Alexander. *For the Life of the World*. New York: St. Vladimir's Seminary Press, 1973.

Short, Rupert. *God's Advocates: Christian Thinkers in Conversation*. Grand Rapids: Eerdmans, 2005.

St. Basil the Great. *On the Holy Spirit*. New York: St. Vladimir's Seminary Press, 2011.

Szerszynski, Bronislaw. *Nature, Technology, and the Sacred*. Oxford: Blackwell, 2005.

Watanabe, Teresa. "Protestants no longer a majority of Americans, study finds." No pages. http://articles.latimes.com/2012/oct/09/local/la-me-protestants-20121010.

Weigel, George. "Reviewing Vatican II." No pages. http://www.firstthings.com/article/2007/01/re-viewing-vatican-iian-interview-with-george-a-lindbeck-2.

Wikipedia. "Stanley Hauerwas." No pages. Online: http://en.wikipedia.org/wiki/Stanley_Hauerwas

Wright, N. T. "How Can the Bible Be Authoritative?" In *The Laing Lecture 1989, and the Griffith Thomas Lecture 1989*. Originally published in *Vox Evangelica* 21 (1991) 7–32. No pages. http://ntwrightpage.com/Wright_Bible_Authoritative.htm.

8

Twentieth-Century Theological Method

Interpretations at the Beginning of the Third Millennium[1]

JUSTIN SCHWARTZ

INTRODUCTION

Twentieth-century theology is a topic fraught with disagreements concerning many issues: the nature of revelation and reason, grace and nature,

---

1 The genesis and impetus of this work comes from Dr. John Castelein. I had the pleasure of being under Dr. Castelein's tutelage for an independent study in twentieth-century theology. At this time I was also his graduate assistant. This paper is a result of thoughts and insights gleaned from reading, conversations in and out of the office space we shared, and the theology-philosophy forum that John began in the seminary of Lincoln Christian University, which I was able to present the seeds of this paper to. I would also credit bringing Bernard Lonergan into this paper to John, at its roots, and also to Dr. Steven D. Cone. Needless to say, I owe much more than I can possibly repay or account for to my academic mentors that have invested in me, who I gladly call friends. I am especially to Dr. Castelein for this paper, who has seen in me what I could not and has encouraged me more than he can possibly know.

illumination and evidentialism, etc. Most of these disagreements in twentieth-century theology spring from methodological issues; thus, a clear understanding of these disagreements, especially those concerning methodology, are essential for navigating the spectrum of contemporary theology. To "set sail" and to "navigate" the treacherous waters of twentieth-century theology, one must have a clear "map," or interpretation, of these complex issues that exist in the present if one wishes to emerge unscathed, their "ship of faith" intact. From hindsight at the end of the twentieth-century, two interpretations of modern theology have provided maps that have especially garnered my interest and attention: an introduction to modern theology by James C. Livingston and company, *Modern Christian Thought: Volume II–The Twentieth Century* (2nd ed.),[2] and the work of a group loosely known as Radical Orthodoxy, specifically inaugurated by the book *Radical Orthodoxy: A New Theology*.[3] Livingston and his group of scholars have provided a great service to scholarship, an excellent introduction and interpretation of contemporary theology that judiciously handles the different schools and methods of theology, while Radical Orthodoxy has provided an additional focused critique of contemporary theology at the end of the twentieth-century and beyond to explain such fragmentation, attempting to "fill in" the foundational gaps that, in my interpretation, are left as more of a history of theology by Livingston and friends. The goal of this paper is to "chart" the path of two of twentieth-century theology's methodologies by the "stars" of two interpretations, Livingston and his group's and Radical Orthodoxy's, and to offer a possible further critique for research to pursue for the future. First, Livingston and Fiorenza's interpretations will provide a basic outline for an overview of the back-and-forth nature of methodological disagreements in contemporary theology in Karl Barth (Neo-Orthodoxy), Paul Tillich (correlation theology), and Hans Frei (Postliberalism). Second, Radical Orthodoxy will provide a critique of these methods, calling theologians to recognize Radical Orthodoxy's interpretation that modern theology is built upon a dualistic metaphysics that has essentially caused methodological disagreements. Third, I will offer a critique and avenues for further research, in which I put forth that Radical Orthodoxy is correct to critique Duns Scotus concerning his metaphysics, but theologians, in the vein of Bernard Lonergan's work *Method in Theology*, should look beyond a metaphysical critique to understanding the cognitional theory supporting the epistemology and metaphysics of each method or theologian.

---

2. Livingston et al., *Modern Christian Thought: Volume II*.
3. Milbank et al., *Radical Orthodoxy: A New Theology*.

LIVINGSTON AND FIORENZA'S NARRATIVES: BARTH, TILLICH, AND FREI

Karl Barth (Neo-Orthodoxy)

Karl Barth's work as a theologian effectively marks the end of nineteenth-century theology and the beginning of twentieth-century theology in Europe. Emerging from the context of nineteenth-century theology and the Great War, Livingston writes that "Karl Barth . . . was concerned to free theology from the worship of human ideals and subjective values."[4] This meant that, according to Livingston, "For Karl Barth the theology of the nineteenth-century no longer had a future."[5] In Barth's work one can mark off early and late periods of his theology, the second half coming to maturity after 1930,[6] which has had an unprecedented influence on the future course of twentieth-century Christian theology.[7]

Barth's first goal was to deconstruct Liberal Protestant theology. The crux of this conflict is in anthropology, which Barth refused to ground theology in. Barth would not begin theology with anthropology, with nature, but with revelation; with grace. So then, first of all, Barth's critique of nineteenth-century theology, according to Rudolph Bultmann, was "fighting on two fronts, against both the *psychologizing* and the *historicizing* of Christian faith. This expressed itself in Barth's polemic against mystical experience and his renunciation of all forms of immanence and pantheism."[8] "The crucial issue," Livingston writes, "between the new generation of dialectical theologians and the Liberal theologians . . . concerned the question of historical consciousness, its claims, and its limits. For . . . Barth, this was the crux of the problem." Due to this, Barth would break from his friends in the dialectical movement, including Bultmann and Tillich, writing that "All of you . . . are trying to understand faith as a human possibility, or, if you will, as grounded in a human possibility, and therefore you are once again *surrendering theology to philosophy*. . . . For me there can be no question but that I can only oppose it in the future."[9] Barth rejected all philosophy, as he perceived it, and much that he had written in the second edition of Romans, though he valued its combating of "the subjectivism and the an-

4. Livingston, *Modern Christian Thought: Volume II*, 58.

5. Ibid., 62.

6. This section of the paper will examine Barth's theology from this mature standpoint, the period of his Church Dogmatics.

7. Livingston, *Modern Christian Thought: Volume II*, 96. Emphasis added.

8. Bultmann, "Karl Barth's Epistle to the Romans in its Second Edition," 36.

9. Livingston, *Modern Christian Thought: Volume II*, 65.

thropocentricism of the prevailing Neo-Protestant theology."[10] Continuing from Livingston's narrative: "This latter theology continued to speak of a human religious *a priori* immanent in the human subject or in history and by which theology could judge Christianity from *outside* Scripture and the Church. In short, it failed to let God be God. Barth struggled for thirteen years . . . with the problem of establishing theology free of the last vestiges of his own Neo-Protestant subjectivism."

Positively, Barth would then construct his own theological method in place of those that he had rejected. By Livingston's account, Barth "sought . . . a theology that would stand on its own feet, so to speak, free of the support of other philosophical or anthropological sources."[11] "The reason for the change," Livingston writes, "was Barth's growing conviction that the world of theology is a function of the Church. It is not, he writes, "A 'free' science, but one bound to the sphere of the Church"—and this meant for Barth that he had to "cut out of his second issue of the book [The Commentary on Romans] that in the first issue might give the slightest appearance of giving to theology a basis, support, or even a mere justification in the way of existential philosophy."[12] This freeing of theology, for Barth, was found in his own study and interpretation of Anselm, who confirmed in Barth's mind "the conviction that the theologian does not begin outside the faith of the Church and then attempt to show, with the help of philosophy or anthropology, that the faith is true. One begins, rather, with the belief of the Church."[13] This Anselmian condition necessary for theology consists, according to Barth, of the following position: "The knowledge that is sought cannot be anything but an extension and explication of that acceptance of the *Credo* of the Church, which faith itself already implied. . . . A science of faith, which denied or even questioned the Faith [the *Credo* of the Church], would *ipso facto* cease to be either "faithful" or "scientific." . . . *Intelligere* [understanding] comes about by reflection on the *Credo* that has already been spoken and affirmed."[14]

For Barth, only one criterion can determine whether a theological statement is admissible or not, namely, "the text of the Holy Scripture, which . . . forms the basic stability of the *Credo* to which the *credere* and therefore the *intelligere* refer. While it is the decisive source, it is also the determining

10. Ibid., 96.
11. Ibid.
12. Ibid., 98.
13. Ibid.
14. Barth, *Anselm: Fides Quaerens Intellectum*, 26–27.

norm of *intelligere*."[15] Livingston then has a section which deserves to be quoted in full:

> Although *intelligere* means a *reflection upon* what has already been said in the *Credo*, this "reflection upon" is not possessed by the believer, nor can the believer seek it outside the *Credo* of the Church, that is, outside of Holy Scripture. Anselm's method is that which Barth now adopts in the writing of the *Church Dogmatics*. He believes that it avoids the errors of both the Neo-Protestants and the orthodox biblical "positivists." One escapes the error of the former by insisting that theological reflection be exclusively on the *Credo* of the Church. The "positivist" error is the belief that the reading and hearing of the written text of Scripture, when assisted by faith, absolves the believer of the task of understanding its meaning and its truth *by human means*. For Barth, as for Anselm, the task of theology is a human reflection on what is given in the written text of Scripture, but only by virtue of a special grace. For Barth, theology can remain neither an unreflective recital of the biblical text nor a purely historical-critical exegesis of the Bible. Theology must proceed to reflect on the relation between the biblical text and the meaning and truth of the object to which the text points and witnesses. True interpretation thus exists only where the perception of the literal text of Scripture and the understanding of its meaning are one. Furthermore, such an understanding remains dependent upon divine grace, whereby human reason is given the capacity to stand under and be mastered by the Word of God (emphasis original).[16]

What this then means for Barth is that "dogmatics is to be understood *as a science of the Church*,[17] and therefore, that it is committed to submitting only to that which is valid for its object. For Christianity, that object is the Word of God as revealed in Holy Scripture (emphasis original)."[18] The

---

15. Livingston, *Modern Christian Thought: Volume II*, 98.

16. Ibid., 98–99.

17. It is important to note that this is not the only interpretation of Anselm: "Not surprisingly, Anselm has been interpreted in two strikingly different ways by modern interpreters. The philosopher Étienne Gilson has characterized Anselm as an arch-rationalist who tried to prove the doctrines of the Incarnation and the Trinity from reason alone. The Reformed theologian Karl Barth, meanwhile, has tried to show that, for Anselm, reason always moves within a circle of faith and not outside it. . . . [B]oth of these readings are perhaps oversimplifications." Allen, *Theological Method*, 97.

18. Livingston, *Modern Christian Thought: Volume II*, 104. Stated in another way by Dr. Castelein, "'theology within the bounds of the Confession only'—versus Kant's

doctrine of predestination is also intertwined with his theological method, because for Barth, theological thinking must express the doctrine of predestination, which encapsulates the whole of the revelational approach—what man "achieves" in relation to God is due to God. In connection to this, Livingston notes that "Barth holds that revelation is a relational concept, and thus God does not, so to say, reveal himself independently of the human apprehension of his self-manifestation. *Consequently, the knowledge of God is itself given by God through grace.* Thus, the *analogia entis* [the analogy of being] is replaced by the *analogia fidei* (the analogy of faith); faith gives us understanding of the nature of God and is God-given. Thus, *God is the cause of true theological assertions, as well as their ground* (emphasis mine)."

Overall, to "rescue" theology from Protestant Liberalism, Barth rejects any grounding of theology in nature and opts for a passive reception of God's word,[19] a form of fideism.

Paul Tillich (Correlation Theology)

In complete contrast and response to Karl Barth, Paul Tillich developed a theological method that was genuinely correlative. In 1950, the first volume of his systematic theology was published,[20] which explicates this theological method. Livingston explains that for Tillich, "Theology follows . . . the 'method of correlation,' which seeks to explain the contents of faith through existential questions and theological answers in mutual interdependence. The Christian theologian thus proceeds by making an analysis of the situation out of which the human existential questions arise and then seeks to demonstrate that the symbols used in the Christian message are the answers to these questions."[21] This method of correlation is, as Livingston indicates, "In opposition to Karl Barth," because "Tillich is emphatic that a Christian theology must be genuinely correlative"[22] and not simply a passive and revelational approach, meaning that theological method must begin with anthropology, not revelation. The existential human situation *first* proposes questions that are then answered by theology, not in the reverse sequence.

This method of correlation is not simply a philosophy, but must begin with philosophy and end with theology because, as Livingston writes concerning Tillich, "The 'answers' to our existential situation cannot . . . be

---

book *Religion within the Bounds of Reason Alone."*

19. Livingston, *Modern Christian Thought: Volume II*, 110.
20. Tillich, *Systematic Theology*, Vol. 1.
21. Livingston, *Modern Christian Thought: Volume II*, 143.
22. Ibid.

simply deduced from the 'questions' that emerge from that situation. The answers are provided by the Christian message."[23] It is this existential dimension of theology that distinguishes it from philosophy and the stance of the philosopher of religion. Therefore, first and foremost, "Theology is existential and never strictly scientific."[24] The task of theological method includes an anthropological, existential foundation. In summarizing this point for the method of correlation, Tillich writes that for contrast, "In every assumedly scientific theology there is a point where individual experience, traditional valuation, and personal commitment must decide the issue."[25]

The method of correlation is grounded in an existential philosophy, yet this theology differs from philosophy because, as Livingston writes, "The theologian ... approaches being existentially and is concerned with the meaning of being for us. Therefore, the theologian "must look where that which concerns him ultimately is manifest ... that is, the logos manifesting itself in a particular historical event" or events. Unlike the philosopher, the theologian stands within a tradition, a community of faith or theological article whose symbols express a soteriological answer to our existential questions." Philosophy in itself cannot provide the answers to the questions it can propose concerning human existence, but in correspondence to these questions, Tillich writes that "The Christian message provides the answers to the questions implied in human existence. These answers are contained in the revelatory events on which Christianity is based. . . . *In respect to content the Christian answers are dependent on the revelatory events in which they appear; in respect to form they are dependent on the structure of the questions which they answer.*"[26] The key insight is that revelation is not simply given, but is given in response to particular questions and situations, and in particular forms, that it may be received as the receptor receives, or is signified so that the sign may be understood. The point being made here is that revelation is not ahistorical. In commenting on this aspect of Tillich's method, Livingston writes that "Tillich rightly holds that revelation is spoken to us and not by us to ourselves. But he is also correct in asserting that we cannot receive answers to questions we never ask. The Christian answers must therefore be couched in a form that speaks to the contemporary situation. In the twentieth century, Tillich affirms, that form is what we call existential."

Therefore, in contrast to Barth, Tillich takes seriously the historical and human/cognitional side of theology, attempting to answer what

---

23. Ibid.
24. Ibid.
25. Tillich, *Systematic Theology*, Vol. 1, 8.
26. Ibid., 64. Emphasis added.

humans are doing when they are "doing theology" within the structure of an existential philosophy contemporary to his own time. Thus, a major debate in twentieth-century theological method was brought forward in the figures of Barth and Tillich. Livingston writes that "Tillich has generated an important debate over theological method that harks back to his break with Karl Barth. Many contemporary theologians have pursued one or another form of Tillich's method of correlation as the only responsible way of addressing the religious questions of our largely secular culture. Other theologians believe, however, that such 'theologians of correlation' inevitably distort the content of the Christian method, because the theological 'answers' that such theologians offer are substantially shaped by the 'questions' posed by the secular culture itself."[27] It is this issue concerning method that continued to occupy center stage in the theological debates of the latter decades of the twentieth century,[28] the time period which this paper now turns to.

Hans Frei (Postliberalism)

In the 1970s and 80s, a school of theology named Postliberalism came to the forefront of theological method as an alternative to the method of correlation in Catholic and Protestant theologies. This movement to return to Karl Barth began with the publication of Hans Wilhelm Frei's *The Eclipse of Biblical Narrative: A Study in Eighteenth and Nineteenth Century Hermeneutics;*[29] his full critique of the method of correlation would come in his posthumously published Edward Cadbury lectures that he gave in Birmingham, England, entitled *Types of Christian Theology.*[30] In Postliberalism's negative and deconstructive stance, Livingston writes that, "following the lead of Karl Barth—and with the help of some postmodernist writers—the Postliberal theologians . . . *refuse to begin by correlating Christian theology with modern philosophy and science, or with the "religious dimension" of our contemporary situation, in the manner of Paul Tillich or Karl Rahner."*[31] Generally, "Post-liberals . . . oppose modern apologetic schemes that are based on appeals to some *common ground of religious experience* [phenomenology], such as one finds in both Transcendental Thomism and in many forms of Protestant

---

27. Livingston, *Modern Christian Thought: Volume II*, 153.

28. Tillich, *Systematic Theology*, Vol. 1.

29. Frei, *The Eclipse of Biblical Narrative: A Study in Eighteenth and Nineteenth Century Hermeneutics.*

30. Frei, *Types of Christian Theology.*

31. Livingston, *Modern Christian Thought: Volume II*, 526. Emphasis added.

Liberalism."[32] So then, constructively and positively, "For the Postliberal," Livingston continues, "theology is a discipline of *Christian* self-description and re-description, within the community, the Church. So governed, Christian theology is able to use philosophy in *a subordinate and improvised way* depending on the specific context."[33]

Hans Frei attempted to retrieve Karl Barth[34] in the face of those contemporary theologies of correlation between the particularities of Christian faith and wider human experience. This took place in the context of hermeneutical theories that were seeking to counteract the emphasis on the proclamation of kerygmatic theology (Neo-Orthodoxy) and to take account of a wider, more universal context of human experience. In contrast to critiques and theologians such as Pannenberg and others concerned with an anthropological grounding, Frei critiqued the method of correlation and called for a return to Barth's methodology, which had been critiqued as a form of fideism by the hermeneutical theologians; Barth's methodology needed to be re-appropriated in a new context. Therefore, prior to commenting on Hans Frei, several continual criticisms of Barth that were proposed to escape a "Barthian fideism" will be noted.

Fiorenza places Frei in his context of theological methodology, writing that

> Frei argues against the theological use of the method of correlation and the grounding of Christian faith in a *general anthropology or concept of human nature.* To the extent that the theological positions of Pannenberg and Tracy and the hermeneutical theories of Gadamer and Ricoeur can be viewed as efforts *to go beyond or criticize Neo-Orthodox theology*, Frei's constructive view of hermeneutics and theology can be seen as an effort *to retrieve and to reformulate Karl Barth's theology* (emphasis added).[35]

Frei has many more targets for critique, including "Gordon Kaufman's constructive theology and David Tracy's revisionist theology, both of which are unacceptable to Frei because both allegedly *subject Christian self-description to philosophical foundations and to external descriptions*

---

32. Ibid., 519. Emphasis added.

33. Ibid., 526. Emphasis added. This is in opposition to Schleiermacher's phenomenological attempt to root the faith in deep and broad common human experience.

34. Frei's interest in Barth is especially noted by his doctoral studies under H. Richard Niebuhr, by which his dissertation at Yale Divinity School is titled "The Doctrine of Revelation in the Thought of Karl Barth, 1909–1922: The Nature of Barth's Break with Liberalism."

35. Fiorenza, "History and Hermeneutics," 373.

(emphasis mine);"[36] an "*Anthropological grounding of theology* in the transcendental Thomism of Karl Rhaner and Bernard Lonergan, and Wolfhart Pennenberg's attempt to go beyond what he considers to be *the fideism of Neo-Orthodoxy* (emphasis added)."[37]

Pannenberg and Tracy are especially interesting as contemporaries of Frei. Pannenberg, a student of Barth, criticized Barth's method, which, as Fiorenza notes, "had criticized "the point of connection" of the Liberal theology of the preceding generation of theologians. Wolfhart Pannenberg, reacting to Karl Barth's position as *a form of fideism*, argues for an anthropological grounding of the Christian kerygma."[38] In fact, Fiorenza notes, "Pannenberg's whole work can be conceived as an attempt to provide a foundational and systematic theology that grounds the Christian kerygma *in anthropology and in history*."[39] This is in opposition to his criticism of Neo-Orthodoxy's separation of faith and reason.[40] David Tracy, a student of Bernard Lonergan's transcendental philosophy of interiority and consciousness, moves toward the analogical character of the imagination and the conversation required by cultural pluralism. Hans Frei stakes out a position *against* what he perceives as *the grounding of meaning and religion in a general transcendental anthropology*.[41]

Essentially, Frei is concerned that the external description of Christianity not become the criterion of the internal self-description, or become the basic standard of theological understanding. Overall, "Frei is opposed to a method of correlation that seeks to ground the Christian faith in general anthropology. Such a procedure, Frei argues, undermines *the autonomy of God's Word* and often adopts *an external description of Christianity* as normative for its own self-description."[42]

Positively, Hans Frei's "constructive work can be seen as an interpretive and theological alternative . . . [that] centers on the importance of narrative for biblical interpretation and on the understanding of theology as redescription or as 'thick' description *rooted in the biblical narratives* (emphasis added)."

"In describing theology's function," Fiorenza writes, "Frei notes that theology involves first- and second-level statements. First level statements

36. Ibid.
37. Ibid.
38. Ibid., 377. Emphasis added.
39. Ibid. Emphasis added.
40. Ibid., 342.
41. Ibid., 377.
42. Ibid. Emphasis added.

are the communal beliefs that are found in the creeds and confessions. Although they are the basic Christian beliefs and practices, they should not be thought of as constituting the essence of Christianity. In addition, theology has second-level statements and these in turn have two aspects."[43] Quoting Frei, these are that "theology is a given Christian community's second-level appraisal of its own language and actions under a norm internal to the community itself. This appraisal in turn has two aspects. The first is descriptive: an endeavor to articulate the 'grammar' or 'internal logic,' of first-level Christian statements. The second is critical: an endeavor to judge any given articulation of Christian language for its success or failure in adhering to the acknowledged norm(s) of Christian language use."[44]

"Thick description," Fiorenza writes, is a description that "describes a society's beliefs and practices in a way that show the logic of its identity."[45] This then "leaves room for philosophical categories, but does not allow them to subvert the ascriptive identity descriptions ... " and "It neither makes one's own internal self-description wholly dependent upon an internal self-description nor does it avoid all reference to external description."[46] This balance allows Frei to place first the affirmation of the kerygma and keep an emphasis upon the autonomy of the kerygma in relation to any historical and anthropological foundation; philosophy is kept in check and controlled by revelation.

RADICAL ORTHODOXY'S CRITIQUE OF TWENTIETH-CENTURY THEOLOGY

Radical Orthodoxy began as a High Anglican "movement" in theology at Cambridge in the 1990s. It was birthed by a membership of three profound thinkers: John Milbank, Graham Ward, and Catherine Pickstock. Radical Orthodoxy, as a "movement," has existed for a mere fifteen or so years, yet has had a significant impact on contemporary theology. The movement gained wide recognition with the publication of the collection of essays in 1999, *Radical Orthodoxy: A New Theology*, which also included authors from the Roman Catholic church tradition. At its core, Radical Orthodoxy is a critique of the ontology they propose modern day thought is built upon. Included in this denunciation of a dualistic metaphysics is Radical Orthodoxy's critique of twentieth-century theology, especially in response

43. Ibid., 374.
44. Frei, *Types of Christian Theology*, 124.
45. Fiorenza, "History and Hermeneutics," 375.
46. Ibid.

to Neo-Orthodoxy and correlation theological methodologies, while taking *nouvelle théologie* as their exemplar model.

John Milbank sets out the methodological problem at the beginning of the twenty-first century, writing that

> Much of twentieth-century theology showed a bias toward one pole or the other [nature or grace]. A stress on the primacy of nature, the universal, and a neutral philosophy characterized the world of "correlationist" theologies. . . . Yet conversely, over-fideistic theologies, tending to see theology as having its own special, positive domain of concern with belief and salvation, appear now to leave the Christian with too little guidance in other domains and to hand these over to secular authority. . . . In [the modern] situation the thinking Christian requires a response that is not simply pure (supposed) Biblicist condemnation on the one hand nor flaccid accommodation on the other.[47]

Radical Orthodoxy's critique cuts both ways, neither taking sides with Neo-Orthodoxy/ Postliberalism or correlation theology.

Backing these proposals is Radical Orthodoxy's narrative of a genealogy of a participatory metaphysics (neo-platonic) that needs to be retrieved so that the modern dualisms in theology (grace/nature, revelation/reason, etc.) that are based in ontology that bred the secular, and thus the methodologies of twentieth-century theology, may be overcome. Roughly, in their interpretation of the teaching of Augustine (a so-called postmodern Augustinianism) and a neo-platonic Aquinas who hold to a realist metaphysic, there exists a connection between God and the world. At the same time, there is a strong distinction between Creator and creature; yet, the Creator "suspends" the created, essentially transcendence giving meaning to immanence. God is *esse* (being) and creatures are not; hence, creatures exist by participating in God; creatures do not have their own existence, but are created *ex nihilo*. The *analogia entis* (analogy of being) allows creation to know analogously and participate in the divine. With this realist metaphysics, there does not exist a duality or separation of grace/nature, theology/philosophy, or revelation/reason. All knowledge, then, is by illumination; in a Christian sense, participation in the divine mind.

Yet, this vision of God and the world did not remain. The "turn to the secular" was solidified when Duns Scotus developed a cogent nominalistic metaphysics with the univocity of being. This "flattened" ontology, hence everything, to immanence by making God and creatures to be of the same being (univocal). This eliminated transcendence; the link between God and

47. Milbank, "Foreword" 12.

the world when the analogy of being was lost and brought about a neutral, or secular, space for everything. Humans, then, cannot know what God is like: he is arbitrary. Grace, revelation, etc., are seen as something extrinsic, added to, or "stacked onto" the natural. Humans are then given a goal, *telos,* that was natural, being apart from God. With this nominalistic metaphysics, there was created a duality or separation of grace/nature, theology/philosophy, revelation/reason. As a result, God became understood as first will/ power/sovereign to control this chaos. This shift to a univocity of being, therefore, provided the space needed that was taken advantage of for the secular, which lead to the hyper-modernism (so-called postmodernism) of today. This is the metaphysics that created modernism and which much of twentieth-century theology has been built upon, leading to a separation between grace and nature along with revelation and reason.[48]

So then, Radical Orthodoxy, according to James Smith, "undercuts much of the project of twentieth-century theology and Christian cultural engagement—particularly in its correlationist modes . . ."[49] He continues, writing that, "this is because theology and the church have been insufficiently radical in these engagements—they have not penetrated to the roots on matters of either theoretical frameworks or perspectival commitments. According to Milbank, this is because Christian theology and practice have accepted the dogma of the autonomy of theoretical thought—and the autonomy of philosophy in particular." "Modern theology on the whole," Milbank observes, "accepts that philosophy has its own legitimacy, its own autonomy apart from faith."[50] The problem with correlation theologians, then, Smith writes, is that they

> assume the neutrality of other sciences (whether philosophy, sociology, economics, or, increasingly, the natural sciences), receive the objective findings of such neutral sciences, and then seek to correlate the claims of Christian confession with these facts—thus furnishing, indirectly, an apologetic demonstration of the truth of Christian revelation. In particular, the broad shape of what it means to know, or questions of being, are determined by the neutral discourse of philosophy and metaphysics; Christian theology then builds on these neutral or natural

48. This is a condensed summary/interpretation. For a more detailed narrative, see: Cunningham, *Genealogy of Nihilism* ; Smith *Introducing Radical Orthodoxy*; Pickstock, *After Writing*; Milbank, *Theology and Social Theory.*

49. Smith, *Introducing Radical Orthodoxy,*149.

50. Milbank, "Knowledge," 21.

axioms and offers a theological supplement of what it means to know Christ, or what it means to say that God "is."[51]

Here is the key point, for Smith: "Correlation theology retains a dualism between reason and revelation: Reason, the domain of the sciences, is conceded as an autonomous sphere that revelation either supplements or overwhelms. In either case, the autonomy of theoretical thought goes unchallenged,"[52] and "by retaining the wall of dualism between reason and revelation, theology in its Barthian mode cannot call into question the assumptions of the 'secular' sciences, and theology itself remains demarcated by the shape of secular science."[53] In critique of the Postliberals, who fall into the Barthian mode, Milbank writes that "There is no such thing as a 'pure first order discourse,' as the Yale school's somewhat barbaric deployment of Wittgenstein would have us suppose. Conversely, the 'second order discourse' of the theologian is no tidily circumscribed exercise . . . but rather more consciously elaborates the existential and the perplexity of belief as such."[54]

Therefore, in a sweeping critique of twentieth-century theology, Smith, summing up the point by Radical Orthodoxy, writes that "Christian theological discourse . . . has uncritically appropriated theoretical frameworks and philosophical categories that, in fact, are funded by commitments that are deeply antithetical to Christian confession and revelation . . . [because] Twentieth-century theology . . . was colonized by the 'liberal' correlationist paradigm."[55]

In the recently published *The Radical Orthodoxy Reader*, John Milbank has provided the newest and most concise summary of the relationship between Radical Orthodoxy and twentieth-century theology, specifically in critique of a Roman Catholic grace/nature dualism and a Protestant influence of this same framework stemming from Karl Barth.[56] From a survey of twentieth-century theology, Milbank explains Radical Orthodoxy's fondness for *nouvelle théologie* and the methodological reasons behind this choice, writing that "Initially, Radical Orthodoxy took the view that what was to be salvaged from twentieth-century theology was mainly the contribution of the *nouvelle théologie* and above all the work of Henri de Lubac. The *ressourcement* carried out by this school has an initial priority, because

51. Smith, *Introducing Radical Orthodoxy*, 149.
52. Ibid., 150.
53. Milbank, "Knowledge," 33.
54. Milbank, foreword to *Introducing Radical Orthodoxy*, 14.
55. Smith, *Introducing Radical Orthodoxy*, 149.
56. Milbank, "Afterword," 367–404.

most modern theology since the seventeenth century has been captive to a false grace/nature, faith/reason dualism that is itself partially responsible for ushering in secularization. The resulting extrinsicism assumes that first one must prove God by reason, then show that revelation is possible *de jure* and finally provide 'sound reasons' . . . for revelation *de facto*."[57] Here, Milbank explains Radical Orthodoxy's claims to a false dualism that modern theology "has been captive" to. This extrincisim, which Karl Barth attempted to remedy in his rejection of liberal Protestantism, leads to Milbank's critique of Barth:[58]

> The Barthian influence on knowing God from revelation alone did not escape a hidden negative determination of what revelation must mean by the seemingly abandoned extrinsicist framework. A double sense that revelation involves something "positive" in contrast to the deliverancies of reason and yet that it discloses knowledge beyond the scope of reason was not entirely expunged. . . . [T]his took the form of the notion of "self-revelation." Here the at-once positive and cognitive content is thoroughly subjectivised: God shows only himself and his showing of himself is himself[;] . . . no longer does God communicate to us "information" and no longer do we accept this communication because it is *a priori* plausible.[59]

Barth's focus on "knowing God from revelation alone" did not escape his own dualistic foundations due to his link to Immanuel Kant, for Milbank narrates that "there is a post-Kantian nuance in the Barthian notion that throws everything askew . . . " and that "Kant's thought is itself one ultimate outcome of the late medieval separation between reason and faith: 'pure reason' can know only its own limits, only its own subjective capacity, only the way in which being 'appears' to it."[60] Milbank levels the charge against Barth that he is Hegelian, "in accordance with his post-Kantian perspective,"[61] due to the fact that "the Hegelian paradigm places something cognitive first, still in keeping with modern extrincisim."[62] Furthermore, Milbank writes that "Hence, even though, for Barth, revelation must include our acknowledgement of revelation and indeed is only possible through the full acknowledgement made by the God-man, he tended to confine this to recognition

57. Ibid., 369.
58. For an earlier critique of Barth by Milbank, see Milbank, "Knowledge," 33.
59. Milbank, *Afterword*, 368.
60. Ibid.
61. Ibid., 369.
62. Ibid.

of a hyper-cognitive disclosure, absolutely (and apocalyptically) relativising his own self-understanding . . . "[63] Hence, in Barth's quest to eliminate any foundations of theological method that include anthropology, or anything other than divine revelation, he is giving into a dualism of nature/grace, reason/revelation. According to Milbank, this is the case because

> Paradoxically then, it might seem, the playing down of human mediation and exaltation of human passivity reduces the revelation event to the scope of categories of reason, whilst inversely the insistence that the human response is strangely there "with" what it is responding to, permits us to see revelation as an "excess" emergent through human action and so exceeding any human rational gap—even of a formally negative kind. In relation to finite causes, response coincides with prompting; it is the very mark of the strange absolute remoteness of divine revelation that here active response is co-original with passive being-prompted, because the latter entirely overwhelms the former.[64]

Barth also failed, Milbank writes, and I think this is his key point, "to embrace the traditional structure of analogy and participation which over-arched the reason-faith divide and so disallowed either pure rational foundations for faith . . . " and he embraced "a fideism which he perpetuated."[65] This is all important for methodology in Protestant and Catholic theology for Milbank, because by his interpretation "Much of twentieth-century Catholic thought remains a hybrid between persistences of the older extrinsicism and an importation of Barth."[66] In the end, Milbank writes, "[Barth] remained essentially the prisoner of German idealism,"[67] and therefore, so did much of twentieth-century theology. Barth did not escape correlation as he thought he had. There is then no place for Protestants to turn to for theological models but for the *nouvelle théologie* model.

In summary of Milbank's critique, "Radical Orthodoxy and Twentieth-Century Theology," he writes that "the point here . . . is . . . there is a resulting loss of a true participatory vision and a concomitant rise in fideism and extrinsicism."[68] This is exactly what Radical Orthodoxy tries to replace with a participatory metaphysics to overcome dualistic methodologies in twentieth-century theology.

63. Ibid.
64. Ibid., 369–70.
65. Ibid., 370.
66. Ibid.
67. Ibid., 372.
68. Milbank, *Afterword*, 373.

CRITIQUE AND RECOMMENDATIONS

Livingston and Fiorenza have done an admirable job of initially putting Barth, Tillich, and Frei in conversation concerning their methodologies and alerting one to the importance of theological method. Though, this has left contemporary theologians with a problem: what methodology, if any, should be followed, or how should they be synthesized? Methodology rooted in Neo-Orthodoxy proposes that religion mediates philosophy and methods of correlation seemingly have philosophy mediating religion.[69] Radical Orthodoxy has proposed one possible way forward; to rethink the foundations of twentieth-century theology. John Milbank labels Radical Orthodoxy as an "always . . . uneasy and possibly aporetic synthesis . . . between theology and philosophy (understood as the coordination of all merely natural enquiries)."[70] This is because, for Milbank, "Our knowledge of things of this world can always be qualified by knowledge of God as he is in himself (given by revelation), but equally, our knowledge of God, since it is analogically mediated, is *always and only* given through a shift in our understanding of the things of this world (emphasis original)."[71] Radical Orthodoxy has taken the seemingly incommensurable views of two branches of theological method in the twentieth century and tries to find a synthesis between them based in a "natural desire for the supernatural." By Radical Orthodoxy's interpretation, the split between nature and grace causes the debates with these methodologies and is the beginning point of the problem. To give into modern enlightenment categories of ontology and epistemology is to give into a science that was defined apart from God, in their opinion. This attention to methodological foundations is long overdue, but I believe it is insufficient in overcoming the root of the methodologies they critique.

Radical Orthodoxy begins with a series of three questions while critiquing the secular: What is the politics? What is the epistemology? What is the metaphysics?[72] Taking a cue from Bernard Lonergan in *Method in Theology*, I believe that what he writes should, instead, be heeded: "Transcendental method is not the intrusion into theology of an alien matter from an

69. See Lonergan's five models of integration, as explained by David Tracy in Tracy, *The Achievement of Bernard Lonergan*, 17–19.

70. Milbank, "Foreword," 13.

71. Ibid.

72. Smith, *Introducing Radical Orthodoxy*, 99–100 fn. 42: "Behind the *politics* of modernity (liberal, secular) is an *epistemology* (autonomous reason), which is in turn undergirded by an *ontology* (univocity and the denial of participation)." "The same is true of the alternative that RO envisions: behind the *politics* (socialism) lies an *epistemology* (illumination), which is in turn undergirded by an *ontology* (participation) (ibid., 100).

alien source. Its function is to advert to the fact that theologies are produced by theologians, that theologians have minds and use them, that their doing so should not be ignored or passed over but explicitly acknowledged in itself and its implications."[73] This approach should lead to Lonergan's three questions: "What am I doing when I am knowing? Why is doing that knowledge? What do I know when I do it?"[74] This reverses the structure of critique by Radical Orthodoxy, the answers to Lonergan's questions consisting of first, a cognitional theory, second, an epistemology, and third, a metaphysics. At the root is a cognitional theory, as opposed to Radical Orthodoxy's ontology. This should bring further attention to what it is, in fact, that theologians are doing when they are "doing theology."

Lonergan forces the theologian to pay attention to the operations of their own mind and not break them into grace and nature dualities. Intense studies in foundational studies and what leads up to them are needed instead of trying to bypass them. In Lonergan's eight functional specialties, "foundations" (what Radical Orthodoxy considers ontology) comes fifth in order of procedure. The point being is that the cognitional theory behind Scotus' ontology led to the univocity of being; Radical Orthodoxy may not have asked the correct question. Also, instead of rejecting all of the secular sciences *tout court*, as Radical Orthodoxy does, one should seek to identify the causes of decline in those systems and seek to correct them.[75] I believe this complete rejection is due to what Lonergan terms a classical paradigm of culture, whereas a pluralist paradigm would be helpful at this juncture, which Lonergan advocates.[76] Allen summarizes Lonergan's contrast, stating, "Whereas classicist views of culture assume a normative meaning for shared values and formulations of revelation, a modern view of culture sees the control of meaning as a process, containing the distinction between core meanings and changeable formulations."[77]

Radical Orthodoxy is on the right track; Duns Scotus should be critiqued, since modern genealogies have proven that he is a pivotal character is the history of ontology.[78] But, to get to the issue, his cognitional theory needs to be studied.[79] The same holds for the other theologians in this paper

73. Lonergan, *Method in Theology*, 24–25.

74. Ibid., 25.

75. Lonergan, *Insight*.

76. Lonergan, Method in Theology, xi; *A Second Collection*. See various chapters in *A Second Collection*.

77. Allen, *Theological Method*, 224.

78. Multiple treatments include one by Gillespie, *The Theological Origins of Modernity*.

79. Initial work has been completed by Peters, "Scotus: An Initial Lonerganian

and studies in cognitional theory should follow for Barth, Tillich, and Frei. Behind their theological methods are cognitional theories, or a lack thereof, that grounds their methodologies; the point here is that Barth and others try to completely bypasses a cognitional theory, while Tillich may have an insufficient epistemology.

It must be noted that Radical Orthodoxy is not completely an illuminationist movement in its epistemology, but has different approaches. Milbank and Pickstock's interpretation of Aquinas is highly contested. They make Aquinas into a wholesale illuminationist.[80] On the issue of perception, of evidentialism versus illumination in Radical Orthodoxy, where one begins depends on if one takes Augustine or Aquinas as one's exemplar model for epistemology. Illumination is marked in the introduction to *Radical Orthodoxy: A New Theology*[81] and the movement has been known as postmodern critical Augustinianism under Milbank.[82] Milbank has criticized phenomenology in general, yet this is not a uniform critique in Radical Orthodoxy. Those giving positive attention to perception and phenomenology that align themselves with Radical Orthodoxy include Phillip Blond,[83] Graham Ward,[84] and James K. A. Smith.[85]

Behind the ontological critique, at its core, Radical Orthodoxy's methodology is built upon a "radicalization," as Millbank admits, of de Lubac's work on grace; yet Milbank's interpretation of de Lubac[86] is just that, an interpretation, and it has not gone uncontested. This stance must be further studied and questioned. Other interpretations of this issue include Lonergan's work on Aquinas and response to de Lubac on the issue of the supernatural, in the article "The Natural Desire to See God,"[87] and a synthesis of his early grace theology and interaction with de Lubac.[88]

In conclusion, examining the methodologies, interpretations, and critiques of twentieth-century theology has been highly beneficial. These

---

Treatment," http://www.loneranresource.com/pdf/articles/Peters%2c%20Scotus%20-%20An%20Initial%20Lonerganian%20Treatment.pdf [accessed April 17, 2012].

80. Milbank and Pickstock, *Truth in Aquinas.*

81. Milbank et al., *Radical Orthodoxy*, 2

82. Milbank, "Postmodern Critical Augustinianism," 225–37.

83. Blond, "Introduction," 1–66; "Perception," in *Radical Orthodoxy*, 220–42; "The Primacy of Theology and the Question of Perception," 285–313; "Theology and Perception," 523–34.

84. Ward, "The Beauty of God," 35–65; Ward, "The Schizoid Christ," 228–56.

85. Smith, *Speech and Theology.*

86. Milbank, *The Suspended Middle.*

87. Lonergan, "The Natural Desire to See God," 81–91.

88. Stebbins, *The Divine Initiative.*

conflicts may be calling out for a higher synthesis or another method for theology. Paul Allen, a Lonerganain who teaches theological method, has identified five fundamental questions at issue in theological method through the course of the history of Christian theology that are well worth pondering today:

1. The role of philosophy and related epistemological and metaphysical presuppositions in theology

2. The coherence of individual criteria that serve as theological starting points (e.g., Barth's Word of God)

3. How one emphasizes various sources of theology such as the Bible

4. The nature of the theological task (e.g., Tillich's conception of critical correlation with other disciplines)

5. Procedure (e.g., Lonergan's functional specialties).[89]

These issues require examining one's own foundations and methods when studying and performing the ever changing science known as Christian theology.

---

89. Allen, *Theological Method*, 208.

BIBLIOGRAPHY

Allen, Paul L. *Theological Method: A Guide for the Perplexed*. London: T. & T. Clark, 2012.

Barth, Karl. *Church Dogmatics*. Peabody, MA: Henderickson, 2010.

Blond, Philip. "Introduction." In *Post-Secular Philosophy: Between Philosophy and Theology*, 1–66. London: Routledge, 1998.

———. "Perception: From Modern Painting to the Vision of Christ." In *Radical Orthodoxy: A New Theology*, edited by John Milbank et al., 220–42. London: Routledge, 1999.

———. "The Primacy of Theology and the Question of Perception." In *Religion, Modernity, and Postmodernity*, 285–313. Oxford: Blackwell, 1998.

———. "Theology and Perception." *Modern Theology* 14 (1998) 523–34.

Cunningham, Connor. *Genealogy of Nihilism*. London: Routledge, 2002.

Frei, Hans. *The Eclipse of Biblical Narrative: A Study in Eighteenth and Nineteenth Century Hermeneutics*. New Haven, CT: Yale University Press, 1980.

———. *Types of Christian Theology*. Edited by George Hunsinger and William C. Placher. New Haven, CT: Yale University Press, 1994.

Gillespie, Michael Allen. *The Theological Origins of Modernity*. Chicago: The University of Chicago Press, 2008.

Livingston, James C., et al. *Modern Christian Thought: Volume II—The Twentieth Century*. 2nd ed. Upper Saddle River, NJ: Prentice Hall, 2000.

Lonergan, Bernard. *Insight: A Study of Human Understanding*. Collected Works of Bernard Lonergan 3. Edited by R. Doran and F. Crowe. Toronto: University of Toronto, 1992.

———. *Method in Theology*. New York: Seabury, 1972.

———. "The Natural Desire to See God." In *Collection*, Vol. 4 of *The Collected Works of Bernard Lonergan*, 81–91. Toronto: University of Toronto Press, 1988.

———. *A Second Collection*. Collected Works of Bernard Lonergan 13. Toronto: University of Toronto Press, 1996.

Milbank, John. "Afterword: The Grandeur of Reason and the Perversity of Rationalism: Radical Orthodoxy's First Decade." In *The Radical Orthodoxy Reader*, edited by Simon Oliver and John Milbank 367–404. London: Routledge, 2009.

———. Foreword to *Introducing Radical Orthodoxy: Mapping a Post-Secular Theology* by James K. A. Smith. Grand Rapids: Baker Academic, 2004.

———. "Knowledge: The Theological Critique of Philosophy in Hamann and Jacobi." In *Radical Orthodoxy: A New Theology*, edited by John Milbank et al., 21–37. London: Routledge, 1999.

———. "'Postmodern Critical Augustinianism': A Short *Summa* In Forty Two Responses To Unasked Questions." *Modern Theology* 7.3 (1991) 225–37.

———. *The Suspended Middle: Henri de Lubac and the Debate concerning the Supernatural*. Grand Rapids: Eerdmans, 2005.

———. *Theology and Social Theory: Beyond Secular Reason*. Oxford: Blackwell, 1990.

Milbank, John and Catherine Pickstock. *Truth in Aquinas*. London: Routledge, 2001.

Milbank, John and Catherine Pickstock, and Graham Ward, editors. *Radical Orthodoxy: A New Theology*. London: Routledge, 1999.

Peters, Matthew. "Scotus: An Initial Lonerganian Treatment," No pages. http://www.loneranresource.com/pdf/articles/Peters%2c%20Scotus%20-%20An%20Initial%20Lonerganian%20Treatment.pdf

Pickstock, Catherine. *After Writing: On the Liturgical Consummation of Philosophy.* Oxford: Blackwell, 1998.

Smith, James K. A. *Introducing Radical Orthodoxy: Mapping a Post-Secular Theology.* Grand Rapids: Baker Academic, 2004.

———. *Speech and Theology: Language and the Logic of Incarnation.* London: Routledge, 2002.

Stebbins, J. Michael. *The Divine Initiative: Grace, World-Order, and Human Freedom in the Early Writings of Bernard Lonergan.* Toronto: University of Toronto Press, 1996.

Tillich, Paul. *Systematic Theology, Vol. 1.* Chicago: University of Chicago Press, 1973.

Tracy, David. *The Achievement of Bernard Lonergan.* New York: Herder and Herder, 1970.

Ward, Graham. "The Beauty of God." In *Theological Perspectives on God and Beauty*, 35–65. Harrisburgh, PA: Trinity, 2003.

———. "The Schizoid Christ." In *The Radical Orthodox Reader*, edited by Simon Oliver and John Milbank 228–56. London: Routledge, 2009.

9

Fugue and Faith

On the Found(er)ing of Reflection

CHRISTOPHER BEN SIMPSON

The Dialectic of Beginning
Scene in the Underworld . . .

> **Socrates**: With what presupposition do you begin?
>
> **Hegel**: None at all.
>
> **Socrates**: Now that is something; then you perhaps do not begin at all . . .[1]

Last Spring, my wife bought a tree that was to be the centerpiece of the backyard of our home in Illinois. It was delivered in a plastic pot. For several weeks, the tree sat in its pot beside the hole in the ground where it was to be planted. Several times, the tree, top-heavy in its small pot, was blown over in the night. We were anxious to plant it in its hole in the earth so that it could be held upright, that its roots could find purchase, that it would grow and its branches not be broken by a fall . . .

---

1. Kierkegaard, *Journals and Papers*, III:3306 [volume and entry number].

I. REFLECTION GROUNDED IN IMMEDIACY

At the bookends of modernity stand two thinkers foundational to our philosophical tradition in the West: René Descartes and Edmund Husserl. It is with what I see to be their common foundational project that I will set the scene and define what is at stake in the thoughts that follow.

René Descartes, seeking "to establish [a] firm and permanent structure in the sciences," endeavored a project "to build anew from the foundation"—to find a fixed and immovable Archimedean point as the basis for knowledge.[2] This would be achieved through a method of doubt—of "withhold[ing] assent from matters which are not entirely certain and indubitable."[3] For Descartes, this path of doubt lead to the "certain" and "definite conclusion" expressed in the proposition: "I am a thing which thinks."[4] Regarding this foundational proposition, he explains: "there is nothing that assures me of its truth, excepting the clear and distinct perception of that which I state."[5] With this statement, with the conjunction of the self's thought and being, Descartes set forth an indubitable foundation for reflection—a founding and grounding self-evident and immediate.

Edmund Husserl, in his *Cartesian Meditations*, presents his project of transcendental phenomenology as "a neo-Cartesianism."[6] Like Descartes, he sought to reform philosophy into "an all-embracing science grounded on an absolute foundation"—to found reflection on "a necessary and indubitable beginning."[7] Again following Descartes, Husserl took up a kind of absolute doubt, an "absolute poverty [or] lack of knowledge" as the "prototype" for beginning a philosophy.[8] His investigation of phenomenologically reduced consciousness lead him to the transcendental ego as the "prior" and "underlying basis" for human thinking that ultimately grounds human knowledge in a self-present immediacy.[9] On the basis of the transcendental ego, Husserl could present reflection as self-grounding, "resting on itself and justifying itself by itself."[10] Thereby, Husserl claimed to produce a "new *meditationes de prima philosophia*" that had "actual autonomy" and

2. Descartes, *Meditations*, 165, 171.

3. Ibid., 166.

4. Ibid., 171, 173, 179.

5. Ibid., 179.

6. Husserl, *Cartesian Meditations*, 1.

7. Ibid., 1, 152.

8. Ibid., 2.

9. Ibid., 27.

10. Ibid., 156.

was "absolutely self-responsible."[11] Thus, both Descartes (historically and symbolically in the middle of the seventeenth century) and Husserl (at the beginning of the twentieth) present the reflection of thought upon itself as leading to *a founding immediacy*, a final self-evident self-presence that is the a priori ground of reflection.

II. DERRIDA'S FUGUE

It is precisely this modern conception of philosophical reflection as self-founded, internally grounded on "the self-certainty of the thinking subject" and thus autonomous and utterly independent of any other discipline[12] that is called into question by Jacques Derrida. In sketching out Derrida's work on immediacy and reflection, I will focus particularly on the representation put forth in Rodolphe Gasché's, *The Tain of the Mirror* (1986).

Derrida's work is (to say the least) "a critique of the Cartesian dream of a self-foundation and [the] self-justification of philosophy."[13] For Derrida, there is, in the philosophical discourse epitomized by Descartes and Husserl, an essential naivety and blindness in that supposed fundamental philosophical concepts are in fact dependent on what they exclude.[14] Philosophy's desire for "plenitude and not lack, presence without difference" is at odds with what makes philosophy itself possible.[15]

To that which makes philosophy or, indeed, any reflection possible, Gasché, synthesizing many of Derrida's own concepts, gives the name, "infrastructures." The Derridean "infrastructures" include such "concepts" as: the "trace,"[16] *differance*,[17] the "supplement,"[18] and "iterability."[19] These infrastructures are at once the conditions of possibility *and* of impossibility

---

11. Ibid., 5, 6.

12. Gasché, *The Tain of the Mirror*, 13, 15, 17.

13. Ibid., 176.

14. Ibid., 125, 128.

15. Derrida, *Of Grammatology*, 131.

16. Or the "arche-trace"—that "the self's . . . own identity is a function of its demarcation from the Other" (Gasché, *The Tain of the Mirror*, 187, see 186–94).

17. See ibid., 194–205. *"The (pure) trace is differance"* (Derrida, *Of Grammatology*, 194).

18. The "supplement" at once adds to and takes the place of. Derrida, *Of Grammatology*, 144–45. Supplement is "another name for differance" (Ibid., 150). See Gasché, *The Tain of the Mirror*, 205–12.

19. That all thought is always already a repetition and alteration. See Gasché, *The Tain of the Mirror*, 212–17.

for reflection—they are the un/ground of reflection.[20] This is so because the infrastructures of thought "limit what they make possible by rendering its rigor and purity impossible."[21] The grounds of thought will always keep one from achieving its most lofty goal—namely, "an all-embracing science grounded on an absolute foundation" founded on "a necessary and indubitable beginning."[22]

For Derrida then, reflection *founders* when seeking to examine its necessary structure, the very conditions for its possibility. The founding immediacy that is sought is perpetually lost in the unreflective infrastructures of reflection ("the tain of the mirror").[23] The infrastructures of thought allow no phenomenological presentation of immediate presence—there appears no "*as such*."[24] As opposed to consciousness being grounded in a "living present"—reflection founded in immediacy—presence and immediacy are *products* of reflection. Derrida writes:

> We thus come to posit presence—and, in particular, consciousness, the being-next-to-itself of consciousness—no longer as the absolutely matrical form of being but as a "determination" and an "effect." Presence is a determination and effect within a system which is no longer that of presence but that of difference.[25]

For Derrida, the immediate "present" is constituted by un/grounded reflection and reflection is grounded in something other to itself that is not immediacy.[26] The infrastructures, uncover not immediacy but the loss "of self-presence, in truth the loss of what has never taken place, of a self-presence which has never been given but only dreamed of and always already split."[27] In human thinking there is "an irreducible reference to Other, anterior to an already constituted subject."[28] The infrastructures constitute an "origin" (in scare-quotes) "without a present origin, without an *archē*."[29] Derrida writes that even "the desire for the origin becomes . . . a function

---

20. Ibid., 100, 155, 161. See Derrida, *Dissemination*, 168.

21. Gasché, *The Tain of the Mirror*, 175.

22. Ibid., 1, 152.

23. Ibid., 238.

24. Ibid., 150.

25. Derrida, "Differance," 147.

26. Ibid., 142–43.

27. Derrida, *Of Grammatology*, 112. "The originary trace" is the condition of "plenitude" or immediacy (ibid., 62).

28. Gasché, *The Tain of the Mirror*, 158.

29. Derrida, "Differance," 141, 146.

situated within a syntax without origin."[30] In a reflection without immediacy, the origin emerges only "as an aftereffect"[31] to supplement the lack
of self-presence—to *construe* an immediacy and a unity.[32] Infrastructures
are at once the conditions of possibility *and* of impossibility for reflection
in that they make reflection possible but are not immediately present, therefore severely limiting reflection's claim to "rigor and purity"[33]—to being
"absolutely self-responsible."[34]

In the process of reflection, immediacy, instead of presenting itself,
flees one even as one tries to grasp it. The infrastructures of thought are
constantly withdrawing, disappearing, fleeing—not sticking around to account for themselves.[35] They are "anterior" to phenomenology; they cannot be made to present themselves of themselves.[36] In the end, digging for
immediacy in the ground of reflection is "a strategy without finality"—"an
endless calculus."[37] I depict this continual flight and bottomless reflecting
as a *"fugue"*—always chasing but never finding its founding repose in im-
mediacy/presence. Thought is grounded on "a non-fundamental" "bottomless" structure, such that, "even as it is carried away of itself by its desire,
it founders there in the waters of this its own desire, unencounterable—of
itself."[38] The endless fugue of reflection, ever seeking its certain, indubitable
founding in immediacy, ever founders—chasing dubious myths and phan-
toms in its own mirror-play.

III. KIERKEGAARD'S FAITH

Kierkegaard (like any good Hegelian) was fond of ruminating on Cartesian
meditations on first philosophy—on the project of grounding reflection in
immediacy. Near the end of the section "Something about Lessing" in the
Concluding Unscientific Postscript, Johannes Climacus gives perhaps his
clearest account of reflection and immediacy as they impinge on the foregoing "fundamental" discussion. Spinning his narrative, Climacus writes that

30. Derrida, *Of Grammatology*, 243.
31. Gasché, *The Tain of the Mirror*, 209.
32. Derrida, *Of Grammatology*, 165–66; Gasché, *The Tain of the Mirror*, 232–33.
33. Gasché, *The Tain of the Mirror*, 175.
34. Husserl, *Cartesian Meditations*, 6.
35. Gasché, *The Tain of the Mirror*, 150, 175; Derrida, "Differance," 134.
36. Gasché, *The Tain of the Mirror*, 249; Derrida, "Differance," 134.
37. Derrida, "Differance," 135.
38. Derrida, *Spurs*, 117.

"the system, so it is said, begins with the immediate."[39] So, if reflection is to get off the ground it must start with the prior ground of immediacy. But, Climacus continues, reflection does not begin with the immediate immediately. "The beginning of the system that begins with the immediate *is then itself achieved through reflection*."[40] So, now in order for reflection to get off the ground (to stand) in a properly grounded manner, reflection must *find its ground* through a kind of "retrogressive reflection"—a Cartesian doubting in order to find immediacy.[41] This, of course, doesn't make a lot of sense. Put simply, if immediacy is a *product* of reflection then reflection is not grounded in the immediate. Climacus states: "This thought in all its simplicity is capable of deciding that there can be no system of existence and that a logical system must not boast of an absolute beginning."[42] If immediacy is a product of reflection, then "the immediate never is but is annulled when it is."[43] Reflection of itself cannot ground itself in immediacy, for "reflection is immediacy's death angel."[44]

For Climacus, reflection then "cannot stop of its own accord"—it is a "spurious infinity"—a fugue.[45] Reflection does not terminate in an immediate and self-evident origin. Instead, the infinity of reflection is only stopped by *a resolution*. So, Climacus continues, "what if, rather than speaking or dreaming of an absolute beginning, we speak of a leap?"[46] But, Climacus infers, "if a resolution is required, presuppositionlessness is abandoned"— "the leap itself makes the ditch [infinitely] broad."[47] This is so because as soon as a "leap" or "decision" enters into the equation, into the building of the foundation, the project of reflection founded in immediacy becomes impossible—it founders.

Here a new element enters in—a third in excess of reflection and immediacy. Climacus states: "Every beginning, when it is *made* . . . does not occur by virtue of immanental thinking but *is made* by virtue of a resolution, essentially by virtue of faith."[48] This general structure of "faith" includes

39. Kierkegaard, *Concluding Unscientific* Postscript, 111.

40. Ibid., 112 (emphasis his); see 150n.

41. Thulstrup, "Beginning of Philosophy," 74.

42. Kierkegaard, *Concluding Unscientific Postscript*, 112.

43. Ibid. "All immediacy is anxiety." One "is most anxious about nothing" (Kierkegaard, *The Sickness Unto Death*, 25).

44. Kierkegaard, *Stages on Life's Way*, 157.

45. Kierkegaard, *Concluding Unscientific Postscript*, 112–13.

46. Ibid., 115.

47. Ibid., 113, 115.

48. Ibid., 189.

within itself the concepts of the leap, transition and decision.[49] Furthermore, this faith "in the ordinary sense"[50] is inherently risky, uncertain, devoid of foundational guarantees. Thus the end of the, of itself, necessarily endless movement of reflection—of fugue—is not a necessary and self-evident founding immediacy but a possible movement of resolution or decision or a leap—that is faith.

In connection with his conception of faith, Kierkegaard speaks of a "new immediacy"—one not *attained* through the fugue of reflection but *acquired* "after reflection."[51] Climacus writes: "When a beginning with the immediate is achieved by reflection, the immediate must mean something different than it usually does."[52] This "new immediacy" is a different kind of immediacy—one that is neither anterior to, "founding," reflection nor passively "found" *by* reflection—but is rather based on *resolution* and "reaches far beyond any reflection."[53] It is not directly immediate but is "a later immediacy" which "has reflection in between" itself and the prior, phantom immediacy.[54] Thus Kierkegaard calls faith "immediacy . . . after reflection"[55]—what we might properly name an *immediacy of affirmation*.

IV. FUGUE AND FAITH

For Descartes and Husserl, what is at stake in the project of grounding reflection in immediacy is the very possibility of true knowledge. Both Derrida and Kierkegaard observe the impossibility of this final/founding immediacy that is both the ground and the goal of reflection. Both recognize this impossibility, yet they draw very different conclusions.

For both Derrida and Kierkegaard, the foundation of thought is invisible. For Derrida what make visibility/immediacy/presence possible is itself invisible, as Gasché writes, for "that which, as the absolute ground, does not belong to the totality of what it makes possible cannot possibly offer itself

---

49. The leap is a "qualitative transition" (Kierkegaard, *Concluding Unscientific Post-script*, 12). The leap is "the category of decision" (ibid., 99). Faith is rooted in decision (ibid., 21). The leap is a transition, a movement (*kineisis*) (ibid., 342). De Silentio comments that, "no reflection can produce a movement" (Søren Kierkegaard, *Fear and Trembling*, 42).

50. Kierkegaard, *Philosophical Fragments*, 87–88.

51. Evans refers to faith as "an *acquired* immediacy" (Evans, *Kierkegaard's* Fragments *and* Postscript, 21). See also Kierkegaard, *Stages on Life's Way*, 162.

52. Kierkegaard, *Concluding Unscientific Postscript*, 113–14.

53. Kierkegaard, *Stages on Life's Way*, 163.

54. Kierkegaard, *Fear and Trembling*, 99, 82; Kierkegaard, *Stages on Life's Way*, 162.

55. Kierkegaard, *Journals and Papers*, II:1123, V:6135.

to perception."[56] Likewise, for Kierkegaard, faith is "always related to that which is not seen."[57] Derrida points to the absence, the invisibility of immediacy; Kierkegaard points to the same absence and then goes on to make an affirmation beyond this negation.

More deeply, both Derrida and Kierkegaard present paradoxical situations. Derrida's analysis "ends" in the paradox that that which is necessary for reflection (immediacy) is impossible. The founding immediacy that is sought is perpetually lost in the unreflective infrastructures of reflection. Reflection *sans* the anchor of immediacy is a bottomless and unending *fugue*. For Kierkegaard, however, faith presents another possibility in the face of this impossible necessity (and necessary impossibility) of reflection. Beyond doubt's "beginning" which takes up the fugue of chasing an ever receding immediacy/presence down the mirrored halls of reflection—beyond this, faith "hold[s] fast to possibility"—to the possibility of having a new beginning.[58] "Faith's possibility"[59] consists of rejecting the modern equating of reflection grounded in immediacy with the possibility of "truth"—it consists of holding open the possibility of true relation without certain foundations.

Kierkegaard's position implies that inasmuch as there is any affirmation about existence/actuality, faith ("leaping" beyond the necessary impossibility of reflection) is itself *necessary*. This is implicit in Kierkegaard's statements, that "all cognition requires an expression of will" and that "knowledge comes after faith."[60] Keeping with the *metaphor* of "a founding immediacy," Kierkegaard presents faith as a "new immediacy."[61] Beyond modernity's phantom unconditional and self-evident first immediacy, beyond the utter conditionality of the fugue of reflection, faith presents a second immediacy that is an affirmation in the face uncertainty, a commitment and a risk.[62] Faith's founding is the *immediacy of affirmation* and is fundamentally different than the foundered founding of doubt—whose sought immediacy is never found. Kierkegaard writes: "The method of beginning with doubt in order to philosophize seems as appropriate as having a soldier slouch in order to get him to stand erect."[63] As fallible as it may be, faith is

---

56. Gasché, *the Tain of the Mirror*, 230–31.

57. Kierkegaard, *Journals and Papers*, II:1119.

58. Ibid., II:1126, II:1136.

59. Ibid., II:1123.

60. Ibid., II:1094, II:1111.

61. Kierkegaard, *Concluding Unscientific Postscript*, 347n.

62. Kierkegaard, *Journals and Papers*, III:3715.

63. Ibid., I:775.

the only possible road to affirmation—to truth.[64] So, for faith, *that which is impossible (immediacy) is possible and this possible impossibility is necessary.* Faith affirms a new immediacy as a "non-foundational" founding for reflection "beyond reflection." Philosophy does not begin with the negative, with doubt, but with an affirmation, a "yes"—something, Kierkegaard writes, like wonder.[65]

There is a sense in which here, with Kierkegaard's thoughts on reflection and immediacy, modern philosophy comes full circle. He, like Derrida, is "postmodern" in the sense of modernity become powerfully if not radically self-critical. The postmodern exposes modern philosophy as fundamentally self-defeating—as creating its own fatal problems. Starting with doubt to find something indubitable yields only a bottomless fugue—an endless chasing and fleeing. The founding of doubt founders and is rendered dubious. This postmodern end of the modern road is prefigured even where we began—in Descartes' *Meditations*. He writes: "I shall ever follow in this road until I have met with something which is certain, or at least, if I can do nothing else, until I have learned for certain that there is nothing in the world that is certain."[66]

Modernity comes full circle insomuch as all modern philosophy that yields knowledge is actually (despite itself) founded on a "pre-modern" conception—on Augustine's "if you do not believe you will not understand"[67]—on Anselm's "I believe so that I may understand."[68] Thought emerges from an adolescence seeking independence into a more childlike maturity—into a position of fundamental dependence—for faith always rests in an-other that establishes it.[69] In the end, *De omnibus dubitandum est* rests and breaks on the foundation of *credo ut intelligam*. Doubt will only founder and only faith can found.

So I conclude as I began, imagining yet another dialogue in the underworld . . .

---

64. Ibid., III:3315.

65. Ibid., III:3284.

66. Descartes, *Meditations*, 170–71.

67. Augustine, *On Christian Doctrine*, 39.

68. Anselm of Canterbury, *Proslogion*, 87.

69. Kierkegaard, *The Sickness Unto Death*, 82, 131.

A modern philosopher states: "Philosophy as a whole is like a tree."[70]

A postmodern thinker asks: "In what soil do the roots of the tree of philosophy take hold?"[71]

A premodern prophet warns: "If you do not stand in faith, you will not stand at all."[72]

70. René Descartes, *Principles of Philosophy*, 305.

71. Heidegger, "Introduction to 'What is Metaphysics?'" 277.

72. Isa 7:9 (NRSV, slightly modified).

BIBLIOGRAPHY

Anselm of Canterbury. "Proslogion." In *The Major Works*, 87. Oxford: Oxford University Press, 1998.

Augustine. *On Christian Doctrine*. Translated by R. P. H. Green. Oxford: Oxford University Press, 1997.

Derrida, Jacques. "Differance." In *Speech and Phenomena*, translated by D. Allison, 129–60. Evanston, IL: Northwestern University Press, 1973.

———. *Dissemination*. Translated by B. Johnson. Chicago: University of Chicago Press, 1981.

———. *Of Grammatology*. Translated by G. C. Spivak. Baltimore: Johns Hopkins University Press, 1976.

———. *Spurs: Nietzsche's Styles*. Translated by B. Harlow. Chicago: University of Chicago Press, 1979.

Descartes, René. "Meditations on First Philosophy." In *The Essential Descartes*, edited by Margaret D. Wilson, 154–223. New York: Meridian, 1983.

———. "Principles of Philosophy." In *The Essential Descartes*, edited by Margaret D. Wilson, 301–52. New York: Meridian, 1983.

Evans, C. Stephen. *Kierkegaard's Fragments and Postscript: The Religious Philosophy of Johannes Climacus*. New Jersey: Humanities, 1989.

Gasché, Rodolphe. *The Tain of the Mirror: Derrida and the Philosophy of Reflection*. Cambridge: Harvard University Press, 1986.

Heidegger, Martin. "Introduction to 'What is Metaphysics?'" In *Pathmarks*, translated by Walter Kaufmann, 277–90. Cambridge: Cambridge University Press, 1998.

Husserl, Edmund. *Cartesian Meditations: An Introduction to Phenomenology*. Translated by D. Cairns. 6th ed. The Hague: Nijhoff, 1977.

Kierkegaard, Søren. *Concluding Unscientific Postscript to* Philosophical Fragments. Translated by Howard V. Hong and Edna H. Hong. Princeton: Princeton University Press, 1992.

———. *Fear and Trembling* and *Repetition*. Translated by Howard V. Hong and Edna H. Hong. Princeton: Princeton University Press, 1983.

———. *Philosophical Fragments* and *Johannes Climacus*. Translated by Howard V. Hong and Edna H. Hong. Princeton: Princeton University Press, 1985.

———. *The Sickness Unto Death*. Translated by Howard V. Hong and Edna H. Hong. Princeton: Princeton University Press, 1980.

———. *Søren Kierkegaard's Journals and Papers*. 6 vols. Translated and edited by Howard V. Hong and Edna H. Hong. Bloomington, IN: Indiana University Press, 1967–78.

———. *Stages on Life's Way*. Translated by Howard V. Hong and Edna H. Hong. Princeton: Princeton University Press, 1988.

Thulstrup, Niels. "Beginning of Philosophy." In *Bibliotheca Kierkegaardiana 3: Concepts and Alternatives in Kierkegaard*, 74. Copenhagen: Reitzels, 1980.

10

The Virtue of Metaphysical Patience
COREY B. TUTEWILER

T HIS ESSAY CONSIDERS THE meaning and significance of *metaphysical patience*. It will be helpful to provide a provisional explanation of this term at the outset, specifically inasmuch as it applies to human beings. Metaphysical patience is not reducible to an action, but it does determine the nature of actions. It is not intent, but it does determine the nature of how and what we intend. Metaphysical patience is perhaps best understood when it is thought of as fundamentally definitive for how human beings constitute themselves relationally. For this reason, I prefer to speak of such patience as a *way of being*—that is, as a way human beings can situate themselves in relation to themselves, other beings, the world, truth, to God, and so forth. The meaning and significance of metaphysical patience is considered here, moreover, as I am convinced that when human beings are patient with being, they *are* true to themselves and true to what is other, such that they have become receptive to the truth of being. Indeed, "The truth demands metaphysical patience."[1]

The concept of metaphysical patience is largely absent from the major movements of modern and postmodern philosophy—the former due to its endeavors to bring being into absolutely determinate categories and the latter due to the fact that, even in all its attempts to subvert and overcome the modern manner of thinking, it simply perpetuates a similar drive for

1. Desmond, *Being and the Between*, 499.

metaphysical totality. There are, on the other hand, ways of thinking meta-physically that are hospitable to the concept of metaphysical patience. In the present essay, for instance, I will continually make reference to the work of William Desmond and Søren Kierkegaard. The essay comprises three sections. The first section analyzes the difference between metaphysical patience and the common understanding of patience. In the second section I examine Kierkegaard's example of the man who willed to be Caesar (found in *The Sickness unto Death*) in order to clarify how human beings are capable of improperly constituting themselves relationally (that is, the man who willed to be Caesar can be understood as a personification of meta-physical impatience). In the final section, I examine what Desmond calls *passio essendi* [suffering of being] in an attempt to articulate the meaning of metaphysical patience with greater precision.

PATIENCE AND PATIENCE

It is important to note that I am here concerned with a metaphysically qualified sense of patience, which is to be contrasted with how the word is commonly understood and applied. This does not mean that the common understanding is somehow lacking and ought to be done away with, because it has its place. It simply lacks the resources to give full expression to, and can hence divert our attempt to understand, patience as a kind of metaphysical virtue.

On the common understanding, patience is instrumental. We often make use of patience in order to achieve some end, and we refer to it as a virtue because some ends cannot be realized on our demand. It is, however, important to note that, within this common understanding, the goal shares no essential relationship with the patience that assists in bringing it about; patience is taken here to be a midwife whose very purpose dissolves upon delivery. Supposing we were able to hook a fish immediately, what use or significance would patience then have? Or, some say, "Everything comes to those who wait." But, on the common understanding, once "everything comes" waiting is certainly of no use, and patience can be swiftly jettisoned without loss. This actually does not to put the matter strongly enough, for on this view it would be meaningless to preserve patience after achievement is reached. It is but mere wasted time once it has no goal outside itself.

By way of contrast, metaphysical patience is not to be regarded as a tool to discard once some goal is attained, since here a posture of patience is continually required for the human being who seeks out metaphysical and theological truth. Why this difference? On the common understanding of patience, matters are much simpler since goals can be fixed more determinately. You either have or have not caught the fish, and there is no *uncertain middle ground* standing between these absolute alternatives. But the end or goal of metaphysical and theological truth cannot be fixed so determinately, and so the question as to whether one has or has not possessed metaphysical and theological truth in such a manner is not to the point. The human being, as finite and contingent, is situated within the *uncertain middle ground* just mentioned, and here both understanding and patience quite simply take on a different type of meaning.[2] Instead of inquiring as to whether one has or has not caught the fish, the truth of the matter is rather that *one is always fishing*.

This being said, we need not doubt that metaphysical and theological truth can be known and that we can live accordingly. The claim that *one is always fishing* does not imply that *one is always lacking*.[3] We can rather become sensitive to the fact that being is excessive in relation to the human being and the limits of discursive thought. Always fishing, always catching, always yearning—such is life for the human. For this reason, even when truth reveals itself, patience will always insist, "and yet, there is more." And this "more" cannot be done away with. This "more" will always stand between mind and being, as a witness to a certain disproportion or lack of commensurability between the self and that which is other to the self. As metaphysically and theologically qualified, then, patience shares an essential relationship with the goal. Moreover, this goal is forever beyond us, without being irrelative to us, as that which we continually strive toward in patience. For human beings, patience paradoxically expresses both the way

---

2. This *uncertain middle ground* corresponds to what William Desmond calls the *metaxu*. For Desmond, the *metaxu* (meaning "middle" or "between") is where the human being is situated and, hence, where philosophical discourse must be grounded. On the contrast that I am speaking of in this paragraph (between determinate, absolute alternatives and the uncertain middle ground), Desmond writes: "It is also significant that the moments when Plato often resorts to myth are at the extremities of the *metaxu*, where *logos*, with its drift to fixed determination, might falsify the truth of what is appearing at the limit of the between" (ibid., 42).

3. "Our mindfulness here is *doubly* mediated. On the one hand, our perplexity shows us to be *distanced* from the truth we seek. We undergo a kind of indigence at the heart of our being; in that respect, perplexity reveals our being-other to the truth of being. Yet this being-other is not absolute vacancy; rather it is a paradoxical indigency of transcending power. Our lack, it might be said, generates the drive beyond itself. However, what drives the lack beyond lack cannot be itself mere lack. The lack points backwards to an inward otherness in perplexity itself that is the promise of a relativity to being that is beyond mere indigence" (ibid., 6).

to become true and a way of being that is true—a paradoxical synthesis of both *means* and *end*.[4]

THE MAN WHO WILLED TO BE CAESAR

Let us now consider the concept of despair as it is presented in *Sickness unto Death* and *Either/Or*, both of which were penned pseudonymously by Kierkegaard. In the former work, in an attempt to communicate that despair is a self-inflicted condition that occurs when one is not truly oneself, a condition ensuing from "the misrelation in the relation of a synthesis that relates itself to itself,"[5] Kierkegaard provides the example of a man who willed to be Caesar.[6] This example is particularly pertinent for our consideration, because it focuses on how a human being can improperly constitute himself relationally (in the case of the man who willed to be Caesar this pertains specifically to how this individual relates to his destiny). In other words, Kierkegaardian despair *is* the existential dissonance and duplicity that ensue when a human being does not properly relate to himself, to others, to God, to his destiny, and so on. In light of these inadequate conceptions of how human beings should constitute themselves relationally, then, Kierkegaard offers a positive alternative. This alternative, then, will help us to clarify our understanding of metaphysical patience.

In *Sickness unto Death*, Kierkegaard presents an ambitious man whose motto is "Either Caesar or nothing."[7] At the beginning of this text, we find a would-be Caesar (and there is no accident in the power associated with such a position) wholly committed to *his* end on *his* terms. He is entirely determined to possess the end of that which he desires, to assume complete control over his own destiny. He will be Caesar—or nothing. Hence, he allows only a single unnerving thought to cross his mind: that he might not achieve this end, that he might not become Caesar. Then, in what seems only a moment, he loses everything. The possibility of becoming Caesar vanishes. As a result, he is shaken and comes to terms with the "nothing" of his motto.

When the man who willed to be Caesar finds misfortune, he despairs over it. But, according to Kierkegaard, *this* despair simply signals that a deeper conception of despair that was at work in the man from the very

4. As Kierkegaard says so very well, "Patience inseparably joins the "condition and the conditioned." Kierkegaard, *Eighteen Upbuilding Discourses*, 169.

5. Kierkegaard, *The Sickness unto Death*, 16.

6. Ibid., 19.

7. Ibid.

beginning. Kierkegaard insists that despair, the sickness of the spirit, is not rooted in some incidental, external circumstance (e.g. not getting to become Caesar); rather, it is rooted in the improper internal orientation of the man's willing itself—that is, rooted in a misrelation in the relation of a synthesis that relates itself to itself. Despair is founded upon this man's refusal to be himself (for, in truth, he is *not* Caesar). This despair is, one could say, rooted in the man's obstinate endeavor to become the artificial, constructed being he has made himself out to be and, along with this, his refusal to be who he truly is. It is in this very elemental refusal to be who he is that the man who willed to be Caesar attempted to assume complete control over his own destiny in the first place. Thus, in willing to be Caesar and in failing to be Caesar, this man exhibits the same despair, albeit in different guises.

It is important to realize that, although the man who willed to be Caesar was shaken in his disappointment, he was not adequately shaken. That is, in being shaken, he is loosened from *his* particular end, but he is not loosened from himself. He questions the external and incidental, lamenting that he did not get to be Caesar, but never does he question that which should have been challenged in the very first moment: his orientation, his disposition, himself. As Kierkegaard writes shortly after, "To despair over oneself, in despair to will to be rid of oneself—this is the formula for all despair."[8] In his "despair," then, the man who willed and failed to be Caesar misses the fuller meaning of his disappointment.

I would like to emphasize a crucial point here. There is something significant in the very formulation of this man's motto: "Either Caesar or nothing." According to the despairing man, there are only these two imaginable outcomes. As Kierkegaard indicates, however, there is another possible outcome that goes unaccounted for. There are, more specifically, two ways in which the reader can interpret the motto's "nothing." Indeed, there are two ways in which one can *become as nothing*. There is here an important distinction to be made; as Judge William writes, "there is a difference between despair and despair."[9]

Kierkegaard's *Either/Or* helps clarify this distinction. In the example of the man who willed to be Caesar, the man's form of despair, his becoming as nothing, is not such that it can usher in a true transformation of self, but rather it simply perpetuates his despairing condition. There is another kind of despair in which this *becoming as nothing* delivers the possibility for true self-transformation.[10] The first becoming as nothing is "the result of a despair

8. Ibid., 20.

9. Kierkegaard, *Either/Or, Part II*, 194.

10. Judge William makes this distinction throughout his half of *Either/Or*. For

that was not carried through, the result of the soul's continuing to quake in despair and of the spirit's inability to achieve its true transfiguration."[11] In the second, positive and provisional sense of despair, one loses not only the goal one wished to achieve (e.g., becoming Caesar), but also—and this is the most essential point—*one relinquishes the very underlying conditions that provided the possibility for such an inordinate goal in the first place.* This latter kind of despair, this positive kind of becoming as nothing, is precisely what Judge William urges the esthete A to come to terms with when he explicitly commands him to despair.[12] This kind of despair or becoming as nothing, due to its *positive* potential to extirpate the perilous conditions which give rise to disordered selfhood, carries with it an overtone of surrender, subordination, and breaking down that is utterly absent in the first, limited form of despair. With this in mind, Judge William's seemingly bizarre exhortations to despair become intelligible.[13] Of course, the *positivity* of this kind of despair does not cancel the element of risk it necessarily involves; it rarely comes without fear, trembling, and a leap. The promise and hope is that—although confronted with the possibility that one will simply lose everything and become as nothing *and remain as nothing*—"in the very next moment the despair proves to be not a break but a metamorphosis. Everything comes back again, but transfigured."[14]

This "becoming as nothing" or "coming to nothing," as it happens, is a central theme in the metaphysics of Desmond as well. He even discusses the two senses of despair as they are found in Kierkegaard (although he does not make reference to Kierkegaard when discussing them): "Despair may destroy; despair may also bring one to the bottom, to a crisis, hence to a turning point. What can happen then? The idol of autonomy can be broken

---

instance: "The person who despairs about something in particular runs the risk that his despair will not be authentic and deep, that it is an illusion, a distress over the particular. You are not to despair in this way, for no particular thing has been taken from you, you still have it all. If the despairing person errs and thinks that the trouble is somewhere in the multiplicity outside himself, then his despair is not authentic and it will lead him to hate the world and not love it, for however true it is that the world is an oppression to you because it seems to want to be something different for you that it can be, so is it also true that when in despair you have found yourself you will love it because it is what it is" (ibid., 208).

11. Ibid., 210.

12. Ibid., 208–9, 211, 219,

13. "[I]t is despair to gain the whole world and in such a way that one damages one's soul, and yet it is my deep conviction that to despair is a person's true salvation" (ibid., 221).

14. Ibid., 271.

open. The shattered idol shows us nothing, shows us our own nothingness. Coming to nothing may be the reopening in us of the porosity of being."[15]

Moreover, like Kierkegaard, Desmond insists that this resurrected state of being and mind "demands a sacrifice of any claim to . . . being absolute. It relativizes in an extreme sense, in showing the powerlessness of the human to effect what it most needs to be itself, to be itself as fulfilled."[16] It is, therefore, the false, autonomous, self-sufficient notion of the self and its drive toward totality that are put to rest when one becomes as nothing in the most appropriate manner.[17] This self endeavors to give itself to be and to be absolute, but the process of becoming as nothing "can recall us to something of the *passio essendi* [suffering of being]" that is ontologically constitutive for created beings.[18] And at this point we are conditioned to break through and become receptive to the truth of being; indeed, Desmond writes, "One has to suffer to see."[19]

PASSIO ESSENDI AND METAPHYSICAL PATIENCE

In order to gain a better understand metaphysical patience, let us now examine more closely this notion of the *passio essendi*. The self is complexly situated between *suffering of being* and *striving to be*, what Desmond refers to as *passio essendi* and *conatus essendi* respectively.[20] That is, we are doubly mediated beings—as both given to be what we are (*passio essendi*) and, concomitantly, continually giving ourselves to be what we are (*conatus essendi*). Consider the expression: "You can choose your friends, but you cannot choose your family." The self is constituted by conditions both unchosen and chosen. The *passio essendi* stresses what is unchosen—that we inevitably undergo a *suffering of being*. He writes, "we do not first choose our being or freedom; both are first given to us; and being given, we begin to give ourselves to ourselves. . . . I say this is a suffering, for there is a *patience to being* at this elemental level, and a patience to the good of being."[21] The *conatus essendi*, on the other hand, stresses that, in addition to suffering

15. Desmond, *God and the Between*, 29.

16. Desmond, *Ethics and the Between*, 113.

17. Desmond, *God and the Between*, 30.

18. Ibid., 87.

19. Desmond, *Ethics and the Between*, 111.

20. Ibid., 371: "We might say that the *passio essendi* and the *conatus essendi* are promiscuously wedded in the tensed singularity of the body."

21. Ibid., 368.

being, we *strive to be* or "endeavor to be."[22] The *passio essendi* is an unwilled aspect of being human; it pertains to a certain inevitable receptivity of the self. The *conatus essendi* properly pertains to the self's willfulness—that is, the assertiveness or determination of the self.

Moreover, while they can be seen as opposites in some respects (the unwilled, unchosen, and received as opposed to the willed, chosen, and asserted), the *passio essendi* and *conatus essendi* are not to be conceived, purely and simply, as opposites. There is an important sense in which the *passio essendi* is prior to the *conatus essendi*.[23] That is to say, the latter, our endeavoring to be, always takes shape subsequent to, and is defined within the given parameters of, our suffering of being—the latter of which is the being that we are given to be, with or without our consent. We choose to be who we are only within confines to which we are subjected from the start.[24]

It is not uncommon for human beings to express resentfulness toward the *passio essendi*, a hatred toward the very limiting, constitutive conditions that are beyond their control (Jean Paul Sartre is perhaps a prototypical example of such). The *passio essendi* exposes the self to an original, unavoidable vulnerability, which is often undesired and hated by individuals who would instead assert and determine themselves absolutely.[25] "The modern quest . . . for the most complete autonomy of knowing," for instance, is often characterized by such hatred for the *suffering of being*, regarding the latter as a blight on human condition.[26] Hence, philosophers "often have sought

22. Ibid., 369.

23. Ibid.

24. This corresponds to Kierkegaard's claim that the human being is a doubly mediated synthesis of finitude and infinitude, necessity and possibility. There are given ontological conditions beyond our control (necessity and finitude), as well as freedom to assume the self of our choosing within these limitations (the possibility and infinitude). Kierkegaard, *The Sickness unto Death*, 29–42.

25. In *Repetition*, for instance, Kierkegaard's pseudonym Constantin Constantius expresses such a resentful attitude toward the *passio essendi*: "Where am I? What does it mean to say: the world? What is the meaning of that word? Who tricked me into this whole thing and leaves me standing here? Who am I? How did I get into the world? Why was I not asked about it, why was I not informed of the rules and regulations but just thrust into the ranks as if I had been bought from a peddling shanghaier of human beings? How did I get involved in this big enterprise called actuality? Why should I be involved? Isn't it a matter of choice? And if I am compelled to be involved, where is the manager? To whom shall I make my complaint? After all, life is a debate—may I ask that my observations be considered? If one has to take life as it is, would it not be best to find out how things go?" Kierkegaard, *Fear and Trembling/Repetition*, 200.

26. "While the ancient philosophical ways were not devoid of a theoretical will to master the world as other, in modernity the will to make knowing the master of itself is more pronounced. The modern quest is for the most complete autonomy of knowing. There is also a praxis to this. Beyond every patience in knowing, anything other is to

to escape this suffering into knowing, rather than coming to know in the suffering"; that is, for these thinkers, philosophy "is a therapy for suffering."[27] The *conatus essendi* is to overcome and eliminate the *passio essendi*.

This suffering is unavoidable, however, and we cannot simply philosophize our way out of it. We did not give ourselves to be, just as we cannot prevent ourselves from eventually succumbing to death and losing our being. In fact, as Desmond points out, it is sometimes when one is confronted with the inevitable reality of death that the attempt to overcome and eliminate the *passio essendi* manifests itself most clearly.[28] He writes in response to this:

> We suffer from ourselves, but we should suffer from ourselves, and not spuriously seek ourselves. I am not saying we should not find ourselves or not be true to what we are, but there is a kind of seeking of oneself indistinguishable from a distraction from oneself. I ought to take a good look in the mirror. (I am going to die.) I need not go elsewhere to do that. I am the Everest I must climb. Horace: *Caelum non animum mutant qui trans mare currunt*: they change their sky, not their soul, those who run across the sea.[29]

When one strives to be the absolute—in being, thought, or both—and escape the ineradicable bearing of the *passio essendi*, one paradoxically diminishes, not only one's relationship to otherness, but also one's very own being. "In seeking to eliminate suffering," Desmond writes, "it risks dehumanizing us, dulling us to the promise of the gift in the *passio essendi*."[30]

What, then, is metaphysical patience? It is the willful (think of the *conatus essendi* here) consent to the *passio essendi*, or, as Kierkegaard eloquently writes, "patience is the courage that freely takes upon itself the suffering that cannot be avoided . . . and in just that way finds itself free in the unavoidable suffering."[31] Fully aware of the fact that impatience resists

---

be redefined in terms of knowing that is fully self-determining." Desmond, *Ethics and the Between*, 372.

27. Ibid., 371.

28. "Patience is an anticipation of the radical amen that is asked of us in the face of the absolute negation of death." Desmond, *Being and the Between*, 454–55.

29. Desmond, *Ethics and the Between*, 75. Once again, the point Desmond is making with the quotation from the Roman poet is identical to the point Kierkegaard makes with the man who willed to be Caesar. Despair is not extirpated through an alteration in one's external conditions, but rather it is the individual who needs to undergo an internal reconfiguration.

30. Ibid. 373.

31. Kierkegaard, *Upbuilding Discourses and Various Spirits*, 119.

the truth of one's being and impairs one's sense of judgment, the patient thinker continually suspects his own familiar manner of reasoning. Instead of primarily (or even exclusively) bringing to question to externalities, the patient thinker primarily puts the question to himself, such that his thought is humbled and rid of the "hubris of absolute knowing."[32] And, perhaps most importantly, in putting the question to himself, he challenges the underlying conditions that give rise to the desire for autonomous knowing in the first place. Patience, far from being the "defeat or humiliation" of the once self-determined subject, is consent to the *passio essendi*.[33]

CONCLUSION

Metaphysical patience is a way of being by which human beings by which human beings are true to themselves and true to others, such that they have become receptive to the truth of being. It is not, therefore, simply a means to some unrelated end. Nor is it a tool to be discarded once some goal is attained, but rather it expresses a way of being by which we continually consent to the original givenness of our being. For human beings complexly situated in existence, it is both the way to become true and a way of being that is true. For, although we can relate to the origin and end of our being, we can never become this origin and end for ourselves. In patience, in the *passio essendi*, we give ourselves back to the divine and, paradoxically, receive ourselves back in return, for "Dependence on God is the only independence."[34] In patience, the soul comes to terms with God and "sufferingly accepts itself from him."[35]

32. Desmond, *Being and the Between*, 192.
33. Ibid., 454.
34. Kierkegaard, *Upbuilding Discourses and Various Spirits*, 182.
35. Kierkegaard, *Eighteen Upbuilding Discourses*, 172.

BIBLIOGRAPHY

Desmond, William. *Being and the Between*. New York: SUNY, 1995.

———. *Ethics and the Between*. New York: SUNY, 2001.

———. *God and the Between*. Malden, MA: Blackwell, 2008.

Kierkegaard, Søren. *Eighteen Upbuilding Discourses*. Translated by Howard V. Hong and Edna H. Hong. Princeton: Princeton University Press, 1990.

———. *Either/Or*. Translated by Howard V. Hong and Edna H. Hong. 2 vols. Princeton: Princeton University Press, 1987.

———. *Fear and Trembling/Repetition*. Translated by Howard V. Hong and Edna H. Hong. Princeton: Princeton University Press, 1983.

———. *The Sickness unto Death*. Translated by Howard V. Hong and Edna H. Hong. Princeton: Princeton University Press, 1983.

———. *Upbuilding Discourses and Various Spirits*. Translated by Howard V. Hong and Edna H. Hong. Princeton: Princeton University Press, 1993.

PRACTICAL ESSAYS

11

The Postmodern, Missional (Emerging) Church Movement and the Epistle of James

or

"Hey Brian, You've Got a Friend in Me"

WILLIAM R. BAKER

T HE CHURCH MOVEMENT WITH the most impact today, and which has potential to extend well into the future, is what has come to be termed as the "missional" movement. This movement has mushroomed out of a small, think-tank of sorts, dubbed the Emergent Village, then became known as the emergent or emerging movement. The term that seems to have staying power and which has described the movement as it has impacted even partially churches of every stripe, particularly evangelical churches, is "missional." In this sense the emerging movement can be understood as the original missional movement.

This emerging/missional movement epitomizes theology of the present age because it has been born out of the realization that the church today needs to re-think about how it does its business, particularly, how it can be most effective in a postmordern era. Those targeted are young, urban professionals, both churched and unchurched. However, the philosophy and strategies are beginning to make their way into traditional, suburban churches as well.

Emerging church literature likes the Old Testament, loves Jesus, for the most part reacts against Pauline literature, and like most other historic church movements ignores the rest of the New Testament, including the Epistle of James. With the Old Testament, emerging literature resonates well with principles of creation, Abraham, the people of God, and the prophets.[1] Jesus' kingdom teaching and lifestyle expectations are the heart and soul of the emerging church movement; he is the "J-Factor."[2] The dominance of Pauline literature in creating divisive, Protestant, evangelical doctrine has caused most emerging church writers to steer clear of it.[3] The thesis of Ray Anderson embracing Paul is stunning in this regard.[4] He projects that the Pauline movement is the first emergent movement of the church. He believes the need to articulate a Christian message and lifestyle within a dominating Greek culture, oriented around Antioch emerged over against the incalcitrant form of Jewish Christianity centered in and controlled by Jerusalem.

Careful examination of fifteen key books from prominent emerging church thinkers revealed just one use of the Epistle of James, this unreferenced. Given its many prominent themes that resonate with emerging church ideals, it is surprising to find is so neglected. Sidelining this vibrant, little book from emerging church dialog probably demonstrates the long shadow of Luther still, who all but removed this little book from the Protestant canon. He reacted against James because it did not embrace his revolutionary cry of justification by faith alone and because Roman Catholics theology saw the grounding for the sacraments of confession and extreme unction in James (5:14–16).

---

1. Kimball, *Emerging Church*, 38; McLaren, "Method," 201–4; Sweet, et al., *Abductive*, 147, 221.

2. Sweet et al., *Abductive*, 169, coins this term and then follows with, "Everything we have said in the A to Z primer that seeds to adjudicate the imperative of postmedernity and the claims of christ can be reduced to one word: Jesus." Selmanovic, "Sweet Problem," 192–93.

3. McLaren, "Method," 198.

4. Anderson, *Emergent Theology*, 21–28; Carson, *Becoming Conversant*, 44, who for the most part takes issue with emerging church ideas, surprisingly agrees, saying, "Even within the first Christian generation, the church emerged from a Jerusalem-bound Jewish body to an international community made up of Jews and Gentiles all over the Roman Empire and beyond."

However, as this study will show, James makes a delightful conversation partner with emerging church voices. This will be seen in its own, unique efforts to instill in its community the ideals of Jesus teaching seen its emphasis on love of neighbor, friendship with God, justice for the poor, cautions against consumerism/materialism, and more. James also has a thing or two to say that might provide balance to emerging/missional church thought.

This study will begin with an analysis of emerging churches and their core ideals before creating a conversation with those found in James.

THE EMERGING CHURCH: DEFINITIONS AND IDEALS

What is now dubbed the emerging church has expanded from a few prominent, young, evangelical church leaders in the early 1990s who became disenchanted with the mega-churches with which they were involved. This expanded into a network of mature, culturally savvy church leaders and thinkers who lead congregations. Most are in large cities, which in divergent ways attempt to embody the gospel within the challenges of a postmodern world.[5] The crisis these leaders were experiencing it turns out was the impact of postmodernism on Western culture, on the church, and themselves personally. This crisis they saw as creating a gorge that cut off younger, postmodern, urban people from Christianity because of the modern fence that entangled it. This is epitomized by the middle-aged baby boomers attending technically driven, brilliantly produced mega-churches and living the modern suburban dream.

This crisis called both for disentangling the church from modernism and also recreating Christianity in a way that embraced the reality of people living postmodernly, both unbelievers outside the church and believers who no longer fit into a modern church. This whole process still evolving has produced a flurry of literature, both practical and theoretical, a think tank of authors, called Emergent Village, and growing number of extremely innovative and highly eclectic congregations striving to be "missional" churches, now the more generic slowly replacing "emerging" and "emergent."[6] With no official organization, the numbers emerging/missional congregations is difficult to estimate, but these do cut across all Christian traditions, evangelical, Protestant, Catholic, and Orthodox.[7]

5. Gibbs and Bolger, *Emerging Churches*, 27–40, 82–87; Jones, "Introduction," 12.

6. McLaren, *Orthodoxy*, 115–25; Zustiak, "Missional Emphasis"; See Also McKnight, "Five Streams," 35–39, for clarification of terminology.

7. Kimball, "Emerging Church," 83; Scandrette, "Growing Pains," 24.

The definition of emerging churches from Gibbs and Bolger is commonly cited: "Emerging churches are communities that practice the way of Jesus within postmodern cultures."[8] If one asks what are these churches emerging from, the best answer is that they are emerging from the modern world to a postmodern world.[9] Yet, thinkers about this emerging also want to place this mantra on the church, both past, present, and future.[10] Thus, the Hellenistic church emerged from the Jewish church,[11] the Protestant Reformation church emerged from the Catholic church,[12] and now the church is emerging again.

Each emergence comes out of a static situation in which the church got bogged down and entrenched in its times and needed rethinking and reordering. In this sense, the church never fully arrives; it is always in some state of discovering itself within the varied cultures and communities into which it is striving to be both relevant and authentic. It must continue to question itself both in how to articulate genuinely relevant doctrine and how to live Christianly within its environment. The ultimate sin is for the church to be sanctimoniously overconfident of where it has situated itself within an ever changing cultural environment.

The current emerging church as articulated by emerging thinkers encompasses the often cited, three traits articulated by Gibbs and Bolger:[13] identify with the life of Jesus, transform the secular realm, live highly communal lives. Mark Scandrette overlaps and expands these traits to include: interest in communal living, open-source approach to community, theology, and leadership, revitalized interest in the social dimensions of the gospel of Jesus, renewed interest in contemplative and bodily spiritual formation, renewed emphasis on creation theology, cultivation of the arts, and reexamination of vocation.[14] Anderson describes emergent theology as messianic, revalational, kingdom coming, and eschatological; emerging churches as missional, reformational, kingdom living, and incarnational.[15]

Tony Jones articulates a central ideal of the emerging church as "a call to friendship—friendship with God, friendship with one another, and with

---

8. Gibbs and Bolger, *Emerging Churches,"* 44.

9. McLaren, "Church Emerging," 149.

10. Kimball, "Emerging Church," 84; McLaren, *Orthodoxy,* 323

11. Anderson, *Emergent Theology,* 21–28; Carson, *Emerging Church,* 46.

12. McLaren, *Orthodoxy,* 323.

13. Gibbs and Bolger, *Emerging Churches,* 45.

14. Scandrette, "Growing Pains," 28.

15. Anderson, *Emergent Theology,* 17.

the world."[16] As he also puts it, "We want to be friends in the Jesus way, and we need others to tranform us so that we may find and join in God's hopes and dreams for the world."[17] Jones's idea of friendship embraces humanity in the sense that friendship cuts across religions, cultural, and social borders; it functions outside and inside the church; it is internalized as a way of life manifesting Jesus' primal teaching about loving one another and loving neighbor.

CONVERSING AS FRIENDS: OVERLAPPING PASSIONS

Despite being ignored by emerging church thinkers, the Epistle of James is a ready dialog partner anyway, sharing central themes and concerns and many traits. Most intriguing initially is the emphasis on friendship as an all-encompassing theme. For James, friendship with God is the life-goal of every person. To be called "God's friend" as Abraham was (2:24) is the goal of life's journey to be manifested in a myriad of ways. For James, friendship with God is language of salvation.

The route to becoming God's friend in James is varied,[18] but it certainly begins with Jesus and his ethic of love, which strikes a chord with the emerging church.[19] Though a classic criticism of James, stemming from Luther through German scholarship, that James has no Christology is false, James's dependence on the teaching of Jesus is impossible to overlook. Without citing Jesus even once, but probably quoting him at least in 5:12, James displays an understanding of Jesus' teaching, particularly the Sermon on the Mount, that is fully integrated into its own teaching. However, central is Jesus' teaching on loving neighbor, which James terms "the royal law" (2:8), a nod to its centrality in Jesus' kingdom ethics. He also calls it "the law of freedom (1:25; 2:12), emphasizing a person's internalization of God's way rather than being a mere statute to be obeyed. That love is the controlling life principle in James is evident when it labels discrimination of others to be a violation of it and speaking spitefully against "neighbors" to be sitting in judgment over it" (4:11–12).

16. Jones, "Introduction," 19.

17. Ibid.

18. Kimball, *Emerging Church*, 179, emphasizes theocentricity in emerging church preaching. Roxburgh and Romanuik, *Missional Leader*, 117, say, "Our *telos* is to know God."

19. Gibbs and Bolger, *Emerging Churches*, 47–64; Anderson, *Emergent Theology*, 138–57; McLaren, *Orthodoxy*, 206, states, "For me the 'fundamentals of the faith' boil down to those given by Jesus: to love God and to love our neighbor." See also, McLaren, "Method," 215–16.

Loving neighbor also manifests itself in care for the poor and widows (1:27) as well as demanding just wages for workers (5:1–12). These matters of social and economic justice are also dear to the hearts of emerging church thinkers.[20]

Treatment of others in James draws not only on the rule of neighbor love but also on principles of creation. The God-given ability of speech should be used to bless others and not curse them because all are created in God's image (3:9). To do anything other than to try to uplift others—whether fellow believers or not—is to denigrate God, the creator of all. Emerging church voices also draw upon creation theology at numerous points.[21]

One of the major emphases of emerging church voices extols total integration of Jesus' kingdom principles into the lives of believers, which should then emerge in positive personal, moral, social and community action.[22] Faith must manifest itself in behavior. Holiness is wholeness.[23] One cannot fail to miss the emphasis in James 2:14–26 on the necessity of corresponding behavior matching up with the faith of believers. James's cry of "Faith without works is dead!" is probably the most well-known saying of in James.

More recent work on James is moving to a consensus that the cry for behavioral changes climaxes James's deeper call for wholeness in believers. Twice James employs a unique word that may well be the key to the book's purpose. Being "double-minded" (literally, "double souled") appears to be the ultimate failing of James's original readers, the all-encompassing sin that separates them from being saved, or being God's friends.

In James 1:8, those who are divided do not trust God enough to implement its requested counsel when trouble invades their lives. They may ask, but they do not trust enough to hear and do. Instead, they blame God for their trouble (1:13–15), which in itself shows how little they know his good nature or even recognize the wonderful things he has provided for them (1:16–18), which employs more creation theology. The only solution for such people is a complete change in their relationship with God. To instill this change, James's lays out a ten-imperative call for its readers to repent (4:4–10), within which they are once again declared "double-mind" (4:8). The radical change they must undergo means no longer being doubtful regarding their trust in God. To become one, whole being, fully trusting in God, is to be God's friend.

---

20. Gibbs and Bolger, *Emerging Churches*, 142–44; Anderson, *Emergent Theology*, 195–96; Carrasco, "Social Justice," 248–58; Bolger, "Following Jesus," 132–41.

21. Sweet et al., *Abductive*, 78, 113, 147.

22 McLaren, *Orthodoxy*, 182–83; Sweet et al., *Abductive*, 116.

23. Sweet et al., *Abductive*, 147–48.

The opposite of divided is whole. God himself is wholly good and undivided in his nature (1:13–15). Indeed, he is "One," as even demons believe (2:19). On the positive side, James desires it readers to be whole and that means that faith is not divided from work—personally (2:14–26), the poor are not divided from the wealthy—communally (2:1–13), the tongue is not divided from personal control—ethically (3:1–13), people are not divided in their motives for prayer—spiritually (4:1–4), nor from God—vocationally (4:13–17; 5:1–6), and as a local body of believers they function—communally—to praise, confess, heal, and restore (5:13–20). Hearing God's wisdom (3:13–18) will make them whole in all these life challenges. All this resonates with the emerging church emphasis on incarnating Jesus in the lives of believers and their communities.[24]

Emerging church voices correspond with this emphasis on wholeness that manifests itself in many of the same ways that James describes. Emerging church voices react against a Christianity that thinks Christians are defined by believing a list of things.[25] This is not against rationality or being intellectual but is against a false sense of security about salvation simply because people have said certain words or subscribed to certain doctrines. Instead, in insisting that Christians be incarnational believers emerging voices and James coincide, and it is on this point that one emergent voice, Leonard Sweet, uses an unreferenced paraphrase of James (2:19) to make his point: "If you have faith in something it transforms how you live. You cannot *not* act upon it. Satan believes in God. But Satan doesn't believe God. Believing is living faith."[26]

Emerging church voices and the Epistle of James coincide on a number of other emphases. First, emerging church voices encourage hospitality—to friends and strangers alike—as action that incarnates the way of Jesus to others.[27] In this regard, James 2:25 poignantly promotes Rahab, specifically identifying her as a prostitute, but also being woman and a pagan, yet a model believer—right alongside Abraham—because she showed hospitality to strangers, even enemies (like "Jewish spies). She could also provide a model for emerging church thought that promotes such a generous

---

24. Gibbs and Bolger, *Emerging Churches*, 146–50; McLaren, *Orthodoxy*, 58, 210–22.

25. Samson, "Reinvention," 158–59; Kimball, "Humble Theology," 222; Sweet et al., *Abductive*, 116, 231; Roxburgh and Romanuk, *Missional Leader*, 121.

26. Sweet et al., *Abductive*, 43.

27. Gibbs and Bolger, *Emerging Churches*, 120; Crouch, "Life," 89; Roxburgh and Romanuk, *Missional Leader*, 158.

orthodoxy in Christianity that is willing to dialog with other religious faith and recognize their virtues, despite their differences from Christianity.[28]

Second, emerging church voices emphasize local communities of believers working together to minister to one another and beyond.[29] James 4:1–4 pictures a hateful, divided community that is separated from one another and from God and demands change. James 5:13–18 pictures the ideal, local community of believers who praise God together, pray together, confess sins to one another, heal one another, and restore those who are straying.

Third, emerging church voices decry the commercialism and materialism of the contemporary mega-church.[30] James 4:13–17 calls ambitious businessmen to task for planning to "make money" apart from seeking God's wisdom for their lives. James 4:1–3 blasts so-called believers for dominating their prayer lives with requests for material goods for their pleasure. James 5:1–6 censures wealthy landowners from cheating their workers.

Fourth, emerging church voices encourage tactile manifestation of worship and ministry.[31] James 5:14 encourages congregational representatives (elders) to visit those who are seriously ill among them and anoint them with oil along with their prayer to the Lord for restoration to health.

Fifth, the cross and atonement is noticeably absent from emerging church literature, replaced it seems with incarnating Christ in the church and in the lives believers.[32] James contains no reference to the cross, nor to Jesus' resurrection, though in its teaching it does depend on the certainty of Christ's return and on his roll in judgment, particularly in 5:7–11.

The Epistle of James, then, has many major and minor themes that resonate with themes emphasized by those who write about the emerging church. James is willing "friend" to embrace them in their thinking at many levels.

28. Ibid., 123–24; Selmanovic, "Sweet Problem," 196.

29. Sweet et al., *Abductive*, 140; Roxburgh and Romanuk, *Missional Leader*, 73, 116.

30 .Gibbs and Bolger, *Emerging Churches*, 136–38; Kimball, *Emerging Church*, 94–95; Horton, "Better Homes," 108–9; Crouch, "Life," 88–90.

31. Kimball, *Emerging Church*, 129.

32. Driscoll, "Emerging Church," 29–35, criticizes some emerging church voices of downplaying the cross and atonement.

CONVERSING AS FRIENDS: SPEAKING THE TRUTH IN LOVE

A truly personal conversation between trusting friends such as Brian (McLaren), the most prominent voice on the emerging/missional church, and James (the brother of Jesus), as represented by the Epistle of James, would include frank criticism. Thus, in this section, then, simply in the name of true friendship James has a few comments that Brian needs to hear.

First, the most prominent matter is the failure of Brian and other emerging church voices to draw a needed distinction between Christ and culture.[33] In the desire to save Christianity from its unholy alliance with modern culture, they are guilty of making another unholy alliance with postmodern culture. A glaring distinction between the vision of friendship of Tony Jones, referenced earlier, and that of James surfaces right here. Jones's call to friendship includes friendship with the world. However, James makes the point more forcefully than any other place in the New Testament that a believer cannot be a friend of the world, saying in 4:4, "Anyone who chooses to be a friend of the world becomes an enemy of God" (NIV). Friendship with world, James says, influences people, so-called believers, to be selfish, materialistic, boastful, and pleasure-seeking. This puts them in complete antagonism to the way of God, the way of Jesus.

An exegetical fight might occur over how "the world" is defined. It would be interesting to see what an emerging church thinker would make of James 4:4, but no one wrestles with this in their literature. The emphasis of this verse cuts to the heart of the criticism of many in the church who question emerging church thinkers on their soften attitude toward the world and culture.

Second, and somewhat connected to the issue of the emerging church stance toward the world, is the matter of repentance. Emerging church voices tend to urge an incarnational form of evangelism and dialog across the religious spectrum as ways of lowering barriers to Jesus that will bring people slowly into the Christian community.[34] On the other hand, James calls for people to turn about immediately from their sinful behavior in 4:7–10. Full of remorse and sorrow, people are to race away from dalliance with the world and rush into the waiting arms of a merciful God.

Third, also James would have a different perspective on someone who doubts God. Emerging church voices embrace uncertainty and perhaps even

---

33. Bolt, "Emerging Critique," 218.

34. Gibbs and Bolger, *Emerging Churches*, 124–26, 129–30; Sweet, McLaren, Haselmayer, *Abductive*, 45.

healthy doubt as a positive situation within believers.[35] This position is an understandable attempt to balance the sometimes overconfident, dogmatic assertions of the church in the past and the many divisive factions within its history. James, however, shouts loud and clear that friendship with God requires complete trust in him, his character, his wisdom, his justice, and more. James does not leave room for doubt. The person who doubts God is self-deceived (1:6–8; 4:1–3). Critics of the emerging movement would love to hear a response to this conflict between doubt and trust. It would be a compelling dialog.

Fourth, emerging church voices want to enfold an incarnational sense of justice into an incarnational sense of eschatology. Some would label this an overrealized eschatology. This comes from the noble purpose of being motivated to enact Jesus' kingdom teaching as it involves social issues, especially the Beatitudes.[36] James tries to help its readers deal with the dreary reality of suffering in the world, for example, of workers like them who are underpaid and poorly treated (5:1–5). However, patience is invoked, not social reform. Judgment will rain down on the abusers, not today but in a certain future judgment. Patience involves waiting, trusting patiently for that day to come when Jesus will return and mete out justice on God's behalf (5:1–11). Can God and the church help now? James would say, yes, through the community of the church (5:13–20) remaining united against oppression, but not grumbling (5:9), and upholding one another to trust in God's justice and promise to right the wrongs in a future judgment if not now. No doubt, emerging church voices believe both in a present and future eschatology. However, James would suggest some of their teaching needs an adjustment that balances a present judgment with the future one

So, Brian (McLaren), as a representative of the emerging/missional movement, face your friend James. Try to listen to him. Talk with him about the challenges he brings to your emerging theology that is ever-emerging.[37]

---

35. Burke, "Response to Driscoll," 36, advocates allowing Christians "time and space to process beliefs" as opposed to the old way of "browbeating people into unquestioning belief compliance." See also Kimball, "Emerging Church," 90–95; Pagitt, "Emerging Church," 119–43; Sawyer, "Huckleberry," 43–48; Condor, "Existing," 106; Kimble, "Humble Theology," 222.

36. McLaren, *Orthodoxy*, 70–71. This comes through more clearly than ever in McLaren, *Secret*, throughout but esp. 117–24.

37. Pagitt, "Emerging Church" 122, 137, comments that theology continues to evolve.

CONCLUSION

The Epistle of James makes an intelligible conversation with Brian (McLaren) and the voices of the emerging/missional church. To a great extent, this is because James is so penetrated by the teaching and voice of Jesus like they are. James and the voices of the emerging/missional church share a central theme to live out their commitment to Jesus holistically. They share a central goal in being God's friend. They share a drive to live out an ethic of loving others that positively affects the lives of those around them, to help the poor and be hospital to people generally.

Yet, questions James and others have raised about the emerging/missional church direction need to be answered. How can a Christian be a friend to the world and to God at the same time? How is this distinction to be nuanced? How can a person come into friendship with God without repentance from a sinful lifestyle of cavorting with the world? Does a gradual warming to friendship with God require a clear point of grief and turning away from former ways? How can Christians be honest with doubts and yet not doubt their relationship with God? How do Christians truly show God's love to the poor? How do Christians balance to be patient in misery with provision for improving quality of life?

The conversation needs to continue . . .

Finally, some emerging/missional thinkers, like Ray Anderson, and even critic like Donald Carson, need to take caution about depicting the Jerusalem church as the foil against which "Antioch" Christianity "emerges."[38] If the author of Epistle of James is James, the Lord's brother, this means he was also the leader of the Jerusalem church. If he has written an epistle like this to his this dispersed church that is so compatible with emerging/missional church ideals, then some adjustment to this theory is necessary.

To be more fair, perhaps if Paul's writings are to be baptized into emerging/missional church theology because they represent the re-thinking required for Hellenistic believers to adapt their principles and lifestyle into Greek culture and away from Jewish culture, then the Epistle of James should be read as an effort to aid Jewish Christians to emerge from Jewish culture into a Jewish Christian culture due to the impact of Jesus. James is an emerging voice, then, in the same way Paul is.

James also does a pretty good job of setting its readers on their incarnational journey, a compatible goal with the emerging/missional church.

---

38. See earlier comments.

BIBLIOGRAPHY

Anderson, Ray. *An Emergent Theology for Emerging Churches*. Downers Grove, IL: InterVarsity, 2006.

Bolt, John. "An Emerging Critique of the Postmodern, Evangelical Church: A Review Essay." *Calvin Theological Journal* 41 (2006) 205–21.

Burke, John. "Response to Driscoll." In *Listening to the Beliefs of Emerging Churches*, edited by Robert Webber, 36–38. Grand Rapids: Zondervan, 2007.

Carrasco, Rodolpo. "A Pound of Social Justice: Beyond Fighting for a Just Cause." In *An Emergent Manifesto of Hope*, edited by Doug Pagitt and Tony Jones, 248–58 Grand Rapids: Baker, 2007.

Carson, D. A. *Becoming Conversant with the Emerging Church*. Grand Rapids: Zondervan, 2005.

Conder, Tim. "The Existing Church/Emerging Church Matrix: Collision, Credibility, Missional Collaboration, and Generative Friendship." In *An Emergent Manifesto of Hope*, edited by Doug Pagitt and Tony Jones, 98–107. Grand Rapids: Baker, 2007.

Crouch, Andy. "Life After Postmodernity." In *The Church in Emerging Culture: Five Perspectives*, edited by Leonard Sweet, 63–104. Grand Rapids: Zondervan, 2004.

Driscoll, Mark. "The Emerging Church and Biblicist Theology." In *Listening to the Beliefs of Emerging Churches*, edited by Robert Webber, 21–35. Rapids: Zondervan, 2007.

Gibbs, Eddie, and Ryan Bolger. *Emerging Churches: Creating Christian Community in Postmodern Cultures*. Grand Rapids: Baker, 2005.

Horton, Michael. "Better Homes & Gardens." In *The Church in Emerging Culture: Five Perspectives*, edited by Leonard Sweet, 105–31. Grand Rapids: Zondervan, 2004.

Jones, Tony. "Introduction: Friendship, Faith, Going Somewhere Together." In *An Emergent Manifesto of Hope*, edited by Doug Pagitt and Tony Jones, 11–16. Grand Rapids: Baker, 2007.

Kimball, Dan. *The Emerging Church*. Grand Rapids: Zondervan, 2003.

———. "The Emerging Church and Missional Theology." In *Listening to the Beliefs of Emerging Churches*, edited by Robert Webber, 35–39. Grand Rapids: Zondervan, 2007.

———. "Humble Theology: Re-Exploring Doctrine While Holding on to the Truth." In *An Emergent Manifesto of Hope*, edited by Doug Pagitt and Tony Jones, 213–24. Grand Rapids: Baker, 2007.

McLaren, Brian. *A Generous Orthodoxy*. Grand Rapids: Zonervan, 2004.

McNight, Scott. "Church Emerging: Or Why I Still use the Word Postmodern but with Mixed Feelings." In *An Emergent Manifesto of Hope*, edited by Doug Pagitt and Tony Jones, 142–52. Grand Rapids: Baker, 2007.

———. "Five Streams of the Emerging Church." *Christianity Today* 51.2 (2007) 35–39.

———. "The Method, the Message, and the Ongoing Story." In *The Church in Emerging Culture; Five Perspectives*, edited by Leonard Sweet, 191–224. Grand Rapids: Zondervan, 2004.

———. *The Secret Message of Jesus: Uncovering the Truth That Could Change Everything*. Nashville: Word, 2006.

Pagitt, Doug. "The Emerging Church and Embodied Theology." In *Listening to the Beliefs of Emerging Churches*, edited by Robert Webber, 119–43. Grand Rapids: Zondervan, 2007.

Pagitt, Doug, and Tony Jones, editors. *An Emergent Manifesto of Hope*. Grand Rapids: Baker, 2007.

Roxburgh, Alan, and Fred Romanuk. *The Missional Leader*. San Fransisco: Jossey-Bass, 2006.

Samson, Will. "The End of Reinvention: Mission beyond Market Adoption Cycles." In *An Emergent Manifesto of Hope*, edited by Doug Pagitt and Tony Jones, 154–61. Grand Rapids: Baker, 2007.

Sawyer, Annette. "What Would Huckleberry Do? A Relational Ethic as the Jesus Way." In *An Emergent Manifesto of Hope*, edited by Doug Pagitt and Tony Jones, 42–50. Grand Rapids: Baker, 2007.

Scandrette, Mark. "Growing Pains: The Messy and Fertile Process of Becoming." In *An Emergent Manifesto of Hope,* edited by Doug Pagitt and Tony Jones, 22–40. Grand Rapids: Baker, 2007.

Selmanovic, Samire. "The Sweet Problem of Inclusiveness: Finding our God in the Other." In *An Emergent Manifesto of Hope*, edited by Doug Pagitt and Tony Jones, 190–99. Grand Rapids: Baker, 2007.

Sweet, Leonard, editor. *The Church in Emerging Culture: Five Perspectives*. Grand Rapids: Zondervan, 2004.

Sweet, Leonard, Brian McLaren, and Jerry Haselmayer. *A is for Abductive: The Language of the Emerging Church*. Grand Rapids: Zondervan, 2003.

Webber, Robert, editor. *Listening to the Beliefs of Emerging Churches*. Grand Rapids: Zondervan, 2007.

Zustiac, Gary. "The Missional Emphasis of Emerging Churches." No pages. *Christian Standard* (September 2007). Online: http://christianstandard.com/2007/09/cs_article-673/

12

Rekindling a Sacramental Imagination

ISAAC GAFF

Fire is a fickle lover. She requires a combination of factors to burn. She requires constant attention. If you get too close, too fast, you will get burned; and if you stay away too long, the fire will go out. Things that provide an illusively complex joy often require this kind of mindful and artful care. It is no wonder that many cultures before the Industrial Revolution placed fire in the middle of their daily lives. A tended fire, when just on the edge of either breaking into a blaze or dwindling to an ember, captivates its caretaker in a way a modern scientifically engineered flame cannot do.

While modernity did its best to place our humanity into one common and totalizing location (for Kantians: the mind, for romantics: the heart, for moralists: the will), the project ultimately failed to fracture humanness into one clean and unilateral compartment. Although the three attempts (heart, mind, and will) when kindled together come close to an experience of full humanity, a key fourth component, the imagination, almost flickered out during modernity. Imagination became either 1) folded completely into the life of the mind and, in some cases, synonymous with the reality-creation claimed within minds; or 2) cut loose from any connection to the embodied, communal, or tangible life. Imagination was either the same as the mind or it had no tether, no reference, and no boundary in relation to the non-imaginative. Nietzsche speaks about both of these disconnects when he describes the reality we constantly create—our "works of art" that are:

> A mobile army of metaphors, metonyms, and anthropomorphisms—in short a sum of human relations, which have been enhanced, transposed, and embellished poetically and rhetorically, and which after long use seem firm, canonical, and obligatory to a people; truths are illusions of which one has forgotten that this is what they are; metaphors which are worn out and without sensuous power; coins which have lost their pictures and now matter only as metal, no longer as coins.[1]

For Nietzsche, the imagination's connection to reality had flickered out and had lost its "sensuous power." When imaginations are not formed and tended by a vigorous and vibrant sacramental life, this kind of disconnect is inevitable. As beings who are and operate in hearts, minds, wills, and imaginations; the sacraments become both the imaginative fuel for our human fire as well as the practice by which we tend our fires. While the sacraments certainly form our hearts, minds, and wills; our imaginations—at this point in history—have the greatest need for tending. This essay will explore the connections between the careful observances of the sacraments and the healthy imaginations they ignite. While the number of sacraments varies according to tradition, three lend themselves well to this exploration of the imagination: Baptism, the Eucharist, and Sacred Reading.

Baptism is our origin story. Whether adult, infant, or somewhere in between; Baptism is the sacramental act that begins and marks our formation as disciples of Jesus. When we engage our imaginations, a good part of what we hope for in the future is shaped by our formation in the past. Modernity in general, and the Christian Protestant variant of it in specific, relocated our origin story to the awakening of the rational or relational mind. Our own skepticism (or our own rejection of that skepticism redirected toward romantic hopes) became the furnace in which we were forged. Our boundaries for reality and our map for living were set along the lines of the rational method or the romantic rejection of that method. Both options produce narrative orphans who are left to fend for themselves and are disconnected from those around them.

The sacrament of Baptism plunges us into a story that is both as comfortable as the skin we live in and as alien as the furthest star. Baptism places us squarely in the middle of the incarnation, death, and resurrection of Jesus. The visceral nature of the water itself connects us with Christ's incarnation. Jesus took on flesh to validate the redemptive potential of our bodies.

1. Nietzsche, "On Truth and Lie in an Extra-Moral Sense," 46–47.

Water is the elemental connection to our flesh that unites us with Christ's incarnation. Water is a beautiful sacramental participant because it offers both the potential for death and life simultaneously. When the Apostle Paul describes baptism, he uses the image of a grave and a resurrection. The water of Baptism brings death, but it also becomes the bedrock of resurrection. Our origin story in Baptism is filled with unlimited fuel for our imaginations. Our forging in the practice of incarnation, death, and resurrection binds our imaginations to things like empathy (incarnation), self sacrifice (death), and restoration (resurrection). When we let our Baptism set the course for our imaginations, the possibilities for beauty in art, politics, ecclesial connections, economics, etc., become tangible.

While Baptism provides the origin story for our imaginations, the Eucharist continually renews and retells our story in both word and deed. When the dominant discussion of the Eucharist became the "how" of Christ's presence in the bread and wine, we lost the Eucharistic connection to our imaginations. Limiting our imaginations to how or if Christ is present in the bread and wine confines us to a modern scientific narrative and not the narrative the Eucharist offers. The Eucharist offers us a unique combination of descriptive and prescriptive imaginative *telos*. The elements of bread and wine are both described ("this is my body") and prescribed ("broken for you"). It is the interplay of description and prescription in the Eucharist that helps our imaginations run towards God's *telos*. While Baptism reminds us of our origins, the Eucharist points us and nourishes us toward our future. When our imaginations are fed on the Eucharist, pictures of the future (both near and far) come into sharper focus. When the story of Christ's nourishing death and resurrection intersect with our imaginations through the incarnated symbol of bread and wine, our imaginations become catalysts for our hearts, minds, and wills. Alexander Campbell relates a unique confluence of this Eucharistic heart, mind, will, and imagination when he describes what he considers an ideal communion service:

> To every disciple he (Jesus) says, "For you my body was wounded; for you my life was taken." In receiving it the disciple says, "Lord, I believe it. My life sprung from thy suffering; my joy from thy sorrows; and my hope of glory everlasting from thy humiliation and abasement even to death." Each disciple, in handing the symbols to his fellow disciple, says, in effect, "You, my brother, once an alien, are now a citizen of heaven; once a stranger, are now brought home to the family of God. You have owned my Lord as your Lord, my people as your people. Under Jesus the Messiah we are one. Mutually embraced in the everlasting arms, I embrace you in mine; thy sorrows shall be my sorrows, and thy

joys my joys. Joint debtors to the favor of God and the love of Jesus, we shall jointly suffer with him, that we may jointly reign with him. Let us, then, renew our strength, remember our King, and hold fast our boasted hope unshaken to the end."[2]

When our imaginations are fed by the Eucharist, our actions and dispositions become the incarnations of the *telos* to which the Eucharist points. We experience, in part, the restoration of the future in our actions and attitudes today.

Perhaps no other sacrament has been as deeply affected by the modern project as Sacred Reading. Many would even question whether or not Scripture reading is essentially sacramental. Since the onslaught of the grammatical/historical method of interpretation, Scripture reading has been left to the realm of the literary critic, not the disciple seeking a means of grace. The grammatical/historical interpretive method and a sacramental reading of Scripture are not mutually exclusive, but when the grammatical/historical method sets the course and prescribes the boundaries, little room is left for a sacramental reading of Scripture. Invoking our imaginations in Scripture reading has had a varied past. Some point to fantastical and irresponsible allegory while others point to sterile and detached historical criticism. A sacramental reading of Scripture lies in between these two extreme poles and relies on the partnership of the imagination to fully encounter the text.

Imagination, in some ways, is the sacramental means of grace in Scripture reading. One way to describe the imagination's role in this sacramental exchange is to apply the components of Speech Act Theory to the imagination in Scripture reading. Generally speaking, Speech Act Theory breaks down a text into three basic parts: the illocution (intent behind the written text), the locution (the text itself), and the perlocution (the result of the text fulfilling its intention). When we encounter the text sacramentally, we need our correctly formed imaginations (imaginations formed through other sacramental acts like Baptism and the Eucharist) to bring out both illocutions (the intent) and perlocutions (the effects of the text on the world). When we engage our imaginations (along with our minds) in the search for illocutions in the text, we empathize with the text's author and begin to share and adopt the intent of the author. Our imaginations help us do things like place ourselves in the Apostle Paul's shoes and plead for Euodia and Syntyche to reconcile. Our imaginations help us identify empathetically with Paul's illocution and by doing so, help us encounter and understand the text more fully. But our imaginations play an even stronger role in our completion of perlocutions. Because a sacramental reading of Scripture assumes that a

2. Campbell, *The Christian System*, 274.

channel of grace is still open and functioning, our imaginations play a pivotal role in bringing that grace into the world as a result of our encounter with the text. This kind of perlocutionary imagination goes much farther than what has commonly been called "application of the text." In application, we simply look around the world for illocutionary or locutionary analogs to the text and map them as close as possible to our understanding of the text. Sacramental perlocutionary imagination extends beyond preexisting analogs and seeks to create new effects from the text based on the situation we find ourselves in. This is not relativistic interpretation, this is responsible reading that engages our full humanity. For example, Barbara Brown Taylor wrestles with the "standard" interpretation of the parable of the talents in light of migrant workers in Nicaragua and those protesting for rights for the poor. At the end of her sermon she demonstrates the use a sacramental illocutionary and perlocutionary approach to the text:

> I have been trying to imagine Jesus coming up to one of them and saying, "I've come for my profit. What? No profit? Then you ought to have invested my money with the bankers, and on my return I would have received what was my own with interest. Somebody take away the little bit they have here in Mosier and give it to those with ten times as much. For to all those who have, more will be given; but from those who have nothing, even what they have will be taken away." And you know what? I can't imagine it. I can't imagine it at all. So maybe this is not a sermon about the parable of the talents at all. Maybe it is a sermon about how we read Scripture—about why we are so reluctant to challenge established meanings, about what is at risk if we do, about what would happen if we stopped thinking of the truth of Scripture as something already set down for good in an old, old book and re-conceived it as something fresh that happens every time we get together and let the sharp edges of our lives poke at Scripture until it yields new and living truth—maybe even something that would upset the (little "m") master?[3]

In order to move ahead beyond modernism and the stasis of deconstruction-only response, we need to reignite our sacramental imaginations. A vibrant sacramental imagination moves us from simple rebellion against a former view to the celebration of a wider embrace. Many first waves of imaginative endeavors in postmodernism were simply about rejecting the modernism before it. They merely broke the rules of art and architecture to dismantle the unified theory those rules were built on. But now, where do

3. Taylor, "The Parable of the Fearful Investor."

we go from here? How long will simple rebellion against the what-was be able to sustain us? Unfortunately, the question of "what or who will become the object of our wrath in order to ignite our imaginations" is still driving much of our current engagement of the imagination. While a healthy part of our imaginations is the testing of the old ways in new and, as yet, unrealized situations; we need to shift the focus of our imaginations toward a new reality that moves toward something instead of away from something. Shifting that focus takes careful tending in two kinds of expressions of imagination. First, we must learn how to let the sacraments shape our interior imaginative life and second, we must learn how to let the sacraments shape our communal imaginative life.

The sacraments shape our interior imagination through creating healthy intimacy with the physical world around us. Our interior worlds are often left disconnected from the physical location and condition of our bodies. Some Christian traditions have set out to create an almost dualistic mind/body split because the body and the world it resides in is not helpful to the growth and vitality of the interior life. In these kinds of traditions, the body and the world it lives in is even more harmful to the imagination because the body cannot help but awaken the potential for evil and sin that the imagination carries with it. After all, many of Jesus' edits to the Law in his Sermon on the Mount relocate the offense to the realm of the imagination and not simply the physical action. These highly ascetic traditions seek to pull us out of the physical world so our imaginations are not ignited by the spark of greed, lust, anger, etc. They see the imagination as a highly flammable wood pile ready to burn the whole house down if it is not covered and keep away from a spark. This policy of containment ultimately renders the imagination almost useless.

The sacraments can be the connective tissue that help unite the body and the imagination while, at the same time, protecting the imagination from being set on fire by the potential evil this connection introduces. The sacraments accomplish this by showing us how to rightly interact with and care for our bodies and the world they reside in. For example, when we interact with water in remembrance of our baptism, the water can help form our interior world when it brings along the narrative of incarnation, death, and resurrection that Baptism itself infuses in the material of water. Our imaginations are not limited by just a strict ceremonial interaction with water; when the sacrament of Baptism becomes formative for our interior world, suddenly all interactions with water—whether ceremonial or not— are pregnant with the incarnation, death, and resurrection of Jesus. Both the physical substance of the sacrament (in this case, water) and its associated narrative set our imaginations on a healthy and active course to engage the world around us while, at the same time, continually reforming our interior life around the life of God as revealed in the sacraments.

Likewise, the sacraments shape our communal imagination through creating healthy relationships with those who share in the sacraments. The idea of having a communal imagination is not new, but with the rise and influence of evangelicalism's emphasis on personal relationships with God, a communal imagination has been largely unexplored in the recent past. Many times we have traded proper communal imagination for somewhat utilitarian mechanisms such as brainstorming, surveying, and market research. These things are not harmful or even unhelpful, but they are not a replacement for a healthy communal imagination. Again, the sacraments provide the connective tissue for communal imagination in the form of tangible symbol and shared narrative. For example, the Eucharist is, in both its tangible and narrative form, a communal act that gathers our individual imaginations and knits them together into a communal imagination that shares a common *telos*. The Apostle Paul tells us the unified one loaf of bread is both a goal and a description of who we are as the church. Augustine tells us to "be what we see and receive who we are" when the bread and wine are shared at the Eucharist.

These interactions with God's grace lay down shared values that point to who we are and how we live into the future—something that only the imagination can nurture and foster appropriately. For instance, a properly formed sacramental communal imagination lets us speak about the "not yet" and discern it together. This kind of imaginative forecasting is helpful because it leaves room for us to ask questions we might not otherwise ask with data driven discernment. Our future (and present) is circumscribed by the nature of God's grace encountered in both the material and narrative of the sacrament, which is ultimately a wider frontier and horizon than our empirical gathering of data about the world could be. A communal imagination forged in the sacraments helps us move past relational roadblocks or stalemates we often encounter as the church. It moves us beyond the narcissistic tendencies of Kant's categorical imperative to empathy. Many times apathy, indifference, and disagreement are seldom resolved by rational and logical arguments with one another. We must appeal to our shared communal imagination to remind ourselves of where we are going and what our *telos* is if we hope to substantially move beyond apathy, indifference, and disagreement. Even Nietzsche recognized the power of communal imagination to spur creativity and agreement among us when he said:

> Without myth every culture loses the healthy natural power of
> its creativity: only a horizon defined by myths completes and

unifies a whole cultural movement. Myth alone saves all the powers of the imagination and of the Apollonian dream from their aimless wanderings. The images of the myth have to be the unnoticed omnipresent demonic guardians, under whose care the young soul grows to maturity and whose signs help the man to interpret his life and struggles. Even the state knows no more powerful unwritten laws than the mythical foundation that guarantees its connection with religion and its growth from mythical notions.[4]

While Nietzsche fails to anchor his notion of myth in the sacramental life of the church, his observations about how myth works as the background of meaning for all our interactions is helpful. This working is not incredibly overt or flashy. Communal imagination is not a shared mission or vision statement splashed on a wall or masthead; it is shared wonder, shared hope, and a shared *telos*—all of which are primarily shaped by a shared sacramental life.

In conclusion, when our imaginations are fueled and ordered by the sacramental life, our world as Nietzschian "work of art" is not left to float as a disembodied metaphor or illusion. Our world painted by the sacraments tethers us to God's reality, even though we cannot call out with objective certainty the whole of that reality. We celebrate the beauty the sacramental life ignites for us and we give thanks for the narrative it ties us to—namely the incarnation, death, and resurrection of Jesus. When we carefully and artfully tend to our sacramental imaginations both alone and with others, our fires burn and we see a present future where God's *telos* invades our hearts, minds, wills, and imaginations.

4. Nietzsche, *The Birth of Tragedy and the Case of Wagner*, 135.

BIBLIOGRAPHY

Campbell, Alexander. *The Christian System*. New York: Arno, 1969.

Nietzsche, Friedrich. *The Birth of Tragedy and the Case of Wagner*. Translated by Walter Kaufmann. New York: Vintage, 1967.

———. "On Truth and Lie in an Extra-Moral Sense." In *The Portable Nietzsche*, edited by Walter Kaufmann, 46–47. New York: Penguin, 1976.

Taylor, Barbara Brown. "The Parable of the Fearful Investor." No pages (January 2012). Online: http://chapel-archives.oit.duke.edu/documents/BBT—FearfulInvestor. pdf

13

Uncommon Sense

How Proverbs Can Help Emerging Adults Find a Meaningful Life

BRIAN MILLS

The proverbs of Solomon son of David, king of Israel: for attaining wisdom and discipline; for understanding words of insight; for acquiring a disciplined and prudent life doing what is right and just and fair; for giving prudence to the simple, knowledge and discretion to the young—let the wise listen and add to their learning, and let the discerning get guidance—for understanding proverbs and parables, the sayings and riddles of the wise. The fear of the Lord is the beginning of wisdom. (Prov 1:1–7)

INTRODUCTION

Proverbs is a neglected book. It is overlooked by preachers who are eager to inspire hearts. It is pushed out of the way by scholars who are eager to dig through more interesting theology. It is irrelevant to children who aren't yet reflective about life's responsibilities or ready for warnings about seductive women. But Proverbs is well-suited for emerging adults. Throughout the book, the teacher emphasizes three key values: wisdom is valuable, discipline is good, and fear is necessary. Dealing with the unraveling of the American culture and unique developmental needs, emerging adults can find a meaningful life by applying the values taught in Proverbs.

UNRAVELED IN AMERICA

There is a perceived "unraveling" in American culture. This is likely the result of multiple factors, including postmodernism, growing secularism and generational shift. The effect on America's youth is that the path to adulthood is not as clear or direct as it once was.

Postmodernism

Stanley Grenz summarized the effects of philosophical postmodernism by saying:

> Postmodern philosophers applied the theories of the literary deconstructionists to the world as a whole. Just as a text will be read differently by each reader, they said, so reality will be 'read' differently by each knowing self that encounters it. This means that there is no one meaning of the world, no transcendent center to reality as a whole. . . . This sweeps away the "uni-" of the "universe" sought by the Enlightenment project. It abandons the quest for a unified grasp of objective reality. It asserts that the world has no center, only differing viewpoints and perspectives. In fact, even the concept of "world" presupposes an objective unity or a coherent whole that does not exist "out there." In the end, the postmodern world is merely an arena of "duelling texts."[1]

This shift has had far-reaching implications in every area of life. Old assumptions have been questioned in every conceivable discipline: psychology, sociology, anthropology, history, political science, the natural sciences, the fine arts, economics, etc. There has been a general sense that old certainties are not so certain. What might have felt absolute and objective in the past was analyzed into deconstructed perspectives. Then it was marginalized as hopelessly subjective perspective. There is no longer a

1. Grenz, *Primer on Postmodernism*, 6–7.

credibly shared metanarrative to provide a strong center or firm grounding for the American culture. Instead, we are fractured into a kind of ideological tribalism. Jean-Francois Lyotard described the essence of the postmodern condition as "incredulity toward metanarratives."[2] Consequently, the nation has struggled to develop a shared sense of the meaning of life regarding art, technology, business, government, politics, family, entertainment, etc. Older generations have been left wondering what they can teach with certainty. Younger generations are left wondering what they can believe with certainty. There are no commonly shared ways of understanding the whole of reality, with coherence and integrity.

Growing Secularism

Secularism is not new in America. Even though Christianity has enjoyed a position of privilege in this country for more than three centuries, officially the country has always been a secular state, serving as the sponsor for no specific religion. We have been a Christian nation by virtue of our personal heritage through our representative form of government, but not by our charter. Jill Lepore describes a renewed interest in the life and thought of Thomas Paine, who was a profoundly revolutionary figure. In 1776 Paine published the best-selling *Common Sense*, which argued for the independence of the American colonies from Great Britain. "Without the pen of the author of common sense, the sword of Washington would have been raised in vain."[3] But Paine wrote *The Age of Reason* just seventeen years later from a French prison where he sharply criticized Christianity and made a strong case against institutionalizing religion along with the new republic. Even though the work earned him many enemies, it was quietly a best-seller. He said, "Soon after I had published the pamphlet 'Common Sense,' in America, . . . I saw the exceeding probability that a revolution in the system of government would be followed by a revolution in the system of religion."[4] That second revolution did not take place as quickly or as publicly as he might have expected. But we see clear fruit that the revolution is bearing fruit today through increasing American secularism, even among those who recently have declared that American evangelicals have finally lost the culture wars of the 1960s.[5]

2. Ibid., 46.
3. Lepore, "Sharpened Quill," para. 7.
4. Ibid., para. 28.
5. Landsberg, "Focus on the Family."

Secularism from the government is no surprise. But there is a growing secularism from within Christianity that is disturbing. In Christian Smith's analysis of the National Study of Youth and Religion (NSYR) the effects of our cultural unraveling are clearer. According to the research, there is good news and bad news. The good news is that parents are successfully passing on their religious orientation to their students.[6] This is true for every religious and non-religious background represented. The bad news is that the students have not evaluated the beliefs that found their orientation . . . and they do not want to. They have "backgrounded" the big questions in life, preferring to deal with the more pressing agenda of self-fulfillment.[7] In fact, this orientation toward self has resulted in a new religion, of sorts, called "moralistic, therapeutic, deism."[8] It is the "do good, feel good, God-is-far-enough-away-not-to-interfere-but-is-close-enough-to-help" religion of American young people. It is a common denominator kind of faith that values the self at the center and isn't sure of much else. In his follow-up work Smith reports on the same students five years later in order to understand how their spiritual journey has progressed. He finds that there are multiple pathways to becoming adults who are "highly committed"[9] to their religious beliefs. But not many students progress to that level. The key elements that seem to make the difference are: having parents with a strong religious commitment, meaningful relationships with other non-parental adults who have strong religious commitments, maintaining regular personal devotional practice, having the ability to connect faith to everyday life, having the opportunity to wrestle doubts, and various sexual behaviors. It seems that when students have many of these elements as part of their adolescent development, they become more highly committed than those who do not.[10]

Kenda Creasy Dean also participated in the NSYR. She describes the faith of teenagers as the "cult of nice" where students see God either as a butler or a therapist.[11] Consequently, they are not terribly committed to him, though they want him to be committed to them. Dean further notes, "it's not because they have misunderstood what we have taught them in church. *They practice it because this is what we have taught them in church.* . . . Our religiously conventional adolescents seem to be merely absorbing

---

6. Smith, *Soul Searching*, 34.

7. Ibid., 129.

8. Ibid., 162–70.

9. Smith, *Souls in Transition*, 224–29.

10. Ibid., 231–41.

11. Dean, *Almost Christian*, 33–34.

and reflecting religiously what the adult world is routinely modeling for and inculcating in its youth."[12]

David Kinnaman and Gabe Lyons, along with the Barna Group, conducted a three-year research project to understand the perceptions young people have about Christianity. They explained that American young people believe the church does *not* display qualities that are Christian. Instead, they are hypocritical, overly concerned with "salvation," antihomosexual, sheltered, too political and judgmental.[13] Interestingly, these critiques were not coming from outside the church. The young people making these claims are frustrated Christian young people. When Kinnaman listened closely, he discovered that 65 percent of these young people have made a personal commitment to Jesus Christ that is still important to them. But only 3 percent of them have a biblical worldview.[14] Furthermore, their attitudes have changed significantly from the previous generation about such lifestyle issues as cohabitation, gambling, sexual fantasies, sex outside of marriage, getting drunk, viewing pornography, homosexuality, and abortion.[15] In a follow up work, Kinnaman further explains that the younger generation of Christians is a "disengaged" or a "dropout" generation from the American church.[16] There is a strong sense that the Christian faith of our children is not the Christian faith of our fathers. There has been a general unraveling that leaves the younger generation in a vulnerable position.

Generational Shift

In 1997 William Strauss and Neil Howe built on their pioneering research into generational theory to help us understand how our development is influenced by the events in our world at significant growth stages. They propose that each generation shares certain characteristics as a result of their shared developmental stages through a shared history. This results in a revolving typology that they have traced back hundreds of years.[17] They use these types to anticipate future developments in generational shift.

---

12. Ibid., 29–30.

13. Kinnaman, *Unchristian*, 29–30.

14. Ibid., 76. A "biblical worldview" was defined as eight specific orthodox doctrines regarding the identity of Christ, rule of God, nature of salvation, the reality of Satan, responsibility for evangelism, reliability of Scripture, existence of unchanging truth, etc.

15. Ibid., 53.

16. Kinnaman, *You Lost Me*, loc. 112.

17. Howe and Strauss, *Fourth Turning*, 71–98.

In 2000, they published *Millennials Rising: The Next Great Generation* to suggest that the Millennial generation will make a profound impact on the world. "[T]he Millennial Generation will entirely recast the image of youth from downbeat and alienated to upbeat and engaged—with potentially seismic consequences."[18] They were specific, identifying seven distinct qualities that give this generation a unique profile: special, sheltered, confident, team-oriented, conventional, pressured, and achieving. Again, in 2003 they proposed in *Millennials Go to College* that Millennials "are probably the most all-around capable teenage generation this nation, and perhaps the world, has ever seen."[19] Yet, others observe that in spite of their potential Millennials display a concerning difficulty with finding direction. Since they are used to having the steps marked out for them they struggle to problem solve and assess strategic steps on their own. Even with great ambition and ability, they seem to lack direction or enduring passion.

Terri Apter, in *The Myth of Maturity: What Teenagers Need from their Parents to Become Adults,* suggests that some parenting styles may be partly to blame for the problem. She says that adolescents who are at the threshold of adulthood need continued parental support in order to cross the threshold. Apter believes that this space in between the two developmental stages is legitimate and that maturity is a myth. By reinforcing the myth through forced independence, many parents actually rob their students of the support they need to make this important transition. Some people wring their hands over this new period between adolescence and adulthood, calling them thresholders, tweeners, adultescents, kidults, or Peter and Priscilla Pans. While acknowledging the difficulties with this dynamic, Apter suggests that there's nothing wrong with it as a phase. Instead, it is carrying baggage from old orders. Rather than pushing adolescents out of the nest to force them to learn to fly, she suggests that the fear of a "failure to launch" is overplayed and can actually cause a stunted maturity.[20]

Jeffrey Arnett also recognizes the delayed maturity. He has included it as a new stage in his popular textbook on human development. Recognizing that it is simply a fact that adolescence begins earlier than in the past for industrialized societies, and various sociological issues have delayed the traditional qualities of adulthood, he has developed a theory of emerging adulthood with five main qualities. He calls it a self-focused age of identity

---

18. Howe and Strauss, *Millenials Rising*, 4.

19. Howe and Strauss, *Millenials Go to College*, 123.

20. Apter, *Myth of Maturity*, 37–51.

explorations, instability, feeling in-between, and possibilities.[21] He remains hopeful about their future.

Dr. Jean Twenge is more concerned. She does not accept all of the hype. She asserts that the problems with this generation may be more about their orientation to the self than their delay to accept the historic marks of maturity. They are narcissists. In contrast to the Baby Boomers, who only became fixated on the self in their youth after having been firmly oriented to the priority of duty, Millennials have been oriented to the priority of their own wants and needs from birth.[22] Twenge suggests that today's youth (anyone born after 1971) have never known a world where some duty or higher purpose came before their own development or desires. This is a profound shift for a culture that was historically oriented to the Modernist objective, rational mind and the Judaeo-Christian wordview.

UNLEARNING IN BIBLICAL WISDOM LITERATURE

Biblical wisdom literature was written to explore and to share reflections about the meaning of life for the Hebrew people. It looks a lot like other oriental wisdom literature from Egyptian, Sumerian, Akkadian, and other traditions, with a strong practical orientation.[23] It was written from the reality of practical experience and its curious difference from common perceptions about the world in the dominant culture.

It has been suggested that Song of Songs, Proverbs, and Ecclesiastes function together as a set, representing three phases of Solomon's life, "with the explanation that 'when a man is young he composes songs; when he grows older he makes sententious remarks; and when he becomes an old man he speaks of the vanity of things.'"[24] In Ecclesiastes the writer vents, "Everything is meaningless. What does man gain from all his labor at which he toils under the sun? Generations come and generations go, but the earth remains forever. . . . There is no remembrance of men of old, and even those who are yet to come will not be remembered by those who follow." The teacher in Ecclesiastes is cynical about the dominant culture's definitions of the meaning of life: pleasure, knowledge and work. He has decided that they do not work. But the teacher is not completely cynical. In the end he concludes that meaning is possible when life is put into perspective by the

---

21. Arnett, *Emerging Adulthood*, 8.

22. Twenge, *Generation Me*, 1.

23. Longman, *Proverbs*, 52.

24. Ibid., 24.

right orientation: "Fear God and keep his commandments, for this is the whole duty of man" (Eccl 12:13).

The teacher in Proverbs also critiques common definitions of the meaning of life, but he approaches them much differently. He is more encouraging about alternatives. He is confident that meaning is possible. He is more direct with his advice. He attempts to engage his audience in a developmentally appropriate way.

Even though the book refuses categorization, there are clearly two sections. Most scholars agree that chapters 1–9 are post-exilic while the rest is pre-exilic. Though the original writing of Proverbs may have been from Solomon or his contemporaries, it is widely believed that later editing was an attempt to cast the wisdom of Israel in the same light as the wisdom of other oriental cultures, especially in the post-exilic time period.[25] The leaders of the reconstruction in post-exilic Jerusalem found it helpful to apply this old teacher's lessons in Proverbs to their new circumstances.

In many ways, the situation for today's Christian emerging adults parallels the postexilic situation for ancient Hebrews that fueled a renewed interest in the book of Proverbs. They had been in exile for only seventy years. But their culture had been disintegrating for more than four hundred years, since they watched Solomon's national inheritance divide under his failed leadership. Two hundred years after Solomon, the Assyrians conquered and exiled the ten tribes of the Northern Kingdom. One hundred and fifty years later, Babylon conquered and exiled the two tribes of the Southern Kingdom. And for seventy years in exile, the Jews were systematically acculturated by the Babylonian empire. Their older leaders were deposed or dead. Their young leaders had been taught in Babylonian schools while serving the Babylonian king and enjoying the comfort of his Babylonian palace. The writings of Moses were distant memories. The Temple was a pile of rubble. The priesthood was scattered and disempowered. And the sacrificial system was dismantled. God's ways were far away.

But after Persia defeated the Babylonians, they began allowing the Jews to return to their homeland. After many years of exile in the Babylonian world, the Jews returned to Jerusalem and began to rebuild their way of life. They rebuilt the Temple. They rebuilt the walls of the city of Jerusalem. They recovered the Law and the priesthood. And they reinstituted the sacrificial system. The Jews dug for roots that could provide new life for a renewed era of flourishing in God's favor. As they worked through old texts for guidance they stumbled onto the wisdom literature, finding some old lessons from good teachers for a new time. The old questions resonated with theirs. The

25. Waltke, *Book of Proverbs*, 64.

advice seemed to speak to their circumstances. The lessons provided the guidance they needed. The young generation needed to unlearn the Babylonian culture. They also needed to unlearn the unfaithful culture of the Hebrews that resulted in God's judgment in the first place. They turned to the forgotten-but-familiar Proverbs.

UNCOMMON SENSE IN PROVERBS

In an unraveled culture where the old ways are questioned, "common sense" is not so common anymore. Where old systems have been discredited, new systems are developed. Where people have "unlearned" a culture they bring an "uncommon" perspective to bear on shaping a new culture. Where God's people find themselves in a culture with divergent values, their perception of the world looks odd. Their values are foreign. Their way of life is fragile. In that setting, uncommon sense can uniquely provide the way forward. But it needs encouragement, reinforcement and direction. The values of Proverbs give direction to emerging adults, helping them to find a meaningful life through wisdom, discipline, and fear.

Wisdom is Reliable

While in Proverbs wisdom may not meet the Modernist epistemological criteria for certainty, it certainly meets criteria for confidence. The possibility, practicality and benefits of wisdom are assumed. It is reliable because it has been tested in the real world by real people. It works. "Listen, my son, to your father's instruction and do not forsake your mother's teaching . . . whoever listens to me will live in safety and be at ease, without fear of harm" (1:8, 33). "My son, preserve sound judgment and discernment, do not let them out of your sight; they will be life for you. . . . Then you will go on your way in safety, and your foot will not stumble; when you lie down, you will not be afraid; when you lie down, your sleep will be sweet. Have no fear of sudden disaster or of the ruin that overtakes the wicked, for the Lord will be your confidence and will keep your foot from being snared" (3:21–26). Wisdom is not speculative or purely rational. It is the result of shared experience and the product of shared reflection.

Throughout the book the teacher in Proverbs uses many words as synonyms for concepts related to wisdom (understanding, knowledge, judgment, insight, discernment, discretion, prudence, etc.). This is important for emerging adults who live in the information age to be clear about wisdom. Information is more available today than at any other time in history. Many of the largest companies in the world are those that provide storage, access, tracking, and analytics of information. For the first time in history, the youngest generation does not need an adult to give them information about their world. Students only need electricity and a computer to learn. And they are quick learners with the technology; they seem to intuitively know how to "Google it" as "digital natives." But while information may be power, it is not wisdom. Understanding comes from experience. Judgment comes from mistakes. Discernment comes through practice.

Proverbs does not present wisdom in a neatly organized topical encyclopedia format, or in the format of a sectioned legal code. It is more like the popular "for Dummies" format—"where you'll find [our] proven experts presenting even the most complex subjects in plain English . . . making everything easier."[26] The teacher presents wisdom as a practical perspective on the world. Its lessons present wisdom like a tutorial for the meaningful life. Instead of an obvious intentional design for the book he invites the reader to consider the Proverbs as more random, reflecting the messiness of life. He gives guidance that is often contingent on conditions or context, rather than being absolute or universal. Likely developed as an oral tradition, the proverbs "come alive again" when they are "spoken orally in the right context," with the application to be determined by the wise person.[27] Proverbs shares observations about cause and effect, choices and consequences, relationships and work. The teacher discusses leadership, business, politics, government, economy, marriage, parenting, friendship, health, neighborhood, home, and heart. He presents wisdom as a reliable, coherent, accessible view of the world that corresponds to reality. Proverbs shares a worldview.

According to David Naugle, in *Worldview: The History of a Concept*, "worldview" has almost always been a project attempting to describe a view of the whole of human experience in the world. In the late eighteenth century, Immanuel Kant used the concept "to refer to a 'world-intuition in the sense of contemplation of the world given to the senses.'"[28] In the early nineteenth century, G. W. F. Hegel described how "Reason then unites this objective totality with the opposite subjective totality to form the infinite world-intuition . . ."[29] In the late nineteenth century, Wilhelm Dilthey's work on epistemology was "rooted in the issues of real life and what he called 'lived experience'" where "'Every true world-view . . . is an intuition which

26. "About For Dummies," http://www.dummies.com/about-for-dummies.html
27. Longman, *Proverbs*, 40–42.
28. Naugle, *Worldview*, 59.
29. Ibid., 69.

emerges from the standing-in-the-middle-of-life."[30] And Søren Kierkeg-aard, in the mid-nineteenth century, considered that "Life-view emphasizes the duty and importance of the individual to understand himself, both his 'premises' and his 'conclusions,' his conditionality and his freedom. Each man must answer for himself about the meaning of life, and thus he cannot take his cue from the spirit of the age which will all too readily answer on his behalf."[31] Proverbs is like this. Practicality and the meaning of life are related to reality somehow. The teacher presents a view of the world that reliably corresponds to reality suggesting that wise people will adopt the view and conform their life to its ways.

The exchange of this wisdom is passed along relational lines. Proverbs speaks from a paternalistic posture. Waltke believes that Proverbs originat-ed in a royal court setting, but was disseminated through "folk" settings like the family. "In sum, Solomon intended to transmit his wisdom to Israel's youths by putting his proverbs in the mouths of godly parents (1:8–9), even as Moses disseminated the law in the home (cf. Deut 6:7–9)."[32] Most schol-ars believe some version of this.[33] Much later it was disseminated through schools. In each setting the experience of the older generation is informing the ignorance of the younger generation. In that process, the young are not just asked to test the reliability of spoken words but to test the reliability of the speakers themselves.[34] Much of the language is "father-son," which is probably both literal and figurative for wide use. When people were sepa-rated from land, Temple, and cult parents had to assume role of priest for their families and households. In the absence of the cultus, character be-came the focal point and objective for teaching about God's way.[35] Proverbs was used to help train the character of the next generation. In some ways it may have been like a tutor or a nanny since the law and the rituals were not readily available and no longer credible. Postexilic Hebrews sought to rees-tablish the credibility of their unique worldview. And Proverbs continued to provide valued guidance for New Testament writers, showing up in their teachings more than sixty times through quotes, allusions and other uses.[36]

Strauss and Howe may be most known for their description of four generational archetypes, which develop and shift according to a specific

30. Ibid., 82–83.

31. Ibid., 74.

32. Waltke, *Book of Proverbs*, 58–63.

33. Longman, *Proverbs*, 54. Murphy, *Proverbs*, xix–xxii.

34. Waltke, *Book of Proverbs*, 119.

35. Bland, "Formation of Character," 227.

36. Waltke, *Book of Proverbs*, 126.

pattern. They trace this pattern back through many generations in American history, but also see it in other cultures and times. While this typology has received most of the attention on their work, a specific part of the dynamic is actually more helpful for our discussion. They explain that the parent-child generational relationship is primarily competitive and fraught with tension, often producing rebellion to some degree. However, the grandparent-grandchild generational relationship is more complementary. The grandparent has developed both wisdom and grace, both of which the youth need. The youth have idealism and vigor, which are both waning for the older generation. In one of Strauss and Howe's archetypes, this looks like a "prophet" grandparent generation complementing a "hero" child generation.[37] The hero has strength, achievement and potential, but the prophet has guidance for direction. Because the human life span is so short, and the human learning process is so long, young people benefit from the accumulated learning of generations before them. Though information can be transmitted through impersonal medium, wisdom requires more of a contextualized, experiential learning. Each generation depends on their ancestors to teach them, understanding that every successive generation will continue to test and develop that body of wisdom. As time passes the formally expressed worldviews may change, but there remains a core of wisdom that consistently and reliably corresponds to reality. Proverbs is about that wisdom.

Discipline is Good

Proverbs values discipline and correction as both the means to wisdom and the result of wisdom. This is often understood as verbal admonition, "A rebuke impresses a man of discernment more than a hundred lashes of a fool" (17:10). But it is sometimes also physical punishment, "The rod of correction imparts wisdom, but a child left to himself disgraces his mother" (29:15).[38] It is motivated by love: "He who spares the rod hates his son, but he who loves him is careful to discipline him" (13:24). "My son, do not despise the Lord's discipline and do not resent his rebuke, because the Lord disciplines those he loves, as a father the son he delights in" (3:11–12). And it is fueled by hope—hope that a foolish person can become wise, that an unmanaged life can become orderly, that a person can learn self-discipline and lead a profitable life that is personally rewarding and benefits others. But the hope is only realized with care. Discipline is not only punitive, it is

37. Howe and Strauss, *Fourth Turning*, 75–78.
38. Longman, *Proverbs*, 564–65.

also considered training, "Train a child in the way he should go and when he is old he will not turn from it" (22:6). It is often training through difficult experience, "As iron sharpens iron, so one man sharpens another" (27:17). Also, "the crucible for silver and the furnace for gold, but the Lord tests the heart" (17:3). And there are clear consequences associated with it: "He who ignores discipline comes to poverty and shame, but whoever heeds correction is honored" (13:18) and "How I hated discipline! How my heart spurned correction! I would not obey my teachers or listen to my instructors. I have come to utter ruin . . ." (5:12–14). Discipline helps wisdom to work. It helps knowledge to effect real change.

Proverbs values work as a training program for wisdom. There are many difficult interpretive and theological issues related to this work, like the guarantees of prosperity and poverty, their strange relationship with oppression, and the true estimation of wealth.[39] But for our purposes, the most relevant lessons concern laziness and foolishness that lead to poverty or temporary wealth.[40] Diligent and honest work is understood as part of a wise lifestyle. "He who gathers crops in summer is a wise son, but he who sleeps during harvest is a disgraceful son" (10:5). "He who works his land will have abundant food, but he who chases fantasies lacks judgment" (12:11). "All hard work brings a profit, but mere talk leads only to poverty" (14:23). "One who is slack in his work is brother to one who destroys" (18:9). "A sluggard does not plow in season; so at harvest time he looks but finds nothing" (20:4). "Go to the ant, you sluggard; consider its way and be wise! It has no commander, no overseer or ruler, yet it stores its provisions in summer and gathers its food at harvest" (6:6–8). Discipline and work are related programs for developing wisdom.

This dynamic is becoming more understood with recent neurological research. Daniel Goleman explored the significance of findings by Joseph LeDoux, a neuroscientist at the Center for Neural Science at New York University. LeDoux pioneered research into the role of the amygdala and the limbic system in relation to the neo-cortex and other areas of the brain.[41] He discovered that the amygdala influences how we understand what is happening around us, but also how we respond to it. Bypassing the cognitive processes for a slower rational assessment, the amygdala makes quick decisions based on cursory feelings from a storehouse of other experiences. These snap judgments stimulate neural and physical responses that influence rational interpretation of the events or circumstances. LeDoux calls it "pre-

39. Ibid., 573–76.
40. Ibid., 561–62.
41. Goleman, *Emotional Intelligence*, 15.

cognitive emotion," because of its instinct-like response in "fight-or-flight" situations. But he believes the response can be trained by cognitive processing and physical conditioning. Goleman refers to other research to suggest that the amygdala responses can be conditioned "with the right experiences."[42] For the teacher in Proverbs, the "right experiences" come in the forms of punishment, rebuke, pious worship, and good old-fashioned hard work. They impact a person's "emotional intelligence," or awareness and ability to manage his own emotions in relationship with those of others. They also help a young person to develop wisdom through training.

James K. A. Smith proposes an anthropological view of human and cultural development where young people develop themselves and their world as *homo liturgicus*.[43] People are reciprocally shaped by the liturgical activities and habits that are originally stimulated by the desires in their heart. These habits are not necessarily the random, unintentional practices of the human heart in its non-structured, impulsive, instinctual operations. Instead, the habits that make a difference are the intentional habits that orient space (the body with the world) and time (schedule) toward a specific, ultimate end (*telos*). These intentional habits are liturgies. They are worship activities. They are not initially habitual. They begin as selective exercises with meaningful objectives that involve amygdala and limbic responses. Over time they become a routine, automatic way to pursue the heart's desires. While in pursuit of its desires, the heart is shaped by them. Then, the person begins to shape the world around them with structure and intentionality.

Spiritual disciplines are the practical mechanism to explain how Smith's liturgy of desire operates. Dallas Willard writes about spiritual disciplines as the chief means of discipleship in, "In general, then, we 'put on' the new person by regular activities that are in our power, and we become what we could not be by direct effort."[44] The heart directs behavior and behavior shapes the heart, both empowered by grace. By employing specific behaviors to focus the mind and heart into productive physical actions, the heart and mind are trained to pursue certain objectives and respond to certain situations in a conditioned way. This looks like Godly restraint and ambition. As these behaviors become automatic, they reciprocally shape the heart by integrating the person's desires, thoughts, and behaviors. He is known for the quip, "Grace is opposed to earning, not to effort."[45]

42. Ibid., 221.

43. Smith, *Desiring the Kingdom*, 40.

44. Willard, *Great Omission*, 30.

45. Ibid., 34.

Sport is an example of another effective liturgy of desire. While study-ing and working at the YMCA training center in Massachusetts, James Naismith studied the philosophical side of physical education in order to help mature the listless, aimless, feminized young men of his day—"incorrigibles."[46] In 1891, he developed the game of basketball in order to give boys something to do with their time that would produce good char-acter. He believed it would help them become men who could work hard and succeed at a goal together. He saw the reciprocal relationship between physical training and character. Intentional training toward a specific goal shapes the heart of a young person. Then the heart influences new behav-iors that are seen as helpful toward achieving the goal. In that way, desire is cultivated and leveraged by discipline.

Work can also be a liturgy of desire. At work a person is engaged in the productive focusing of his abilities, skills and desires for accomplishing a specific goal. Miroslav Volf suggests "the various activities human beings do in order to satisfy their own needs and the needs of their fellow creatures should be viewed from the perspective of the operation of God's Spirit."[47] He develops a theology of work based on pneumatology and eschatology. He explains that our work can be cooperation with God's work toward his ultimate goal of transformation. When we work like that, our work is em-powered by his Spirit for his goals. We are transformed by the activities and He transforms the world around us at the same time.

Discipline is good. By integrating a person's desires, beliefs, thoughts and behaviors with actual impact on the real world, a person finds integrity in their soul and a meaningful existence in the world. By highlighting pain-fully practical, ordinary disciplines in life the teacher in Proverbs gives the younger generation examples of wisdom.

Fear is Necessary

The "fear of the Lord" is an important concept in Proverbs. It holds together rational and non-rational elements. On the one hand, it is "a co-referential term to 'law,' 'statutes,' 'commands,' and 'ordinances.'" But on the other hand, it is used synonymously with "love of the Lord" and humility.[48] This dual nature is both a sense of duty and a sense of desire. A young person is called cognitively to recognize God's superior wisdom, judgment and knowledge,

46. "Who We Are." http://www.ymca.int/ http://www.ymca.int/who-we-are/history/basketball-a-ymca-invention/
47. Volf, *Work in the Spirit*, 88.
48. Waltke, *Book of Proverbs*, 100.

affectively to trust and respect his care and behaviorally to submit his will and life. Together, these qualities direct objectives, define means and provide the motives for a meaningful life. A clear pathway to adulthood, along with the support of the community's cultural reinforcement and the incentive of compelling benefits helps young people to navigate the transition from adolescence into adulthood.

Proverbs 1:7 says, "The fear of the Lord is the beginning of wisdom." In 9:10 the teacher repeats the statement but extends it to say, "knowledge of the Holy One is understanding." In 2:1–5, the son is encouraged to "accept, store up, turn your ear to, apply your heart to, call out for, cry aloud for, look for and search for" wisdom, insight and understanding. The son is promised, "then you will understand the fear of the Lord and find the knowledge of God." In a surprising way, it seems that wisdom is found only *after* a person accepts that it can be found, commits to seeking, and submits to conformity. So, fear is both the beginning of wisdom and the result of its pursuit. The heart must be in its proper posture to find and respond to wisdom rightly. In Deuteronomy, there appears to be synonymous uses of "love of the Lord" and "fear of the Lord." The twin motivations of fear and love are significant.[49] In this way, "the fear of the Lord" functions more like an epistemology than a blunt reference to the effects of divine retribution. "The oft-maligned wisdom literature is not simply secular or profane or self-centered. It is anthropological and creational, and the pertinence of the divine to these areas should be clearly evident."[50] The posture of the heart influences its pursuit of wisdom and its ultimate fulfillment.

The relationship between a man and a woman provides the perfect metaphor for the potency of fear and desire. The teacher in Proverbs chooses this metaphor to illustrate a young man's relationship with wisdom. She "calls aloud in the street" (1:20), "will not answer" (1:28), "she will protect you; love her, and she will watch over you" (4:5), "Esteem her, and she will exalt you; embrace her, and she will honor you" (4:8), "Does not understanding raise her voice? . . . Listen, for I have worthy things to say; . . . Choose my instruction instead of silver, knowledge rather than choice gold, for wisdom is more precious than rubies and nothing you desire can compare with her . . . " (8:1, 6, 10–11). She calls out. She can be pursued. She can be found. She should be treasured. She provides many benefits.

Since the second century, "Sophia" (the Greek word for wisdom) in Proverbs 8 is often identified with Jesus.[51] This interpretation became a

49. Ibid, 101.
50. Murphy, *Proverbs*, 256.
51. Waltke, *Book of Proverbs*, 127.

major part of significant theological debates (i.e., Arians vs. Nicenes, Prov 8:22), though recent scholarship tends to interpret the teacher's lady as his own body of teachings. At other times the teacher's lady Sophia was related to the *logos* in Greek philosophy. But the word does not appear one time in John's gospel, where the Greek concept of *logos* is developed in Christian Scripture. And there are big differences between Sophia in these writings and the *logos* in John's writings. At best, Sophia may be a type of Christ. But there is no clear or direct Christology in the woman wisdom. Christ is distinct and superior.[52] By characterizing wisdom as a lady the teacher develops an epistemology that is more than ideal or intellectual. Wisdom is more than knowledge and information or quotable platitudes. Wisdom is highlighted as understanding, discernment, good judgment in relationship with the real world, practical life issues and internal concerns. Wisdom is a meaningful life.

David Naugle responds to the history of the worldview concept with his own biblical summary. He says, "From a scriptural point of view, therefore, the heart is responsible for how a man or woman sees the world. Indeed, what goes into the heart from the outside world eventually shapes its fundamental dispositions and determines what comes out of it as the springs of life. Consequently, the heart establishes the basic presuppositions of life and, because of its life-determining influence, must always be carefully guarded."[53] A worldview is not a highly abstracted, analytical, intellectual or idealized system for beliefs and knowledge. Instead, it is a pre-reflective commitment of the heart. They are initially accepted uncritically, but with commitment. Naugle follows the Augustinian tradition where faith is a grace gift that enables understanding. He locates the existence and development of a worldview in a biblical theology of the heart. James Sire agrees and further defines the process of worldview formation in *Naming the Elephant*. He defines worldview as "a commitment, a fundamental orientation of the heart, that can be expressed as a story or in a set of presuppositions (assumptions which may be true, partially true or entirely false) which we hold (consciously or subconsciously, consistently or inconsistently) about the basic constitution of reality, and that provides the foundation on which we live and move and have our being."[54] The human heart contains the beginning point for a worldview. The orientation of a person's heart is what matters first, and so it matters most.

James K. A. Smith's anthropology is again relevant at this point:

52. Ibid., 131.
53. Naugle, *Worldview*, 272.
54. Sire, *Naming the Elephant*, 122.

> We need a nonreductionistic understanding of human persons as embodied agents of desire or love. This Augustinian model of human persons resists the rationalism and quasi-rationalism of the earlier models by shifting the center of gravity of human identity, as it were, down from the heady regions of mind closer to the central regions of our bodies, in particular, our *kardia*— our gut or heart. The point is to emphasize that the way we inhabit the world is not primarily as thinkers, or even believers, but as more affective, embodied creatures who make our way in the world more by feeling our way around it.[55]

That being the case, then, we must pay attention to what we fear and what we love as ultimate and the intentional practices or habits we engage in that love relationship. If we are truly *homo liturgicus*, then the activities born from our deepest duties and desires shape us at the most fundamental levels, impact our beliefs and thoughts, and shape our world.

The "fear of the Lord" is a fundamental orientation of the heart. It is a fundamental recognition of and respect for God's existence, presence and power. It is the orientation that allows for a more conscious, theoretical processing of life and beliefs. It properly directs us toward the possibility of meaning through understanding and motivates us toward the integrity of living consistently with that understanding. When our understanding and our lifestyles mutually reinforce each other, while also corresponding to the realities of the world around us, we find a meaningful life. But it must be lived before it can be proven. The suspected understanding (by faith) will not be justified with certainty through a rational, objective process alone. It must be tested through intention and discipline. What proceeds behaviorally by discipline must begin in the heart by the twin motivations of desire: fear and love. And it does not have to be a strong desire. A *want* to desire (a want-to-want) may be a sufficient starting point. According to the wisdom of Proverbs, when desire, intention, and behavior work together successfully for practical benefit a person finds themselves and their meaning. When young people accept the wisdom of the parent and grand-parent generations, they have a head-start in the process of finding a meaningful life. In Proverbs, individuals and the community are oriented around the fear of God. The vision of the teacher is that this center will hold life together more productively and effectively than other centers. Specifically, if the pursuit of pleasure is at the center, laziness, sloth, poverty and irrelevance are the consequences. When achievement is at the center, quarreling, cheating, dishonest gain, loneliness and ruin are produced. But where the fear of the

---

55. Smith, *Desiring the Kingdom*, 47.

Lord is the center, wealth, love, satisfaction, respect, honor, influence, and integrity are the reward.

CONCLUSION

I have to admit, I really do love the Proverbs. And I think the values expressed in Proverbs can be immeasurably helpful for emerging adults at our unique time in American history. I enjoy reading Proverbs, marking verses in my Bible and journaling prayers from the text. But there would be no text without a teacher. The most important value in Proverbs is the value of a relationship with a teacher. When that teacher is wise, he presents a reliable worldview with confidence, even if without certainty. When he is disciplined, he models for them a life consistently shaped by a worldview and graciously shaping the world. And when he is in relationship with God, he shows how life can have meaning even if we do not always have answers. Emerging adults need teachers who invest in their development by assuring them wisdom is valuable, discipline is good and fear is necessary.

It appears in Proverbs that wisdom is not possessed. It is produced. And we do not control it. But we can cultivate it through relentless pursuit. The pursuit makes all the difference. The quest itself is valuable. The need to search for meaning is vital and life-giving. Like a hunger pang, it compels us to interact with our world and with each other for something or someone to satisfy its craving. Viktor Frankl observed in *Man's Search for Meaning*, that deep and lasting meaning cannot be found in oneself. "The more one forgets himself—by giving himself to a cause to serve or another person to love—the more human he is and the more he actualizes himself. . . . According to logotheraphy, we can discover meaning in life in three different ways: 1) by creating a work or doing a deed; 2) by experiencing something or encountering someone; and 3) by the attitude we take toward unavoidable suffering."[56] Somehow, we must be oriented outside ourselves in order to find true meaning. After months in a Nazi prison camp, he decided these three paths led a person outside himself. In the search for meaning, a person is perpetually drawn forward by his soul's appetite . . . and sometimes his starvation . . . unless he loses hope that he will be satisfied.

Ironically, it is often the absurdity of suffering that causes us to despair of meaning in the first place. Frankl notes that our hope regarding meaning has profound implications for the actual meaningfulness of our lives. He describes his observation that when a man would smoke "his own cigarettes, we knew he had given up faith in his strength to carry on, and, once lost, the

56. Frankl, *Man's Search*, 109–10.

will to live seldom returned."[57] Cigarettes to a prisoner were bargaining chips to leverage the critical exchange of goods, like purchasing extra soup. Or, they were elite rewards to be protected and preserved until there was reason to enjoy them. When a person gives up hope, they give up the search and the struggle for meaning. When they give up meaning, they give up everything.

The postmodern unraveling of our time has disturbed our naïve contentment in certainty. For many, this has resulted in directionless disillusionment. But for others, it has awakened their appetite for meaning. It has actually helped them by drawing into a quest with desire—a search that ultimately finds its fulfillment in Christ. Proverbs may appear to give easy answers to practical questions. But that is a superficial reading of the book. Chapters 7 and 31 paint a related picture of something deeper. They paint man's search for meaning—the search for wisdom—as a romantic love relationship charged with desire. She might tease and seem elusive. But she hides in plain sight. She can be found in the everyday and mundane. She has many layers in a complex and mysterious, intriguing character. The more you learn about her, the more you are stupefied. The more you know her, the more she surprises you. She is a bit intimidating, but relentlessly intriguing. Young men struggle to know how to relate with a woman when so much is uncertain. But as long as they believe she is desirable, they will pursue. And they will love the pursuit.

In a similar way, man finds his meaning in the search for wisdom. We are invited into a respectful and loving relationship with the world, with each other and with God. That relationship may not be marked by certainty, but it is reliable. We may find more mystery than mastery. We may not understand fully, but we can know. Us younger men need a good teacher to show us what a mature relationship looks like. Thank you, Dr. John Castelein for teaching us like that.

57. Ibid., 7–8.

BIBLIOGRAPHY

Apter, Terri. *The Myth of Maturity: What Teenagers Need from Parents to Become Adults.* New York: Norton, 2001.

Arnett, Jeffrey Jensen. *Emerging Adulthood: The Winding Road from Late Teens through the Twenties.* Oxford: Oxford University Press, 2004.

Bland, Dave. "The Formation of Character in the Book of Proverbs." In *Restoration Quarterly* 40.4 (1998) 221–237.

Dean, Kenda Creasy. *Almost Christian: What the Faith of our Teenagers is Telling the American Church.* Oxford: Oxford University Press, 2010.

For Dummies. "About For Dummies." No pages. (January 2013). http://www.dummies.com/about-for-dummies.html

Frankl, Viktor E. *Man's Search for Meaning.* Boston: Beacon, 2006.

Goleman, Daniel. *Emotional Intelligence.* New York: Bantam, 1995.

Grenz, Stanley J. *A Primer on Postmodernism.* Grand Rapids: Eerdmans, 1996.

Howe, Neil and William Strauss. *The Fourth Turning: What the Cycles of History Tell Us about America's Next Rendezvous with Destiny.* New York: Broadway, 1997.

———. *Millenials Go to College.* Great Falls, VA: Life Course Associates, 2007.

———. *Millenials Rising: The Next Great Generation.* New York: Vintage, 2000.

Kinnaman, David. *Unchristian: What a New Generation Really Thinks about Christianity . . . and Why it Matters.* Grand Rapids: Baker, 2007.

———. *You Lost Me: Why Young Christians are Leaving the Church . . . and Rethinking Faith.* Grand Rapids: Baker, 2011.

Landsberg, Mitchell. "Focus on the Family head takes conciliatory tone after the election." *LA Times* 10 November 2012. No pages. Online: http://www.articles.latimes.com/2012/nov/10/news/la-pn-focus-family-jim-daly-20121109.

Lepore, Jill. "The Sharpened Quill: Was Thomas Paine too much of a freethinker for the country he helped free?" *The New Yorker* 16 October 2006. No pages. Online: http://www.newyorker.com/archive/2006/10/16/061016crbo_books?currentPage=1.

Longman, Tremper. *Proverbs.* Grand Rapids: Baker Academic, 2006.

Lyons, Gabe. *The Next Christians: How a New Generation is Restoring the Faith.* New York: Doubleday, 2010.

McCuaig, Donald S. "Who We Are." No pages. Online: http://www.ymca.int/who-we-are/history/basketball-a-ymca-invention/.

Murphy, Roland Edmund. *Proverbs.* Word Bible Commentary 22 Nashville: Nelson, 1998.

Naugle, David K. *Worldview: The History of a Concept.* Grand Rapids: Eerdmans, 2002.

Sire, James W. *Naming the Elephant: Worldview as a Concept.* Downers Grove, IL: InterVarsity Press, 2004.

Smith, Christian, with Melissa Lundquist Denton. *Soul Searching: The Religious and Spiritual Lives of American Teenagers.* Oxford: Oxford University Press, 2005.

Smith, Christian, with Patricia Snell. *Souls in Transition: The Religious and Spiritual Lives of Emerging Adults.* Oxford: Oxford University Press, 2009.

Smith, James K. A. *Desiring the Kingdom: Worship, Worldview, and Cultural Formation.* Grand Rapids: Baker, 2009.

The Committee on Bible Translation. *The Holy Bible.* New International Version. Grand Rapids: Zondervan, 1984.

Toffler, Alvin. *Power Shift: Knowledge, Wealth, and Violence at the Edge of the 21st Century*. New York: Bantam, 1991.

Twenge, Jean M. *Generation Me: Why Today Young Americans are More Confident, Assertive, Entitled—and More Miserable than Ever Before*. New York: Free, 2006.

Volf, Miroslav. *Work in the Spirit: Toward a Theology of Work*. Eugene, OR: Wipf & Stock, 2001.

Waltke, Bruce K. *The Book of Proverbs: Chapters 1–14*. New International Commentary on the Old Testament. Grand Rapids: Eerdmans, 2004.

Waltke, Bruce K. *The Book of Proverbs: Chapters 15–31*. New International Commentary on the Old Testament. Grand Rapids: Eerdmans, 2005.

Willard, Dallas. *The Great Omission*. San Francisco: HarperSanFrancisco, 2006.

14

Reading Scripture Together

How It Is That Acknowledging Ignorance Can Restore Us to Community

JASON RODENBECK

For my teacher, friend, and mentor, John Castelein.
With great respect and appreciation for what you have given me—
but even more for the manner with which you gave it.

IN THE SUMMER OF 2008, I bought a new CD by my favorite music group, a band called King's X. Though I had only been following them since the early 90s, they had been recording for over ten years achieving some success as a Christian rock band and even some success in the secular music world. What I liked best about King's X had always been their combination of powerful melodies and very thought-provoking lyrics. So I was as excited to read the lyric sheet as I was to listen to the CD.

When I opened the CD jacket, I became extremely interested in a song titled "I Don't Know," which turned out to be a lament over the way the lyricist had acted in judgment with a friend. Though the issue is unstated in the song, as is the nature of the relationship, it was hard not to assume that the band's history had had an impact on the theme of the song. In 1998, the lead vocalist and bassist of the band, Doug Pinnick, declared that he was a homosexual and had come to acknowledge questions about his faith that he could no longer answer. He declared himself an agnostic based on those questions and doubts and on his experiences as a Christian dealing with homosexual feelings.[1]

It was not long before Christian radio stations and Christian music distributors dropped King's X from their playlists and store shelves, sometimes even publicly encouraging listeners to abandon their music.[2] By that time, the thematic progression of questions, frustration, and even anger had become, and would continue to be, prominent in their lyrics. While their early albums were full of overtly Christian references, by 2005 their album *Ogre Tones* contained a song entitled *Get Away*, which consisted of a series of questions for God about where he goes when people suffer. The first question asked God why his people are so cruel.[3]

The song *I Don't Know* seems to reflect on the kind of pain that Doug and countless others have experienced in coming out of their own closets from the perspective of the person causing that pain. Sung by the guitarist of the band, it is a penitent reflection on the sorrow the lyricist feels over the way he had damaged the relationship with his friend by assuming that he knew (or completely understood) what was wrong with his friend and what his friend should do about it. The song reflects that, in retrospect, he does not know as much as he once thought he did and seeks, with that admission, to restore the friendship.

In other words, the song implies three things. First, judgment is rooted in our sense of knowing, or the assumption that we can have complete epistemological certainty about our perception of reality, or even God. This certainty breeds an arrogance that makes us feel that we can so fully understand the context of another person and their issues or problems (such as a neighbor's homosexuality) that we can stand on the outside and make claims about why they have those issues and how they might change them. The result is the second implication: that that certainty-rooted judgment is a destroyer of relationships, a destroyer of community. The solution is the third: that admitting ignorance is a means of avoiding judgment and restoring community through compassionate humility.

1. Van Pelt, "No Room Inside a Box." See also Andy Langer, "Heaven's Metal."
2. Steve Ruff, "Doug Pinnick: There Is No Room Inside a Box."
3. King's X, "Get Away."

THE DESTRUCTIVENESS AND ARROGANCE OF CERTAINTY

The destructiveness of this type of certainty is often revealed in political discourse. As this essay is being written the Unites States is embroiled in another election season. Issues of health-care, the economy, taxes, and war combined with deep-seated fears about socialism and the broad range of attitudes about issues like homosexuality, homosexual marriage, and abortion have stirred the nation into near frenzy. The dialogue one sees on the news channels, hears on the radio talk-shows, and reads in print and on social media outlets reveals the truth that, while we may have passionate convictions, the public's ability to talk reasonably about the issues is radically underdeveloped. Instead, fear is the currency of the political economy. The candidates play on the fears of their constituents and the talk-show hosts exacerbate them. As a result, voters are convinced of their convictions, even if they cannot always articulate in peaceful dialogue why they hold them. The people I talk to (on either side of the issues) don't seem to be as interested in their own candidate as they are in stopping "the other guy," whom they have been assured is going to systematically dismantle their nation.

The church is not immune. Many conservative and fundamentalist Christians have associated belief in God with a Republican vote, hoping to illegalize abortion or stop the seemingly inevitable government affirmation of homosexual marriage. In contrast, many moderate and liberal Christians have assumed a Democratic agenda, hoping to usher in a new age of equality, peace, and opportunity. Ironically, it seems one can justify a vote for either party based completely on Christian convictions.

But when one talks to Christians (in either camp), what often emerges is that they see it differently. Moderate and liberal Christians often find it difficult to understand why their conservative or fundamentalist brothers and sisters do not always seem to be very reflective about the ethical and theological implications of the current wars; or they cannot understand why the teaching of Jesus about the poor should not translate into public policy, but Christian teaching about homosexuality should. Fundamentalist and conservative Christians, conversely, often assume that purging American capitalism of anything smelling of socialism is a Christian ideal and are often stumped by the fact that there are Christians who do not see the legalization of homosexual marriage as a horrendous evil.

In a recent post on his blog, one prominent conservative minister lamented what he felt was the "silence" of many preachers regarding the controversy surrounding Dan Cathy (CEO of Chic-fil-A) after Cathy made a few public statements about homosexual marriage.[4] Bob Russell supposed that the primary reasons many preachers refused to publicly support Cathy was that they were simply "fearful of criticism," or afraid to "feel awkward." He was extremely critical of a Christian blogger who felt that the culture war is polarizing and destructive, sarcastically referring to the suffering of John the Baptist and Dietrich Bonhoeffer to infer that she had lost her nerve. In quoting Mark 8:39, he implied that her approach to the culture war meant that she was "ashamed of the words of Jesus." In other words, if we don't publicly support those who publicly denounce homosexual marriage, we're chickening out on Jesus, and caving in to cultural pressures.

Ironically, someone who feels differently from Russell might refer to the words of Jesus in John 8. In that situation, a woman caught in adultery had been found and dragged before Jesus. Clearly she had sinned—that was "certain." What was "uncertain" was how to approach it. According to Hebrew law, she should be stoned to death. However, Israel was under Roman rule and was forbidden from carrying out capital punishment. She had been brought to Jesus as a sort of trap. "Jesus, we know she's sinned. We know what's right. What should we do?"

The question was loaded with first-century Israel culture war significance. As in Russell's worldview, there were only two options. An answer of leniency put him in tension with Hebrew culture and law, just as Russell claims that those ministers who don't publicly support Dan Cathy's views on homosexual marriage are in tension with their Christian faith. An answer in support of the law put Jesus in tension with the pagan culture and law, as Russell believes those ministers who don't support Cathy are being influenced by. The pressure must have been profound. There were two options, and Jesus must choose. However, rather than "take a *side* and stand for what we know is right" (as was expected of him) Jesus said, "Let any of you without sin cast the first stone." Later, when the mob had left, he turned to the woman and said, "go and sin no more," but only after saying, "I do not condemn you." Jesus had found a third option, one which emphasized mercy, understanding, and forgiveness and which dismantled the tension of their culture war.

Russell's argument assumes that not only are there only two options, there is only one Christian position regarding the culture war: to make bold public statements about the people on the other side of the war, their morals, and the moral obligation to enforce our own perspective. For Russell, to not take this position is to sit in cowardly silence and allow evil to flourish. He readily dismisses 1) anyone who reads in the Gospels a Jesus who

---

4. Russell, "Cathy and Silence."

demonstrates a more humble, communal, and compassionate approach to sin and culture issues or 2) Christians who feel that there are more Christ-like ways to demonstrate that we are not ashamed of the words of Christ. For Russell, and many others, we are just *right*. We know what's right. We know how people ought to live. Let's get out there and say it. Any disagreement, any other perspective at all, can only be a tacit denial of what "we know" is right.

It seems that people like Russell (on both sides of any issue) find it difficult to imagine a perspective other than their own and are quick to categorize and judge anyone who sees things differently from them. It is a disease that has infected all of us, to some degree. At the heart of our inability to hear other perspectives is an arrogant certainty about our understanding of the reality we perceive. That kind of arrogance destroys dialogue and makes it impossible for people to commune with one another when there is any tension between their perspectives. It assumes "We know the truth; and anyone who doesn't know the truth is either deceived, a liar, or has no integrity." Further, anyone who does not believe as we do must first be corrected; but if they will not receive correction we must treat them as an enemy in a kind of *war* (like a culture war). For Christians like Russell who assume that belief in Christ means taking a side in the culture war, right Christian belief means that we, necessarily, have enemies whom we must battle. They are often quick to quote Pauline statements about our battle "not being against flesh and blood," but go right on warring with real flesh and blood people, forgetting that Jesus told his disciples that their attitude about their enemies should be one of love and service toward them. In the words of Christ, Christians are forbidden to treat enemies as enemies (Matt 5:38–48). They must, instead, humbly pray for and serve them. They must be willing to sit and eat with them. They must be willing to die for them.

Instead, many Christians have concluded that being the church means aligning themselves with other people who hold to exactly the same propositions that they do. Rather than dialogue (which has the potential to lead to the mutual growth of the participants), they opt for monologue—surrounding themselves with other people and teachers who believe exactly as they do. Why? They are quite convinced about the propositions they hold. That certainty precludes any tension between them and their neighbor. Or, rather, any tension between them and their neighbor precludes peaceful community and brotherhood. Those with different perspectives are enemies. Surrounding ourselves with like-minded people reinforces our certainty and makes us feel less afraid of our enemies.

My proposition has it quite the opposite. I begin with the assumption that no human being can claim certainty about any proposition. We are all limited persons with limited perspectives on the issues at stake in our world. None of us knows all that God knows. Part of becoming a Christian is the acknowledgement (confession) that God is God (with Jesus as the ultimate revelation of God) and we are not. Therefore, the acknowledgement of Jesus as Lord ought to remind us not that we are certain of what we hold to be true (arrogant), but that we are, in fact, limited and fallible. I believe that the capacity this acknowledgement has to restore community is in direct proportion to its capacity to instill humility.

CERTAINTY AS DECONSTRUCTIONISM

Popular Christian attitudes about things like homosexuality are often drastically oversimplified. Homosexuality is seen as nothing more than a simple choice with no physiological or sociological factors; people who have abortions are simply murderers; and those who support whichever political party I do not are clearly idiots or faithless heathens. Moreover, the teaching of Scripture seems quite clear on these issues—even when the issue is hardly inferred. To support a position on a specific issue, a Scripture containing a key-word or key-concept related to the issue is often found, unreflectively ripped out of its context, and messily applied with a sense of self-righteous indignation.

These oversimplifications are necessary to convince ourselves of our sense of certainty in the face of the multiplicity of perspectives we encounter each day. Life is scary for someone seeking the security of epistemological certainty in an individualistic culture in which each person sees himself as an authority on every issue. When people of faith who feel certain about their beliefs are exposed to people with radically different worldviews they are sometimes unable to find any common ground which might help them scare up a sense of compassion. As a result Christians exegete Scripture, as well as culture with a very simplistic and arrogant lens.

In *Is There a Meaning in this Text?* Kevin Vanhoozer reveals a parallel in his thorough analysis of the deconstructionism of Jacques Derrida. Concisely, for Derrida it is the reader who determines the meaning of a text, not the author of that text. This implies that people who follow Derrida (and many follow him without knowing they follow him) assume that they themselves are, ultimately, the authority on the text (whether that "text" is a written text or culture itself).[5] Ironically, many Christians are quick to call

5. My project assumes that the hermeneutical process is not merely something we apply to the texts we read. It is also applied to the people we read the texts for and to. In doing hermeneutics, we must become skilled exegetes of text . . . but also self, neighbor,

"postmodernism" on the culture in which they live while they themselves, in their claim to certainty about the biblical text they read and the people they meet, are just as influenced by Derrida's deconstruction.

Vanhoozer rightly notices that there is an inherent arrogance in that kind of solipsist assumption. He states, "Pride does not listen. It knows."[6] In other words, reading Scripture (or culture) with a sense of certainty about its meaning reveals an inner arrogance. Succinctly, the subject of the phrase "I know" is "I." Building on Vanhoozer, to claim to "know" requires that we root our certainty in our own ability to discern what is true without reflecting on the ramifications of perspectives we might be ignorant of (as in Derrida's deconstruction where the reader is responsible for meaning). Conversely, the thing known is an object to be handled, manipulated, even wielded as a weapon to protect the insecurity we feel deep inside when we realize how unprepared we are to answer the questions raised by those of a different perspective (our "enemies"). Generally, the response is to look to people who hold our own perspective who can provide us with convincing arguments to bolster our sense of certainty, creating a powerful "us-against-them" mythology that refuses to listen to a neighbor or differing perspective in dialogue. I cannot listen or learn when I already "know."

The kind of deconstructionist arrogance Vanhoozer refers to, in its radical individualism, is ultimately a deconstructor of community and relationship. The assumption the individual reader of text or culture makes is that his certainty of interpretation, no matter how great or poor the quality of his exegesis, qualifies him as an authority sitting in judgment of anyone with whom he disagrees. By contrast, Paul, in dealing with the issue of meat sacrificed to idols in 1 Cor 8, begins by noting that "knowledge puffs up," but "love builds up." His point is, ultimately, that love for one another is more important than "knowing the truth," "proving I'm right," or even "feeling secure in my belief." That Paul thinks it is necessary to say so gives the impression that Christians, even in the first century, were liable to this kind of arrogance.

In fact, Derrida's philosophy is not new—just well-articulated. Bonhoeffer might argue that Derrida is merely philosophizing the original sin. In *Ethics*, Bonhoeffer closely associates *all* sin with this solipsist certainty, which he calls participation in eating from the Tree of Knowledge of Good and Evil. According to Bonhoeffer, the original sin was not a test involving forbidden fruit. Instead, it was the choice all people make to become the

---

or culture. I propose that Christians are often just as apt to eisegete their neighbors as they are the text they believe in.

6. Vanhoozer, *Is There a Meaning in This Text?* 462.

source of knowledge of good and evil themselves. And it is this knowledge which is a destroyer of relationship. For Bonhoeffer, "Man at his origin knows only one thing: God. It is only in the unity of his knowledge of God that he knows of other men, of things and of himself. . . . The knowledge of good and evil shows that he is no longer at one with his origin."[7] Humans, as image-bearers of God, were created to have access to life, drawing their identity and purpose from God. Therefore their inherent value, which they were able to recognize within themselves and in their neighbors, was only apparent because of their relationship to God as image-bearers. They were created to live in that healthy relationship with God (their source), with one another, with themselves, and with nature in relationships defined by the selfless love of God. Eating from the tree of Knowledge of Good and Evil, however, meant that man had "forgotten how he was at his origin and has made himself his own creator and judge. What God had given man to be, man now desired to be through himself."[8]

In *Ethics*, Bonhoeffer is stating that sin is denying the authority of God on matters of good and evil and becoming the source of that authority ourselves. This means that we are now also cut off from God as the source of life, which means that each person must now create his own meaning and identity as well. To become that authority in and of ourselves—to take what is God's and make it ours—is a destroyer of the relationship we were created for. "Originally man was made in the image of God, but now his likeness to God is a stolen one."[9] In fact, the claim to certainty makes us "a god against God."[10] This stolen, god-like authority, then, creates within man "disunion with God, with men, with things, and with himself."[11] The Genesis fall account shockingly describes in Gen 3 how, after this fall, the lives of humans were now defined by death, dysfunction, isolation, insecurity, and disunion. When each person is the source of "knowledge of good and evil" for himself, there cannot be anything but disunion.[12]

7. Bonhoeffer, *Ethics*, 21.

8. Ibid., 22.

9. Ibid.

10. Ibid., 23.

11. Ibid., 24.

12. Greg Boyd's *Repenting of Religion* does a masterful job defining how Bonhoeffer's description of the fall is reenacted whenever Christians sit in judgment over those they deem wrong. He describes that what we often define as "standing for Jesus" against this or that issue because we "know the truth" is really just a baptism of the original sin—it is the effort to make ourselves the source of knowledge of good and evil over and against God as well as culture.

Derrida deals, primarily, with the reader being the source of meaning when reading a text. But, according to Bonhoeffer, he is only stating philosophically what people have believed since the Fall—it is *we* who know—it is *we* (or, rather, *I*) who sit in God's seat—and no one else can or should take that authority from us. This sounds remarkably like Nietzsche's *Overman*, the human who, having killed God must now replace him with his own authority. "Must we not become gods simply to appear worthy of it?"[13] Nietzsche asks in the "Parable of the Madman." For Nietzsche, it is the *Overman* who rises above the slave morality of Christianity and finds in himself the source of meaning (as in *Zarathustra*), ethics (as in *Beyond Good and Evil*), and ultimately motivation: "Suppose, finally, we succeeded in explaining our entire instinctive life as the development and ramification of one basic form of the will—namely, of the will to power . . ."[14] It isn't hard to see how the culture war is, ultimately, a struggle between autonomous selves for the power to control culture.

COMPASSIONATE COMMUNITY THROUGH MANUDUCTION

Peter Candler's book *Theology, Rhetoric, Manuduction, or Reading Scripture Together on the Path to God* illustrates a far different approach to reading and applying Scripture than the individualistic arrogance I have defined. His thesis is that the "notion of participation is embodied in a grammar, in the way in which texts are organized as structures for the manuduction ('leading-by-the-hand') of readers along an itinerary of exit and return from creation to eschatological beatitude."[15] His project is to see in certain medieval theological works (primarily two of St. Thomas Aquinas) an example of a communal approach to writing and reading a text.

The primary analogy in Candler's book is that of the map vs. the itinerary. He proposes that there are always two options for finding directions to a specific place, such as the National Gallery in London.[16] One is to draw a map "or production of a *London A-to-Z*." The other is to receive a "narrative description of how one comes to the National Gallery by making a journey according to various signs and markers along the way." This Candler describes as a detailed set of instructions, such as "Coming out of the tube station onto Long Acre, turn left . . . you will come to the intersection of

13. Nietzsche, *The Gay Science*, 181.
14. Nietzsche, *Beyond Good and Evil*, 48.
15. Candler, *Theology*, 4.
16. What follows is a summary of a lengthy analogy in ibid., 41–43.

several smaller roads with St. Martin's Lane . . . you will know you are on the right path if you can see the hexagonal steeple of St. Martin-in-the-Fields."

Studying Michel de Certeau, Candler states that "The map is a spatial depiction of a place, a 'totalizing stage on which elements of diverse origin are brought together to form the tableau of a "state" of geographical knowledge, [which] pushes away into its prehistory or into its posterity, as if into the wings, the operations of which it is the result or the necessary condition. It remains alone on the stage. The tour describers have disappeared.'"[17] Put another way, a map purports to be a complete picture of a territory, including all of the elements of that territory, articulating exactly (to scale) their position in space. As map-makers learn more of the territory, and find better methods of drawing, their maps become more and more accurate representations of reality until, finally, we feel that when we look at the map, we understand the whole of the reality. Importantly, Candler's quotation of de Certeau reveals the impersonal nature of such certainty as the final product of the map is divorced from the person who drew it. "Gradually these 'tour describers' fall out of the picture, literally, and the map becomes a kind of panoptic image of the whole of a place."[18]

For my project, let the map be representative of a person's sense of certainty. It stands for what a person "knows," such as a specific set of theological propositions they apply to a specific issue. The map claims to know the ins-and-outs of the entire territory (reality). It claims to have complete knowledge of every road, river, nook, and cranny. A well-drawn map (and we all believe our maps to be excellent) has neglected no perspective. It reflects the territory and every possible destination or starting point within the territory. The map is, when it comes to the territory, omniscient. The reader's identity soon becomes wrapped up in his ownership of the map and his proper use of it. To further define my micro-analogy, the "certain" person analyzing an issue such as "what the Bible says about his neighbor's homosexuality" must feel he completely understands the map he holds, which accurately reflects the Bible and the cause of his neighbor's homosexuality. *He* has a map, *he* reads it correctly, and there is simply no reason to question its accuracy.

Note, however, Candler's caveat that the distinct mental operation of the map is that one is required, first, to find oneself on it.[19] The assumption of most "map" users is that they are equally as sure of their own position on the map as they are of those whom they are trying to direct. The map is the

17. Candler, *Theology*, 42. With quote from de Certeau, "*Practice*," 119.
18. Ibid.
19. Ibid.

fullness of perspective on the territory, and their ability to read it enables them to precisely locate their own position, as well as their neighbor's position and the proper path to their perceived destination. The project is a decidedly individualistic one assuming the precision of the map and the accurate hermeneutical discernment of the reader.

The map-reader simply "has all the answers." And because of his confidence in the map and his own interpretation, any questions put to him which he cannot immediately answer must be perceived as criticisms of the inadequacies of his own interpretation or else attacks on the map itself. If he sees the question as a critique of the map, he may find the need to improve his map (redefine his theology), or set about to defend his map with a mix of apologetic and polemic arguments. Most often, however, he will experience it as an attack on his own interpretive acumen and react out of insecurity. He may lash out, talk louder, restate his position in bolder terms, or seek out like-minded voices which sooth the insecurity with a sense of safety-in-numbers. The map-reader is inherently insecure, precisely because he is his own authority.

By contrast, Candler's other option, the itinerary, is a more communal and narrative approach. Where "the map" required locating oneself on the map, the itinerary requires a "performance of the memory."[20]

> In order for the traveler to get . . . to the National Gallery, she must in some way reenact the narrative which she has heard. Thus as the narration of the journey resides in the memory, the traveler performs the operations which make the narration intelligible, and by doing so, traces a 'route' through a series of mnemonic signs. . . . As she performs the itinerary from memory, she becomes coextensive and coterminous with it, and is led towards the destination of her route by enacting her memory.[21]

His claim is that classic theologians, such as Aquinas, do not see themselves as map-makers precisely defining the whole of a territory with absolute certainty, but *manuductors* holding hands with their readers on the pathway to God *together*. He defines the terms *ductus* and *skopos*: the former being "the flow and movement of a composition . . . within and through awork's various parts," and the latter being "the goal to which the *ductus* of a composition leads."[22] Candler's thought is that in Aquinas, "the reader is not simply provided with a deposit of doctrine independent of an interpretive community, nor a 'summary map' of all theology. Rather, . . . [the] texts have

20. Ibid., 43.
21. Ibid.
22. Ibid.

a specific rhetorical purpose, and their authors and their interlocutors act as the reader's guides along the way, her manuductors, towards their common *skopos* . . ."[23] Furthermore:

> By the process of reading, or the memorial performance of the itinerary, the reader becomes in a sense identical with the text, though in a rhetorical sense and not (obviously) a physical one. And though the "tour guide" is not physically present, he is nevertheless the manuductor in memory, insofar as to trace the route is to recall the voice of the one who has narrated it. And as far as rhetorical activities, itineraries are also acts of mediation and devotion, ways "marked out by the schemes and tropes of Scripture."[24]

Whether Candler has accurately defined the intent of theologians like Aquinas, the subtitle of his book, *Reading Scripture Together on the Path to God*, concisely states the entire point of his project. Theology is intended to be an act of community. Its subject is a communal God, its object is to define ourselves in relationship to this God, and its purpose is to draw us into more perfect community with God and with one another. It isn't intended to be done by individuals studying impersonal "maps" with the purpose of articulating cold propositional arguments, or simply finding biblical principles defining right and wrong behaviors which we can then apply to our neighbors to, inevitably, find them lacking.

If our radical individualist/deconstructionist approach to reading Scripture as well as neighbor is a destructive, isolating force, then *Reading Scripture Together* should be seen as the solution. The former requires a map-maker/map-reader, certain about the precision of his map, certain that he is not eisegeting his interpretation of the map, and certain about his own position on the map. With it he can claim to know all that needs to be known to make a proper directive decision about his neighbor's life. The latter requires him to reach out his hand to his neighbor to hold it in a process of coming to the text *together*. It requires two things: 1) an admission that he is also in the process learning where he is, where he is going, and how to get there (an admission of ignorance, rather than certainty), and 2) a humble willingness to actually care enough about his neighbor to withhold judgment about his neighbor's ignorance. The first is a prerequisite of the second.

As in Candler's interpretation of Aquinas, we must not see ourselves as map-makers or map-readers. Rather, we must see ourselves as itinerary

23. Ibid., 44.
24. Ibid., 45.

receivers and communicators: at best guides in a type of communal reading and remembering of the text (and one another), holding hands as we work our way through the text on the path to God. It requires at least two willing parties to "clasp hands."[25] And, while I may have no control over whether my neighbor is willing to join me, my responsibility is only my willingness to join him.

Manuduction is an inherently communal and humble act. It requires humility to slow down and consider the welfare of the one whose hand we are holding. We may urge and tug on our neighbor's hand to convince him to come a certain way, but we may not jerk or squeeze his hand too tightly in an effort to control him. There may be tension, but not violence. Ultimately, he may decide that he is no longer willing to continue this community— our thoughts on which path to take to God may be too clearly different for him to continue with me. But it is up to him whether he will continue the relationship, because I am always more concerned with him than I am with myself.

This kind of humility can be seen in the tenderness of a loving mother holding hands with a child on the way through a grocery store. The mother will most certainly know several paths through the store or will be far better prepared to navigate than the child. In other words, she has reason to believe she is less ignorant than the child. However, the loving mother holds the child's hand firmly but gently because she desires to help the child, to protect him from harm, and to guide him to the proper goal (the purchase of groceries for the common good). She tugs and guides firmly, but humbly and patiently because she understands that she, too, was once a child and needed guidance. She understands that there are contextual reasons why the child is ignorant and doesn't judge the child as "stupid" or a "problem." Though she is sometimes firm, she is careful how she speaks to him because she doesn't want to cause him harm. The child may resist her manuduction at times because he is distracted by something that piques his curiosity or interest. Sometimes she urges him to keep going. But sometimes she explores with him; either anticipating what he will discover or curious to discover it with him. Her tender actions are rooted in love and humility. She must stoop a little to hold his hand; she must slow her pace, and she must be willing to learn along with him—even things she believes she has already learned. And there are times when the child asks questions. Sometimes she will know the answers, and sometimes she will have to respond with "I don't know," implying, "let's find out together."

25. In Candler, the "clasping" is inferred between reader and writer whenever we read the text. For my project, it is inferred when a humble acknowledgement of common ignorance of one-another and the text is made.

By contrast, a dysfunctional parental relationship looks far different. A selfish, insecure mother is far more concerned with controlling the child than guiding the child. The selfish mother yanks at the child's arm and exhibits no patience with him. She wants him to do exactly what she wants him to do and doesn't understand why he can't see her perspective. The relationship may become violent as the child reacts in his frustration and pain. Because of her insecurity, any question he asks must be given an authoritative response in order to maintain the proper sense of authority—she cannot bear any question of "why" which would pose a challenge to her authority.

In the two scenarios, it is only the acknowledgement of ignorance, and the humility of love that enables the first mother to manuduct her child on a specific path through the store. Similarly, it is the acknowledgement of our own ignorance in our search for God and for answers for ourselves, as well as a humility that flows out of that acknowledgement that will enable us to read Scripture in community, within the church and with our neighbors. We must be patient enough to go over it again and again, remembering the itinerary together. We must be secure enough to ask questions and be asked questions—to get to know our neighbor's context, rather than assuming we already do. We must be less individualistic, less likely to assume we already know the answers or the meanings if we are to begin to restore the kind of community Jesus exhibits. We must refrain from judgment in dealing scripturally with the hot-button issues of our day, rather than assuming that our neighbor is an enemy in a culture war whom we must fight.

In other words, contra Russell, taking a stand for Jesus is far more than being willing to make bold public statements about which actions are evil and good—it is far more than merely taking sides in the culture war. That kind of approach is exactly like the approach of the Pharisees who saw themselves at odds with Jesus when he ate with tax-collectors and touched lepers. Jesus, rather, saw himself in a manuducting relationship, his humility demonstrated in his willingness to empty himself, become a human . . . a servant . . . obedient to death (Phil 2). This Jesus was a messiah who had come to reveal the compassion of God, who knows far more about the people in our culture and why they make the decisions they do than I know. Jesus represented God reaching out his hand to his beloved fallen children, inviting them to come with him on the path to the Father.

Of course, many whom he reached out to ultimately rejected him. He expected they would. He fully expected (and predicted) that the powers would crucify him. In fact, most of those he reached out to withdrew their hand. However, that did not change the fact that his was always extended toward them. The cross itself is an invitation, "pick up your cross and follow me" (Matt 10:38; 16:24; Mark 8:34; Luke 9:23; 14:27). Just like Jesus, those we reach out toward may also withdraw the hand. But that should not change the position of our own hands. Even when they "crucify us," our approach to culture, to neighbor, should be one of humble invitation, rather than knowing condemnation and control.

The culture warriors, in their self-assured certainty, are sure to cry "postmodernism." Any attempt to appeal to perspectives tends to be viewed as a denial of absolute truth. I am not denying truth. I am not advocating relativism. This essay is not either of those things. Rather, what I am proposing is an attitude of humility that begins with the admission that "I am only human." Even Paul was willing to say, "not that I have already obtained all this, or have already arrived at my goal, but I press on to take hold of that for which Christ Jesus took hold of me. Brothers and sisters, I do not consider myself yet to have taken hold of it. But one thing I do: Forgetting what is behind and straining toward what is ahead, I press on toward the goal to win the prize for which God has called me heavenward in Christ Jesus."[26]

Postmodernist relativism denies the positive ontological status of truth. I am suggesting only that we change our epistemological assumptions about it. We are all searching for truth, for God. Some of us may be more familiar with the territory than others, but none of us can be arrogant in our perception of the territory because none of us is omniscient as God is. We are working with itineraries, not maps, and none of us has, yet, "taken hold of it."

Nor is this simply a way of being nicer in our approach with people. Stanley Hauerwas, in a Q/A style lecture entitled "Being a Christian in Today's World" rightly notes that being a church committed to peace is not the same as being a "nice" church.[27] In fact, "nice" churches are often ineffective ones. Being "nice" precludes honest truth-telling for a co-dependent "peace-keeping" approach that makes us afraid of genuine conflict. I am not advocating silence about Scripture for the purpose of not offending those sensitive to the message of Christ. I am advocating, instead, humble dialogue that is aware that we, in ourselves, are not the authority on truth. This means that we will often be forced into greater conflict—and that conflict will be all the more uncomfortable because we are in conflict with someone whose hand we are holding, rather than the easy, self-righteous, "us-against-them" hatred of worldly conflict. That held hand means that the person with whom we are in conflict is never the enemy. They are, instead, my brother or sister. And I am as liable to be mistaken as they are.

---

26. *The Holy Bible: Today's New International Version*, Phil 3:12–14.
27. Hauerwas "Being a Christian in Today's World."

If anyone had a right to arrogance, it was Jesus Christ. If anyone had a right to solipsism, it was the son of God. Yet, in his mind his authority could only be derived from his special relationship to the Father. Everything Jesus had that he passed on came from the Father (John 17:6–7). What Jesus did was only what he saw the Father doing (John 5:19). In the temptation narratives, Jesus looked to God's authority and will for what was right (Matt 4; Luke 4). Even in Jesus' prayer in Gethsemane; when he was afraid and alone; it was the Father's will which was paramount (Luke 22:42). Jesus never founded his authority, purpose, or knowledge of right and wrong within himself. Instead, his mission was always founded on the will of God and his authority came only from the Father. As a result, his life was always revealing the love of God, rather than judgment and condemnation. That love was one of humility, selflessness, and an invitation to blessed community.

None of us knows the Father as Jesus did. In fact, our only way to know the Father is through Jesus. Therefore, we must consider ourselves humble (and often ignorant) seekers striving to be at least as humble as Jesus. And since we are not Jesus, it would appear that we have even more reason to be humble. If we are going to do as Jesus did; if we are going to follow him on the way of the cross, then we must put aside our arrogant self-righteous certainty (our maps) and see ourselves as we are: lonely and easily confused seekers, working with itineraries as we struggle to find community with God and with one another. Our seeking, the act of remembering the itinerary, is something that can only be done together as the community of the fellow disciples and with hands outstretched humbly to those outside that community.

BIBLIOGRAPHY

Bonhoeffer, Dietrich. *Ethics.* 1st Touchstone ed. New York: Touchstone, 1995.

Boyd, Gregory A. *Repenting of Religion: Turning from Judgment to the Love of God.* Grand Rapids: Baker, 2004.

Candler Jr., Peter M. *Theology, Rhetoric, Manuduction, or Reading Scripture Together On the Path to God.* Grand Rapids: Eerdmans, 2006.

De Certeau, Michel. *The Practice of Everyday Life.* Translated by Steven Rendall. Berkeley: University of California Press, 1984.

Hauerwas, Stanley, and David Crabtree. "Being a Christian in Today's World" Lecture given at the Anglican Episcopal House of Studies (November 2009). No pages. http://deimos.apple.com/WebObjects/Core.woa/BrowsePrivately/new.duke.edu .2718649575.02718649580.2702913654?i=1878366516 (accessed November 19, 2010).

King's X. "Get Away." On the album *Ogre Tones.* Composed by Doug Pinnick, Ty Tabor, and Jerry Gaskill. InsideOut Music. Released September 27, 2005. Compact disc.

———. "I Don't Know." On the album *XV.* Composed by Doug Pinnick, Ty Tabor, and Jerry Gaskill. InsideOut Music. Released May 20, 2008. Compact disc.

Nietzsche, Friedrich. *Beyond Good and Evil.* Translated by Walter Kaufman. New York: Random House, 1989.

———. *The Gay Science.* Translated by Walter Kaufmann. New York: Vintage, 1974.

Ruff, Steve. "Dug Pinnick: There Is No Room Inside a Box." *Down the Line* (May 2010). No pages. Online: http://downthelinezine.com/archives/dug-pinnick-there-is-no-room-inside-a-box/

Russell, Bob. "Dan Cathy and the Silence of Many Churches." *Bob Russell Ministries* (August 2012). No pages. Online: http://www.bobrussell.org/2012/08/05/dan-cathy-and-the-silence-of-many-churches/

Vanhoozer, Kevin J. *Is There a Meaning in This Text?: The Bible, the Reader, and the Morality of Literary Knowledge.* Grand Rapids: Zondervan, 1998.

Van Pelt, Doug. "No Room Inside a Box." *HM Magazine* (May/June 1999). No pages. Online: http://www.hmmagazine.com/oe/archives/000367.php?page=all

15

Business and the Beatific Vision

ERIC A. TEORO

HAPPINESS

There are many ways to pursue happiness. One could focus on physical pleasure. Left unchecked, however, the pursuit of physical pleasure could devolve into a form of slavery in which the person seeking it needs ever-greater sources of stimulation, and, never satisfied, the fulfillment of pleasure becomes the primary driving force in the individual's life. One could focus on achieving goals, be they money, fame, power, or some other tangible or intangible temporal good or status. Such attainments are tenuous. As circumstances change, so could one's standing in relation to these goods. The fragility of achievement could entrap a person in perpetual comparisons with others, reducing individuals or communities to people who must be beat, enemies in the battle for success. The instability of achievement could foster feelings of anxiety or insecurity, feelings that are contradictory to happiness. In-and-of-themselves, money, fame, and power are not evil, but an undo focus on them prevents people from achieving the ultimate goal of deep-seated contentment, peace, and joy. In the pursuit of happiness, one could focus on relationships with others. As creatures created in the image of a Triune God, humans are meant for fellowship. Regardless of how meaningful a relationship with another can be, however, human relationships can never completely fulfill the inherent drive for happiness. No human is sufficiently good enough to never disappoint; at the minimum, no human relationship will last forever.

There is only one source to which humans can look for complete fulfillment of happiness: God. To see God uninhibited, that is to experience the beatific vision, will fulfill the innate human drive for happiness, for only the infinitely good and loving God is capable of surpassing human desire and need. Humans were created to commune with God for eternity, and for this reason, only the beatific vision is proportionate to human longing. While on earth, the path to union with God is found in the theological virtues of faith, hope, and love. Through the infusion of these virtues into the human soul, God directs humans toward a rightly ordered relationship with him, others, creation, and the self.

In this essay, I will briefly outline the three theological virtues, and offer some thoughts on their implications for business. This essay is neither meant to be a detailed treatment of faith, hope, or love, nor a fully developed theology of business. My goal is to stimulate discussion on the nature of business by couching business in the larger narrative of God's design for humanity. I am heavily indebted to the sources in the reference section for the material on happiness, faith, hope, and love, and I highly recommend them if a more nuanced understanding of the virtues is desired.

FAITH

For humans to be fulfilled, they must live lives appropriate to their natures. Because humans are created by God and for union with God, and because the full truth concerning God transcends human reason and human ability to discover on its own, humans need divine revelation, a breaking into human consciousness of the First Truth of God. This First Truth, however, is not self-evidential and does not compel assent.

Though human reason can attain knowledge of reality, that knowledge is incomplete. Faith enables individuals to understand truth that exceeds what they can know through human reason alone. Faith makes possible the reception of revelation in which God communicates a fuller truth concerning reality. This truth transcends the human intellect's natural capacities. It cannot be tested or verified according to natural standards for evidence. Faith enables believers to understand reality according to divine norms, resulting in objective knowledge. When God infuses individuals with faith, the infusion not only provides the access to, and understanding of, revealed truth, but the ability to assent to revealed truth. Assent leads to believers living lives in accordance to the realities expressed in revealed truth.

The Holy Spirit provides two gifts to believers to aid their faith: understanding and knowledge. While understanding enables believers to more deeply comprehend the articles of faith, the object of understanding is faith itself. Understanding simultaneously illumines the intellect of believers concerning doctrine and helps believers appreciate the inability of doctrine to fully capture the reality of God. It simultaneously strengthens believers while deepening mystery. In this way, understanding does not undermine the character of faith. Knowledge enables believers to move beyond mere subjective understanding by unifying disparate doctrines concerning God's interaction with creation. It helps believers move from effects to causes, and in so doing, facilitates proper judgments concerning created goods. Knowledge equips believers to interact with God's creation in ways that are consistent with God's character and design for creation, and, thereby, to interact with God himself more appropriately.

Human reason, operating outside of faith can understand genuine principles of human conduct. However, sin, and its perverting nature, distorts the truth about human conduct and inhibits a full understanding of the life for which humans were created to live. Faith informs individuals that the goal of virtue is unity with God, that human action should conform one to God's character and prepare one to share in the beatific vision. To these ends, God blesses believers with the gift of the Holy Spirit and the commands of Scripture. Through the Holy Spirit, believers can fulfill the commands of Scripture with joy and understanding, recognizing the true nature and outcome of obedience.

Humans are responsible to use their reason to guide their behavior, to understand and implement the virtues. When under grace, however, humans are not left alone or restricted by their natural capacities. Through grace, God transforms human capacities, and allows believers to use these transformed capacities in creative ways. The Holy Spirit prompts and enables human action that surpasses natural limitations, human action that accords with a fuller, deeper understanding of virtue. God does not inhibit human autonomy, but enables authentic human freedom by empowering humans to fulfill their created purpose, to actualize their fullest potential.

A gap exists between human nature and the requirements of experiencing God in his fullness, of experiencing the beatific vision. Human nature, in itself, is not proportionate for such a task. On their own, that is without the gift of the Holy Spirit, believers are more prone to pursue created goods than to pursue God. Human reason is limited in its ability to control or direct the will toward the eternal. The Holy Spirit enables believers to transcend the boundaries of natural inclinations and judgments. Not only does the Holy Spirit prompt human will, he helps shape human character to where the will readily receives his promptings.

HOPE

For humans to be fulfilled, they must live lives appropriate to their natures. Because humans are created by God and for union with God, and because the goodness of God transcends human ability to achieve or to embrace on its own, humans need divine help. This help comes in the form of theological hope. Hope enables humans to pursue the good that is God himself. Hope enables humans to fulfill their potential by activating their will according to God's will, and by helping humans overcome any hardship that impedes them from reaching their perfection in God.

Hope shapes the human appetite so that humans will the good, and it shapes the emotional response humans experience when pursuing that good is difficult. Moreover, when hope looks to God for help amidst the difficulty of achieving the good, the act of looking to God already reaches a good, that is human dependence upon God and a degree of communion with him. Dependence on, and communion with, God are appropriate actions for humanity. They are part of God's design for human experience. In this way, humans approach the ultimate fulfillment they will know when they experience the beatific vision.

Hope ultimately seeks God for himself. Hope does not subordinate God to humans or relegate him to an instrumental purpose. It is right for humans to desire God because he is their reason for existence. He is their terminal good. Humans can have hope of seeing God because of the Incarnation. Redemption through Christ makes the beatific vision possible, because through Christ's sacrifice, God communicated his desire to return creation to himself.

Hope relates to several emotions in unique ways. Hope focuses on that which perfects humanity. Anything that can destroy or hinder human progress toward its ultimate good, that is God and the beatific vision, is met with fear or hatred. Hope looks forward to the future. If the good hope seeks is attained, hope is replaced by joy. Hope exists due to difficulty in attaining the good. If reaching the good is unhindered or easy, hope gives way to simple desire. Hope seeks that which is attainable. If the good hope seeks is impossible to realize, despair ensues.

When an individual experiences despair in relation to God, however, it is due to a failure of properly appropriating God's gift of faith. By refusing to believe that God will fulfill his promises in Christ, the individual assumes a posture toward God that is disordered. The individual rejects God's goodness. When an individual presupposes God's mercy without concern for God's wisdom and justice, the individual, similarly, assumes a disordered posture toward God. Such a posture fails to take seriously God's desire for human transformation, that God enables a capacity for action that transcends human ability alone, and that such a transformation and such actions prepare one for the beatific vision. Whenever an individual assumes a posture toward God that is disordered, the individual hampers the actualization of his or her fulfillment and ultimate happiness.

LOVE

For humans to be fulfilled, they must live lives appropriate to their natures. Because humans are created by God and for union with God, and because the ability to love God above all else transcends human ability to achieve or to embrace on its own, humans need divine help. This help comes in the form of theological love. Theological love is not love for an abstract construct or idea, but for a person, a friend. If humans love someone solely for the good it brings to them, what they actually have is desire, not love. Similarly, if humans love someone in a way that wishes goodness to the other in exclusion of any reciprocity, what they have is simple benevolence, not love. For love to be truly love, humans must wish the good to a friend, to someone with whom they share a reciprocating relationship, a unity, a communion. Humans have been created to love God as a friend, to love God as he loves himself, and to receive from God his love for them.

To love God as God loves himself is to recognize the perfection of his divine goodness, to recognize that God does not need anything other than himself to experience perfection. Because God's divine goodness cannot increase, no greater basis for loving him exists. To love God as God loves himself is to recognize that when God acts, he does so in freedom, that no created good can compel God to do anything. Everything God does, he does because of his own goodness, because of his own love. When God acts, it is not to fill some emptiness or lack within him. When God acts, it is to communicate what he already has, what he already is, to communicate his fullness. Humans can love God by enjoying him as he is, and by desiring that all of creation be ordered to him properly. When creation is ordered to God according to his will, it is in a state of flourishing and of glorifying God.

Humans are capable of love because God first loves them. They are called to love others and themselves because God has created all of creation to return to him so that he can be all in all. By being all in all, God does not diminish or marginalize the other, but fulfills the other, resulting in the other's ultimate happiness. God's goodness forms the basis for genuine friendship and love; he loves humanity because he is good, not because humanity is good. Humans, in turn, are to love others as friends because others are God's friends. Believers are to even love nonbelievers, for believers should hope that nonbelievers would turn to God and share in the beatific vision. They should not love nonbelievers as sinners, but as potential members of the believing community. Whereas humans can love other humans as friends, they should love other created goods only with reference to humans, only as those goods promote human flourishing. Human reason, enlightened by faith, enables humans to understand the purpose of created goods, and to relate to created goods appropriately.

BUSINESS

If humans are created to share in the beatific vision, finding their fulfillment of happiness through intimacy with God, proceeding from him only to return to him, then every facet of human existence must be interpreted, understood, or valued in light of, or in relation to, this ultimate end. Every segment of human life must conform to the beatific vision. This includes business. It is imperative for believers, individuals called to be friends of God, to discern what is the purpose of business, and to structure business according to that discernment.

One facet of God's original design for work is that work serves as a means through which humans subdue the earth, that is to ensure all of creation conforms to God's character. Business is a mechanism for structuring work, as well as a product of work or human ingenuity. At a minimum, therefore, businesses should provide goods and services that move creation toward greater conformity to God's character. Insurance, for example, should be such a service. Through insurance, individuals should have the opportunity to bring some measure of order into their lives by mitigating potential loss through the spreading of risk among participants. In turn, the measure of protection derived from insurance should facilitate the risk-taking that often accompanies human progress and flourishing. Insurance should provide a measure of peace, reducing anxiety about the future. It is important, however, to recognize the distinction between *should* and *does*. The insurance industry, as are all industries, is affected by sin and does not fully accord to God's character. Due to the fall, humans not only have the charge to subdue the earth, but to redeem it.

Faith provides the awareness of business' original calling, enabling believers to transcend popular beliefs that the sole purpose of business is to maximize profits or that business becomes legitimate solely by engaging in social responsibility. Profits are important for the sustainability of businesses, and as one of several measures of efficiency and effectiveness. Engaging in socially responsible projects could be worthwhile uses of profits and organizational resources. Faith, however, enables believers to understand the inherent value of business as business, that regardless of how profitable or how engaged in socially responsible projects a business might be, its primary purpose is to produce goods and services and to enable humans to work. Its success is to be judged on the coherence of its products, services, and organizational culture and processes with the character of God.

The beatific vision does not supplant the original design for work and, by extension, business, but subsumes it in a larger narrative, that is business does not just engage reality as it proceeds from God, but also engages reality as it returns to God. For the believer, love becomes the primary reason for engaging in business. Because love desires that all of creation is ordered to God appropriately, it supports business' original calling. Because love recognizes that God desires friendship with all humans, it animates the additional calling of returning everything, particularly humans, to God. At a minimum, love requires that believers give primacy to humans over other created goods. This should impact how believers structure the work environment and influence the choice of goods and services a business provides. For example, believers should recognize that humans are not resources for businesses, but that businesses are resources for humans. Humans, be they employees, partners, or customers, are to be treated with the highest respect and consideration, not seen as dispensable or reduced to instrumental goods, but seen as proximate terminal goods, a reason for one's existence as a business person. Love precludes taking advantage of others, using them for personal or corporate gain, and compels believers to consider how their behavior and decisions inhibit or promote others' friendship with God.

Love calls believers to treat others as friends, desiring and facilitating their flourishing. For example, love would prevent a believer from engaging in the pornography industry regardless of potential profits. Pornography objectifies humans, reducing them to simple means, and not treating them as invaluable ends. It views humans solely through the lens of sexuality, ignoring their complexity and richness as image bearers of God with bodies and souls that will live eternally. Pornography promotes a disordering of human sexuality, and, thereby, a disordering of human relationships with God and each other. Instead of preparing one for the beatific vision by developing characters and passions proportionate to God, pornography enslaves individuals in a deepening darkness that pushes God away.

In the midst of a fallen world, surrounded by evil structures and patterns of being that seem destined to overtake all of creation, believers easily could feel impotent in ever fulfilling God's calling for business. In such a world, to structure business according to God's goodness could seem impossible at best and utterly ludicrous at worst. God, however, has not left believers without hope. He has given believers his Spirit who is truly greater than he who is in the world. God has given believers the church and his truth, against which all of hell shall not prevail. When the forces working against God's calling for humanity and business appear to have victory in their grasp, believers need to remember that only the Lamb who was slain has the authority to unseal the book and write the last chapter of history, and that there will be a day in which the waters that give birth to evil and chaos will be no more. Most importantly, when darkness seems to stretch from one end of the horizon to other, and all that God has destined for creation and humanity will be lost, believers must remember that a day is coming when there will be no temple or need for light for God will be among his people, that there will be no tears in their eyes for they will be seeing God.

BIBLIOGRAPHY

Cates, D. F. *Aquinas on the Emotions: A Religious-Ethical Inquiry*. Washington DC: Georgetown University Press, 2009.

Cessario, R. *The Virtues, or the Examined Life*. New York: Continuum, 2002.

Brown, S. F. "The Theological Virtue of Faith" In *The Ethics of Aquinas*, IIa IIae, qq. 1–16. Washington DC: Georgetown University Press, 2002.

Kaczor, C. editor. *Thomas Aquinas on Faith, Hope, and Love: Edited and Explained for Everyone*. Ave Maria, FL: Sapientia, 2008.

Pieper, J. *Faith, Hope, Love*. Translated by F. McCarthy et al. San Francisco: Ignatius, 1997.

Porter, J. "Right Reason and the Love of God: The Parameters of Aquinas' Moral Theology." In *The Theology of Thomas Aquinas*, 167–91. Notre Dame, IN: University of Notre Dame Press, 2005.

Schockenhoff, E. "The Theological Virtue of Charity" In *The Ethics of Aquinas*, IIa IIae, qq. 23–46. Translated by G. Kaplan and F. G. Lawrence. Washington DC: Georgetown University Press, 2002.

16

Influence and Method
The Role of Spiritual Direction in Theological Study

JEFF VALODINE

INTRODUCTION

Theologians tend to be of three types: (1) the *Country Club* theologian, one who treats the vast discipline of theology with only a quick glance in order not to miss his morning tee time, (2) the *Lord of the Ring* theologian who, after finding his "precious" in the ivory tower of theology, works diligently to keep the information to himself, purposely using terminology to keep the content veiled to outsiders, and (3) the *Doctor Universalis* theologian who, after processing through with scholarly diligence the multiple layers of the theological discipline himself, makes his discoveries available and accessible to all. John Castelein is of this third type.

John Castelein taught theology, preached theology, modeled theology, and breathed theology. For him the discipline of discussing the concepts of God was never *the* goal of theology but rather how we can know (understand) God better in order that we may worship and serve him better. His was a theology in praxis that incorporated the Scriptures, his personal journey, his scholarship and his commitment as a pastor. Attending seminary, the most important factor to me was that the professors I placed myself under actually believed the stuff they were teaching. In addition to believing what they taught their lives needed to reflect their theological convictions. John Castelein did both of these well.

In addition to the people we choose to place ourselves under on our theological journey lies the vast body of theological writing covering over two thousand years of church history. When one enters into the study of theology there is a starting place. Most young theologians begin with the basics: Scripture and some book on theological introduction. The body of material used in theological studies may be mapped with concentric circles, with the outer ring being introductory material and the center being original sources. Undergraduate studies usually begin with the outer introductory ring and proceed through background material and end with compilations or readers. Graduate studies begin with compiled material but immediately begin to focus on original sources. This is where the work of the theologian thus begins.

However, the beginning of a theological pursuit cannot start with theology itself. Before a student begins to develop his own map of the theological territory he must determine the necessary if not crucial foundations that make the pursuit possible. Often times these foundations are either unknown or, even if they are known, ignored. We must look behind the curtain to issues of epistemology, hermeneutics, language theory, logic, dialectics and worldviews. We must also consider the different faith-communities involved in the theological tradition.[1] In addition to these fundamental disciplines we must add systematics, method, and application. Without considering these functional specialties[2] it is impossible to converse theologically.

In reflecting on this enterprise I would like to elucidate on three basic categories that shape the theological discipline. First, there is *Direction and Influence*, the launching point and sequence of epistemological revelation to us. Second, there is *Sources and Systematics*, from original thought to our

1. See McBrien, *Catholicism*, 51 (i.e., Catholic, Protestant, Jewish, Islamic theologies). "Every self-conscious attempt to come to a better understanding of what one believes about God, about the ultimate meaning of life, about our hopes for the future, and about our sense of moral obligation to others, is a work of theology at one level or another."

2. See Lonergan, *Method in Theology*, 125–36. Lonergan proposes eight functional specialties in theology: (1) research, (2) interpretation, (3) history, (4) dialectics, (5) foundations, (6) doctrines, (7) systematic, and (8) communications.

thought within categories we can communicate. Third, there is *Method and Application*, the operational processes undertaken to "articulate in a specific historical-cultural context the unchanging faith commitment of the church to the God revealed in Jesus Christ."[3] Because this is intended to not only paint a broad picture of the theological enterprise but to also honor my colleague John Castelein, the category of direction and influence will be given primacy.

DIRECTION AND INFLUENCE IN THE THEOLOGICAL ENTERPRISE

There are many different starting points and structures of the theological system.[4] Do we begin with Scripture or with natural theology? How do we weigh the denominational presuppositions that most theologians begin with? How do we judge the historical climate a particular individual had when he wrote? What kind of influence guided the theologians of generations past? What material was available to these men in their historical-cultural setting? Who were their peers and with whom did they take advice from? With whom did they disagree? To what extent did science, philosophy, art, and literature shape the development of theology? These and many other questions are very important issues to consider when assessing the theological enterprise and there are many who have attempted to do so with extreme vigor.[5] Let us look at theological influence, from those living and dead, both modeled and written.

I find it interesting that, with all of the written discussion on method in theology, I am unaware of much attention given to the influence that a mentor has over his student, the influence that the socio-politic-economic climate of his lifetime has on his theological perspective, nor the intimate

3. See Grenz, *Theology for the Community of God*, 16. Grenz puts forth three sources or norms for theology: (1) the biblical message, (2) the theological heritage of the church, and (3) the thought-forms of the historical-cultural context in which the contemporary people of God seek to speak, live and act.

4. See Erickson, *Christian Theology*, 62–84 (Reformed); Oden, *Classic Christianity: A Systematic Theology*, xiii–xxvi (Paleo-Orthodox); Grenz, *Theology for the Community of God*, 1–25 (Baptist); Lonergan, *Insight: A Study of Human Understanding* and *Method in Theology* (Catholic, conservative); Meyendorff, *Byzantine Theology*, 1–15 (Orthodox); Tillich, *Systematic Theology, Volume One*, 3–68, esp. 34–68 on Method and Structure of Systematic Theology (Catholic, liberal).

5. See Augustine, *City of God, Confessions, On the Trinity*, and *On Christian Doctrine*; St. Thomas Aquinas, *Summa Theologiæ* and *Summa Contra Gentiles*; Barth, *Church Dogmatics* (14 vols.); Calvin, *Institutes of the Christian Religion*; Balthasar's systematic theology trilogy (*Glory of the Lord, Theo-Drama*, and *Theo-Logic*).

and personal factors that so greatly influence any theological voice. Much of the time these "factors of influence" are addressed within a brief biographical introduction of the individual prior to the "real dialogue" that takes place within the pages of his written work. We are familiar with the influence St. Anthony and mother Monica had on St. Augustine, Kant's claim that "Hume interrupted my dogmatic slumber," and the role of the *studium generale* in Naples and Albertus Magnus in Paris had on St. Thomas.[6] The modernist method of limiting our dialogue to that which is written is understandable. We have difficulty communicating with people directly. When ask if he had a "soul mate . . . someone who could open things up for you," Will Hunting replied, "Plenty of them . . . Shakespeare, Nietzsche, Frost, etc." His mentor Sean then asks, "Well that's great, they're all dead," to which Will responds, "Not to me." Contemporary theologians focus their attention on the writing of authors past because we simply cannot have a lot of dialogue with them without a heater and some serious smelling salts.[7]

The modernist methods of textual interaction (and the surrender of authorial intent), has now eroded into postmodern concept of reader-response. However, we must insist on ascertaining the context, mood, climate, and setting that make up our initial situation in order to derive the proper understanding of the author, text and meaning. It may be considered counterproductive or too speculative, but consider if Augustine would have articulated his treaty on original sin without Pelagius? Would Kant have developed his speculative metaphysics without Hume? Would Aquinas have produced his brilliant and prolific work had he followed his uncle into the Benedictine monastery at Montecassino? So much emphasis is placed on the written work of the past and present that it overshadows the theological influence of the living spiritual director like an eclipse. In addition to these factors, thought must be given to the special circumstances that have existed throughout church history that provide insight into the development of theological method. The Desert Fathers provide a unique perspective on method. The age of the medieval monasteries provide not only a locative significance but also influential method. Even the twenty-one ecumenical church counsels provide an incredibly layered and rich platform for the development of theology as a whole, as well as the advancement of theological method.[8]

6. See Chadwick, *Augustine of Hippo: A Life*; Kant, *Prolegomena to Any Future Metaphysics*; Copleston, *Aquinas: An Introduction to the Life and Work of the Great Medieval Thinker*. Biographies on influential theologians provide crucial insight into the circumstances that existed before and during their time of writing.

7. From *Good Will Hunting*, written by Matt Damon and Ben Affleck.

8. See Joseph Kelly, *The Ecumenical Counsels of the Catholic Church: A History*;

In addition to largely ignoring personal influences that shape theologians, and thus theology in general, contemporary theologians tend to dismiss the cultural, religious, economic, political, and scientific climate of the past and present while they focus on texts. We need be aware that sound theology must consider the setting and circumstances that allow the theological enterprise to flourish. For example, I have been particularly interested in the ascetics and in monasticism during my theological studies. Perhaps this is because I see the value of a person's calling to embrace this way of life; it is so encompassing, so paradigmatic, so purposeful and so directed. This is not to suggest that this is the only context to engage in theological study or whether this context is perhaps too limiting. However, the monastic structure, the spiritual mentors, the religious Rule, and their ecclesiastical associations have greatly influence theological development and content.[9] This type of influence is not limited to ancient and cloistered orders of the medieval period. Contemporary theologians have chronicled similar experiences in which the academic discipline of theology proper and the influence of spiritual direction and ministry context have been united.[10] Often times the theological community passes off figures like Henri Nouwen, C. S. Lewis, St. John of the Cross and Eugene Peterson because they practice a kind of spiritual, mystical, or practical theology.

As much distance as there seems to be between the philosophical theology of Aquinas, the mystical theology of Dionysius, and the Reformed theology of Calvin, there is even a further distance between theologians who write and those who do not. Theological legacy and influence is not

---

Burton-Christie, *The Word in the Desert: Scripture and the Quest for Holiness in Early Christian Monasticism*; McGinn, *The Essential Writings of Christian Mysticism*; Brooke, *The Age of the Cloister: The Story of Monastic Life in the Middle Ages*; the *Rule of St. Benedict*; St. Ignatius of Loyola and Anthony Mottola, *Spiritual Exercises of Saint Ignatius*; Bernard of Clairvaux, *Cistercians and Cluniacs: St. Bernard's Apologia to Abbot William*

9. For example, see Lawrence, *Medieval Monasticism: Forms of Religious Life in Western Europe in the Middle Ages*. The Benedictine Abby at Cluny (est. 910) led by only four abbots over the first 200+ years, practiced a strict Rule, enjoyed autonomous government, and become the prime example of western monasticism. Nicholas Herman, the cook and sandal repairman at the Discalced Carmelite monastery in Paris (1614–91), otherwise known as Brother Lawrence, was a common man who greatly affected the learned clerics of his order.

10. See Nouwen, *In the Name of Jesus*. Henri Nouwen, after teaching at Notre Dame, Yale and Harvard, went to the L'Arche community in Toronto. Here he had a profound experience that changed the course of his life. In the account of C. S. Lewis we see several influences, (1) *fictional literature* such as MacDonald's *Phantastes*, (2) *non-fiction literature* such as Chesterton's *Everlasting Man*, and (3) *spiritual direction* provided by his friends J. R. R. Tolkien and Hugo Dyson. These influences were added to the foundation laid when Lewis attended the Church of Ireland as a child.

reserved exclusively for those who were fortunate to write their thoughts out during their lifetime. It is also reserved for those who modeled their theological convictions at the highest level and discipled others to do the same.[11] This form of theological legacy is not only admirable, but thoroughly biblical. John Castelein represents this type of theological influence.

John Castelein taught graduate level theology at Lincoln Christian Seminary and I was blessed to sit under him for several classes. John was an excellent teacher, outstanding mentor, and thoroughly biblical theologian. My time with John was not merely reading theology written by a bunch of dead guys; nor was it simply a matter of "knowing the several schemes on interpreting the creation narratives" or understanding terms like *anknupfungspunkt*, *homoousios*, or *sublapsarianism*. John Castelein prepared each of us and gave us the tools to *become* theologians ourselves.[12] We received more than merely John in our classes . . . we had James Strauss, Martin Marty, Langdon Gilkey, David Tracy, and Peter Berger as well. This is also true of all teaching theologians. However, in addition to teaching, John also served as preaching minister at Lincoln Christian Church. Often times, John would "work out" the content, coherence, and biblical competence of his sermons with us before he delivered them on a Sunday morning. I learned to justify my theological positions by referencing who and where I received my information and how I came to my conclusions. John taught us that objective truth does exist and that we should not seek doubt and embrace skepticism but rather seek reasonable faith and ultimately, truth.

James Sire defines a worldview as "a commitment, a fundamental orientation of the heart, that can be expressed as a story or in a set of presuppositions (assumptions which may be true, partially true or entirely false) that we hold (consciously or subconsciously, consistently or inconsistently) about the basic constitution of reality, and that provides the foundation on which we live and move and have our being."[13] Theologians have a similar foundational context in which they build their theology. We all have a childhood (positive or negative), primary educators (good or bad), personal

11. See articles such as Gerald Hiestand, "Pastor-scholar to Professor-Scholar: Exploring the Theological Disconnect between the Academy and the Local Church," and Michael Alan Shanbour, "Academic Theology: Swimming with Your Clothes On."

12. The popular sentiment at many conservative Bible Colleges, with regard to the study of theology, seems to be, "We don't teach theology, we instruct in doctrine." The liberal sentiment may be the opposite, "Theology . . . we don't need no stinking theology." John established a sound method in teaching by mapping out the theological scope, reading original sources, deconstructing the material, interpreting the data, reconstructing it systematically, sifting it through the filters of faith and Scripture, and implementing the results contemporarily contextually, and culturally.

13. See Sire, *The Universe Next Door*, 20.

relationships, mentors and professors (spiritual or secular, conservative or liberal) and access to a wealth of theological scholarship (some helpful, much hurtful). Influence comes from a life lived, but also from written sources. Direction in theology should encourage students to appropriate the important and influential voices of the past and the present. However, where and what you begin with is crucial.

Life provides us our first breath, first steps, first date, and first child. The journey in theology has similar steps. First, everyone begins with some locative worldview even though most people cannot identify their position. This initial theological position is extremely important because is exercises a great deal of weight or persuasion over the individual. If someone begins their pursuit as a Lutheran, they will most likely take a very Lutheran approach to the task. Perhaps confirmed in the Lutheran tradition, they will be well versed in the Large and Small Catechism, and possibly attend a Lutheran seminary. The books they read will most likely be on Luther himself, the Book of Concord, and the Augsburg Confession. Even their Bibles will be read with Lutheran lenses and the help of R. C. H. Lenski. It is a most peculiar thing—Lutherans beget Lutherans, Baptists beget Baptists, and Catholics beget Catholics. As easy as it is to see why this happens, it is not easy to see if the task of theology is ever breached. Evidence that perhaps shows a young theologian has embraced the task of theology comes when one's own doctrinal position is critiqued. John Castelein helped us do just this.

A grand journey is a metaphor of the theological enterprise—one that begins on one mountaintop and ends on some distant mountaintop. The deep and dark valley between the two peaks provides several options for travel. At the very base, where the mountains come together, there is a black sea. The initial part of the journey is a perilous downward jaunt that is quite unnerving. Here we must leave our initial position of knowing, believing and trusting as we seek information that is challenging and leaves us unsettled. On this descent we must choose from several optional routes. First, we need to identify our personal prolegomena or our initial starting position.[14] Where we are going and how we get there have a lot to do with

14. Augustine and Anselm embraced Platonism; Aquinas had an Aristotelian map. Pascal grounds all communication with God in Christ. Tillich claims that we are not prepared to receive the Word of God without the experiencing participation of the church. Lonergan states that the believer is attentive to the data of his or her own consciousness, and the unbeliever is not, or at least interprets the data differently. Peter Berger argues for an anthropological starting point. Newman adopted his apologetic of conscience. McGrath states that the word prolegomena was not to be understood as "things which need to be said before theology is possible," but rather "the things that must be said first in theology." He grounds this in the Word of God.

who we are and with whom we travel. Second, we must decide upon the structural path(s) of theology that we utilize.[15] These structural paths deal with growing cultural influences and subcategories such as denominational preferences and special interest perspectives. Third, as we approach the dark lake of despair, we are challenged to endure the precarious dominion of the underlying disciplines such as metaphysics, epistemology, hermeneutics, language theory and philosophy.[16] Some would include these disciplines as necessary "vehicles" on the theological path, where others see these as "occupational hazards." John Castelein emphasized these as fundamental to the theological quest.

However, theology is not merely a downhill jaunt into the lake of despair, where we embrace the nothingness of eternal skepticism and doubt. It is the ascent upward towards the place where God inhabits and exists. It is the journey of faith and purpose, the discovery of reality and truth, and the realm of immediate and eternal peace and hope. For after we scale down the mountainside from the peak we started by deconstructing our worldview, our denomination, our tradition, our culture (*sitz in lebem*), our understanding and even our preferred Bible translation, we must confront our own doubts, limits, and fears of unknowing. The surface of the lake represents the line of despair while the bottom of the lake represents the nihilistic pit of philosophical and ethical hopeless. It is important to approach the surface tension on the theological journey, for without it, could be argued, that you ever left home. The abyss of the dark lake, while unnerving to some, is home to many. Those who study theology without any Christian commitment may find satisfaction in its empty, groundless meaninglessness. Those who come to faith as an adult may find the secondary base of the foundation (the primary being the Cornerstone of Christ). However, those who were raised in a strong Bible-based church may feel the foundation of their faith eroding away. Regardless of our commitment, is not this is the place we all must come to? Faith in faith itself is fideism and reason alone, finite rationalism. Whether you dive into the lake, perhaps even to its very depth, or merely walk along its edge, the goal is not to stay here. We must ascend the next peak. A true theologian not only *deconstructs* his thought

15. Theological *systems* that included but not limited to biblical, historical, systematic, apologetic, natural, pastoral, anthropological, mystical, and philosophical. Denominational preferences refer to the "received" archetypal structures used in Roman Catholic, Reformed Theology, Eastern Orthodoxy, Arminian or Wesleyan, Evangelical, and Pentecostal perspectives. Special interest perspectives refer to such categories as liberation, feminist, ethnic, prosperity gospel, and syncretistic camps.

16. See such topics as ontology, cosmology, necessity and possibility, theories of knowledge, justification, rationalism, empiricism, warrant, externalism, internalism, idealism, constructivism, skepticism, existentialism, and phenomenology.

and understanding, but *constructs* a meaningful and comprehensive system . . . and brings disciples along his journey. John Castelein has led many in this way.

SOURCES AND SYSTEMATICS IN THE THEOLOGICAL ENTERPRISE

The theological climb upward is logically more difficult than the descent. It is one thing to deconstruct the critical and fundamental building blocks of our thought than to erect a biblically sound and philosophically constructed method in theology. When constructing something such as a building, workers must clear away all obstruction and dig down to a solid base. On this solid base they will lay a foundation from which the entire structure is built. This foundation must be not only able to support the structure; it must also be true, for if it is not, even by the slightest error, the entire building will, by increasingly larger margins, deviate from true. Contemporary theology has the benefit of two thousand years of church history and thus two thousand years of doctrinal development.[17] When we enter into theological dialogue we have to start somewhere and with something. This starting place is as crucial as the foundation of a one hundred story skyscraper. The initial question a beginner wrestles with is direction, both spiritual and theological, on his journey towards truth. This is where theological influence plays an important part.[18] A good theology professor will recommend not only what to read but also how to read. They decide upon which floor of the building we are to enter constructing our theological paradigm. For none of us begin this journey with an *a prori tabula rasa*. Nor does a person who is uninitiated in the discipline of theology have the necessary categories, framework, or content to properly engage with the theological community. My thought here is of a tall building and the different floors represent different levels of theological involvement. Perhaps the ground floors are basic resources in theology, the upper floors are intermediate works, and the lower floors are

---

17. Beginning with in the first century with *Ignatius of Antioch* who wrote on ecclesiology; *Irenaeus of Lyons* who wrote as an apologist; The Alexandria Three: *Clement*, who had a Platonic expression of the Christian faith, *Origen*, a prolific writer who expressed the faith allegorically, and *Athanasius*, who developed the earliest expression of the Trinity. It was not just what the church fathers wrote theologically but also how they developed their doctrine that matters.

18. Theology is not practiced in a vacuum (although some perspectives seem to come off the bathroom wall). Hence, the initial advice we receive, the first book we read, and the first time we encounter what is behind the grand curtain, we are so enamored with our findings that we often pitch our tents here and venture no farther.

core resources. So you would enter the process with a basic introduction to concepts and terminology then proceed upwardly to discover increasing truths. Once these truths are codified and systematized into understandable sections they are placed in the basement of the building, forming the foundational truths placed at the base, close to the Cornerstone.

There are some who are on the journey that are beginning before even making a commitment to the Christian faith. If a person begins their quest as an atheist or agnostic before deciding on any particular creed or denomination they seem more able to "begin at the beginning" better than Christians who have already settled on some perspective. In any case, studying the "science of divine things" must begin with the Christian Scriptures. Evangelicals are leaders in the Bible-based approach to theology. They would argue that it is impossible to speak theologically without grounding the discussion on the authority of Scripture.[19] Since the scope of theological material is vast, a theological director introduces the subject with some type of primer. Reformers gravitate towards Princeton scholar Charles Hodge, Dallas Seminary founder Lewis Sperry Chafer, or Calvin Seminary professor Louis Berkhof. These three examples are kept alive by the voices of R. C. Sproul, James Montgomery Boice, Millard Erickson, and Wayne Grudem. But these voices of both past and present, although adequate enough in introducing theology, are not the source of theology.

Primary sources are perhaps the most important starting place for theological content. This is why the Bible is foundational to any discussion on Christian theology. The Gospel writers claim to have been eye witnesses themselves or, in the case of Luke, careful to investigate everything from the beginning (see Luke 1:1–4). It is also why theologians need to engage with primary sources in order to adequately discuss doctrine. If the map chosen to navigate the theological territory is from the Reformed tradition, you will eventually encounter John Calvin, John Knox, and Huldrych Zwingli, while also reading the German reformers Martin Luther, Philipp Melanchthon, and Martin Bucer. There is no mystery in this process. The development of theology can be traced throughout church history.[20] What remains is a mystery: the overwhelming sway that certain theological lines have on us.

19. See Stackhouse, *Evangelical Futures*; Erickson et al., *Reclaiming the Center*; Grenz and Franke, *Beyond Foundationalism*; Dorrien, *The Remaking of Evangelical Theology*.

20. See contemporary examples such as McGrath, *Historical Theology: An Introduction to the History of Christian Thought*; Bromiley, *Historical Theology: An Introduction*; Olson, *The Story of Christian Theology: Twenty Centuries of Tradition and Reform*; Allison, *Historical Theology: An Introduction to Christian Doctrine*; McCormack and Kapic, *Mapping Modern Theology: A Thematic and Historical Introduction*.

In other words, how do we get beyond the doctrinal path of our spiritual forefathers in order to see the theological enterprise from 30,000 feet? For if we buy into Calvin, interpreted by Hodge, systematized by Berkhof, and contemporized by Sproul, it could be argued that we are simply too close to *das Ding an sich*, even if hundreds of years have passed. For, with all of our theological gymnastics, we have just reinterpreted the "good old boy" doctrine generation after generation. Not only are we required to have a personal grasp of biblical doctrine but we are also being asked to weigh the understanding of our theology through generations past and present. This is where systematic theology can assist us. John Castelein wrote his systematic on our lives.

Systematic theology is the reflection on and the ordered articulation of faith.[21] Systematic theology deconstructs biblical theology into doctrinal categories or themes and then reconstructs them as topical sets.[22] The advantage to this approach is the ability to see theology as both a sum of its parts and as a unified whole. The disadvantage in systematizing theology is to assign certain semantic and theological loads to concepts and terms, and then to use these terms univocally and interchangeably, thus either removing them from their original context or imposing an inappropriate meaning. In addition to the categorical methods of systematizing theology and the "sub-ologies" that emerge, the systematic approach can also be focused around an organizing theme.[23] By the early twenty-first century the theological community has produced hundreds of systematic works, ranging from (1) the immense, multi-volume editions of Aquinas, Barth, and von Balthasar, (2) the mid-range expositions of de Lubac, Thielicke, and Pannenberg , (3) the contemporary synthesis of Lonergan, Henry, and Geisler, to the (4) the one-volume introductions of Erickson, Grudem, and

---

21. See Grenz, *Theology for the Community of God*, 1–5. The typical subcategories of systematic theology are identified as Paterology, Christology, Pneumatology, Cosmology, Anthropology, Angelology, Demonology, Bibilology, Harmartiology, Soteriology, Theodicy, Ecclesiology, Axiology, Eschatology, and Missiology.

22. Systematic theology could also refer to the attempt to reduce Christian doctrine into a compact and coherent system around fundamental axioms. See Schleiermacher, *A Brief Outline of the Study of Theology*.

23. Some examples are: freewill and responsibility in Augustine; scholasticism in Aquinas; justification by faith in Luther; the problem of boredom, anxiety and despair in Kierkegaard; man's pride and self-centeredness in Niebuhr; generalized philosophical hermeneutics in Schleiermacher; the theological aesthetics of von Balthasar; patristic orthodoxy in Oden; the eschatological community in Grenz.

McBrien.[24] Each of these attempts at "reasoning or discussion concerning the Deity"[25] has helped develop the theological doctrine we have today.

Theological direction plays an important key in choosing what to read, what lenses to wear, and what purpose we have towards the theological process. If you simply want to know a bit *about* theology you could be guided to a basic introduction.[26] If you want to study theology in order to live according to the promises it offers, perhaps one ought to consider the theological mystics.[27] However, if a disciple is already familiar with the basic fundamentals of the theological tradition and would like to explore the development of doctrine, they will have to contend with the original authors and their work. This is where theology becomes more difficult and yet exciting and satisfying all the same. Primary source form the base of the next theological mountain. The theological journey is perhaps chiastic in structure; epistemologically descending down one slope, deconstructing their worldview (from whole or complete into many parts), and then reconstructing these parts systematically and rationally into a cohesive constitution of reality.

METHOD AND APPLICATION IN THE THEOLOGICAL ENTERPRISE

On the ascent of theological reconstruction, away from the lake of despair, we use the organizing schema of biblical, historical and systematic theology. These larger frameworks provide us a necessary set of cohesion and method that orders our progress. However, these frameworks are not sufficient enough to settle the complexity of theological content and application. In other words, even after a theologian traces a particular doctrine biblically, from Genesis to Revelation, the information and perhaps the conclusion is still a matter of question. This is because, with all the good intentions of the theologian, these larger organizing methods must, themselves be deconstructed by the subcategories which make theology possible to begin with. Following our analogy on the ascent up the next mountain, when we reach the summit, it is possible to think "we have arrived." However,

24. See bibliography for recommended sources.

25. Augustine, *City of God, Book VIII* "*de divinitate rationem sive sermonem.*"

26. See Milne, *Know the Truth: A Handbook of Christian Belief*; Erickson, *Introducing Christian Doctrine*; Little, *Know What You Believe*; Olsen, *The Mosaic of Christian Belief: Twenty Centuries of Unity & Diversity.*

27. See Lossky, *The Mystical Theology of the Eastern Church*; Meyendorff, *Byzantine Theology*; St. John of the Cross, *The Ascent of Mount Carmel* and *Dark Night of the Soul*; Symeon the New Theologian, *The Discourses.*

what we find there is a large oak tree. If theology includes this oak tree, the leaves and fruit are what people see (theology as lived out), the branches are the individual doctrines that each theological camp has constructed, the trunk is the main theological pillar from which all traditions receive the Core Doctrine (orthodoxy), and the root system is that immense network of information that forms the basis of theological data.

It is this immense root system that must be nurtured and tended to in order that we can establish a solid theological core and strong doctrinal branches that will produce healthy fruit that nourishes the members of the Body of Christ. This root system is an intricate network itself comprised by the subcategories of epistemology, hermeneutics, logic, language and communication.[28] These important disciplines are crucial to ensuring that our theological root system not only receives the correct information but they also provide the necessary adhesive that unites sound biblical theology with the larger discipline known as natural theology. One goal in incorporating these crucial subcategories is to help the would-be theologian progress from "The Bible says . . ." or "Gregory of Nazianzus states . . . " to establishing a dynamic working model of expression that adequately deals with the complexity of theological doctrine from pre-Genesis to post-Revelation. A good theological director will not only recommend original sources and a helpful systematic, but will also provide instructions on theological method and application. John Castelein guided us in such fundamental subcategories, giving us the ability to properly engage in theological study. He taught us how to properly deconstruct existing worldviews, to critique our personal presuppositions and perspectives, and how to begin constructing a thoroughly biblical, logically coherent, systematically constructed, and personally identified theological position. It is only when we nurture the theological root system of the large oak tree on top of our new mountain home that we can turn around and gaze out over the territory we just endured. We can see our original position, full of childlike naivety and passionate conviction. We long to see God the way we did before our journey but we cannot. It is not that God has changed, it is because we have. There may even be an overwhelming urge to jettison our new position and jump back to the original place where we felt a closeness to God's presence. John Castelein challenged us to go back home to the place we were meant to stand, naked and vulner-

28. Particularly helpful examples of such works are Sosa and Kim, eds., *Epistemology: An Anthology*; Kittel and Friedrich, *Theological Dictionary of the New Testament*; Gadamer, *Truth and Method*; Kreeft, *Socratic Logic*; Lonergan, *Insight: A Study of Human Understanding*; Botterweck, et al., *Theological Dictionary of the Old Testament*; Chisholm, *Theory of Knowledge*; Vanhoozer, *The Drama of Doctrine: A Canonical Linguistic Approach to Christian Theology*

able before God, not to take the easy way of being carried on eagles' wings, but to repeat our journey backwards. In this, we shall surely discover that our faith and theology are rest assured.

Theological method thus becomes crucial to the direction, development, apprehension and conclusion of the theological enterprise. Method incorporates sound biblical exegesis and hermeneutics, proper historical-grammatical linguistic study, general and specific worldview and epistemological concepts, and static and dynamic influence and discipleship. The difficulty in discussing method in theology is that it is hard to pinpoint an exact schema that satisfies enough of the theological participants. In reading through *Evangelical Futures: A Conversation on Theological Method*, you will see little reference to or dialogue with, Catholic, Orthodox, or Anglican theologians on method. The reverse is also true when reading through *The Orthodox Way* by Kallistos Ware. He is deafening silent in dialogue with those outside the Orthodox tradition. Thus, what we have for examples of comprehensive theological methods are the massive theological treaties of Aquinas, Barth, von Balthasar, and Lonergan.[29] In addition to the outstanding contributions of the systematic theologians of past and present, I would argue for including of the work and ministry of the outstanding mystical theologians of the Christian tradition within the theological dialectic. The excellent and insightful work of Origen, Gregory of Nyssa, Bernard of Clairvaux, Evagrius Ponticus, John of the Cross, and Teresa of Avila[30] should be given the same level of attention and authority that we extend to the traditional sources. This inclusion happens when we extend the boundaries of our method in theology to the extent exampled by Aquinas, Barth, et al.

When encountering a deeply committed theologian you should also find an outstanding Bible scholar, linguist, philosopher, apologist, and exegete. However, in addition to these skills, a theologian must be deeply committed to the Christian faith, to the Trinity, to the study and proclamation of Scripture, and to the advancement of God's kingdom. When the study of theology becomes separated from the faith and practice of the fundamental truths that constitute theology it becomes merely philosophical gymnastics. This does not mean that all theologians will practice their faith the same way nor does it mean that they will be consistent. It does however imply that the theologian must live within their theological system. Somehow their faith must identify their theology and their theology must identify their faith. This does not always happen. Whereas theology as a discipline

29. This is not to say that these are the only significant, overarching methods available, but to suggest these are the most comprehensive approaches to the subject.

30. See bibliography for recommended sources.

is usually taken up by committed believers, it is often times practiced in a professional manner. The content of theology can so enamor a person that they become fascinated with the discipline apart from faith. When this happens the rigor of theological discipline becomes more important than the content, faith, and practice of such theology. Theology then becomes an intellectual play thing, something that is discussed among small groups of like-minded men who attempt to convince the theological community to adopt and apply their carefully constructed program. However, theology is the study of God and the ways of God. It is our duty as theologians to set our minds on things above, not on earthly things (Col 3:1–4), to carefully investigate everything from the beginning and write an orderly account for future generations (see Luke 1:1–4), and to make disciples of all nations, teaching them to be obedient to the teaching of the Father, Son and Spirit (see Matt 28:18–20). John Castelein was this type of theologian. Jesus chose not to write down anything in print but to write his testimony and will on the hearts and minds of his disciples; John Castelein wrote his method in theology on the hearts and minds of his students—we are very grateful that he did.

BIBLIOGRAPHY

Allison, Gregg R. *Historical Theology: An Introduction to Christian Doctrine*. Grand Rapids: Zondervan, 2011.

Augustine. *Augustine: The City of God against the Pagans*. Translated by R. W. Dyson. Cambridge: Cambridge University Press, 1998.

———. *Confessions*. New York: Oxford University Press, 2009.

Balthasar, Hans Urs von. *Glory of the Lord—A Theological Aesthetics: Seeing the Form, Vol. 1*. 2nd ed. San Francisco: Ignatius, 2009.

———. *Glory of the Lord—A Theological Aesthetics: Studies in Theological Styles— Clerical Styles, Vol. 2*. San Francisco: Ignatius, 1984.

———. *Glory of the Lord—A Theological Aesthetics: Studies in Theological Styles—Lay Styles, Vol. 3*. San Francisco: Ignatius, 2003.

———. *Glory of the Lord—A Theological Aesthetics: The Realm of Metaphysics in Antiquity, Vol. 4*. San Francisco: Ignatius, 1989.

———. *Theo-Drama—Theological Dramatic Theory: Prolegomena, Vol. 1*. San Francisco: Ignatius, 1989.

———. *Theo-Drama—Theological Dramatic Theory: The Dramatis Personae: Man in God, Vol. 2*. San Francisco: Ignatius, 1990.

———. *Theo-Drama—Theological Dramatic Theory: The Dramatis Personae: Persons in Christ, Vol. 3*. San Francisco: Ignatius, 1993.

———. *Theo-Drama—Theological Dramatic Theory: The Action, Vol. 4*. San Francisco: Ignatius, 1994.

———. *Theo-Drama—Theological Dramatic Theory: The Last Act, Vol. 5*. San Francisco: Ignatius, 1998.

———. *Theo-Logic: Truth of the World, Vol. 1*. San Francisco: Ignatius, 2001.

———. *Theo-Logic: Truth of God, Vol. 2*. San Francisco: Ignatius, 2004.

———. *Theo-Logic: Spirit of Truth, Vol. 3*. San Francisco: Ignatius, 2005.

Barth, Karl, et al. *Church Dogmatics*. Edited by G. W. Bromiley et al. 14 vols. Reprint. Peabody, MA: Hendrickson, 2010.

Benedict, et al. *The Rule of Saint Benedict*. New York: Vintage, 1998.

Bernard of Clairvaux. *Bernard of Clairvaux: Selected Works*. Classics of Western Spirituality. Translated by G. R. Evans. New York: Paulist, 1987.

Bonaventure. *Bonaventure: The Soul's Journey into God, The Tree of Life, The Life of St. Francis*. Classics of Western Spirituality. Translated by Ewert Cousins. New York: Paulist, 1978.

Botterweck, Johannes, et al. *Theological Dictionary of the Old Testament*. 11 vols. Grand Rapids: Eerdmans, 2003.

Bromiley, Geoffrey. *Historical Theology: An Introduction*. Edinburgh: T. & T. Clark, 2000.

Brooke, Christopher. *The Age of the Cloister: The Story of Monastic Life in the Middle Ages*. Snohomish, WA: HiddenSprings, 2003.

Brother Lawrence. *The Practice of the Presence of God with Spiritual Maximums*. Grand Rapids: Spire, 1967.

Burton-Christie, Douglas. *The Word in the Desert: Scripture and the Quest for Holiness in Early Christian Monasticism*. New York: Oxford University Press, 1993.

Calvin, John. *Institutes of the Christian Religion*. Translated by Henry Beveridge. Grand Rapids: Eerdmans, 1989.

Chadwick, Henry. *Augustine of Hippo: A Life*. New York: Oxford University Press, 2010.

Chan, Simon. *Spiritual Theology: A Systematic Study of the Christian Life*. Downers Grove, IL: InterVarsity, 1998.

Chisholm, Roderick. *Foundations of Knowing*. Minneapolis: The University of Minnesota Press, 1982.

———. *Theory of Knowledge*. 2nd ed. New York: Prentice Hall, 1989.

Copleston, F. C. *Aquinas: An Introduction to the Life and Work of the Great Medieval Thinker*. London: Penguin, 1956.

Cross, St. John of the, et al. *The Collected Work of St. John of the Cross*. Washington, DC: ICS, 1991.

De Lubac, Henri. *Medieval Exegesis*. 4 vols. Grand Rapids: Eerdmans, 1998–2009.

Dorrien, Gary. *The Remaking of Evangelical Theology*. Louisville: Westminster John Knox, 1998.

Erickson, Millard J. *Christian Theology*. 2nd ed. Grand Rapids: Baker Academic, 1998.

———. *Introducing Christian Doctrine*. 3rd ed. Grand Rapids: Baker Academic, 2001.

Erickson, Millard, et al. *Reclaiming the Center: Confronting Evangelical Accommodations in Postmodern Times*. Wheaton, IL: Crossway, 2004.

Gadamer, Hans-Georg. *Truth and Method*. 2nd ed. New York: Continuum, 1997.

Good Will Hunting. Directed by Gus Van Sant. Distributed by Miramax Films, 1997.

Grenz, Stanley J. *Theology for the Community of God*. Grand Rapids: Eerdmans, 2000.

Grenz, Stanley, and John Franke. *Beyond Foundationalism: Shaping Theology in a Postmodern Context*. Louisville: Westminster John Knox, 2001.

Gruden, Wayne. *Systematic Theology*. Rev. ed. Grand Rapids: Zondervan, 2000.

Hiestand, Gerald. "Pastor-scholar to Professor-scholar: Exploring the Theological Disconnect between the Academy and the Local Church." *Westminster Theological Journal* 70 (2008) 355–69.

Ignatius. *The Spiritual Exercises of Saint Ignatius*. Translated by Anthony Mottola. New York: Image, 1989.

Lawrence, C. H. *Medieval Monasticism: Forms of Religious Life in Western Europe in the Middle Ages*. New York: Longman, 1989.

Little, Paul. *Know What You Believe*. Rev. ed. Downers Grove, IL: InterVarsity, 2008.

Lonergan, Bernard J. F. *Collected Works of Bernard Lonergan: Insight, Vol. 3*. Toronto: University of Toronto Press, 1992.

———. *Collected Work of Bernard Lonergan: Method in Theology, Vol. 14*. Toronto: University of Toronto Press, 1999.

Lossky, Vladimir. *The Mystical Theology of the Eastern Church*. New York: St. Vladimir's Seminary, 1998.

Kant, Immanuel. *Prolegomena to Any Future Metaphysics*. Translated by Gary Hatfield. Cambridge: Cambridge University Press, 1997.

Kelly, J. N. D. *Early Christian Doctrine*. Peabody, MA: Prince, 2004.

Kelly, Joseph F. *The Ecumenical Counsels of the Catholic Church*. Collegeville, MN: Liturgical, 2009.

Kittel, Gerhard, et al. *Theological Dictionary of the New Testament*. 10 vols. Grand Rapids: Eerdmans, 2006.

Kreeft, Peter. *Socratic Logic: A Logic Text Using Socratic Method, Platonic Questions, and Aristotelian Principles*. 2nd ed. South Bend, IN: St. Augustine's Press, 2005.

McBrien, Richard P. *Catholicism: New Study Edition, Completely Revised and Updated*. New York: HarperCollins, 1994.

McCormack, and Kelly Kapic. *Mapping Modern Theology: A Thematic and Historical Introduction*. Grand Rapids: Baker Academic, 2012.

McGinn, Bernard. *The Essential Writings of Christian Mysticism*. New York: Modern Library, 2006.

McGrath, Alister. *Historical Theology: An Introduction to the History of Christian Thought*. 2nd ed. London: Wiley-Blackwell, 2012.

Meyendorff, John. *Byzantine Theology: Historical Trends and Doctrinal Themes*. New York: Fordham University Press, 1979.

Milne, Bruce. *Know the Truth: A Handbook of Christian Belief*. 3rd ed. Downers Grove, IL: InterVarsity Academic, 2010.

Nouwen, Henri J. M. *In the Name of Jesus*. New York: Crossroads, 1996.

Oden, Thomas C. *Classic Christianity: A Systematic Theology*. New York: HarperOne, 1992.

Olsen, Roger E. *The Mosaic of Christian Belief: Twenty Centuries of Unity and Diversity*. Downers Grove, IL: InterVarsity, 2002.

———. *The Story of Christian Theology: Twenty Centuries of Tradition and Reform*. Downers Grove, IL: InterVarsity Academic, 1999.

Origen. *Origen: An Exhortation to Martyrdom, Prayer, and Selected Works*. The Classics of Western Spirituality. Translated by Rowan Greer. New York: Paulist, 1979.

Pannenberg, Wolfhart. *Systematic Theology*. 3 vols. Grand Rapids: Eerdmans, 1994–2010.

Plantinga, Alvin. *Warranted Christian Belief*. New York: Oxford University Press, 2000.

———. *Warrant and Proper Function*. New York: Oxford University Press, 1993.

———. *Warrant: The Current Debate*. New York: Oxford University Press, 1993.

Scanbour, Michael Alan. "*Academic Theology: Swimming with Your Clothes On.*" *Word Magazine* 45.2 (2001) 4–9.

Schleiermacher, Friedrich. *A Brief Outline of the Study of Theology*. Reprint. Eugene, OR: Wipf & Stock, 2007.

Scoobie, Charles H. H. *The Ways of Our God: An Approach to Biblical Theology*. Grand Rapids: Eerdmans, 2003.

Sire, James W. *The Universe Next Door*. 5th ed. Downers Grove, IL: InterVarsity, 2009.

Sosa, Ernst, and Jaegwon Kim. *Epistemology: An Anthology*. Malden, MA: Blackwell, 2001.

Stackhouse, John G. *Evangelical Futures: A Conversation on Theological Method*. Grand Rapids: Baker, 2000.

Symeon the New Theologian. *The Discourses*. Classics of Western Spirituality. Translated by C. J. De Catanzaro. New York: Paulist, 1980.

Thielicke, Helmut. *Modern Faith & Thought*. Grand Rapids: Eerdmans, 1990.

Thomas Aquinas. *Summa contra gentiles*. 5 vols. Translated by A. C. Pegis (Bk. I), J. F. Anderson (Bk. II), V J. Bourke (Bk. III), C. J. O'Neill (Bk. IV). Notre Dame, IN: University of Notre Dame Press, 1975.

———. *Summa Theologica*. 5 vols. Translated by the Fathers of the English Dominican Province. Notre Dame, IN: Christian Classics, 1981.

Tillich, Paul. *Systematic Theology*. 3 vols. Chicago: University of Chicago Press, 1973–75.

Teresa, St., and Kieran Kavanaugn. *The Collected Works of St. Teresa of Avila*. 3 vols. Washington, DC: ICS, 1980–87.

Vanhoozer, Kevin J. *The Drama of Doctrine: A Canonical Linguistic Approach to Christian Theology*. Louisville: John Knox, 2005.

———. *Is There a Meaning in this Text? The Bible, the Reader, and the Morality of Literary Knowledge*. Grand Rapids: Zondervan, 1998.

Wittgenstein, Ludwig. *Philosophical Investigations*. 3rd ed. Englewood Cliffs, NJ: Prentice Hall, 1958.

PERSONAL ESSAYS

17

Reflecting on a Teacher's Influence

MICHAEL GOWIN

Measuring impact or influence is easier in some areas than others.

In business, McDonald's counts hamburgers ("billions and billions" according to the sign outside my local restaurant) and Apple has more than twenty-eight million songs available for sale in the iTunes store.[1] My favorite college football team, the Notre Dame Fighting Irish, counted a twelve win and zero loss season in 2012 (they've not yet played in the national championship game at the time I'm writing this). This earned the Irish a #1 national ranking. Depending on your line of work, you might count articles published, sermons preached, weekend attendance, free throws sunk, leads converted, cases closed, retweets, likes, your Klout score, or any of a thousand other metrics.

But what measure does a teacher use?

Years in the classroom? Number of students taught? Percentage of "A's" awarded? What can you quantify that sums up a teacher's influence?

Google counts over fifteen million views of a presentation given by Randy Pausch, the Carnegie Mellon professor who gave a moving "last

---

1. http://www.digitalmusicnews.com/permalink/2012/120425itunes

lecture" just months before terminal cancer claimed his life.[2] By comparison, South Korean musician PSY's music video for his song "Gangnam Style" has been viewed more than one billion times, making it the most viewed YouTube video of all time.[3] It would be silly to suggest that the rapper is sixty-six times more influential than the professor—based solely on YouTube viewing statistics—but it does hint at the difficulty of measuring influence.

John Castelein was my teacher and, as a teacher myself, I often wonder what endures. We spend hours reading, culling, preparing, choosing assignments, attempting to determine what's important about a subject and then choosing the best way to communicate that to students. Teachers rarely see the fruit of their labor, and if they do, it is typically not until years after a student graduates.

From 1993 to 1996, I studied theology with John. I took several classes with him and wrote an extended research paper under his guidance on the way to earning a master's degree. This experience will be shared by most (if not all) of the contributors to this volume.

But I also benefitted from John's teaching in a local congregation, Lincoln Christian Church. In 2001 John helped start a Sunday school class for young adults, the Open Door as it came to be known, and my wife and I were part of that. John also took on preaching duties for the church from July 2001 through June 2006 and I heard his sermons many of those Sundays.

Having shared life together with John, my teacher, in these two settings—both in and out of the classroom—offers me a unique vantage point from which to measure this teacher's influence.

Several months ago I received an invitation to write an essay, a "reflection of John's teaching in [my] own thought." So this, then, is an essay about influence and ideas, and one that will trace a line from one teacher's life into that of another.

THE TEACHER

I met Dr. Castelein (as I knew him then) in my very first class at Lincoln Christian Seminary back in January 1993. I'd registered for TP662 Twentieth Century Theology, and the class was team-taught by Dr. Castelein and Dr. Jim Strauss.

My undergraduate journey had led me through four schools and three majors, from engineering to art and finally English. I had read some Bonhoeffer and some InterVarsity Press titles on my own but didn't have the

2. http://www.youtube.com/watch?v=ji5_MqicxSo
3. http://www.youtube.com/watch?v=9bZkp7q19fo

Bible college background of many of my classmates. I had not even grown up in a Restoration Movement church: I was raised Catholic. With this first class, I was stepping off the dock a good distance from shore.

In many ways, the two teachers of this course could not have been more different. Dr. Strauss filled the room with his presence—boisterous, outgoing, and quick with a retort or quippy phrase. He also filled the chalkboard, at times nearly incomprehensibly, with notes, names, dates, titles, and abbreviations. "We'll put this in code," he would declare, "so the outsiders won't know." An idea might lead in one direction at one moment and then a hundred others in the next. Following the path of Dr. Strauss' thought was like trying to capture fireflies with a thimble—an arduous task but still worth the challenge.

By contrast, John was measured, deliberate, intentional—thoughtful with an intellect as powerful as Dr. Strauss' yet revealed in markedly different fashion. While Dr. Strauss was everywhere, John was focused, singular in his direction, linear in his presentation. Dr. Strauss wanted you to see everything at once, connecting apparently random ideas across the centuries: see how this philosopher influenced that theologian, and how that book brought about this idea—and behold!—that's how we got here today!

John, on the other hand, patiently walked students through each idea, each thinker, each development in that thinker's journey, one step at a time. When the time came to summarize and compare, John masterfully synthesized the disparate parts into a whole, easy to understand. I still have a diagram from that class that John created, pragmatically and descriptively entitled, "A Rough Spectrum of the Modern Theological Scene in Relationship to Biblical Authority (only for Protestant Theology)." A precursor to the current hot trend in infographics, it divides the century's theological landscape into quarters (fundamentalism, evangelicalism, neoorthodoxy, liberalism) and then locates theologians, philosophers, thinkers, and movements along its axes.

Disparate parts into a whole, easy to understand.

Aside from learning more about Bonhoeffer, Barth, and Bultmann in that class, I picked up other things from John that semester. These lessons were often repeated in the subsequent classes I took with him as well.

For one, John demonstrated both humility and curiosity in his teaching. I watched as he respectfully deferred to his senior colleague in TP662, inviting Dr. Strauss to offer his thoughts at times when John was lecturing.

And when a student raised a question or idea that John found insightful, he took notes. He stopped to write down the question or thought that had been offered.

I had never seen a teacher do this.

Not once in seventeen years of school had I seen this happen. In college alone, I had sat through hundreds of hours of lectures with dozens of different professors, but I cannot recall a single instance when an instructor stopped to jot down something thoughtful suggested by a student.

This showed me that John was not just a teacher but a learner as well, humble enough to acknowledge and accept a student's insight.

The teacher-as-learner was also disclosed in the books that John passed around the classroom. He'd often bring an armful of books, the most relevant titles on that week's topic, for students to see and flip through. Many of his books were annotated and highlighted in multiple colors (evidencing multiple readings), sometimes with his own indices handwritten in the opening or closing pages. On one occasion, he told us he'd been reading in the tub that week and had become so engrossed in the book that he didn't notice the bath water had gone cold.

All of this was done, I believe, in service to the students. Not to brag ("see how many books I've read!") but to show us that investing time in good books is fundamental to developing one's mind and ministry. He enjoyed and loved learning, and sought to inspire us to love it as well.

In the classroom, John was open about his limitations. If he did not know something, he admitted as much. He shared his knowledge as well as his questions with his students, and did so comfortably. John never appeared embarrassed by not knowing an answer to a question.

At the same time, however, he was not embarrassed to reveal his convictions. In another class I took with John a couple years later, a student disagreed on a point of biblical criticism. I can't remember the specifics of the conversation but she was arguing along the lines of a more developmental/evolutionary view of the canon than traditionally accepted. John responded—politely but firmly, not dismissive—"well, I don't take that view" and that was the end of it. The student's argument wasn't relevant to the discussion at that moment and John wasn't going to waste valuable class time on it.

Humble preparation, making sense of things, inspiring students to learn. This is what good teachers do, and this is what John taught me about teaching.

THE PASTOR

I was fortunate to enjoy John's teaching outside the classroom as well, in a local church.

In 2001, Lincoln Christian Church, a congregation that is nearly as old as the town of Lincoln itself, had many active ministries and classes for people at all stages of life—except young adults. The church had a large and dynamic children's and youth ministry, as well as classes and activities for those with established families and into their thirties and beyond. But a void awaited those who were just out of college, in graduate school, or at some place in their twenties.

John, who attended Lincoln, and a handful of others saw an opportunity to minister to this overlooked group. In the spring of 2001, a new Sunday morning class emerged: the Open Door. The class grew rapidly—for several years attendance averaged around fifty, sometimes peaking in the seventies. This one Sunday school class was larger than many congregations in the area, and we had to meet in the church's fellowship auditorium because we outgrew the available classrooms.

What brought people to the Open Door? In part, it was the community. Young people, many having children for the first time, were drawn together from mutual interests and the desire to support one another. But John's presence and teaching were key components as well. John was thoroughly energized and passionate about seeing this group of people grow and mature in Christ. He saw us as his children in the faith, perhaps as Paul regarded Timothy (1 Tim 1:2; 2 Tim 1:2; 2:1) or the elder John regarded his audience (1 John 2:1, 12, 18, 28; 3:7, 18; 4:4; 5:21).

In those first few months, John taught them using film clips and stories as his texts. One especially memorable series covered the themes of law and grace in Victor Hugo's *Les Miserables* (not a common text for a Sunday school class). Later he taught on baptism and church membership, subjects that aroused some controversy in the group since not all of the class participants were members of the church or immersed believers. John was willing to tackle difficult subjects and could breathe new life into old ones in a creative and innovative way.

I also had the privilege to call John my preacher for a season. From July 2001 to June 2006, John filled the pulpit at Lincoln Christian Church. What initially began as an interim assignment when the previous preaching pastor took a new ministry in New Hampshire became a full-time preaching appointment. All this while John continued in his full-time teaching role at the seminary.

What struck me during this period were John's passion and honesty. While I had always felt that John was honest with students in the classroom, it was a little startling to see this same transparency on display from the pulpit. It is not that the preachers I had heard up to that point had been dishonest. Rather, it was more that John was simply being himself instead of assuming a different persona when he stepped into the pulpit. For me this was like someone had opened a window in a stale, stuffy room, allowing a fresh breeze to fill the place.

In 2003, John preached through the book of Romans. While introducing Romans 5:1–5, he acknowledged that Paul's words portrayed a "spiritual mountaintop" that he had yet to climb himself. But he saw in the text a number of ways that God becomes real to us and then proceeded to preach the passage apologetically and very personally. John was deeply concerned that Paul's words were not just "church words" but that they genuinely worked themselves into and out of the everyday lives of those gathered. He then explained each word or term in the passage (e.g., justified, faith, peace with God, etc.), asked a question about how that might be revealed in his own life, and then offered his evidence. Here is how John described the opening of Romans 5:1:

> The first word is "justified." In a culture where so many people are constantly explaining themselves, excusing themselves, I can't help but think that a lot of people must feel like failures. They feel like they're falling short. Does that describe you? Just this deep sense, even when people are complimenting you still, a sense of failure, of falling short. And yet Paul says if you're living the Christian life, you should have a sense of being justified.
>
> Do you know how that comes out for me? I asked myself, sincerely, "Am I a justified person?" My job at Lincoln Christian Church aside, and my job at the seminary aside, am I truly a justified person? And I came up with this, an unshakeable reality that's really true in my life—not that I deserve it, it's a gift— but there are times that I feel so *accepted*. Accepted . . . we're all looking to be accepted. That's my apologetic for being justified: there are times that, by God's grace, I know I am accepted.[4]

A few months later, John preached from Romans 7 and 8, "the heart of the heart" of the New Testament as he explained it, Paul's comparison between life (or death, really) under the law and life in the Spirit. As he described Paul's struggle with the war being waged in his body, the tension between the desire to do God's will and the sin that draws him away (7:14–25), John was nearly beside himself to explain Paul's dilemma: "I wish I could just sit down in individual face-to-face conversation with each one of you and just ask you, 'Are you aware of how shocking this passage is?!' This isn't just a preacher or elder or deacon or Sunday school teacher, this is

4. LCC audio recording, January 26, 2003.

the apostle, the single most formative person—except from Jesus Christ—through all of Christianity and look at what he's confessing!"[5]

This kind of intensity, excitement, and earnestness was present each week as John preached. His messages were not academic exercises, presentations of interesting but ultimately useless trivia unrelated to daily life. Nor were they lighthearted fare intended to tickle and entertain. A friend once remarked to me that people come to church looking for the Bread of Life and we offer them a Twinkie. John did not do this.

In discussing Timothy's task at Ephesus, correcting some problems in both belief and practice there, Eugene Peterson states that "[nothing] a pastor does is more important than the way she or he uses words."[6] He contends that, in the West, we use words that fall into impersonal knowledge, abstraction, and information (science) as well as words that come from the heart, from experience, from life (wisdom). A danger lies in failing to recognize the difference. "If we don't discern the distinction between these two ways of knowing, we will treat matters of the gospel wrongly and therefore lead people wrongly. All knowledge has content to it. But science depersonalizes knowledge in order to make it more exact, precise, objective, manageable. Wisdom personalizes knowledge in order to live intensely, faithfully, healthily."[7]

John's preaching was so stirring because it married years of thoughtful, deep study with a passion to draw people into closer relationships with Christ. The words of his sermons were not those of a scientist; they were the words of one seeking and sharing wisdom. He was seeking answers for himself: Am I justified? Do I have faith? Do I experience peace? What does Paul's struggle tell me about my own inner conflicts? What do all these things reveal about the God who loves me and who wants me to love him and my neighbor?

Because of his compassion for God's people, John publicly and humbly shared the results of his reflection and study each week. As John worked through his own questions, his journey benefitted those of us in the pews as well.

MEASURING A TEACHER'S INFLUENCE

Ten years ago, I was given the opportunity to speak before the undergraduate students in a Lincoln Christian College chapel service. I spoke about failure

5. LCC audio recording, March 9, 2003.
6. Peterson, "Wise Teachers," 1226.
7. Ibid.

and persevering through it, and I shared some of my own failures—personal stories of mistakes I had made, dumb things I had said or done, but how I still managed to survive in spite of them. One of those stories was about a fight that I had had with my wife, Suzanne, while we were newly married.

Suzanne had "nuked" a hot dog in our microwave until, from my perspective, there was little left of it to eat. That's no way to cook a hot dog, I rebuked. Having painstakingly developed an elaborate system for "properly" cooking a hot dog in the microwave, I had little patience for overcooked, molten masses of food mess. Suzanne, on the other hand, was a fan of the ease and simplicity of the "one minute cook" button the microwave offered and used it liberally. Thus, our fight over how to cook a hot dog.

This was just one brief illustration in the ten-minute message.

Months after that sermonette, two of my students who were then dating and now married told me how helpful that message was for them. They said that whenever they would get into a pointless argument about something, one of them would realize it and then declare, "Dude, that's just a hot dog." Argument over.

In the end, is this what sticks with our students? Should I tell more stories about hot dog fights? How do we measure our influence as teachers?

In the nearly twenty years that I have known John Castelein, Ihavve attended his lectures, heard many of his lessons and sermons, read his words, enjoyed conversation. Though I studied theology with him, I am not now a professor of theology (not formally anyway), and I have retained few of the details from those classes I took in the mid-90s. But John has taught me many things, mostly by modeling them, important things that have helped me grow as a disciple and as a teacher:

- **A disciple of Jesus is curious.** Curiosity is an essential ingredient in learning and faith. A curious mind continues to seek, to ask questions, to explore. A curious disciple, it could be argued, hungers and thirsts for righteousness (Matt 5:6). A curious teacher inspires his students with curiosity as well.

- **Growth requires humility.** At the moment I claim to know enough, I stop growing. If John can learn from a student, so can I.

- **Honesty and transparency are gateways to intimacy.** I respected John for his intelligence and learning. But what I valued so much in him in both the classroom and in the pulpit was his willingness to be real—to have shortcomings (like me), to fail (like me), to have questions and doubts (like me). Sharing my own failures with students, I think, has made me more accessible to them and they in turn more open to me.

- **Passion and enthusiasm inspire learning.** McKeachie claims that the lecturer's main role in higher education is to "communicate the teacher's enthusiasm about the subject."[8] John showed me this not only in the classroom but from the pulpit as well. His energy motivated me and others to learn.

- **Critical thinking brings clarity.** Research shows that "[people] are most likely to learn deeply when they are trying to answer their own questions or solve their own problems."[9] This is confirmed in our experience as well: as learners, we work hardest on the problems we care about. As a teacher, John consistently created environments where questions could be posed and discussed. At the same time, he helped students understand and make sense of the world, even—and especially—when that meant helping students change how they see the world.[10]

A teacher's influence might be measured, then, in his ability to inspire his students to continue to learn, and then in their ability to inspire others to do the same. Some of John's students have become teachers themselves (several are my colleagues at LCU), others serve in churches, others in the marketplace. Even so, this is still difficult to quantify.

As I reflect on John's teaching in my own thought—and life—I'm left with this: the legacy and impact of John Castelein, a curious, humble, honest, passionate teacher who helped his students see God's world more clearly, may well be immeasurable on this side of eternity. To be sure, many sermons have been preached, articles written, students taught. These things can be quantified and may give some indication of influence.

In the end, the one benchmark that truly matters is "well done good and faithful servant." And on this account, I reckon John Castelein measures up.

8. McKeachie, *McKeachie's Teaching Tips*, 73.

9. Bain and Zimmerman, "Understanding Great Teaching," 11.

10. In the Sermon on the Mount (Matt 5–7), Jesus repeatedly uses the formula, "You have heard it said . . . but I tell you." Not only does this reveal his authority vis-a-vis the Mosaic Law, but it also guides his listeners into a new way to understand their relationship to the law and to the world.

BIBLIOGRAPHY

Bain, Ken, and James Zimmerman. "Understanding Great Teaching." *Peer Review* 11.2 (2009) 9–12.

Castelein, John. Untitled sermon on Romans 5:1–5 delivered at Lincoln Christian Church. January 26, 2003. Audiocassette.

Castelein, John. Untitled sermon on Romans 7–8 delivered at Lincoln Christian Church. March 9, 2003. Audiocassette.

McKeachie, Wilbert J., and Marilla Svinicki. *McKeachie's Teaching Tips: Strategies, Research, and Theory for College and University Teachers.* 12th ed. Boston: Houghton Mifflin, 2006.

Pausch, Randy. "Randy Pausch Last Lecture: Achieving Your Childhood Dreams." Recorded September 18, 2007. YouTube video, 1:16:27. Posted December 20, 2007. http://www.youtube.com/watch?v=ji5_MqicxSo.

Peterson, Eugene H. "Wise Teachers, Sound Teaching." *Christian Century* 116.35, December 15, 1999, 1224–27.

PSY. "PSY—GANGNAM STYLE." YouTube video, 4:13. Posted July 15, 2012. http://www.youtube.com/watch?v=9bZkp7q19f0.

Resnikoff, Paul. Digital Music News (blog). http://www.digitalmusicnews.com/.

18

Undone and Redone
on the Way Back to Jerusalem

DAVID PETERS

I T IS HUMBLING TO be invited to participate in a project such as this; first, as an opportunity to give honor to whom honor is due, particularly when the one due honor is due so much more honor than the one giving the honor. It is also humbling to be invited to participate in it by colleagues who themselves are due so much honor. Scholars and faithful disciples, these ... and in contemplating the blessing to the kingdom and myself personally that these are, I become very much tempted towards joining a Sesame Street-like refrain that begins to churn in my heart: "Eleven of these things are kind of special, eleven of these things are kind of the same, one of these things just doesn't belong here ..." Or perhaps the introductory refrain— candid and honest but without shame—of the Great Gonzo: "I'm the ugly disgusting one that catches cannonballs."

After having (almost) resisted that temptation, I am blessed with a graced washed recognition that what I am about to write is more sermonic than academic, and my Sesame Street-like refrain gives way to a Popeye-like one: "I yam what I yam." I am preacher before academic, and I am tempted to be slightly sheepish about that in light of John's scholarship, and the scholarship of others writing to honor him. I am tempted to believe that the best honor to render John is some academic piece that strongly influences those who would read it and then ultimately the church. I fear that I am one of John's black sheep—one whose influence has been more local, personal, practical and pastoral than academic, and I am quickly and happily wrested from these false fears by two additional recognitions:

John's ministry has arguably been as much local, personal, practical, and pastoral as it has been academic. Perhaps even more so. His graduates are indeed testimony to his deft pastoral care (and we are, generally, a lot with great need for a special kind of nurture). Even more so, his life and ministry within the congregations he has served is testimony to this practical ministry.

As I recognize this, I become tempted to lionize and validate my relative disposition towards the practical and away from the writing of papers for meetings of the ETS, AAR, or the various Journals of Tremendous Theological Consequence. I (try to) make John in my own image, at the risk of sounding doubly blasphemous—the first blasphemy that I am engaged in a project of self-justification, and the second that John should be my measure of my discipleship. Beyond the blasphemy, the preposterousness of this is transparent and immediate. For John has written for these journals and more, and is as academic as any I have known. And somehow I suspect that John would be quick to point out how I've simply stumbled into an either-or binary that simply does not exist—either practical/pastoral *or* academic.

Indeed, the fallacy of that now stands clear, and I would do violence to the recent intellectual history of the church—a history that rightly recognizes the obscene perils of some falsely sanctified anti-intellectualism that has crept into the life and practice of much of the American church. Far from bearing or fostering this guilt, John has fought against it and been a virtuous example of what it means to be fully intellectual and deeply thoughtful about the faith, while simultaneously being an integrated doer of his faith. I learned from John in new and clear ways that the Christian faith is not simply a matter of orthodoxy (right believing [however important that is])—but is simultaneously and in equal measure a matter of orthopraxy (right doing, right acting). I learned this via the content of his teaching—what he teaches in word and what he teaches in deed.

So, I remain humbled to stand with these men who are also writing to render honor to John—one who is worthy of that honor. While the sermonic spirit of what follows is transparent, it remains my goal that it be likewise rigorously analytic and fundamentally honest and truthful. It simply cannot honor John if it is the former without the latter, or the latter without the former. More to the point, it cannot honor God. It seems to me that however diverse we beneficiaries of John are in disposition, temperament, giftedness and emphasis, we are united in this chief aim of glorifying God and loving him with all of our hearts, minds, souls and strength. Perhaps our bond can be well summarized as a shared recognition that God does indeed want truth in our innermost being (Ps 51:6) and that from that place he causes rivers of living water to flow (John 7:38). God's Spirit is that living water, and for many of us, John has been a God-sent plumber, helping unclog the PVC pipes of our hearts, clearing the way for that living water to flow.

My time spent under John's tutelage and mentoring was relatively brief (two years, more or less), but life and faith altering. I came from a Bible college that imparted to me a deep love of the Scriptures and knowledge of them, and I regarded seminary as the place where my remaining questions about God, faith, life and the church would be largely answered. Yes, it was a naïve conviction, but lay off me. I really thought along those lines. John had an instinctive awareness of many of my assumptions about life, faith, and my capacities as a knower and a believer, and that awareness blossomed into a forensic understanding of my heart and mind as he invested his life and time in me.

As I got to know John and the vast fields of knowledge that he had surveyed and actually comprehended, I think I got my first chill that perhaps there was more to understand then I had the capacity or even will to understand. Initially undaunted in the unbounded confidence of my relative youth, I believe I expected I would "get there" eventually. However, it took only a handful of class sessions together with John and my classmates for that chill to begin to freeze my watery self-confidence into solid ice. Perhaps indeed, there were more questions than I had imagined, and the answers far more elusive then I could have feared.

My iced confidence threatened to give way to a permafrost of despair sometime near the end of our rather grueling hermeneutics class. I understood what I was learning. I understood the questions the people we studied were presenting. Most of the time, I think I understood their answers to those questions, to the extent that they presented answers. But I found myself unable to agree with many of the conclusions of Foucault, Derrida, Rorty, Fish, Eco, Habermas, West, or Gadamer. At the same time, I was often impressed with the acuity of their grasp of certain problems. These men who didn't know Jesus had thought more earnestly about several problems then I, with my extensive knowledge of offsides rules in hockey, had ever considered. "Too often, too true" was a refrain that I learned to apply to much of what I was reading of these men. While there was substance to criticize, to be preoccupied with that criticism would be to fail to understand why they were being critical—and sometimes, those "whys" demand honest attention.

I was supposed to be a truth seeker as a Christian, and I was humbled by these men John introduced me to. I was supposed to have answers to all the problems and questions, or so I thought, and John helped usher me into a world where the answers I had seemed to be unhearable as I wanted them to be heard. Before I could finish uttering an answer, each of these men would have described and understood my answer in a way that said more about me than about the substance of the answer I had presented. It was bewildering. This wasn't how I needed the world to function. Of course, it escaped my notice that it wasn't the world's modus operandi to march in step with my drum. Less abstractly, I didn't have a guarantee of a rational silver bullet that would defeat the reasoning of those who concluded something other than that Jesus was Lord. I'm reminded of an old Mr. Boffo cartoon strip, captioned "same planet; different worlds," where a man courting a woman was pictured in a single frame in a restaurant, waxing profoundly on some subject, while the thought balloon above the woman's head read only "boing boing boing boing boing." I couldn't tell whether Derrida, Fish, Rorty, and Foucault were the woman, or whether she was me.

I fell into my dilemma unwittingly. In my undergraduate years, I saw some of the weaknesses of the evidentialism to which I had married my faith. Paul's admonition that we not be unequally yoked comes to mind as I now contemplate that union. In coming to rest in my faith, Josh McDowell had been a steadying, confidence imbuing guide. He helped build a bridge from doubt to confidence. The brute facts were the brute facts, after all.

Little did I realize that I was unwittingly committing myself to an understanding of truth and facts that was little different than that possessed by David Hume or A. J. Ayer, hardly two that I would expect to find walking alongside me on the Emmaus Road. I am struck by the strangeness of such bedfellows in retrospect; at the time Josh was molding my intellectual filters, I was oblivious to Hume and Ayer. In my first encounters with them, I learned to refute their arguments against the faith, and particularly dismissively, at least in the case of Ayer's verification principle. Ayer's verification principle—the notion that any non-analytic statement be regarded as meaningful only if empirically verifiable—was closely related to the evidentialist's conviction that the justification for a belief depends solely upon the evidence for it. While I somewhat smugly (I confess) delighted in the self-refuting nature of the former, the gravitational pull of the latter still left me with more in common with Hume and Ayer than I realized.

By no means would McDowell have intended me to be a disciple of Hume, Ayer, or any other empiricist. Nor, do I believe, would he assent to the version of evidentialism where a belief's justification is grounded solely on evidence for the belief. Surely he wanted me to be a disciple of Jesus. But as I started to notice the blindspots and inadequacies of the theories of the empiricists, I began to realize that had some application to the way that I believed in Jesus. No rational person could possibly resist the blunt force trauma of the brute facts of history, could they? Was I a disciple of Jesus, or a disciple of evidence, and of the assumptions necessary about life and the world and rationality to make evidentialism function?

John might not always have been the first to introduce me to each of these authors, forces, challenges and arguments (though he was indeed my first guide through many of these). He did a marvelous job of preventing them from ever being mere academic abstractions. He forced me to understand them and simmer in the depths of the challenges these realities represented.

As I simmered in these challenges while simultaneously being challenged by Derrida, Foucault, Fish, Rorty, and the like, I was totally and utterly thrown. What was there to stand upon any more, if I could not definitively tear through opposing arguments with irresistible reason alone? Sartre's Nausea set in: I could no longer define myself on the foundation of utterly reliable reason. It was gone. I felt sick. It seemed to me like I now had nothing.

In retrospect, as one owned by Jesus, I never should have worried that I had nothing. But I had by then learned the faith in such a reason-reliant/ reliable way that indeed it seemed so. I was in the pit—sitting or laying on my couch in married student housing, emotionally and mentally exhausted, wondering how I could ever believe in anything ever again if I did not have recourse to the kind of reason that delivers indubitable, incorrigible, certain results. John helped me understand deconstruction by analogizing it to a garment from which one thread begged to be pulled. Tug that thread long enough, and there would be no substance left to the garment. Indeed, I felt like there was no substance left to me. I had come undone. I felt that I had been left with nothing.

Finding yourself with nothing is perhaps the most hollow liberation you can experience. It is indeed freeing. There is nothing you have to fight for anymore. It is akin to the faux utopia Lennon unwittingly created in his song "Imagine." There truly is nothing to kill or die for—that is to say, as Lennon himself did to protesters at Berkeley who were at the precipice of experiencing physical harm from the authorities, there's nothing worth dying for. While on the surface this sounds quite life affirming, as you reflect on it, it seems quite life robbing too. "Imagine" is, in this sense, a sweet sounding continuation of another brilliantly crafted song earlier penned by

Lennon and McCartney, "A Day in the Life." While sparing you the lyrics due to copyright and licensure issues, that song is, among other things, a desperate attempt to express horror over things like people committing suicide in their despair, but a frustrated attempt to do so in a world where it seems like death and filling potholes are morally equivalent. If indeed all we are is matter in motion, governed strictly and solely by sociological or biological cause and effect—a view increasingly popularly prevalent at the time Lennon and McCartney were writing "A Day in the Life"—then how indeed can we believe that there is more or less moral significance to despair and suicide than there is going about getting a cup of coffee? While some might grieve in horror, might it be as appropriate simply to laugh? Such is a world where nothing is worth dying for. This is the reduction of life to Turkish delight—a series of visceral, ephemeral pleasures that fill us enough to deny us steak, fruit, and vegetables. There is nothing—abject nothing. Nothing worth living for, and nothing worth dying for. It becomes a vacuum—a horrible place of inertia. There is no reason to move from one place to another, from one position to another. You can find nothing within your reason, ambition, or desire to move you. Precisely because there is nothing.

I was struggling, lacking my tool of ever-reliable reason, to find something guaranteedly reliable that could move me, with all certainty, from one position to the next. I wanted to use that tool to find that first place on which I could stand—that Cartesian foundation, that Archimedian point— but was reminded again through John's faithful instruction that my reason was fallen and finite and forever bound, even on its best day, firmly within my own finite horizons and perspective. I simply could never see enough or know enough to make a solely, sufficiently rational judgment about such a foundation.

Back to the question that continued to dog me: Was I a disciple of Jesus, or a disciple of evidence, and of the assumptions necessary about life and the world and rationality to make evidentialism function? I concluded that I had been more devoted to the deliverances of my own reason than I was to the substance of anything I affirmed. Understanding it in these terms, this seemed a poor outcome for one devoted to Jesus. He, the substance of my conviction, seemed clearly to be second fiddle to the confines and demands of my reason. But I didn't know how to think otherwise without committing what I had long understood to be intellectual suicide. I seemed doomed to inertia.

John had waxed reflective upon Cain and Abel during one season of class. Perhaps he has subsequently—it was so abruptly challenging and nourishing that I really hope that someone brighter than me has taken and developed the seeds that he planted. I know enough to know there is something there to work with. Perhaps John himself has developed it further without my knowledge. What he contemplated was whether Cain himself should be understood as struggling with the very dilemma I found myself faced with—whether Cain could handle the choice between God and nothingness. "Abel," after all, was Hebrew for vanity, that vanity having the sense of fleetingness—of an ephemeral coming and going. Indeed, nothingness and *abel*/vanity are directly related in Isaiah 49:4: "I have toiled in vain, I have spent my strength for nothing and vanity." The nothing here is the *"tohu"* of Genesis—empty, formless, a wasteland. Might somehow God be telegraphing us that we ultimately have a simple choice—between him and nothingness?

Whether this was Moses' intent is a matter I've not yet established with much confidence, but contemplation of the possibility opened up a door of hope to me. Maybe it was little more complex than simply reckoning with the choice of God or nothingness. Skepticism would place priority on choosing nothing, but why give pride of place to skepticism or suspicion over faith? This too was something I had never considered at length, and was one more of John's gifts to us. We treat faith as though it is less intellectually responsible than faith. Yet, on a rather Augustinian note, we are all functioning within the framework of faith in something. Once again, it remains a question of whether the object of that faith can sustain life and faith.

Before I started reckoning with the hope these new ways of thinking were providing to me, I remember wondering, as I writhed in nothingness, how John and some of my classmates could seem to understand all of these challenges even more clearly than I could, yet pass through those fires and apparently have a real relationship with Jesus. It was bewildering. They really seemed to earnestly, seriously, actually believe in the resurrected Jesus, and that living Christ, as I had understood him, seemed to drive their believing, doing, imagining and hoping. This much seemed familiar. I was having such a hard time understanding how that could be authentically mine.

There was a kind patience about John. It was, in my experience, occasionally terse—a patience that cut through garbage very quickly; John called me on some of the dramatic tendencies perhaps even reflected in this brief essay ("aren't you being just a bit over the top here?"). But it was longsuffering. Knowing that John had walked roads as dark and darker provided hope. He was careful never to short-circuit my own journey by telling me precisely where or how he found his footing as a witness of the resurrection. I think he knew that I needed to find my way to Jesus. He was unrelentingly present and stabilizing. And his continual Jesus following was simultaneously bewildering and hope-imbuing.

The simplicity of the choice between God and the nihil reminded me of Paul's warning that we not be led astray from the purity and simplicity of devotion to Christ (2 Cor 11:3). Surely it was all supposed to be so much more simple than I had made it. Perhaps it was a simple choice. I still struggled with the grounds for making a choice. Was it an arbitrary, groundless leap into the dark? Are arbitrary and groundless the same thing?

Certainly Alvin Plantinga's argument concerning the proper basicality of belief in God was an influence on my thinking. He proposes that there are properly basic beliefs that are justifiably held without being grounded on other evidence. Belief in God is one such belief, he asserts. For me, William Alston added a piece to Plantinga's argument. He attempted to demonstrate—with some success, in my opinion—that no beliefs are ultimately warranted on the grounds of evidence or reason. All justification is necessarily, ultimately circular. That recognition fused itself to Anselm's *"credo ut intelligam"* summary of Augustine's notion that we first believe in order to understand.

Together I took these arguments to mean that justification is, at its root, always a matter of faith before it is a matter of reason. Indeed, it would seem that reason is dependent on faith for its progress and order. In light of these convictions, I have often said that it "simply" becomes a matter of the quality of the object of your faith—whether that resting place for faith can sustain the epistemic burdens placed upon it, and whether it can help clarify which burdens are legitimate and which are misguided. All in all, I was being introduced to philosophical reasons to question my devotion to reason as a first principle.

More compelling than the foregoing philosophical reasons were the theological reasons for me to be more tentative about my confidence in the powers of reason alone. I was accustomed to thinking of the impact of sin in more ethical terms than epistemological. The impact of sin was manifest in my life in terms of lust, anger, and any other that might pay me a visit. I was less accustomed to understanding the epistemic/noetic impact of sin. John helped me appreciate more fully and practically that my reason was fallen and in need of redemption, and was/is itself a subject of sanctification.

Additionally, and perhaps obvious enough for most people, I am not God. That has consequences for the scope and expanse of my reasoning powers that I had failed to consider at much length. I did not enjoy an objective view—at least not by myself, fueled solely by my own reason. I was a subject. I was blessed with my own lenses, as every human being is blessed with their own finite, local, socially influenced lenses. I did not have a view from nowhere. John imparted to his charges his sensitivity to the conditions and conditioning that give rise to believing. And here again, my devotion to reason alone seemed unsustainable.

Those significant but fairly basic theological reasons for a tempered perspective on the powers of my reason were accompanied by a couple of practical applications. Some of my classmates shared an appreciation for Bonhoeffer's *Cost of Discipleship.* "When Christ calls a man, He bids him come and die." Bonhoeffer was talking, in part, about needing to die to our epistemic preconditions to responding to Christ's call to come and follow him. In other words, when Jesus says, "come and follow me," you do it. You don't demand that he satisfy intellectual preconditions you have; at that point, you've inverted the relationship of creator and created. You've usurped his role, and subverted the creator to having to fulfill the role of the created. It is you who are supposed to do what he says when he says it—not the other way around. You jump through his hoops—it is not within your province to demand that he first jump through yours before you jump through his. Indeed, how could I hope to reason well if I did not have faith in the author of reason? How would I even know which demands to impose upon him without starting with him? I wouldn't know, and that point began to sink in.

This made sense to me, although I now must note that God lets us taste and see that he is good, and he doesn't condemn the Thomas who first asks to see before he will believe. That aside, if indeed God calls, at least theoretically, we should simply respond. Are we epistemically justified in doing so? If God presents himself—and I concede that the "if" is a major issue here— but if it is indeed God, then it seems we should indeed respond, and somehow in that response questions of epistemic justification would seem to be appropriately, submissively, instantly resolved. Though there remain some very interesting questions related to epistemic justification in such a scenario, that we should respond to the call of God seems clear and simple enough, at least in principle.

Also relatively simple is the fact that I was told that Jesus rose from the dead, and I simply had to choose whether or not I believed that. Someone had borne witness of this possible state of affairs to me. This, at least, was a simple truth. Also simple was the fact that I could either choose to accept that testimony, or reject it. Now, the reasons for accepting or rejecting could themselves be simple or complex, but the choice itself was clear enough. Also clear enough was that there was some sort of a chain of custody of that testimony. It had been handed down to the person bearing witness to me from someone else, and that someone else from an earlier someone else, dating to some point in the finite past where such a belief emerged, however it emerged. This much did I know.

Am I just a reified Cartesian at this point, switching out "I think, therefore I am," for something along the lines of "regardless of whether I think, Jesus rose from the dead, and if God calls, I should respond"? Is this my new foundationalism? Well, perhaps. I suppose it could be described in those terms. I will leave the fully developed answer to those skilled deconstructors who care to ask those questions. Yet even after they do, I will find myself unable to part from these convictions. So, regardless of the complexities previously noted, "I got that goin' for me, which is nice."

Add these convictions together, and what became clear to me is that God calls me to be a witness of the resurrection of Jesus Christ. For someone who came undone and lost all that was once clear, this much clarity is a blessing. And "this much" is all the clarity I have come to ask for or expect. To any extent that I have any more clarity about any matters, I expect that this clarity will be at its root. I am conscious that I have had a tendency to put my faith more in the reason that is part of this faith than in the great subject/object of faith, Jesus—the Logos, the author of reason. Because I'm not yet fully sanctified, I'm confident that there remain things in which I am putting my faith that are not God. Sometimes, it may still be my own reason. But I am more conscious and practiced at resubmitting myself to Christ, rather than my reason, than I have ever been, and I continue to strive to grow. I want my faith to be in Christ, and my reason grounded in his life. There is life in Christ. That's where I want my faith to be. To summarize Lewis, the true attitude of faith is sometimes to believe even in the presence of seemingly good reasons to the contrary. The great debt that I owe John is shepherding me through what I feared was a permafrost, and leading me to a greater faith in the only subject/object capable of sustaining faith—Jesus.

Through the years I have had the opportunity to recommend to many of my seminary bound students that they study with John. I do so because my time with John boils down to this simple testimony: under John's tutelage, I began to recognize many of the things that I put my faith in that are not God. I was blind to these things; sometimes I idolatrously conflated some of these idols with God, and effectively took his name in vain as I attached them to my misplaced faith. John is, in the tradition of Josiah, an idol smasher. He ascends with his students on the high places of his students' hearts. He then smashes the idols, perhaps sometimes in spite of his students protests. His smashing is not always an immediately welcome thing. Then he returns to his home on the temple mount. As we victims of his holy vandalism try to make sense of what just happened to our golden calves, surely the best we can do is simply follow his example and retrace his steps back to the temple and the presence of God.